STIMULUS CLASS FORMATION
IN HUMANS AND ANIMALS

ADVANCES IN PSYCHOLOGY

117

Editors:

G. E. STELMACH

P. A. VROON

ELSEVIER
Amsterdam – Lausanne – New York – Oxford – Shannon – Tokyo

STIMULUS CLASS FORMATION IN HUMANS AND ANIMALS

Edited by

Thomas R. ZENTALL

Department of Psychology
University of Kentucky
Lexington, KY, USA

and

Paul M. SMEETS

Department of Psychology
Leiden University
Leiden, The Netherlands

1996

ELSEVIER
Amsterdam – Lausanne – New York – Oxford – Shannon – Tokyo

NORTH-HOLLAND
ELSEVIER SCIENCE B.V.
Sara Burgerhartstraat 25
P.O. Box 211, 1000 AE Amsterdam, The Netherlands

ISBN: 0 444 82401 4

This book is printed on acid-free paper.

Transferred to digital printing 2005

Preface

This volume would not have been possible without the extensive research program and influence of Murray Sidman. If one adopts the metaphor of authors being the parents of their contributions, then surely Murray Sidman should be considered the grandfather of this book. His research has certainly had an important influence on each of the contributors to this book.

Taking Sidman's lead, the formation of stimulus classes can be thought of as one of the most important capacities of humans (and other animals). Having the capacity to form stimulus classes allows one access to that most powerful tool, *symbolic representation*. That capacity distinguishes human language from mere communication. It embodies that crucial component of language that we refer to as *meaning*. The use of symbols allows us to represent or refer to events in their absence. An appreciation of the implications of stimulus class formation can best be gained from reading the introduction to Murray Sidman's (1994) recent book, *Equivalence relations and behavior: A research story*. In it, Sidman asks rhetorically, "What is interesting about equivalence relations in behavior?" He answers,

> One of the most fascinating observations is that we often react to words and other symbols as if they *are* the thing or events they refer to. Even though we do not treat word and referent as equal in all respects, we attribute some of the same properties to both. This treatment of linguistic forms as equivalent to their referents permits us to listen and read with comprehension, to work out problems in their absence, to instruct others by means of speech or text, to plan ahead, to store information for use in the future, and to think abstractly -- all of these by means of words that are spoken, written, or thought in the absence of the things and events they refer to. (p. 3)

What is remarkable about these symbols is how easily we typically move between treating the symbols as the events they represent while understanding, at least in principle, that there is little actual similarity between the symbol and the event. Sidman's (1994) example of the strong emotion that often accompanies the desecration of symbols (e.g., the American flag) shows how hard that separation can be sometimes.

Sidman (1994) also notes that, "the very definition of equivalence relations requires the emergence of new performances.... [and] the emergence of new behavior that has not been explicitly taught is the defining feature of *creativity*" (p. 14). Thus the emergent relations that come about when we form an equivalence class allows previously unrelated events to take on each other's characteristics. It allows us to understand analogies, similes, and metaphors. Psychologists know very little about the creative process, in part because it is often endowed with mystical properties. At the same time, we are developing a considerable data base about how and when equivalence classes develop and about the nature of some of the underlying emergent relations. Perhaps this analytic approach will provide a better route to understanding creativity.

Stimulus class formation has been studied independently by two groups of researchers. One group has come out of a learning theory approach, best exemplified by the work of Hull (1943) and Tolman (1932). These researchers, who generally work with animals, ask if nonverbal organisms are capable of forming relations among unrelated stimuli in ways that do not obviously follow from the simple associative processes often attributed to animals. These investigators often use the term *animal cognition* to describe their research area and they see themselves operating in the area between animal learning and human cognition (Honig & Fetterman, 1992; Hulse, Fowler, & Honig, 1978; Roitblat, Bever, & Terrace, 1984; Zentall, 1993).

A second group of researchers interested in the development of stimulus classes has come out of a behavior analytic tradition of the type suggested by Skinner (1938) and Sidman (1960). These researchers have focussed on the conditions under which relations among arbitrary, initially unrelated stimuli can emerge as a function of training. They have asked, primarily of humans, what variables control the establishment of these emergent relations. Because language plays such an important role in human behavior, they have also asked about the extent to which stimulus class formation requires a language-able organism (see Horne & Lowe, 1996).

Because these two groups of researchers have come from different backgrounds, they often do not share the same terminology or even the same research goals. Yet the subject of their research has been remarkably similar. This fact was perhaps first recognized by Michael L. Commons, John A. Nevin, and Lanny Fields who organized the *Fifteenth Symposium on Quantatative Analyses: Stimulus Relations* which met in June of 1992 at Harvard University. A version of the papers presented at that conference were published in 1993 as a special issue of the *Psychological Record*.

The purpose of the present volume is to further establish the ties between these two research areas while allowing for differences in approach to the questions asked. We could have chosen as the title of this book, *Stimulus equivalence in humans and animals*. But because the term equivalence often has been used in its formal sense to mean the specific logical operations of reflexivity (identity), symmetry (bidirectionality), and transitivity (mediation) it was felt that the term *stimulus class formation* might be less controversial and more inclusive.

This book is loosely organized around four themes. The first two sections deal with what constitutes functional and equivalence classes in animals and humans. In the third section, the authors attempt to identify stimulus control variables that contribute to the formation of equivalence classes. The last section deals with the complex issue of the role of verbal behavior in equivalence classes.

In the introductory chapter, Catania places stimulus classes in the context of operants -- classes of events that are defined by reinforcement contingencies. He proposes that reinforcers can operate on relations among responses not simply on the current response. As a simple example, case, one can reinforce novelty, a response that has no meaning outside of the context of its relation to responses that came before.

In the section on functional and equivalence classes in animals, the chapter by Zentall focusses on the important distinction between similarity-based and nonsimilarity-based classes. In a similar vein, the chapter by Roberts separates classes into those based on stimulus similarity and those based on associative linkage. In Urcuioli's chapter the development of stimulus classes is interpreted as an example of secondary or mediated stimulus generalization that is responsible for the establishment of the class. This framework allows one to specify the mediator and by so doing predict conditions under which stimulus classes will and will not develop. Pepperberg's chapter approaches stimulus class formation from a more traditional child-development perspective. She asks directly whether classes that are generally acquired by language-able organisms (e.g., same/different, none, numerical competence, relative size) can be acquired by a parrot.

Saunders, Williams and Spradlin's chapter provides a clear transition from the chapters in the first section by addressing the defining conditions of formal equivalence: reflexivity, symmetry, and transitivity. The authors are concerned with what constitutes convincing evidence for each of these components. In the other chapter in this section Astley and Wasserman also address the defining characteristics of a stimulus class but they approach it from the perspective of theories of human cognition. They suggest that evidence for the acquisition of arbitrary stimulus classes cannot be accounted for by the essentialist view that the formation of a stimulus class depends on the convergence of natural characteristics of the stimuli in that class (e.g., the class of young, male, humans).

In the first chapter in the Stimulus Control Variables section, Dougher and Markham review the conditions under which evidence for stimulus equivalence (i.e., the emergence of novel functions) can be found. In the next chapter, Barnes, Smeets, and Leader demonstrate that if stimuli are presented simultaneously, relations can form between them in the absence of reinforcement. This finding has important theoretical implications for contingency accounts of equivalence class formation. In the third chapter in this section Pilgrim and Galizio assess correlations among the incidence of the three hypothesized components of stimulus equivalence. They conclude, perhaps surprisingly, that reflexivity, symmetry, and transitivity do not always appear together but instead, they may represent independent stimulus-control relations. In the final chapter in this section, Dube and McIlvane examine the establishment of equivalence relations from the perspective of *stimulus control topographies* (similar to Harlow's, 1950, error factor theory). According to this view, acquisition of a stimulus class depends on the elimination of irrelevant topographies, or of learning what is not correct.

The last section of the book deals with the complex relation between stimulus class formation and language. In the first chapter, Stromer and Mackay analyze the relation between naming and the formation of stimulus classes and conclude that verbal behavior does not play a unique role in the formation of stimulus classes (as Horne & Lowe, 1996, have recently suggested) but rather it may enhance discriminative control or provide a mediator between the sample and test stimuli. In the next chapter, de Rose concurs with this analysis and adds that verbal control is merely a special case of rule-governed behavior. deRose concludes that Skinner's (1969) distinction between rule-governed and contingency-governed behavior may be a more fruitful distinction to make. In the final chapter of the book, Hayes, Gifford, and Wilson present stimulus equivalence and its relation to language in the context of Relational Frame Theory. According to this view, a relational frame is a functional, overarching operant that is a more powerful concept than an equivalence class because it allows for a broader scope of relations including inequality (e.g., smaller than).

The goal of this book is to provide the reader with a better understanding of the current state of research and theory in stimulus class formation. If, in addition, it serves to stimulate research into how, and under what conditions, stimulus classes can form, we will consider our efforts to have been very well spent.

REFERENCES

Harlow, H. F. (1950). Analysis of discrimination learning by monkeys. *Journal of Experimental Psychology, 40*, 26-39.

Honig, W. K., & Fetterman, J. G. (Eds.). (1992). *Cognitive aspects of stimulus control.* Hillsdale, NJ: Erlbaum.

Hull, C. L. (1943). *Principles of behavior.* New York: Appleton-Century-Crofts.

Hulse, S. H., Fowler, H., & Honig, W. K. (Eds.). (1978). *Cognitive processes in animal behavior.* Hillsdale, NJ: Erlbaum.

Roitblat, H. L., Bever, T. G., & Terrace, H. S. (Eds.). (1984). *Animal cognition.* Hillsdale, NJ: Erlbaum.

Sidman, M. (1960). *Tactics of scientific research.* New York: Basic Books.

Skinner, B. F. (1938). *The behavior of organisms; an experimental analysis.* New York: Appleton-Century.

Skinner, B. F. (1969). *Contingencies of reinforcement: A theoretical analysis.* New York: Appleton-Century-Crofts.

Tolman, E. C. (1932). *Purposive behavior in animals and men.* New York: Appleton-Century.

Zentall, T. R. (Ed.). (1993a). *Animal cognition: A tribute to Donald A. Riley.* Hillsdale, NJ: Erlbaum.

Contents

I

INTRODUCTION

Stimulus Class Formation in Humans and Animals
T.R. Zentall and P.M. Smeets (Editors)
© 1996 Elsevier Science B.V. All rights reserved.

1

On the Origins of Behavior Structure

A. Charles Catania

University of Maryland, Baltimore County

The emergence of structure from undifferentiated beginnings has long been a fundamental problem in science. For example, the priority of form or function was once a divisive issue in biology (e.g., Bonner, 1961; Catania, 1973a, 1978; Russell, 1916). Debates over the development of the embryo pitted the unfolding of pre-existing structure (preformationism) against the functional differentiation of unstructured systems (epigenesis), and gave rise to the widely cited but usually misleading generalization that ontogeny recapitulates phylogeny (Gould, 1977). The debates waned as it became clear that both structure and function are relevant at all levels of development (cf. Medawar & Medawar, 1983, p. 113-114).

With the advent of Darwin's (1859) account of evolutionary process in terms of selection, both structure and function in biology came to be seen as derivatives of selection, each reciprocally constrained by the other. For example, the properties of animal locomotion, whether on land or at sea or in air, are jointly determined by common functions (e.g., capturing prey, escaping predators) and by structural limitations that arise from differences in vertebrate and invertebrate body plans (e.g., muscle configuration, number of limbs). In psychology, the relative provinces and provenances of structure and function remain controversial, but the controversies are perhaps amenable to the same sorts of solutions that worked for biology.

One expression of the problem of the emergence of structure from undifferentiated beginnings is familiar to psychologists in the form of William James's metaphorical description of the newborn's response to the world as "one great blooming, buzzing confusion" (James, 1890, p. 488; cf. p. 224: "Consciousness, from our natal day, is of a teeming multiplicity of objects and relations"). It is a peculiar metaphor, because James precedes it with a description of the "pristine unity" of the infant's first impressions of the world, in the sense that all sensory input "will fuse into a single undivided object" until its parts become discriminated: "...so prominent may our consciousness of its composition be, that we may hardly believe that it ever could have appeared undivided" (p. 488). A confusion, however, implies many separate but disorganized entities rather than the unity that James argues for in his prelude to the metaphor. In any case, James appeals to the child's discriminations among the parts of that unity and therefore to the child's organization of what had been disorganized. "Discriminative acts" are at the core of his account of the emergence of structure.

We know much more about discrimination than was available to James more than a century ago. In his writings on discriminating as telling things apart or as noticing, his terms are not far removed from colloquial usages. He operated without the benefit of Thorndike's research on the consequences of behavior, or Pavlov's on the signalling functions of stimuli, or Skinner's on operant classes and three-term contingencies. In three-term contingencies, discriminative stimuli set the occasion on which responses have consequences (e.g., at a traffic intersection, the consequences that may follow from stepping on the gas or stepping on the brakes vary with whether the traffic light is green or red). The three-term contingency brought signalling and consequential functions together in such a way that effects on behavior were not reducible to pairwise relations among the three terms (the joint dependence of behavior on both stimulus antecedents and on consequences distinguishes operant from respondent relations). Our quest for the sources of structure can therefore be extended to the interactions among the familiar terms of that contingency: discriminative stimuli, responses and consequences.

The argument begins by considering how discriminated operant classes are established by contingencies. We must deal not only with what separates one class from another, in the speciation of behavior classes, but also with what holds the responses within a single class together (cf. Keller & Schoenfeld, 1950. p. 155). We must examine how classes can intersect and can nest within other classes in higher-order relations. Behavior classes are created by common contingencies. That fact has implications not only for arbitrary classes but also for classes that seem to be structurally constrained by sensory capacities and/or properties of the environment. Both the former and the latter classes necessarily involve common contingencies, and the evidence forces the conclusion that, as in the analogous Darwinian account, behavior structure is a derivative of selection (selection operates in both phylogenic and ontogenic domains: cf. Skinner, 1981; Catania, 1994).

CONTINGENCIES AND CONSEQUENCES

The operant, as a class of behavior selected by its consequences, is a fundamental unit of behavior (Catania, 1973b; Skinner, 1935). If a pigeon's pecks produce food, for example, pecking may become established as an operant. As an operant, it must be distinguished from classes of pecking that have other sources (e.g., elicited pecking engendered by autoshaping). The class is defined in terms of both response properties (e.g., force of the key peck) and the stimuli in the presence of which responses occur (e.g., key pecking in the presence of green may be established as a different discriminated operant from key pecking in the presence of red). The stimulus term of the discriminated operant sometimes remains implicit (e.g., key pecking depends on various stimulus properties of the key even when the stimuli displayed on it remain constant).

Operants are often characterized in terms of relevant stimuli or in terms of properties of the response (for some reason, we rarely discuss reinforcers in terms of classes of consequences). Such usage is always shorthand, but even though that shorthand is used freely here, it is important to remember that the operant class is defined by all three terms of the three-term contingency.

Novel operant classes can be produced by shaping, the differential reinforcement of successive approximations to a response (e.g., Eckerman, Hienz, Stein & Kowlowitz, 1980; Platt, 1973; Stokes & Balsam, 1991); fading provides analogous procedures for successive approximations with respect to stimulus dimensions (Terrace, 1963). New behavior can also be produced through emergent behavior engendered by higher-order classes, as in the imitation of behavior that the imitator had not seen before (generalized imitation: Poulson & Kymissis, 1988), and through the recombination and/or reorganization of existing response classes, as in the novel intersection of stimulus dimensions each of which determines a different response dimension (adduction: Andronis, 1983; Catania & Cerutti, 1986; Esper, 1973). The taxonomy of processes that can generate new behavior is yet to be exhausted. In any case, the processes that generate new behavior must be distinguished from those that maintain it.

Operant classes are selected by their consequences, but the common consequences of responses within the class must not be confused with common contingencies. Common consequences are not sufficient for creating differentiated classes, because different response classes can be maintained by the same reinforcer. In concurrent performances with pigeons, for example, pecks on a left key may be in a different class from those on a right key even though both are maintained by the same food reinforcer, as is demonstrated whenever the performances on the two keys vary separately with changes in the contingencies arranged for them. Thus, operant classes are created not by common consequences but rather by common contingencies.

Operant classes are defined functionally rather than topographically. For example, a rat's press of a lever with left paw, right paw, both paws, chin or rump is a member of the class of lever pressing provided only that the same contingencies operate for all of these topographies. The common contingencies define the class. We tend not to think of all of these variations as arbitrary, but it is appropriate to do so because they all depend on the arbitrary environment that exists within the experimental chamber (arbitrary environments must not be conflated with arbitrary responses: "Such responses are not wholly arbitrary. They are chosen because they can be easily executed.... In such a bird as the pigeon, pecking has a certain genetic unity": Ferster & Skinner, 1957, p. 7).

Let us turn to another example, in which the variants that enter into the common contingencies are not different response topographies, as in the lever-pressing example, but instead are arbitrary stimulus sets. In Vaughan (1988), photographic slides were divided into two arbitrary sets of twenty each. The slides were presented one at a time, and pigeons' pecks were reinforced given slides from one set but not the other. Occasionally the correlation between slide sets and reinforcement was reversed. After several reversals, pigeons began to switch responding from one slide set to the other after only a few slides. The common contingencies arranged for the twenty slides in a set made them functionally equivalent, in that changed contingencies for just a few slides in the set changed behavior appropriately for all of them.

This procedure created two arbitrary discriminated operants, pecks to one slide set and pecks to the other, by arranging common contingencies for the members within each set: "...the presentations of food were basically the only way the two sets could be distinguished" (Vaughan, 1988, p. 42; cf. Wasserman, DeVolder & Coppage, 1992). We tend to think of classes differently when the constituents are arbitrary, like Vaughan's, than when the constituents have some natural coherence (e.g., when they are selected from a narrow band of spectral stimuli or are all instances of some natural category: Herrnstein, Loveland & Cable, 1976). Yet the point is still that common contingencies select the members of operant classes. In a sense that is both straightforward and profound, Vaughan's experiment is merely about the use of common contingencies to create discriminated operant classes; it differs from other differentiation and discrimination procedures mainly in the particular stimulus classes that it established.

PROPERTIES OF OPERANT CLASSES

Operant contingencies make all of the members of the operant class functionally equivalent, to the extent that they become interchangeable. This functional equivalence extends to both stimulus and response properties of members of the class. That is what defines operant classes: All members of an operant class are *by virtue of that membership* functionally equivalent.

Once an operant class has been created, it can be analyzed into component subclasses (as when, in a procedure called topographical tagging, contingencies move some but not all responses maintained by a reinforcement schedule from one location to another: e.g., Catania, Sagvolden & Keller, 1988). Such procedures, however, arrange new contingencies for the subclasses: they do not necessarily imply that the subclasses had functional integrity before the change in contingencies.

Many operants created experimentally are defined in terms of some property of individual responses (e.g, force or location), but classes have also been established in which the relevant property is the relation of the current response to earlier responses. For example, in reinforcement of response variability (Page & Neuringer, 1985), no single response can have variable properties. A given response can be variable only in the context of prior populations of reinforced and unreinforced responses.

A similar point holds for reinforcement of novel responses. When novel performances of porpoises were shaped by reinforcing in each session some class of responses not reinforced in any previous session, the porpoises eventually began to emit responses in each new session that the experimenters had never seen before (Pryor, Haag & O'Reilly, 1969). But reinforcers are produced by individual responses, whereas novelty cannot be a property of single responses: A given response might be novel in the context of one sequence of past responses and stereotyped in the context of another. Thus, the differential reinforcement of novelty, like that of variability, implies that contingencies can operate on properties of behavior manifested only over successive instances of responding that are extended both in time and over multiple instances of reinforcement. In these cases, the issue is that the reinforcer cannot operate simply on current responses; it must select response classes defined by relations among responses.

Classes defined sequentially (e.g., Straub, Seidenberg, Bever & Terrace, 1979) raise similar questions, in that contingencies are based not on properties of individual responses but on responses in relation to earlier responses. Such procedures imply higher-order classes. For example, individual pecks may be functional units, but within a fixed-ratio performance the entire ratio may function as a unit. This illustrates a property of higher-order classes: As long as the higher-order class is reinforced, the subclasses within it may also be maintained even though they are no longer reinforced (the first peck of the fixed ratio does not extinguish, even though by itself it never produces the reinforcer).

Similarly, if a correction procedure makes it likely that an error will eventually be followed by a correct and therefore a reinforced response, the sequence of error followed by correct response may acquire some functional unity by virtue of these contingencies. As a result, the error may not extinguish completely or may extinguish relatively slowly, even though by itself it never produces the reinforcer. Errors from such sources may be reduced by reinforcement schedules in which reinforced correct responses may be preceded by unreinforced correct responses, but usually the problem is dealt with instead by excluding all correction trials after the initial presentation of a given stimulus configuration from the data analysis (e.g., Wasserman, Kiedinger & Bhatt, 1988).

A higher-order behavior class (a higher-order operant) includes within it other classes that can themselves function as operants, as when generalized imitation includes all the component imitations that could be separately reinforced as subclasses (e.g., Poulson & Kymissis, 1988). In a higher-order operant, contingencies arranged for some subclasses generalize to all of the others.

Higher-order classes may also be a source of novel behavior. In fact, the novel production of behavior that is part of a higher-order class (e.g., as in generalized imitation of behavior the imitator had not seen before, or as in behavior that arises from the novel intersection of existing classes) is itself a way of demonstrating the existence of the higher-order class (cf. Estes, 1971, p. 23). Like the various topographies of a rat's food-reinforced lever-pressing, higher-order classes of behavior are held together by the common contingencies. In these cases, however, the contingencies are of different orders. For example, the contingencies that operate on the following of orders in general, which are usually social and verbal, are different from those that operate on the following of a particular order, which may be completely nonverbal (consider the military command to attack a machine gun nest across an open field of fire).

Much research on complex discrimination is concerned with distinguishing between higher-order operants and the component operants that are their subclasses. In matching-to-sample, for example, the matching of green to green or of red to red or of yellow to yellow may each stand as separate operants. They can be treated as instances of identity matching only if they can be shown to be components of a single higher-order operant defined by the identity relation between sample and comparison. Emergent relations such as the matching of novel colors (e.g., blue to blue) may be taken as one test of the higher-order operant; another is the maintenance of all matching subclasses even after reinforcement is discontinued for one or more of them. Presumably common class membership outside of the matching context is relevant to the maintenance of the higher-order class (e.g., problems could probably be designed for humans in which the traffic-light functions of red, green and yellow would limit transfer to blue in certain contexts). Similar issues are involved in the more complex relations that define equivalence classes (e.g., Sidman, 1994; Saunders & Green, 1992).

Other examples of higher-order classes are learning set, where operant classes are defined by relations common to a variety of discrimination problems rather than by the specific stimuli of particular problems (cf. Catania, 1992, pp. 148-150), the following of instructions in rule-governed behavior (e.g., Catania, Matthews & Shimoff, 1990; Skinner, 1969), and classes of verbal responding such as manding, tacting and naming (cf. Horne & Lowe, 1996; Skinner, 1957).

CONTINGENCIES AND STRUCTURE

It is time to return to Vaughan (1988), which demonstrates the creation of arbitrary stimulus classes based on common contingencies. Stimulus structure has often been characterized by common features, and accounts of complex discrimination too often appeal to the relative contributions of the stimulus and the organism without including the contingencies (e.g., Fetterman, 1996). In the absence of common features, the endeavor has moved on to derivatives of stimulus properties, such as information, or to sets of features that are weighted probabilistically, as, for example, in fuzzy sets or polymorphic classes or prototypes (e.g., Rosch, 1973). It is not even clear whether it is possible to identify exhaustive sets of stimulus properties to be sampled for such purposes, especially when relevant properties and their derivatives may include not only particular features of one or more dimensions but also relations among those features.

Many classes that superficially seem to have structural coherence upon examination dissolve into arbitrary subsets. Verbal behavior provides obvious cases. For example, acoustic features have no visual properties, so the various auditory forms of the spoken letter "a" can share no common features with the various visual forms of that letter in upper case or lower case, print or script, and even the several visual forms defy a single characterization (cf. Morgan, Fitch, Holman & Lea, 1976). Another illustration is provided by the task of distinguishing among handwriting samples from different individuals.

The word "chair," whether spoken or written, is an arbitrary class by virtue of the common verbal consequences arranged by verbal communities (Skinner, 1957). Chairs themselves are not verbal stimuli, and they cannot be defined in terms of common features. They range from those small enough to fit in doll houses to those in statuary that could not fit in an ordinary room, and they vary in materials, number of legs, and innumerable other properties (Plato's essentialism illustrates the antiquity and ubiquity of the problem). To make things still more complicated, they can also be imbedded in other classes, as when they are pieces of furniture. Nonverbal examples can easily be extended to many other cases, ranging from facial recognition to quality control in manufacturing to the sexing of chicks in poultry farms.

Even those classes called abstractions, presumably involving discriminations based on single properties of stimuli independent of other properties (e.g., all red stimuli as opposed to specific red objects), have arbitrary properties. The property of color determines the verbal response "red" whether occasioned by red traffic lights or noses, but the property is defined by the practices of the verbal community and not by independent physical dimensions. As illustrated by contrast effects and other visual phenomena such as Hering shadows, no range or distribution of wavelengths exists such that all visual stimuli within that range are called red whereas all those outside are not.

If no common physical features can be identified, however, then all approaches that look to stimulus properties to define how such classes are formed must fail. It is necessary to look instead to the behavioral processes that created these classes, and the *only* consistently common feature of their members is the common contingencies they enter into. If the classes include *any* arbitrary members, common contingencies are the only possible basis for holding them together.

We have just argued that common contingencies can create the sometimes arbitrary functional classes called operants. Let us now consider whether they can also create those structurally coherent classes that are ordinarily regarded as nonarbitrary. When class members share physical properties, nonarbitrary functional classes may arise not because of direct effects of those shared properties but rather because, by virtue of those shared properties, all class members are necessarily involved in common contingencies. For example, running one's hand over a sphere has consequences that differ from those of running it over a cube; only in the latter case does one encounter an edge. Thus, what seem to be nonarbitrary natural categories may well be established in the same way as arbitrary ones, over a lifetime of experience with the common contingencies they engender (cf. Catania, 1988, pp. 480-481).

In this context we must recall that contingencies do not involve only those sorts of major events that usually constitute the reinforcers in laboratory studies of behavior (cf. Catania, 1992, pp. 86-89, 331-349). Given different stimuli in the visual field, for example, eye movements produce changes in what is seen. One of Skinner's early illustrations of the three-term contingency involved reaching for a pencil in light or in darkness (Skinner, 1938, p. 178). The contingencies that operate in the reaching for and touching of seen objects are repeated throughout life. So also for attending, listening, and the innumerable little adjustments and posturings by which we interact with our environments (evidence is also emerging that such interactions are critical to the structural organization of sensory areas in the nervous system: e.g., Catania, K. C., 1995).

Now consider the contingencies that operate on a newborn's eye movements, or its vocalizations, or the coordinations of its limbs, or its subsequent interactions with caregivers. Is there anything significant that does *not* involve contingencies, and is there not plenty of time over which these contingencies can act to bring order, in the form of discriminated operants, out of the "great blooming, buzzing confusion"?

CONSTRAINTS, COMPLICATIONS AND CAUTIONS

Of course there must be constraints on the establishment of classes through operant selection. Certainly stimulus classes are limited by sensory capacities, and response classes by motor and neural constraints. Visual stimuli for the blind and auditory stimuli for the deaf will be ineffective as discriminative stimuli, and some coordinations may be out of reach for those whose motor coordinations are impaired by damage or disease. Perhaps other aspects of operant selection are constrained by properties of the sensory and motor systems and neural organizations that have been selected phylogenically. The history of behavior analysis suggests, however, that ontogenic contingencies are sufficiently pervasive that they must never be discounted when the task is to identify the origins of behavior.

Accounts of origins must also consider the effects of other contingencies. For example, respondent classes, which are established by stimulus-stimulus rather than three-term contingencies, may involve structures that differ from those engendered by discriminated operant classes. Studies of operant and respondent interactions provide some hints about compatibilities across such behavior classes.

What about cases in which subclasses of higher-order classes seem insensitive to their consequences? To the extent that higher-order classes maintain their integrity, their subclasses are maintained even if they are not consistently involved in the contingencies that maintain the higher-order class. For example, if a class has been established through reinforcement of members ABCDEFGHI... and reinforcement is then continued for all but, say, F, F *by definition* will be maintained as long as it remains a member of the class; to the extent that it does so, it will seem insensitive to the changes in contingencies that have been arranged for it (in generalized imitation, for example, particular imitations may persist long after they are excluded from the reinforcement contingencies that continue for other instances).

In arbitrary classes, we expect the members for which contingencies have changed eventually to be differentiated from the rest of the class. This might not happen, however, if the class is defined not only by those changed contingencies but also by additional contingencies that it shares with a variety of other classes. In other words, the continuation of class membership when members no longer share common contingencies with the class may not imply that nonarbitrary structural properties determine their class membership. The integrity of the class may be maintained if the class, originally determined by nonarbitrary properties, has a long enough history and has itself become a member of other interlocking higher-order and conditional classes within which different and overlapping common contingencies continue to operate for various members.

Any instance of generalized imitation, for example, shares class membership not only with the imitative class but also with other classes in which that particular imitation functions, as when the imitation of what someone has said also participates in social contingencies that involve other verbal interactions. It is reasonable to expect that interlocking structures will be sturdier than those existing in isolation.

Arbitrary matching procedures (e.g., Zentall & Urcuioli, 1993) may be particularly appropriate for the experimental exploration of issues of interlocking classes. Such procedures may involve not only individual samples each correlated with individual correct comparisons in one-to-one matching, but also multiple samples with a common correct comparison in many-to-one matching, or individual samples each with multiple comparisons in one-to-many matching, or multiple samples with multiple comparisons in many-to-many matching. Thus, such procedures allow the creation of many different kinds of overlaps among different classes (it might be expected, for example, that the relaxation of contingencies in one-to-many matching would be less likely to disrupt class membership if the common sample also participated as the common comparison in maintained many-to-one matching).

As for the priority of structure or function, for classes of behavior as for species, both are derivatives of selection. One implication is that those who study the structure of discriminated operants must focus on the contingencies that create those structures. Analyses that are restricted only to the antecedent stimulus term of the three-term contingency are necessarily incomplete. To see how stimuli can enter into the creation of behavior structure, we must examine how those stimuli share in common contingencies.

This argument has concluded that behavior structure is inevitably determined by contingencies. It does not follow that contingencies are independent of environmental structure. In fact, to acknowledge that the contingencies that determine behavior structure depend themselves on environmental structure is to acknowledge the central and vital role of contingencies. After all, in mediating between environmental structure and behavioral structure, contingencies define the very subject matter of behavior analysis.

REFERENCES

Andronis, P. T. (1983). *Symbolic aggression by pigeons: Contingency coadduction.* Ph.D. dissertation, University of Chicago.

Bonner, J. T. (Ed.) (1961). *"On growth and form" by D. W. Thompson: An abridged edition.* Cambridge: Cambridge University Press.

Catania, A. C. (1973a). The psychologies of structure, function, and development. *American Psychologist, 28*, 434-443.

Catania, A. C. (1973b). The concept of the operant in the analysis of behavior. *Behaviorism, 1*, 103-116.

Catania, A. C. (1978). The psychology of learning: Some lessons from the Darwinian revolution. *Annals of the New York Academy of Sciences, 309*, 18-28.

Catania, A. C. (1988). Problems of selection and phylogeny, terms and methods of behaviorism. In A. C. Catania & S. Harnad (Eds.), *The selection of behavior: The operant behaviorism of B. F. Skinner* (pp. 474-483). New York: Cambridge University Press.

Catania, A. C. (1992). *Learning* (3rd ed.). Englewood Cliffs, NJ: Prentice-Hall.

Catania, A. C. (1994). The natural and artificial selection of verbal behavior. In Hayes, S. C., Hayes, L., Sato, M., & Ono, K. (Eds.) *Behavior analysis of language and cognition* (pp. 31-49). Reno, NV: Context Press.

Catania, A. C., & Cerutti, D. (1986). Some nonverbal properties of verbal behavior. In T. Thompson & M. D. Zeiler (Eds.), *Analysis and integration of behavioral units* (pp. 185-211). Hillsdale, NJ: Erlbaum.

Catania, A. C., Matthews, B. A., & Shimoff, E. (1990). Properties of rule-governed behaviour and their implications. In D. E. Blackman & H. Lejeune (Eds.) *Behaviour analysis in theory and practice* (pp. 215-230). Hove & London, UK: Erlbaum.

Catania, A. C., Sagvolden, T., & Keller, K. J. (1988). Reinforcement schedules: retroactive and proactive effects of reinforcers inserted into fixed-interval performances. *Journal of the Experimental Analysis of Behavior, 49*, 49-73.

Catania, K. C. (1995). Magnified cortex in star-nosed moles. *Nature, 375*, 453-454.

Darwin, C. (1859). *On the origin of species.* London: John Murray.

Eckerman, D. A., Hienz, R. D., Stern, S., & Kowlowitz, V. (1980). Shaping the location of a pigeon's peck: effect of rate and size of shaping steps. *Journal of the Experimental Analysis of Behavior, 33*, 299-310.

Esper, E. A. (1973). *Analogy and association in linguistics and psychology.* Athens, GA: University of Georgia Press.

Estes, W. K. (1971). Reward in human learning: Theoretical issues and strategic choice points (pp. 16-36). In R. Glaser (Ed.) *The nature of reinforcement.* New York: Academic Press.

Ferster, C. B., & Skinner, B. F. (1957). *Schedules of reinforcement.* New York: Appleton-Century-Crofts.

Fetterman, J. G. (1996). Dimensions of stimulus complexity. *Journal of Experimental Psychology: Animal Behavior Processes, 22*, 3-18.

Gould, S. J. (1977). *Ontogeny and phylogeny.* Cambridge, MA: Harvard University Press.

Herrnstein, R. J., Loveland, D. H., & Cable, C. (1976). Natural concepts in pigeons. *Journal of Experimental Psychology: Animal Behavior Processes, 2*, 285-311.

Horne, P. J., & Lowe, C. F. (1996). On the origins of naming and other symbolic behavior. *Journal of the Experimental Analysis of Behavior, 65* (in press).

James, W. (1890). *The principles of psychology.* Volume 1. New York: Holt.

Keller, F. S. & Schoenfeld, W. N. (1950). *Principles of psychology.* New York: Appleton-Century-Crofts.

Medawar, P. B., & Medawar, J. S. (1983). *Aristotle to zoos: A philosophical dictionary of biology.* Cambridge, MA: Harvard University Press.

Morgan, M. J., Fitch, M. D., Holman, J. G., & Lea, S. E. G. (1976). Pigeons learn the concept of an "A." *Perception, 5*, 57-66.

Page, S., & Neuringer, A. (1985). Variability is an operant. *Journal of Experimental Psychology: Animal Behavior Processes, 11*, 429-452.

Platt, J. R. (1973). Percentile reinforcement: paradigms for experimental analysis of response shaping. In G. H. Bower (Ed.), *The psychology of learning and motivation.* Volume 7. New York: Academic Press.

Poulson, C. L., & Kymissis, E. (1988). Generalized imitation in infants. *Journal of Experimental Child Psychology, 46*, 324-336.

Pryor, K. W., Haag, R., & O'Reilly, J. (1969). The creative porpoise: training for novel behavior. *Journal of the Experimental Analysis of Behavior, 12*, 653-661.

Rosch, E. H. (1973). Natural categories. *Cognitive Psychology, 4*, 328-350.

Russell, E. S. (1916). *Form and function.* London: John Murray.

Saunders, R. R., and Green, G. (1992). The nonequivalence of behavioral and mathematical equivalence. *Journal of the Experimental Analysis of Behavior, 57*, 227-241.

Sidman, M. (1994). *Equivalence relations and behavior: A research story.* Boston, MA: Authors Cooperative.

Skinner, B. F. (1935). The generic nature of the concepts of stimulus and response. *Journal of General Psychology, 12*, 40-65.

Skinner, B. F. (1938). *The behavior of organisms.* New York: D. Appleton-Century.

Skinner, B. F. (1957). *Verbal behavior*. New York: Appleton-Century-Crofts.

Skinner, B. F. (1969). An operant analysis of problem solving. In B. F. Skinner, *Contingencies of reinforcement* (pp. 133-171). New York: Appleton-Century-Crofts.

Skinner, B. F. (1981). Selection by consequences. *Science, 213*, 501-504.

Stokes, P. D., & Balsam, P. D. (1991). Effects of reinforcing preselected approximations on the topography of the rat's bar press. *Journal of the Experimental Analysis of Behavior, 55*, 213-231.

Straub, R. O., Seidenberg, M. S., Bever, T. G., & Terrace, H. S. (1979). Serial learning in the pigeon. *Journal of the Experimental Analysis of Behavior, 32*, 137-148.

Terrace, H. S. (1963). Errorless transfer of a discrimination across two continua. *Journal of the Experimental Analysis of Behavior, 6*, 223-232.

Vaughan, W., Jr. (1988). Formation of equivalence sets in pigeons. *Journal of Experimental Psychology: Animal Behavior Processes, 14*, 36-42.

Wasserman, E. A., DeVolder, C. L., & Coppage, D. J. (1992). Non-similarity-based conceptualization in pigeons via secondary or mediated generalization. *Psychological Science, 3*, 374-379.

Wasserman, E. A., Kiedinger, R. E., & Bhatt, R. S. (1988). Conceptual behavior in pigeons: Categories, subcategories, and pseudocategories. *Journal of Experimental Psychology: Animal Behavior Processes, 14*, 235-246.

Zentall, T. R., & Urcuioli, P. J. (1993). Emergent relations in the formation of stimulus classes by pigeons. *Psychological Record, 43*, 795-810.

II

FUNCTIONAL AND EQUIVALENCE CLASSES IN ANIMALS

Stimulus Class Formation in Humans and Animals
T.R. Zentall and P.M. Smeets (Editors)
© 1996 Elsevier Science B.V. All rights reserved.

2

An Analysis of Stimulus Class Formation in Animals

Thomas R. Zentall

University of Kentucky

A stimulus class can be broadly defined to include any case in which a common response is made to a set of discriminably different stimuli. Such a definition has functional value because, if one knows the likelihood of the occurrence of each of the stimuli in the class, it allows one to predict the occurrence of the response. More often, however, one is interested in identifying which aspects of a stimulus that result in its inclusion in the class. Of particular interest are characteristics of the organism and of training result in the development of untrained *emergent relations* among stimuli in a class.

SIMILARITY BASED CLASSES

For the most part, psychologists interested in basic learning processes have studied stimulus classes for which the defining characteristic has been stimulus similarity. These classes have received considerable study (see e.g., Honig & Urcuioli, 1981; Mostofsky, 1965), in part, because the degree to which training with one stimulus *fails* to extend to other similar stimuli indicates the ability of the training stimulus to exert control over responding. In fact, if one trains an organism to make a response in the presence of single stimulus (under a variety of Pavlovian and instrumental training conditions) one can often show that the strength (or probability) of the response decreases in direct proportion to the decrease in similarity between the test stimulus and the training stimulus. This function, relating strength of response to stimulus similarity, is known as a gradient of stimulus generalization. It can be viewed, as well, as a direct measure of the subjective similarity among stimuli. The generalization gradient, together with a few assumptions about its theoretical shape and rate of development (Spence, 1937), can be shown to have considerable explanatory power (see Riley, 1968).

Depending on one's level of analysis, similarity-based classes can be explained in terms of the number of stimulus elements shared by the training and test stimuli (Estes, 1950), or in the degree to which an organism fails to discriminate between them (Lashley & Wade, 1946). There is even evidence that the function relating response strength to stimulus similarity is predisposed and does not require previous experience with stimulus dimension (Peterson, 1962; Riley & Leuin, 1971). Thus, it may be that similarity-based classes form automatically and depend either on confusion between the training and test stimuli or on judged commonality of stimulus elements. For this reason, if one is interested in the formation of stimulus classes, the study of arbitrary or nonsimilarity-based classes may be of more value.

NONSIMILARITY BASED CLASSES

The defining characteristic of nonsimilarity based classes is that there is an imperfect correlation between the similarity of the test stimuli to the training stimuli and the strength of the response. In some cases, the correlation is so poor that one would describe the relation as arbitrary and dependant on factors other than the physical features shared by the training and test stimuli.

Categorical classes

Categorical classes differ from similarity based classes in that there is little change in the strength of the response over a broad range of stimulus values (i.e., the range of stimulus values that define the category), but at the boundary of the category there is an abrupt change in response strength. Examples of such classes are pigeon color "naming" categories (Wright & Cumming, 1971; Zentall & Edwards, 1984; Zentall, Jackson-Smith, Jagielo, & Nallan, 1986).

Wright and Cumming (1971), for example, trained pigeons on various identity matching tasks, each involving two hue stimuli. In identity matching each sample stimulus has the same stimulus properties as (i.e., matches) one of the comparisons, and a response to the matching comparison is reinforced. Following acquisition, they tested the pigeons by varying the wavelength of the sample between the two training values and noted the point of indifference (i.e., the value of the sample at which the pigeons responded equally often to the two hue comparisons). When Wright and Cumming compared these points of indifference over a number of hue pairs, they found that those crossovers were relatively independent of the training values. Instead, there appeared to be two relatively stable points of subjective equality, one at about 540 nm and the other at about 595 nm. The presence of fixed points of indifference suggests that the subjective hue dimension is discontinuous and consists of broad regions to which the pigeon will naturally respond in a categorical fashion. Such color categories or color "names" are routinely found with human subjects (i.e., the bandwidth over which a single response, e.g., red, is used to describe a range of different-valued stimuli). Although it is tempting to ascribe the formation of these categories to the use of language labels (i.e., when a range of wavelengths is consistently referred to as "red," it may take on that common property, Lawrence, 1963), the similarity of the categories that humans use, over a large number of unrelated and often isolated cultures, suggests that these color categories are probably determined more by our biology than by our experience (Berlin & Kay, 1969; Heider, 1972).

For pigeons, there appear to be three natural groupings of colors: one comprising the reds, oranges, and some of the yellows, a second comprising the rest of the yellows and some of the greens, and the third comprising the rest of the greens, the blues, and the violets (Wright & Cumming, 1971; Zentall & Edwards, 1984; Zentall, Jackson-Smith, Jagielo, & Nallan, 1986; see also, Zentall, Jackson-Smith, & Jagielo, 1990). These color "names" are natural classes in the sense that pigeons appear to respond categorically to the stimuli without having been trained to do so. Thus, these classes too, tell us little about how classes are formed.

Natural polymorphic classes

Pigeons also appear to be able to "classify" large numbers of natural stimuli (i.e., photographic slides of natural scenes) in ways that would seem to defy simple judgements of stimulus similarity (e.g., Herrnstein & Loveland, 1964). In this experiment, pigeons were trained to peck at pictures when a human form (or a part of a human form) was present and to refrain from pecking when no human form was present. Herrnstein and Loveland went to great lengths to rule out the possibility that a simple common feature (other than person present) was the basis of the appropriate sorting behavior (e.g., by testing with novel stimuli). Given the complexity of the stimuli used, however, one can not be sure that the pigeons' discrimination performance was not controlled by a simple alternative feature (or by the physical similarity between each of the test stimuli and one or more of the training stimuli; see Astley & Wasserman's chapter in this volume).

Furthermore, the ability of the pigeon to learn to assign one of two responses to each of a large number of different photographs is not sufficient to conclude that a stimulus class has been formed. There is evidence, for example, that pigeons are capable of "memorizing" how to respond to each of a large number of natural stimuli (i.e., they may learn the specific response associated with each photograph). There is also evidence that background cues (what human sorters might consider to be irrelevant cues) exert significant control over the pigeons' sorting behavior (Greene, 1983). Specifically, if pigeons are trained to respond to a set of pictures based on a person-present rule and the test set involves pictures of previously shown (person-absent) backgrounds, now presented with a person present (S- -> S+) or the reverse (S+ -> S-), they show some tendency to persist in responding the way they did in training rather than according to the person-present rule.

Thus, a critical test of the formation of stimulus class formation is a high level of sorting accuracy when trained animals are presented with new member and nonmember exemplars. But even with such transfer tests, the complexity of the stimuli makes it virtually impossible to specify all of their elements. The fact that humans appear to be so predisposed to sort stimuli conceptually (i.e., by functional category, such as, "forms of transportation"), may make it particularly difficult to detect a potentially parallel nonconceptual sorting rule in other organisms. Furthermore, the larger the set of training stimuli, the more likely it will be that some of the test stimuli will be physically (as well as conceptually) similar to one or more of the training stimuli. Finally, important species differences between pigeons and people in visual systems, behavior, and motivation may make it difficult to determine which elements of the photographs control responding. The implication of this uncertainty is that no test will be adequate to ensure that the data provide evidence for the formation of a true nonsimilarity-based stimulus class.

Rather than looking for definitive evidence for the existence of polymorphic stimulus classes, a more fruitful approach has been to look for convergent supporting evidence. One source of such supporting evidence is the degree to which pigeons can learn to sort photographs representing a wide range of different polymorphic stimulus classes. There is evidence, for example, that pigeons can learn to sort a variety of other "conceptual" categories. For example, following training to sort natural pictures of trees (of different species in many different contexts) versus pictures in which no tree appears, pigeons are able to sort correctly novel exemplars of trees and nontrees (Herrnstein, Loveland, & Cable, 1976). Similar findings have been reported by these researchers following training to sort pictures containing images of water versus those with no water. Pigeons have also been trained to sort photographs of pigeons (of a number of quite different looking human-bred strains) from other bird species (Poole & Lander, 1971), underwater photographs of fish from similar photographs without fish (Herrnstein & de Villiers, 1980), and silhouettes of the leaves of different tree species (Cerella, 1979).

Another source of supporting evidence for polymorphous stimulus-class sorting comes from examination of the pattern of errors in such a task. Herrnstein et al. (1976) have found that sorting errors made by pigeons involve exemplars that humans might assign to the boundaries of the class (e.g., a TREE response might be made to a picture of a bunch of celery or of an ivy-covered wall).

Common coding classes

Pigeons also appear to be able to learn to categorize stimulus sets that are completely arbitrary (i.e., that are not based on the physical similarity of the members of the class). The only common physical characteristic of non-similarity based stimulus classes is that, as a result of training, a common response occurs to all the members of the class. One could say that as a result of training, the members of the class "go together." Although a common response is necessary, it is not sufficient. What characterizes these arbitrary classes is the emergence of untrained relations among the members of the class. Common-coding classes are typically defined in the context of conditional discrimination training in which two (or more) conditional (or sample) stimuli are both associated with reinforced responding to the same test (or comparison) stimulus (so-called many-to-one training), and as a result of that training, emergent relations between those commonly associated samples can be demonstrated.

Transfer of training design. A good example of the formation of such stimulus classes in pigeons has been provided by Wasserman, DeVolder, and Coppage (1992). Wasserman et al. trained pigeons to sort natural photographs by pecking one of four response keys located at the corners of the projection screen. The pigeons were first trained to make a particular response (e.g., peck the top right response key) to all exemplars (photographs) of two different categories (e.g., flowers and chairs) and to make a different response (peck the bottom left response key) to exemplars of two other categories (e.g., people and cars). During interim training, the pigeons were trained to make a new response (peck the top left response key) to exemplars of one category (e.g., flowers) and to make a different new response (e.g., peck the bottom right response key) to exemplars of one of the categories from the other category pair (e.g., people). On test trials, the pigeons made the appropriate new responses to exemplars of the two remaining categories (i.e., chairs, top left and cars, bottom right). Thus, the pigeons appear to have learned two arbitrary, superordinate categories based on (but not restricted to) their common association with a particular response location.

The Wasserman et al. (1992) design is actually a special case of the many-to-one (MTO) symbolic matching procedure. Evidence that the samples associated with the same comparison also form a stimulus class can be shown, as did Wasserman et al., by training the animals (during an interim training phase) to respond to a new comparison following the presentation of one member of each hypothesized sample stimulus class, and then demonstrating that the remaining samples are also associated with the new comparisons (Urcuioli, Zentall, & DeMarse, 1995; Urcuioli, Zentall, Jackson-Smith, & Steirn, 1989).

Urcuioli et al. (1995) first trained pigeons to associated plus and blue samples with a vertical-line comparison and to associate square and white samples with a horizontal-line comparison. During interim training, the pigeons learned to associate the plus and square samples with novel red and green comparisons. Evidence for common coding was demonstrated when, on test trials, the pigeons chose the red comparison when the sample was blue, and chose the green comparison when the sample was white. The complete design of the MTO transfer experiment is shown in Table 1.

Interference/facilitation design. Further evidence of common coding of samples associated with same comparisons in many-to-one matching comes from the interference/facilitation design used by Zentall, Sherburne, and Urcuioli (1993). As in the transfer design, following many-to-one matching training, Zentall et al. trained pigeons to associate one sample, originally associated with each of the original comparisons, with a new comparison. A retention interval was then introduced between the offset of the sample and the

Table 1
Common coding: many-to-one transfer design

Group	Phase 1	Phase 2	Test
Consistent	P --> V	P --> R	
	S --> H	S --> G	
	B --> V		B --> R
	W--> H		W--> G
Inconsistent	P --> V	P --> R	
	S --> H	S --> G	
	B --> V		B --> G
	W--> H		W --> R

Note. P = a white line-drawn plus, S = a white line-drawn square, V = three vertical black lines, H = three horizontal black lines, R = red, G = green. Lines were projected on a white background and shapes were projected on a white background. For each trial type the first letter represents the sample and the second the correct comparison. In test, samples from Phase 1 that were not presented in Phase 2 were presented with the comparisons from Phase 2 and reinforced responding was either consistent with or inconsistent with the presumed stimulus classes.

onset of the comparisons, and on test trials, one of the remaining samples from original training was presented during the retention interval. The design of this experiment appears in Table 2.

For pigeons that acquired original many-to-one matching rapidly, facilitation of delayed matching accuracy was found when the interpolated stimulus was compatible with the presumed stimulus classes established during original training, whereas matching accuracy was disrupted when the interpolated stimulus and the presumed stimulus classes were incompatible. Presumably, pigeons that were able to acquire the original matching task quickly, did so by commonly coding samples associated with the same comparison.

For pigeons that acquired many-to-one matching slowly, however, interpolation of the remaining samples from original training consistently interfered with matching accuracy. This finding is consistent with the hypothesis that these slow learners had not commonly coded sample associated with the same comparisons during many-to-one matching training. Thus, for these pigeons, interpolated stimuli were treated as novel in the context of Phase 2 comparisons.

Partial versus total reversal design. Converging evidence for the formation of stimulus classes during many-to-one matching training comes from the finding that if the sample-comparison associations involving one pair of samples (i.e., the line orientations) are reversed following original training, acquisition of the reversal takes significantly longer than if the sample-comparison associations involving both pairs of samples (i.e., both the hues and the line orientations) are reversed (Zentall, Steirn, Sherburne, & Urcuioli, 1991, Exp. 1). The design of this experiment is presented in Table 3.

Table 2
Common coding: many-to-one interference/facilitation design

Phase 1	Phase 2A	Phase 2B	Test
R --> V	R --> C	R -------> C	R ---------> C
G --> H	G --> D	G -------> D	G ---------> D
V --> V			R --- V --> C
H --> H			G --- V --> D
			R --- H --> C
			G --- H --> D

Note. R = red, G = green, V = three vertical white lines, H = three horizontal white lines, C = a white line-drawn circle, D = a white dot. All lines and shapes were projected on a black background. For each trial type the first letter represents the sample and the second the correct comparison. In Phase 2B, a 2-sec delay was inserted between the sample and comparisons. In Phase 3, the delay was filled with either of the two remaining samples on some trials or remained empty on others. Other groups received line-sample training in Phase 2 and were tested with hues inserted during the delay. For half of the pigeons the Phase 1 line-sample/line-comparison task was mismatching rather than matching.

Table 3
Common Coding Many-to-One Partial Versus Total Reversal

Phase 1	Phase 2		
All Groups	Group Hue	Group Line	Group Hue-Line
R --> C	R --> D	R --> C	R --> D
G --> D	G --> C	G --> D	G --> C
V --> C	V --> C	V --> D	V --> D
H --> D	H --> D	H --> C	H --> C

Note. The first letter of each pair represents the sample (R = red, G = green, V = vertical, H = Horizontal) and the second letter represents the correct comparison (C = circle, D = dot).

The fact that a similar finding is not found when the partial reversal involves the hue samples suggests that hues form the basis for these common codes (i.e., red and vertical lines are both coded as red, whereas green and horizontal lines are both coded as green). This hypothesis is consistent with the finding that identity matching with hues is generally acquired faster and retained better over delays between samples and comparisons than is identity matching with line orientation (Farthing, Wagner, Gilmour, & Waxman, 1977; Zentall, Urcuioli, Jackson-Smith, & Jagielo, 1989). Thus, pigeons that "encode" the line samples as hues (i.e., as the hue paired with the same correct comparison stimulus as the line) might be expected to have an advantage in their rate of original acquisition.

The advantage of a total reversal over a partial reversal is not reserved for many-to-one matching training. Similar results have been reported when the training task involved a simple successive discrimination in which responding to two stimuli (e.g., red and vertical lines) was followed by a food outcome and responding to two other stimuli (i.e., green and horizontal lines) was extinguished. When the outcomes associated with only the line orientations were reversed, reacquisition was slower than when the outcomes associated with the hues were also reversed (Zentall et al., 1991, Exp. 2; see also Nakagawa, 1986).

Discrimination design. A defining characteristic of a stimulus class is that there is a high degree of generalization of responding *among* members of the class but a relatively low degree of generalization *between* members and nonmembers of the class. If many-to-one matching results in the common coding of samples associated with the same comparisons (i.e., the formation of stimulus classes), then samples associated with the same comparison should be more difficult to discriminate than samples associated with different comparisons. In other words, it should be relatively more difficult to differentiate between two members of the same class than between two members of two different classes (see Lawrence, 1949).

Kaiser, Sherburne, and Zentall (1995) tested this hypothesis by first training pigeons on many-to-one matching in which red and vertical-line samples were associated with a circle comparison, and green and horizontal-line samples were associated with a dot comparison. The pigeons were then trained on a simple successive discrimination involving the four samples. Those pigeons trained with outcomes consistent with the presumed common codes (e.g., with red and vertical-lines as the stimuli associated with food outcomes, and with green and horizontal lines as the stimuli associated with the absence of food outcomes), acquired the discrimination significantly faster than other pigeons trained with outcomes inconsistent with the presumed common codes (e.g., with red and horizontal-lines as the stimuli associated with food outcomes, and with green and vertical-lines as the stimuli associated with the absence of food outcomes). Thus, pigeons learn to discriminate stimuli that are assumed to be commonly coded more slowly than those that are assumed to be differently coded.

Slope of the retention functions. Supporting evidence for the common coding of samples associated with same comparison comes from experiments in which the retention functions for hue versus line-orientation samples have been examined. As mentioned earlier, when a delay is inserted between the sample and comparisons, hue samples are generally remembered better (or longer) than are line-orientation samples (Farthing et al., 1977; Urcuioli et al., 1989; Zentall et al., 1989). When training involves the many-to-one mapping of samples onto comparisons, and one hue and one line-orientation are mapped onto the same comparison, however, very little difference has been found in the slope of the retention functions between hue- and line-orientation-sample trials (Urcuioli et al., 1989; Zentall et al., 1989). Similarity in the slopes of the retention functions for hue and line-orientation samples following MTO training (but not other mapping conditions) is consistent with the hypothesis that under these conditions the memories maintained during the delay are similar (i.e., the samples are commonly coded) following hue and line samples.

Although the evidence from research in which the slopes of retention functions have been compared is less direct than that found when transfer designs have been used, the findings are consistent with the hypothesis that many-to-one matching training results in the common coding of samples associated with the same comparisons.

Stimulus classes defined by a common history of reinforcement. A special case of common coding has been reported by Vaughan (1988). In this experiment, the defining characteristic of each of two stimulus classes (i.e., the value of members of each class) was allowed to vary from session to session of training such that the value of each class over sessions was the same. In fact, the only feature that could be used to distinguish between the two classes was the reinforcement conditions that were constant within a training session but varied between sessions. Vaughan first randomly assigned photographs of trees to two arbitrary sets, A and B. After training pigeons that responses to stimuli in set A were reinforced and those to stimuli in set B were not, the valence associated with each set was reversed, and then reversed again, repeatedly. After a large number of such reversals, Vaughan found that early in a session (i.e., after a small number of stimuli from each set had been presented), the pigeons could identify the contingencies associated with all of the members of each set and could respond appropriately. Thus, these arbitrarily assigned stimuli had become two functional stimulus classes, in spite of the fact that they shared no more in common (in terms of their physical similarity or their overall reinforcement histories) than they did with each member of the other class -- once the current status of each set was determined, the pigeons could respond appropriately to the remaining members.

Equivalence classes

Stimulus equivalence is typically used to define formal relations among stimuli involving three specific kinds of untrained (emergent) properties: reflexivity, symmetry, and transitivity (Sidman, 1990).

Reflexivity, also referred to as generalized identity, involves the principle of "sameness" (i.e., stimulus A is the same as stimulus A). One can demonstrate reflexivity using an identity matching task by first establishing an association between a sample and a comparison stimulus having physical properties in common and then showing that, without further training, an association exists between a different sample and comparison pair that also have physical properties in common with each other. In other words, after training a pigeon to peck comparison A when the sample is A, reflexivity is demonstrated when it now pecks comparison B when the sample is B.

Symmetry, also referred to as bidirectionality or backward associative learning, involves the principle that an association between two events functions in both directions. For example, if a response to comparison stimulus B is reinforced when sample stimulus A is presented, then an emergent relation should be found between comparison stimulus A and sample stimulus B.

Transitivity, also referred to as mediated learning, involves the principle that if a stimulus, A, is associated with a second stimulus, B, and the second stimulus is associated with a third, C, then a direct relation should emerge between A and C.

The purpose of the following discussion is to first examine evidence for the three kinds of emergent relations that define formal stimulus equivalence in animals, and then to attempt to address the question of stimulus equivalence in animals.

Reflexivity. The ability of animals to show generalized identity learning has been of interest to comparative psychologists because such learning is viewed as an important measure of the conceptual capacity of species (see Premack, 1976). Three approaches to this question will be examined, two dealing with the matching of stimuli, and the last dealing with the matching of responses.

The simplest way to test for generalized identity learning is to train animals on an identity matching task and assess the animals' transfer to an identity matching task with new stimuli. Under a variety of conditions, pigeons appear to show significant positive transfer of the matching concept to novel stimuli (Urcuioli & Nevin, 1975; Zentall & Hogan, 1974, 1975, 1976, 1978). The problem with use of a transfer test with novel stimuli is that pigeons have a tendency to be neophobic (i.e., they tend to avoid novel stimuli). Any tendency to avoid the novel test stimuli could result in an underestimation of identity transfer. Although significant positive transfer is often found on early trials of the transfer test (Zentall & Hogan, 1974), to allow for the possibility of a temporary disruption in performance, the rate of acquisition of the transfer task, relative to an appropriate negative transfer control group (a group of subjects originally trained on a mismatching task with the training stimuli and then transferred to the same matching task as subjects in the experimental group, after Zentall & Hogan, 1976 - see Table 4 for the complete design of this experiment). The advantage of this design is that it controls for prior conditional discrimination experience not only with the stimuli used in training but also with the specific stimulus configurations. Furthermore, it controls for whatever difference there might be in the rates of acquisition of matching versus oddity tasks. An example of transfer data obtained with such a design is presented in Figure 1 (the data are from Zentall & Hogan, 1978, Figure 2).

Table 4
Test of reflexivity: matching and oddity transfer

Condition	Group	Phase 1	Test
Nonshifted	M - M	C --> C P --> P	R --> R G --> G
	O - O	C --> P P --> C	R --> G G --> R
Shifted	M - O	C --> C P --> P	R --> G G --> R
	O - M	C --> P P --> C	R --> R G --> G

Note. M = matching, O = oddity, R = red, G = green, C = a white line-drawn circle, P = a white plus sign. The shapes were projected on a black background. For each trial type the first letter represents the sample and the second the correct comparison.

An alternative interpretation of such transfer effects has been proposed by Wilson, Mackintosh, and Boakes (1985). According to Wilson et al., the basis for positive transfer is a relative novelty judgement. In the case of matching, the pigeons learn to look at the sample and to respond to the comparison that is relatively more familiar than the other. Although the odd comparison was presented as recently as the preceding trial, the matching comparison is relatively more familiar because it was presented as the sample on the current trial. Similarly, in the case of oddity, the pigeons learn to look at the sample and to respond to the comparison that is relatively more novel than the other. However, this is really not an alternative account of the transfer data. Rather it is an alternative description of generalized matching and oddity. A matching-trained pigeon might learn to peck the line orientation that was most recently seen, but how does it know to apply that rule to novel transfer stimuli unless relative novelty or relative familiarity is a generalized rule. Furthermore, on the transfer test, the pigeon must be able to recognize that the novel test sample is the same as the matching comparison in order for it to apply the generalized familiarity rule acquired during training. To attribute matching transfer to a mere relative-familiarity discrimination is similar to the suggestion made by a colleague that the pigeons demonstrating transfer of matching are *merely* learning to select the stimulus of which there are two (i.e., they are merely counting, M. J. Moskowitz, personal communication, February, 1974).

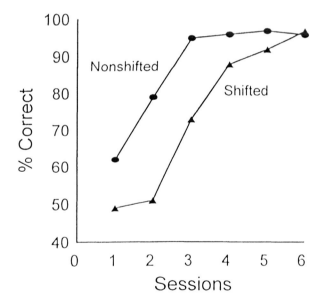

Figure 1. Acquisition of hue matching and oddity following training with shape matching and oddity. Pigeons that were nonshifted were trained with shape matching and were transferred to hue matching or were trained with shape oddity and were transferred to hue oddity. Pigeons that were shifted were trained with shape matching and were transferred to hue oddity or were trained with shape oddity and were transferred to hue matching (after Zentall & Hogan, 1978). The design of this experiment is presented in Table 4.

The second approach to the study of identity in pigeons involves testing pigeons with all familiar stimuli. This approach was discovered in the processes of asking a different question -- namely, What role do the correct and incorrect comparisons play in the acquisition of identity matching and oddity by pigeons. If, as Skinner (1950) has suggested, the identity relation plays no role for pigeons, and matching-to-sample is acquired by learning an association between the sample and the correct comparison, then the incorrect comparison should play little role in what is learned in the acquisition of matching or oddity tasks.

Preliminary evidence suggested that Skinner was correct. Replacement of the sample and the matching comparison with a novel stimulus results in a substantial decrement in matching accuracy, whereas replacement of the odd comparison has little consequence on matching accuracy (Cumming & Berryman, 1961). A similar test following oddity acquisition results in disrupted performance when the odd comparison is replaced (Cumming & Berryman, 1965). When the sample and the matching stimulus are replaced, however, there is only minimal disruption in oddity performance. These latter results suggest that there may be some evidence of oddity transfer. As noted earlier, however, pigeons tend to be neophobic, and these results, as a whole, are also consistent with novelty avoidance.

Zentall, Edwards, Moore, and Hogan (1981) attempted to answer the question of stimulus replacement in a different way. First, only one stimulus was replaced at a time (either the matching or the odd comparison). Second, to control for the effects of novel stimulus presentation on performance of the conditional discrimination when one of the comparison stimuli is replaced data and to ensure that the replacement stimuli were discriminated from the training stimuli, none of the replacement stimuli were novel (though they were new in the context of the sample). In fact, each of the replacement stimuli had appeared as a sample and as a comparison stimulus in matching or oddity training. The design of this experiment appears in Table 5 and it can be described as follows: Pigeons were first trained on either a matching or an oddity task involving four hues as samples. During training, each sample hue appeared with a matching hue comparison and, over trials, two of the three remaining hues appeared as the nonmatching comparison. During test, the remaining hue replaced the matching comparison on some trials and the nonmatching comparison on others.

Test-trial performance for matching-trained pigeons was consistent with Skinner's (1950) prediction. Matching accuracy was severely disrupted when the correct comparison was replaced but it was unaffected by replacement of the incorrect comparison. Test-trial performance for oddity-trained pigeons was just the opposite, however, and was inconsistent with Skinner's prediction. For oddity-trained pigeons performance was severely disrupted when the *incorrect* comparison was replaced but it was unaffected by replacement of the *correct* comparison. The data from this experiment appear in Figure 2.

A simpler way to describe the data from both groups is in terms of the matching and nonmatching comparisons. For both groups, performance suffered when the matching comparison was replaced, regardless of whether, in training, it served as the correct or the incorrect comparison. Thus, it appears that the matching comparison plays an important role for both matching- and oddity-trained pigeons. Matching-trained pigeons appear to look for the matching comparison and peck it (select). Oddity-trained pigeons, however, appear to look for the matching comparison and peck the alternative comparison (reject). Thus, it is clear that the identity relation between sample and matching comparison is not only recognized but is also used by the pigeon.

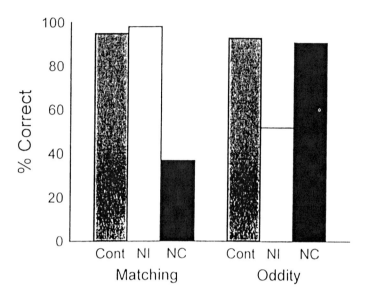

Figure 2. Performance on trial types involving replacement of the correct or the incorrect comparison with a new (but not novel stimulus) for pigeons originally trained on either a matching or an oddity task (after Zentall, Edwards, Moore, & Hogan, 1981). The design of this experiment is presented in Table 3.

Another way to examine reflexivity is from the perspective of generalized response matching. Although response matching, generally referred to as imitation or observational learning, is not typically thought of as an example of reflexivity, the ability to match behavior certainly warrants such characterization. In the case of response matching one looks for the facilitation of acquisition of a response through observation of that response performed by another. Interpretation of the literature on imitative learning in animals is made difficult because of problems with control. Facilitated acquisition following observation could result from a number of motivational or attentional factors. Some, like the facilitation of eating behavior resulting from the presence of others (sometimes called contagion, Thorpe, 1963), are relatively easy to rule out by selection of an arbitrary behavior. Others, like the increase in activity produced by the mere presence of another animal (sometimes called social facilitation, Zajonc, 1965) may more subtly increase the probability of the chance occurrence of the behavior being assessed. In the case of observation of a bar press, for example, the observers attention may be drawn to the location of the demonstrator (local enhancement, Thorpe, 1963), or to the movement of the bar itself (stimulus enhancement, Galef, 1988).

A procedure that adequately controls for all of these confounding factors is the *two-action* method. In this procedure, first described by Dawson and Foss (1965). Animals observe a response (e.g., depression of a treadle for food reward, Zentall, Sutton, & Sherburne, in press) being made in one of two different ways (i.e., by a demonstrator either pecking at the treadle or by stepping on the treadle). The dependent measure is the correlation between observer's response topography and that of its demonstrator. That is, does the observer make the treadle response in the same way as it observed it being made. Using variations on the two-action method, evidence has been found for imitative learning in rats (Heyes & Dawson, 1990), pigeons (Zentall et al., in press), Japanese quail (Akins & Zentall, in press) and budgerigars (Dawson & Foss, 1965).

Table 5
Design of experiment to determine the basis of matching and oddity learning by pigeons

	Samples			
	Red	Green	Yellow	Blue
Training Trial Types	RRG RRB	GGB GGY	YYR YYG	BBY BBR
Test Trial Types	RRY YRG YRB	GGR RGB RGY	YYB BYR BYG	BBG GBY GBR

Note. R = red, G = green, Y = yellow, B = blue. The middle letter in each triad indicates the sample hue. For pigeons in the matching group, the left letter indicates the hue of the correct comparison and the right letter, the hue of the incorrect comparison. For pigeons in the oddity group, right is correct and left is incorrect. For the test trial types, the top line represents new correct comparisons for pigeons in the matching group and new incorrect comparisons for pigeons in the oddity group. The bottom two lines of test trial types represent new incorrect comparisons for pigeons in the matching group and new correct comparisons for pigeons in the oddity group.

Evidence for imitative learning suggests not only that an animal can identify the similarity between two behaviors, but more remarkably, that the animal can identify the similarity between the behavior performed by itself and the behavior performed by the other animal. From the perspective of the imitator the stimulus complex produced by its own behavior must be perceptually quite different from the stimulus complex produced by the demonstrator. The question is, how does the observer detect their similarity. One possibility suggested by Piaget (1928) is that the observer is able to "take the perspective" of the demonstrator. Although such a process could account for imitative learning in adult humans (and perhaps even in children), it is unlikely that rats and pigeons are capable of such extrapolations (see Zentall, 1988). Whatever the mechanism underlying imitative learning in animals, the finding suggest that identity matching is a phenomenon that applies not only to stimuli, but to responses as well.

Symmetry. Although there is some evidence for the development of symmetrical relations following training in the Pavlovian conditioning literature (see Spetch, Wilkie, & Pinel, 1981), the evidence for symmetry in matching-to-sample research with pigeons is not very good. For example, when pigeons are trained on a matching task in which the samples are different from the comparisons and following acquisition, the samples and comparisons are interchanged, typically, little evidence of positive transfer is found (Gray, 1966; Hogan & Zentall, 1977; Richards, 1988; Rodewald, 1974). The problem with this approach to the assessment of symmetry in pigeons is that the exchange of samples and comparisons results in the presentation of those stimuli in unexpected locations (but see Lipkens, Kop, Matthijs, 1988; Sidman, Rauzin, Lazar, Cunningham, Tailby, & Carrigan, 1982).

Zentall, Sherburne, and Steirn (1992) proposed that better evidence of symmetry might be obtained if one of the events entering into the associative relation was biologically important (e.g., it was a reinforcer). In their experiment a differential outcomes procedure was used in which correct comparison responses following one sample were followed by a food outcome, whereas correct comparison responses following the other sample were followed by the absence of a food outcome. The question asked in this experiment was whether there was a symmetry relation established between the comparison stimuli and their associated outcomes. To answer this question the samples were replaced by the hedonic outcomes, and the correlation between those former outcomes and comparison choice was determined. The design of this experiment is presented in Table 6.

Table 6
Design of experiment to test for symmetry (backward associations)

Training	Test	
	Consistent	Inconsistent
Red --> Red ==> Peas	Peas --> Red	Peas --> Green
Green --> Green ==> No Peas	No Peas --> Green	No Peas --> Red

Note. In training, the sample is indicated by the first hue, the correct comparison by the second, and the outcome follows. In test, peas and no peas are presented as samples, the hue indicates the correct comparison, and the outcomes for correct responding are always mixed grain.

Zentall et al. (1992) reported that there was a significantly greater tendency to respond to the comparison associated with the food outcome following a food sample, than following the absence of a food sample. Thus, although these pigeons had never previously experienced food and no-food samples, significant differential control of comparison choice behavior was exerted by these samples (see also, Hearst, 1989; Sherburne & Zentall, 1995).

The advantage of the procedure used by Zentall et al. (1992) is that the samples and comparisons retain their location from training to test. Furthermore, the use of hedonic events may provide additional incentive (or stimulus salience) for the development (or the performance) of symmetry.

Transitivity. Again, as with symmetry, the bulk of the evidence for transitivity in learning comes from the Pavlovian conditioning literature. In two lines of research, sensory preconditioning and second order conditioning, evidence for transitivity has been reported. In sensory preconditioning, one stimulus (CS1) is paired with another (CS2) in Phase 1. Then in Phase 2, the CS2 is paired with, for example, a food outcome (the US). Evidence for transitivity is the elicitation of a conditioned response (CR) to CS1 on test trials (see Seidel, 1959, for a review). In second order conditioning, one of the CSs is first paired with the US, and then that CS is paired with the second). Again, evidence of transitivity is the elicitation of a CR to the second CS (see Rescorla, 1980, for a review).

Recently, evidence for emergent transitive relations in pigeons has been reported in an instrumental context (Steirn, Jackson-Smith, & Zentall, 1991). Pigeons were first trained in a simple successive discrimination to associate a red stimulus, for example, with food, and a green stimulus with the absence of food. In Phase 2, the pigeons were trained on a symbolic matching task involving samples of food and the absence of food, and line-orientation comparisons. Finally, the pigeons were tested in a positive- versus negative-transfer test, with hue samples and line-orientation comparisons. The design of this experiment appears in Table 7.

Table 7
Design of experiment to test for transitivity (mediation)

Phase 1 Train	Phase 2 Train	Test	
		Consistent	Inconsistent
Red --> Fd	Fd --> Vert	Red --> Vert	Red --> Horiz
Green --> No Fd	No Fd --> Horiz	Green --> Horiz	Green --> Vert

Note. Fd = Peas, Vert = vertical, Horiz = horizontal. Phase 1 training involved Pavlovian pairings of hue with outcome. Phase 2 training involved matching-to-sample with peas or no peas as samples and line-orientation comparisons. On matching-to-sample test trials, hue samples were presented with line-orientation comparisons.

On test trials, although there was a strong bias on the part of all the pigeons to respond to the comparison that in training had been associated with the absence-of-food sample (in fact, during the test phase, none of the samples were food), there was also a significant difference in matching accuracy between the positive and negative transfer groups. Thus, although no association between the hue sample and line-orientation comparisons was explicitly trained, an emergent relation apparently developed between them.

The research presented in this section suggests that pigeons are capable of demonstrating emergent relations involving each of the three components of stimulus equivalence. Although the three components of stimulus equivalence were demonstrated in separate experiments, there is no reason to believe that all three could not, in principle, be demonstrated in the same experiment. In fact, Sidman and Tailby (1982) have suggested that both symmetry and transitivity are demonstrated in the many-to-one transfer design (refer back to Table 1) used by

Urcuioli et al. (1995). Transitivity is indicated because the relation between samples must be mediated by the comparison stimulus that is common to both. Symmetry is indicated because the path from one sample to the other must involve a backward association between the common comparison and the second sample.

According to Sidman (1990), one can incorporate a test for both symmetry and reflexivity into the transitivity design by simply reversing the roles played by the samples and comparisons in Phase 3. Thus, Phase 1 consists of training with A samples and B comparisons, Phase 2 consists of training with B samples and C comparisons, and the test involves C samples and A comparisons. Reversing the roles played by A and C on test trials tests for symmetry because it represents a relation that is in the backward direction from that which is hypothesized to occur in training. According to Sidman, this design also tests for reflexivity because in order for positive transfer to occur, an emergent relation between the A sample and A comparison (as well as between the C sample and C comparison) is implied. Emergent equivalence relations have been found in some species of animals when this design has been used (e.g., in sea lions, Schusterman & Kastak, 1993, and in chimpanzees, Yamamoto & Asano, 1995). It is of particular interest that in both studies the animals had initial difficulty in demonstrating emergent symmetry relations (i.e., given AB training, initially, emergent BA relations were not reliably found). Once trained, however, the animals not only generalized the emergent symmetry relation to other stimulus pairs, but also demonstrated both emergent transitive relations (i.e., given AB and CD training, they showed good transfer to AC) and emergent equivalence relations (i.e., good transfer to CA).

The implications of these findings are important not only because they demonstrate emergent equivalence relations in (nonverbal) animals, but also because they suggest that when the spatial location of stimuli change from training to test (as they often do when testing for symmetry) animals may have to be trained not to use spatial location as a relevant cue. This methodological problem may account for at least some of the past failures to find evidence for emergent equivalence relations in animals.

CONCLUSIONS

Although the study of similarity-based classes has played an important role in the assessment of stimulus control, with the recent increased interest in the conceptual abilities of animals, the focus has shifted to the study of non-similarity based classes. An attempt has been made here to classify the research on non-similarity based classes according to characteristics of the class members (predisposed classes, classes of natural stimuli, and arbitrary stimulus classes) and according to the method used to establish the class (e.g., many-to-one matching). Whether equivalence classes are, in fact, psychologically different from other functional classes is not clear and remains to be determined (see Sidman, 1995).

What is clear, however, is that the range of stimuli capable of comprising a stimulus class and the variety of methods that have been successfully used to establish them suggest that the ability to form stimulus classes must play an important role in the survival of animals. Historically, biologists have been primarily interested in the predisposed behavior of animals, while psychologists have been more interested in degree to which behavior is flexible. To account for the evolution of simple associative learning, one need only propose that fluctuations in the environment are sufficiently great to decrease the value to an animal of possessing certain fixed behavior patterns. Similarity-based stimulus classes allow for further flexibility. They permit learning to generalize from one experience to other similar experiences. In cases in which the environment is particularly unpredictable, survival of the animal may depend on the ability to generalize experience over stimulus classes that, although not physically similar, are similar by reason of outcome, or function.

Considerable progress in the study of stimulus class formation by animals has come from the integration of approaches developed in three disparate research areas: animal behavior, human cognition, and traditional learning (see e.g., Axelrod & Hamilton, 1981). Continued progress can only benefit from this cooperative effort.

AUTHOR NOTES

The research described in this chapter was supported by National Institute of Mental Health Grants MH 35376 and MH 45979, and by National Science Foundation Grants BNS 8418275, RII 8902792, BNS 9019080, and IBN 9414589. Important contributions to the research were provided by Peter J. Urcuioli, David E. Hogan, Charles A. Edwards, Joyce A. Jagielo, Pamela Jackson-Smith, Janice N. Steirn, Lou M. Sherburne, Karen L. Roper, Daren H. Kaiser.

REFERENCES

Akins, C., & Zentall, T. R. (in press). Evidence for true imitative learning in Japanese quail. *Journal of Comparative Psychology*.

Axelrod, R. & Hamilton, W. D. (1981). The evolution of cooperation. *Science, 211*, 1390-1396.

Berlin, B., & Kay, P. (1969). *Basic color terms: Their universality and evolution*. Berkeley, CA:University of California Press.

Cerella, J. (1979). Visual classes and natural categories in the pigeon. *Human Perception and Performance, 5*, 68-77.

Cumming, W. W., & Berryman, R. (1961). Some data on matching behavior in the pigeon. *Journal of the Experimental Analysis of Behavior, 4*, 281-284.

Cumming, W. W., & Berryman, R. (1965). The complex discriminated operant: Studies of matching-to-sample and related problems. In D. I. Mostofsky (Ed.), *Stimulus generalization*. Stanford, CA: Stanford University Press.

Dawson,B. V. & Foss, B. M. (1965). Observational learning in budgerigars. *Animal Behaviour, 13*, 470-474.

Estes, W. K. (1950). Toward a statistical theory of learning. *Psychological Review, 57*, 94-107.

Farthing, G.W., Wagner, J.W., Gilmour, S., & Waxman, H. M. (1977). Short-term memory and information processing in pigeons. *Learning and Motivation, 8*, 520-532.

Galef, B. J., Jr. (1988). Imitation in animals: History, definition, and interpretation of data from the psychological laboratory. In T. R. Zentall & B. G. Galef, Jr. (Eds.), *Social learning: Psychological and biological perspectives* (pp. 3-28). Hillsdale, NJ: Erlbaum.

Gray, L. (1966). Backward association in pigeons. *Psychonomic Science, 4*, 333-334.

Greene, S. L. (1983). Feature memorization in pigeon concept learning. In M. L. Commons, R.J. Herrnstein, & A. R. Wagner (Eds.), *Quantitative Analyses of Behavior: Vol. 4. Discrimination Processes* (pp. 209-229). New York: Ballinger.

Hearst, E. (1989). Backward associations: Differential learning about stimuli thatfollow the presence versus the absence of food in pigeons. *Animal Learning and Behavior, 19*, 280-290.

Heider, E. R. (1972). Universals in color naming and memory. *Journal of Experimental Psychology, 93,* 10-20.

Herrnstein, R. J., & deVilliers, P. A. (1980). Fish as a natural category for people and pigeons. *The Psychology of Learning and Motivation, 14,* 59-95.

Herrnstein, R. J., & Loveland, D. H. (1964). Complex visual concept in the pigeon. *Science, 146,* 549-551.

Herrnstein, R. J., Loveland, D. H., & Cable, C. (1976). Natural concepts in pigeons. *Journal of Experimental Psychology: Animal Behavior Processes, 2,* 285-301.

Heyes, C. M., & Dawson, G. R. (1990). A demonstration of observational learning in rats using a bidirectional control. *Quarterly Journal of Experimental Psychology, 42B,* 59-71.

Honig, W. K., & Urcuioli, P. J. (1981). The legacy of Guttman and Kalish (1956): 25 years of research on stimulus generalization. *Journal of the Experimental Analysis of Behavior, 36,* 405-445.

Hogan, D. E. & Zentall, T. R. (1977). Backward associative learning in the pigeon. *American Journal of Psychology, 90,* 3-15.

Kaiser, D. H., Sherburne, L. M., & Zentall, T. R. (1995). *Common coding in many-to-one matching by pigeons as evidenced by reduced discriminability of commonly coded stimuli.* Unpublished manuscript.

Lashley, K. S., & Wade, M. (1946). The Pavlovian theory of generalization. *Psychological Review, 53,* 72-87.

Lawrence, D. H. (1949). Acquired distinctiveness of cues: I. Transfer between discriminations on the basis of familiarity with the stimulus. *Journal of Experimental Psychology, 39,* 770-784.

Lipkens, R., Kop, P. F., & Matthijs, W. (1986). A test of symmetry and transitivity in the conditional discrimination performance of pigeons. *Journal of the Experimental Analysis of Behavior, 49,* 395-410.

Mostofsky, D. I. (Ed.). (1965). *Stimulus generalization,* Stanford, CA: Stanford University Press.

Nakagawa, E. (1986). Overtraining, extinction, and shift learning in a concurrent discrimination in rats. *Quarterly Journal of Experimental Psychology, 38,* 313-326.

Peterson, N. (1962). Effect of monochromatic rearing on the control of responding by wavelength. *Science, 136,* 774-775.

Piaget, J. (1928). *Judgement and reasoning in the child.* New York: Harcourt.

Poole, J., & Lander, D. G. (1971). The pigeon's concept of pigeon. *Psychonomic Science, 25,* 157-158.

Premack, D. (1976). *Intelligence in ape and man.* Hillsdale, NJ: Erlbaum.

Rescorla, R. A. (1980). *Pavlovian second-order conditioning.* Hillsdale, NJ: Erlbaum.

Richards, R. W. (1988). The question of bidirectional associations in pigeons' learning of conditional discrimination tasks. *Bulletin of the Psychonomic Society, 26,* 577-579.

Riley, D. A. (1968). *Discrimination learning.* Boston: Allyn and Bacon.

Riley, D. A., & Leuin, T. C. (1971). Stimulus generalization gradients in chickens reared in monochromatic light and tested with a single wavelength value. *Journal of Comparative and Physiological Psychology, 75,* 389-402.

Rodewald, H. K. (1974). Symbolic matching-to-sample by pigeons. *Psychological Reports, 34,* 987-990.

Seidel, R. J. (1959). A review of sensory preconditioning. *Psychological Bulletin, 56,* 58-73.

Sherburne, L. M., & Zentall, T. R. (1995). Delayed matching in pigeons with food and no-food samples: Further examination of backward associations. *Animal Learning and Behavior, 23*, 177-181.

Sidman, M. (1990). Equivalence relations: Where do they come from? In H. Lejeune & D. Blackman (Eds.), *Behavior analysis in theory and practice: Contributions and controversies* (pp. 93-114). Hillsdale, NJ: Erlbaum.

Sidman, M., Rauzin, R., Lazar, R., Cunningham, S., Tailby, W., & Carrigan, P. (1982). A search for symmetry in the conditional discrimination of rhesus monkeys, Baboons, and children. *Journal of the Experimental Analysis of Behavior, 37*, 23-44.

Sidman, M., & Tailby, W. (1982). Conditional discrimination vs. matching-to-sample:An expansion of the testing program. *Journal of the Experimental Analysis of Behavior, 37*, 5-22.

Skinner, B. F. (1950). Are theories of learning necessary? *Psychological Review, 57*, 193-216.

Spence, K. W. (1937). The differential response in animals to stimuli varying within a single dimension. *Psychological Review, 44*, 430-444.

Spetch, M. L., Wilkie, D. M., & Pinel, J. P. J. (1981). Backward conditioning: A reevaluation of the empirical evidence. *Psychological Bulletin, 89*, 163-175.

Steirn, J. N., Jackson-Smith, P., & Zentall, T. R. (1991). Mediational use of internal representations of food and no-food events by pigeons. *Learning and Motivation, 22*, 353-365.

Thorpe, W. H. (1963). *Learning and instinct in animals* (2nd ed.). Cambridge, MA: Harvard University Press.

Urcuioli, P. J., & Nevin, J. A. (1975). Transfer of hue matching in pigeons. *Journal of the Experimental Analysis of Behavior, 24*, 149-155.

Urcuioli, P. J., Zentall, T. R., & DeMarse, T. (1995). Transfer to derived sample-comparison relations by pigeons following many-to-one versus one-to-many matching with identical training relations. *Quarterly Journal of Experimental Psychology, 48B*, 158-178.

Urcuioli, P. J., Zentall, T. R., Jackson-Smith, P., & Steirn, J. N. (1989). Evidence for common coding in many-to-one matching: Retention, intertrial interference, and transfer. *Journal of Experimental Psychology: Animal Behavior Processes, 15*, 264-273.

Vaughan, W., Jr. (1988). Formation of equivalence sets in pigeons. *Journal of Experimental Psychology: Animal Behavior Processes, 14*, 36-42.

Wasserman, E. A., DeVolder, C. L., & Coppage, D. J. (1992). Non-similarity based conceptualization in pigeons via secondary or mediated generalization. *Psychological Science, 6*, 374-379.

Wilson, B., Mackintosh, N. J., & Boakes, R. A. (1985). Matching and oddity learning in the pigeon: Transfer effects and the absence of relational learning. *Quarterly Journal of Experimental Psychology, 37B*, 295-311.

Wright, A. A., & Cumming, W. W. (1971). Color-naming functions for the pigeon. *Journal of the Experimental Analysis of Behavior, 15*, 7-17.

Zajonc, R. B. (1965). Social facilitation. *Science, 149*, 269-274.

Zentall, T. R. (1988). Experimentally manipulated imitative behavior in rats and pigeons. In T.R. Zentall & B. G. Galef, Jr. (Eds.), *Social learning: Psychological and biological perspectives* (pp. 191-206). Hillsdale, NJ: Erlbaum.

Zentall, T. R. & Edwards, C. A. (1984). Categorical color coding by pigeons. *Animal Learning and Behavior, 12*, 249-255.

Zentall, T. R., Edwards, C. A., Moore, B. S., & Hogan, D. E. (1981). Identity: The basis for both matching and oddity learning in pigeons. *Journal of Experimental Psychology: Animal Behavior Processes, 7*, 70-86.

Zentall, T. R. & Hogan, D. E. (1974). Abstract concept learning in the pigeon. *Journal of Experimental Psychology, 102*, 393-398.

Zentall, T. R. & Hogan, D. E. (1975). Concept learning in the pigeon: Transfer of matching and nonmatching to new stimuli. *American Journal of Psychology, 88*, 233-244.

Zentall, T. R. & Hogan, D. E. (1976). Pigeons can learning identity, difference, or both. *Science, 191*, 408-409.

Zentall, T. R. & Hogan, D. E. (1978). Same/different concept learning in the pigeon: The effect of negative instances and prior adaptation to the transfer stimuli. *Journal of the Experimental Analysis of Behavior, 30*, 177-186.

Zentall, T. R., Jackson-Smith, P., & Jagielo, J. A. (1990). Categorical color and shape coding by pigeons. In M. L. Commons, R. J. Herrnstein, & S. Kosslyn (Eds.), *The quantitative analyses of behavior: Vol. 8. Pattern recognition and concepts in animals, people, and machines* (pp. 3-21). Hillsdale, NJ: Erlbaum.

Zentall, T. R., Jackson-Smith, P., Jagielo, J. A., & Nallan, G. B. (1986). Categorical shape and color coding by pigeons. *Journal of Experimental Psychology: Animal Behavior Processes, 12*, 153-159.

Zentall, T. R., Sherburne, L. M., & Steirn, J. N. (1992). Development of excitatory backward associations during the establishment of forward associations in a delayed conditional discrimination by pigeons. *Animal Learning and Behavior, 20*, 199-206.

Zentall, T. R., Sherburne, L. M., & Urcuioli, P. J. (1993). Common coding in a many-to-one delayed matching task as evidenced by facilitation and interference effects. *Animal Learning and Behavior 21*, 233-237.

Zentall, T. R., Steirn, J. N., Sherburne, L. M., & Urcuioli, P. J. (1991). Common coding in pigeons assessed through partial versus total reversals of many-to-one conditional discriminations. *Journal of Experimental Psychology: Animal Behavior Processes, 17*, 194-201.

Zentall, T. R., Sutton, J. E., & Sherburne, L. M. (in press). True imitative learning in pigeons. *Psychological Science.*

Zentall, T. R., Urcuioli, P. J., Jagielo, J. A., & Jackson-Smith, P. (1989). Interaction of sample dimension and sample-comparison mapping on pigeons' performance of delayed conditional discriminations. *Animal Learning and Behavior, 17*, 172-178.

Stimulus Class Formation in Humans and Animals
T.R. Zentall and P.M. Smeets (Editors)
© 1996 Elsevier Science B.V. All rights reserved.

3

Stimulus Generalization and Hierarchical Structure in Categorization by Animals

William A. Roberts

University of Western Ontario

Several lines of investigation suggest that both humans and animals categorize stimuli. By categorization is meant that stimuli which are perceptibly different are responded to with a common label or response. Human language is a powerful tool for categorization, as we label many different objects, actions, and abstract ideas with verbal categorizing labels, such as "tree", "game", and "justice". These examples indicate that human categorization can be based both on the perceptual similarities of perceived objects and on more complex associative linkages that tie together ideas based on things which have no primary physical resemblance to one another.

The notion to be developed in this chapter is that evidence for categorization based both on perceptual similarity and associative networks may be found in animals. Although the ability to use highly abstract concepts may appear to be one factor which clearly distinguishes humans from animals, non-perceptually based categorization based on relatively simple associative structures can be found in animal cognition. Such structures may be only quantitatively different from associative networks that give rise to complex thought in people.

Much of animal behavior, certainly much of it studied in psychology laboratories, can be described as a response (R) to a stimulus (S) that leads to an outcome (O). Through sequential contiguity and repetition, representations of these three elements become associated as an S-R-O cognitive unit. The importance of such a basic associative structure in animal cognition can be traced back to Tolman (1959), who argued that this unit formed the basis for expectancies in animals. More recently, Capaldi (1992) has defined this associative unit as a *trial chunk*. Trial chunks may be combined to form series chunks, which in turn may be linked together to form list chunks. Although research on categorization and research on chunking in animals have been pursued somewhat independently of one another, the two may be closely aligned if they are dependent upon the same processes. A chunk of information may be formed because its components form a unit that has a single label or response.

Building upon the basic S-R-O unit, what I wish to suggest is that categorization and chunking arise when new stimulus elements are added to such units. Thus, if three different stimuli require the same response and lead to the same outcome, we can express the S-R-O structures as S_1-->R-->O, S_2-->R-->O, and S_3-->R-->O. If three different stimuli are each followed by different responses that yield a common outcome, then the S-R-O structures can be symbolized as S_1-->R_1-->O, S_2-->R_2-->O, and S_3-->R_3-->O.

PROCESSES OF CATEGORIZATION

Given these structures, categorization of stimuli may arise from either of two processes, *primary stimulus generalization* or *associative linkage*. Primary stimulus generalization refers to the well known finding that stimuli which resemble one which already is associated with a response and outcome also will tend to produce that response. Furthermore, the degree of similarity between a new stimulus and a trained stimulus will determine its degree of inclusion within a category. A common metric for determining the degree of similarity between complex stimuli is the number of features they have in common. For example, Stimulus $S_{(A,B,C,D)}$ is highly similar to Stimulus $S_{(A,B,C,X)}$ but dissimilar to Stimulus $S_{(A,X,Y,Z)}$. Primary stimulus generalization gives categorization an open-ended quality (Herrnstein, 1990). Novel stimuli may be included within a category, as long as they bear a resemblance to a trained stimulus.

Even in cases in which stimuli have no perceptual similarity, categorization may arise through associative linkage. Stimuli S_1, S_2, and S_3 may not bear any resemblance to one another but may still form a common category if they have common response and/or outcome links. Of course, both stimulus generalization and association may combine to produce strong categorization of sets of stimuli. That is, a set of similar stimuli may be categorized together even more strongly than they would be by generalization alone, if they give rise to the same response and/or outcome.

EVIDENCE FOR CATEGORIZATION BY STIMULUS GENERALIZATION

In a celebrated experiment carried out by Herrnstein and Loveland (1964), it was shown that pigeons learned to peck a key for food reward whenever pictures of people appeared on an adjacent screen but not when pictures without people appeared on the screen. Since then, pigeons and nonhuman primates have been shown to be able to categorize a number of natural objects, including different classes or species of animals, trees, bodies of water, aerial sites, and human artifacts, such as cars, chairs, and letters and numbers written in different script. The interest this research excited seems to have arisen from the suggestion that there may be considerable isomorphy between animals' perceptual grouping of objects and human perceptual grouping. One might wonder whether this grouping of objects by category is simply a result of rote memorization of rewarded and nonrewarded pictures (Herrnstein, 1990). Although pigeons can remember the reward status of hundreds of pictures (Vaughan & Greene, 1984), two important findings suggest that categorization was not just a product of memorization. First, pigeons are able to correctly categorize novel pictures that fall within learned categories; presumably, this could not occur if pigeons could categorize only those pictures that had been memorized. The other finding involves the *pseudocategory* control procedure. Two groups of pigeons may be taught to discriminate between sets of pictures that fall into natural categories, say trees and people. A category group is reinforced for making one response whenever a tree picture appears but a different response whenever a picture containing a person appears. In the case of the pseudocategory group, however, half of the tree pictures and half of the people pictures form a reinforced group, and the other half form a nonreinforced group. If memorization of which pictures are reinforced and which are nonreinforced is all pigeons use to acquire this task, both groups should learn at the same rate. Experiments of this nature show clearly that the category group learns more rapidly than the pseudocategory group (Herrnstein & de Villiers, 1980; Wasserman, Kiedinger, & Bhatt, 1988). It appears that pigeons and other animals often group objects into the same perceptual categories as humans.

Prior to the demonstration that animals could categorize pictures of complex objects, the perceptual aspect of discrimination learning was viewed as a relatively simple affair. Animals discriminated between stimuli that contained different stimulus elements (triangle versus circle) or combinations of elements (black triangle versus white circle). The same element or combination of elements always defined the reinforced or nonreinforced stimulus. Discrimination between pictures of complex scenes or objects could not be explained by the classical notion of concepts based on necessary and sufficient features. For example, pigeons could classify as "tree" a picture that contained a limb and leaves and a picture that contained a trunk and roots. Pictures that appeared to contain no common features were classified accurately as belonging to the same category.

One explanation of this ability to sort complex pictures is that animals use a *polymorphous* rule to determine inclusion or exclusion of a particular item with respect to a category (Herrnstein, 1984). Thus, limbs, leaves, trunk, roots, and many other features may be remembered as parts of a tree, but only a critical number of these features is necessary to identify a picture as a tree, and, in some cases, even pictures with no common features will be identified as a tree.

Beyond the stimulus attributes of pictures is the question of a higher-order representation of a category of pictures as a *concept* (Lea, 1984). Conceptualization in people often involves the use of a verbal label for objects we perceptually group together. Do animals also have some form of label that identifies trees, water, cars, etc? Such a label in animals obviously could not be based on language, but it might take the form of a visual image of a prototypical tree, body of water, or car. In terms of a neurological or connectionist description of categorization, is there a higher-order cell or node which is activated whenever a tree picture is shown to a pigeon?

Watanabe, Lea, & Dittrich (1993) argue that the evidence for a higher-level representation of concept in animals is inconconclusive.

Wasserman (Wasserman, 1995; Wasserman & Astley, 1994) has argued persuasively that higher-order representations are unnecessary to account for most of the current findings on perceptual categorization. The critical process we do need to utilize is *stimulus generalization* based on stimulus similarity. Stimulus generalization originally was shown along continuous physical dimensions. Animals reinforced for responding to one wavelength, level of sound intensity, or size of stimulus would show monotonically declining response rates as wavelength, sound pressure, or stimulus area became increasingly discrepant from the training value. One reason for the prominent role played by stimulus generalization in a behavioral analysis of learning was the precision with which the value of the stimulus could be measured. Furthermore, it seemed reasonable to assume that different points along single physical dimensions of energy excited neural processes that gave rise to sensations that varied in similarity with distance along the physical dimension.

With complex pictures, however, stimuli vary along multiple dimensions. Such stimuli are said to vary in the number of features held in common; features may include the color, brightness, saturation, size, and shape of parts of the picture. In addition to features, pictures have an emergent or gestalt property that allows the combination of features to display an object or scene (Wasserman, Kirkpatrick-Steger, Van Hamme, & Biederman, 1993). Although ultimately we may be able to find a metric for measuring features and similarity among pictures through multidimensional scaling or other analytic techniques (Sands, Lincoln, & Wright, 1982), we may assume for now that pictures vary in similarity for animals as well as people. This assumption then leads to a rather powerful analysis of animal categorization experiments (Wasserman & Astley, 1994).

A key assumption for this analysis is that pictures which fall into a conceptual category are more similar to one another than they are to pictures which do not fall into the category. At the same time, it is assumed that pictures within a category have varying degrees of similarity to one another. As responses to pictures in category A are reinforced, each item is stored as part of an S-R-O unit with a common response and outcome. When novel stimuli within the same category are presented as test items, the novel stimuli will usually resemble a stimulus already stored as an S-R-O unit and will elicit the appropriate response through stimulus generalization. However, novel members of a category are not identical to those in the training set and sometimes may be only distantly similar to any item in the training set. Thus, some generalization decrement or loss of responding is expected on novel stimulus transfer tests, and this is exactly what happens. Typically, animals respond to novel items above chance or control levels but at a level that is below that found with training items (Bhatt, Wasserman, Reynolds, & Knauss, 1988; Roberts & Mazmanian, 1988).

The degree of similarity among the items in a category strongly affects strength of response to novel items. As an example, Roberts and Mazmanian (1988, Experiment 1) trained pigeons and monkeys to discriminate between pictures of pairs of animals, with the relationship between the pictures varied in degree of breadth or abstraction. At the narrowest level, the positive items were pictures of a single species of bird (common kingfisher), and the negative items were pictures of various other species of birds. At a more abstract level, subjects had to discriminate pictures of birds in general from those of any other species of animal. Finally, the most abstract discrimination involved choosing pictures of animals over pictures of nonanimals. Although pigeons and monkeys learned these discriminations, when transfer tests were carried out with novel pictures, choice of the correct picture was much higher at the lowest level of abstraction. That is, kingfishers were chosen over other birds far more often than birds were chosen over nonbird animals or animals were chosen over nonanimals (See Figure 1). An examination of the pictures used shows that there was far more similarity among the kingfisher pictures than among bird or animal pictures. Although the kingfishers photos depicted kingfishers in different poses or activities, the distinctive shape, color, and markings of this bird were similar from one picture to another. Thus, high intra-category similarity should and does promote strong generalization between training items and most novel items. In an experiment carried out by Cerella (1979), it was found that training with a picture of only a single oak leaf led to accurate classification of several novel oak leaves. However, the distinctive pattern of oak leaves varies only slightly from leaf to leaf.

When categories are used that contain substantial variation in visual appearance, a further observation is that the degree of accurate categorization of novel stimuli is directly related to the number of stimuli used in the training set (Wasserman & Bhatt, 1992). In the extreme, if response to only one flower picture is reinforced, a pigeon is unlikely to respond strongly to a novel flower picture, unless it is nearly identical to the training picture. If responses to twenty or more flower pictures are reinforced, however, response to the new flower picture will be far more vigorous. This finding follows from the observation that as more flower pictures are stored in an S-R-O unit, the probability becomes greater that a novel flower picture will be similar to at least one of the training pictures and yield a response through stimulus generalization.

Bhatt, et al. (1988) showed that pigeons can learn to categorize pictures of people, cats, chairs, and cars when no picture is ever repeated. By using a large pool of pictures from each category, they were able to show pigeons a novel set of pictures on each daily session. The fact that pigeons came to categorize completely new sets of pictures at about 70% accuracy (chance = 25%) after 40 days of training shows the power of stimulus generalization. As pigeons were trained with novel pictures each session, they were able to establish larger and larger libraries of images within each stimulus category. As the size of each category library grew, the

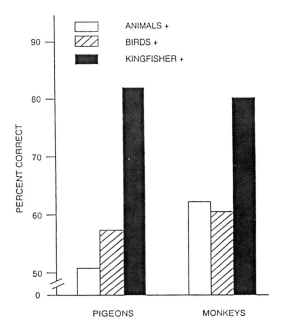

Figure 1. Levels of accuracy shown when pigeons had to discriminate kingfishers from other birds, birds from other animals, and animals from nonanimals. (Adapted from Roberts & Mazmanian, 1988).

probability that a new picture would be similar to one or more pictures in the library became larger and larger. However, novel pictures still were not identical to stored pictures, and some loss of accuracy should arise from generalization decrement. Indeed, Bhatt, et al. did find that accuracy was about ten percentage points lower with novel pictures than with repeating pictures.

As previously mentioned, Roberts and Mazmanian (1988, Experiment 1) initially found poor categorization of novel exemplars when monkeys and pigeons were trained to discriminate between reinforced pictures of animals and nonreinforced pictures of nonanimals. With further training with more exemplars (Roberts & Mazmanian, Experiment 3), however, squirrel monkeys reached a level of 73% accuracy on novel items (chance = 50%). Roberts and Mazmanian argued that a very broad polymorphic rule would be needed to capture all of the animal pictures used, which included insects, fishes, amphibians, reptiles, and mammals. For example, a spider and an elephant have virtually no visual features in common and yet were accurately categorized. However, on reflection, this finding may be explained without the assumption that spider and elephant pictures were somehow recognized as members of the same concept. A simpler explanation is to assume that as monkeys responded to more and more reinforced animal pictures, they built larger and larger libraries of memories within each animal class. With sufficient experience with a wide variety of animal pictures, a subject would have memorized enough mammal pictures to have one stored in memory that would closely resemble a novel elephant picture and have memorized enough insect pictures to have one stored in memory that would closely resemble a novel spider picture.

The important point to be understood from this example is that this account of categorization requires no higher-order label or recognition of a picture as a type of something. It suggests that animals sort pictures because a picture resembles the stimulus component of an S-R-O unit that specifies a particular response and outcome. Concept learning experiments reveal "concepts in animals" only in the sense that they show us how animals lump images together or perceive similarity between visual stimuli (Wasserman & Astley, 1994).

Although considerable evidence of picture categorization by animals can be explained by an exemplar model based on stimulus generalization, an observation made by Roberts and Mazmanian (1988, Experiment 4) may be problematic. The interesting finding was made that monkeys and pigeons found it very difficult to discriminate pictures of birds from pictures of nonbird animals, even after considerable training with novel pictures. Although humans quite easily made the distinction between birds and other animals, it appears that these animal subjects did not readily perceive a visual distinction beteen avians and other animals. Since most of the information on picture categorization suggests that pigeons and monkeys see the same similarities and differences between natural objects that people do, why should they not see a discontinuity between birds and other animals? One possibility is that monkeys and pigeons somehow do not see this visual discontinuity and generalize between birds and other animals. The other possibility is that although monkeys and pigeons perceive the same visual differences we do, they nevertheless lump birds and other animals into a single category. In this case, we would need to entertain the idea that animals code categories by some form of higher-order labels and that these labels may differ between species.

Another means of testing exemplar theory would be to use empirical generalization gradients to predict the ease or difficulty of category acquisition. Stimulus generalization gradients could be measured using pictures that vary within and among human perceptual categories, and predictions from such gradients would be tested in sorting experiments. For example, pigeons could be trained to peck at a single picture within a category and then tested for response rate to pictures in that category and in other categories. The resulting generalization gradient might show a constant, high level of responding to some pictures, with a drop in responding to other pictures. The exemplar model suggests that pigeons then should find it relatively easy to categorize pictures in a choice task when different responses are required to pictures at different levels of responding on the generalization test and relatively difficult when different responses are required to pictures that form a mixture of those from different levels of responding on the generalization test. If categorization difficulty could not be predicted from empirical generalization funtions, we would need to more strongly entertain the possibility that animals use higher-order categories that do not always correspond to perceptual similarity.

CATEGORIZATION THROUGH ASSOCIATIVE LINKAGE

In a typical perceptual categorization experiment, pictures of objects from one category require a particular response and yield a particular outcome, whereas pictures from a different category require a different response and lead to a different outcome. In addition to similarity between pictures within categories, an additional process which may promote category learning is the formation of associative networks based on common responses and outcomes. In successive discriminations, for example, responding to one group of stimuli for reinforcement and nonresponding to another group of stimuli that yield nonreinforcement may serve to divide these stimuli into two different categories based on response and outcome.

In order to examine associative processes aside from stimulus generalization between similar stimuli, stimuli need to be used that do not have higher intraclass similarity than interclass similarity. In other words, we control out the stimulus generalization process. Experiments which use such stimuli are said to be studies of *mediated generalization* or *secondary generalization* (Keller & Schoenfeld, 1950). In most studies of this type, stimuli designated as a particular category require the same response, but, in some studies, only a common outcome is used.

Different Stimuli with A Common Response

Table 1 shows two experimental designs that have been used to study categorization with common responses. Notice that both designs have the same type of learning in Stage 1. Two different stimuli (S_A and S_B) have a common response, and two other different stimuli (S_C and S_D) have a different common response. Although only two stimuli are shown in each potential category in the table, several stimuli may be associated with the same response. The question of interest is the extent to which stimuli with a common response will form a category. The designs differ in the way in which this question is tested. The first design is the *instance to category generalization test* (Lea, 1984), in which Stage 2 involves training subjects to make a new response to one stimulus (S_A and S_C) or set of stimuli from each potential category. Stage 3 is designed to determine to what extent, if any, the response learned in Stage 2 generalizes to the other stimulus trained with the common response in Stage 1. Consistent and inconsistent subgroups are formed from the subjects that completed Stages 1 and 2. In the Consistent Group, the stimuli not used in Stage 2 are combined with the responses learned in Stage 2 in a fashion that should produce positive transfer and rapid learning in Stage 3 if categories based on common responses were formed in Stage 1. Just the opposite is the case in the Inconsistent Group, in which negative transfer and slow learning should occur if Stage 1 training produced categorization.

Evidence for transfer effects suggesting categorization may be found within both the Consistent and Inconsistent Groups on Session 1 performance. If the Consistent Group showed accurate performance above a chance baseline or the Inconsistent Group showed performance below a chance baseline, these findings would indicate immediate transfer of categorization behavior. On the other hand, subjects in Consistent and Inconsistent groups might both perform at chance on early sessions and not show any initial differences in performance. On later sessions, however, these groups may show divergence in the course of learning, with the Consistent Group rising faster than the Inconsistent Group. For example, Roberts, Cheng, and Cohen (1989; Experiment 1) trained pigeons to perform a temporal discrimination based on the duration of either a visual or an auditory signal. A group trained with each signal then was subdivided into consistent and inconsistent subgroups and trained to perform the same temporal discrimination with the alternative sensory signal. Although birds transfered from auditory training to visual training showed immediate transfer of the original discrimination, birds transfered from visual to auditory training showed no differential accuracy over the inital days of tranfer, after which the consistent group learned more rapidly than the inconsistent group. Thus, the consistent-versus-inconsistent groups design is a highly sensitive one that may pull out transfer effects on either early and/or later sessions of transfer.

The second design involves two stages. In the second stage, subjects from Stage 1 are divided randomly into *Total Reversal* and *Partial Reversal* subgroups. In the Total Reversal

Table 1
Tests for Categorization performed when Stimuli (S) differ and Responses (R) are the same within Categories, and the same Outcome (O+) is given for all Correct Responses

	Instance to Category Generalization Test (Consistent versus Inconsistent Groups)	
Stage 1	Stage 2	Stage 3
		Consistent Group
S_A-->R_1-->O+ S_B-->R_1-->O+	S_A-->R_1-->O+	S_B-->R_1-->O+ S_D-->R_4-->O+
		Inconsistent Group
S_C-->R_2-->O+ S_D-->R_2-->O+	S_C-->R_4-->O+	S_B-->R_4-->O+ S_D-->R_3-->O+

	Total Reversal versus Partial Reversal Test
Stage 1	Stage 2
	Total Reversal Group
S_A-->R_1-->O+ S_B-->R_1-->O+	S_A-->R_2-->O+ S_B-->R_2-->O+ S_C-->R_1-->O+ S_D-->R_1-->O+
S_C-->R_2-->O+ S_D-->R_2-->O+	
	Partial Reversal Group
	S_A-->R_1-->O+ S_B-->R_2-->O+ S_C-->R_1-->O+ S_D-->R_2-->O+

Group, the common response learned to one set of stimuli is reversed with the common response learned to the other set of stimuli. In the Partial Reversal Group, only half of the stimuli within a potential category are paired with a new response, while the other half require the same response learned in Stage 1. It is predicted that, if common responses led to categorization in Stage 1, the Total Reversal Group should learn faster than the Partial Reversal Group. The logic behind this prediction is that total reversal requires less new learning than partial reversal. Subjects in the total reversal condition must learn new responses to prestablished categories, but partial reversal subjects must learn both new responses to old stimuli as well as forming totally new categories based on common responses.

Evidence using the instance to category generalization test
    The first design was used by Wasserman, DeVolder, and Coppage (1992). Pigeons viewed 48 slide-projected pictures sequentially on a screen, 12 each from the categories flowers, people, chairs, and cats. At each corner of the screen, a response key was located. During Stage 1 of training, pigeons had to respond to diagonally located keys in order to discriminate between pictures that fell into pairs of categories. For example, a pigeon would be reinforced for pecking the lower-left key whenever a flower or chair picture appeared and for pecking the upper-right key whenever a cat or person was shown. Had the common response requirement caused pigeons to form new flower-chair and people-cat categories? In Stage 2, one set of pictures from each of the potential categories of Stage 1 was reassigned to a new response. Only flower and people pictures were shown, and pigeons were reinforced for pecking the lower-right key when flower pictures appeared and for pecking the upper-left key when people pictures appeared. When pigeons had learned the Stage 2 discrimination, Stage 3 testing was carried out by presenting chair and cat pictures intermixed with flower and people pictures and allowing subjects only to respond to the lower-right and upper-left keys. If the new responses learned to flower and people pictures generalized to chair and cat pictures by virtue of the common response training given in Stage 1, pigeons should prefer to peck the lower-right key when chair pictures are shown and to peck the upper-left key when cat pictures are shown. These preferences were clearly shown, as pigeons responded in agreement with Stage 1 categorization training on 72% of the test trials. Apparently, classes of pictures that had low visual similarity to one another could be combined into a new superclass by requiring they elicit a common response.
    An often-cited experiment carried out by Vaughan (1988) is related to the the initial test shown in Table 1. Although Vaughan's experiment did not contain formally divided stages, it appears to involve above-chance-baseline performance based on instance-to-category generalization. Forty pictures of trees were divided randomly into two sets of 20 pictures each, and pigeons were reinforced for pecking when pictures from one set (Set A) appeared on a screen and were nonreinforced for pecking when pictures from the other set (Set B) appeared. Training proceeded over a number of sessions, with the 40 pictures appearing in different random orders on each session. When pigeons clearly discriminated between Sets A and B by responding to Set A pictures and witholding response to Set B pictures, the reinforcement contingencies were reversed, and pigeons had to learn to peck at Set B pictures and not to peck at Set A pictures. After this reversal was learned, a third and further reversals were trained. The finding of interest is that after a number of reversals, pigeons began to respond accurately to pictures in each set after only a few pictures within the reversal had been experienced. Specifically, after 30 reversals, pigeons began to respond more to reinforced pictures than to nonreinforced pictures after the 12th slide of the first reversal session was shown. In other words, the responses made to the initial pictures of each set within the first reversal session generalized to the remaining pictures in each set. Pigeons had learned to treat pictures in each set as categories based upon the consistency of responses required to them during the earlier stages of training. Note that Stages 2 and 3 in the first instance-to-category-generalization test in Table 1 are telescoped together in each reversal of the Vaughan experiment; Stage 2 training with a subset of items from the categories established in Stage 1 occurs on the initial trials of a reversal, and the Stage 3 test corresponds to performance on the later trials of the reversal.
    Urcuioli, Zentall, Jackson-Smith, and Steirn (1989; Experiment 3) carried out an experiment using the delayed matching-to-sample procedure. In Stage 1, pigeons were taught to match two pairs of sample stimuli to single comparison stimuli. This many-to-one matching required

pigeons to choose a vertical lines comparison stimulus for reinforcement after seeing either red or vertical lines as a sample stimulus and to choose a horizontal lines comparison stimulus after seeing either green or horizontal lines as a sample stimulus. Were categories formed of sample stimuli that required a common response of pecking the same comparison stimulus? To answer this question, one member of each pair of samples became the sample for response to a new comparison stimulus in Stage 2. Thus, pigeons now learned to peck a circle for reinforcement if red had been the sample and to peck a dot if green had been the sample. In Stage 3, the subjects were divided into two equivalent groups and trained with contingencies that were consistent or inconsistent with category formation in Stage 1. In the Consistent Group, the vertical and horizontal samples from Stage 1 were presented, with choice of the circle correct after vertical lines and choice of dot correct after horizontal lines. These contingencies were reversed in the Inconsistent Group, with choice of dot correct after a vertical lines sample and choice of circle correct after a horizontal lines sample. The data provided striking confirmation of category formation in Stage 1 through a common response; there was a significant difference between the consistent and inconsistent groups in the first 16 test trials, with consistent pigeons making about 72% correct responses and inconsistent pigeons making about 35% correct responses.

Evidence using the total reversal versus partial reversal test
         In an experiment carried out by Nakagawa (1986), rats were overtrained on discrimination problems that required them to jump across a gap in the arm of a Y-maze and push down a stimulus card. Two pairs of stimuli were presented on different trials in Stage 1, black and white and vertical and horizontal black-and-white stripes. One member of each pair was reinforced and the other was nonreinforced. In one condition, for example, choice of black was reinforced and choice of white was nonreinforced, while choice of vertical stripes was reinforced and choice of horizontal stripes was nonreinforced. Was categorical association formed between the stimuli that animals learned to approach and the stimuli that animals learned to avoid? In Stage 2, animals were divided into equivalent subgroups, with one group given total reversal and the other given partial reversal of the discriminations learned in Stage 1. In the total reversal condition, rats had to now learn to approach white and horizontal stripes for reinforcement. In the partial reversal condition, rats were reversed on only one of the original discriminations; thus, a group in this condition would have white and vertical stripes reinforced. Animals in the total reversal condition reached criterion significantly faster than those given partial reversal, suggesting that categorization by a common response had occurred in Stage 1.
         Similar findings were reported by Zentall, Steim, Sherburne, and Urcuioli (1991; Experiment 1) with pigeons learning a matching-to-sample task, but the effect interacted with the stimulus dimensions used. When hue and line-orientation samples were used, partial reversal of line samples lead to substantially slower learning of the lines problem than was the case in the total reversal condition, but partial reversal of the hue samples was not more difficult than the reversal of hue samples in the total reversal condition. In a subsequent experiment (Zentall, et al., 1991; Experiment 2), pigeons were trained on a simpler multiple-schedule discrimination, with two stimuli reinforced and two stimuli nonreinforced. For example, red and vertical-line stimuli would both be reinforced when pecked, while green and horizontal-line stimuli would both be nonreinforced when pecked. As in the matching-to-sample study, reversal of the line discrimination required more trials to be learned when the color discrimination was not reversed (partial reversal) than when the color discrimination also was reversed (total reversal). No

differential effect of partial versus total reversal was seen with the color discrimination.

Different Stimuli and Responses with A Common Outcome

All of the tests shown in Table 1 indicate that the same positive outcome (O+) was delivered for responses in both categories. Among the experiments presented, this was true of the Wasserman, et al. (1992), Urcuioli, et al. (1989), and Zentall, et al. (1991) studies, but it was not the case in the Vaughan (1988) and Nakagawa (1986) studies. In these latter experiments, categories were distinguished by stimuli that led to response and reinforcement and stimuli that led to nonresponse and nonreinforcement. Neither type of study allows us to determine whether outcome by itself is sufficient to lead to category formation. In experiments in which the same outcome follows response to stimuli from both categories, outcome is not a variable. In experiments in which response is reinforced and nonresponse is nonreinforced, both response and outcome are varied and thus the effect of outcome cannot be isolated.

That outcome should be an important factor in category formation is suggested by the differential-outcome effect (DOE). In experiments on discrimination learning and the acquisition of delayed matching-to-sample, following one stimulus-response sequence with a particular reward outcome and another stimulus-response sequence with a different reward outcome leads to faster acquisition than following both stimulus-response sequences with the same reward or nondifferential reinforcement with both rewards (Peterson, 1984; Trapold, 1970). We may ask then whether a reward outcome associated with two or more different stimulus-response sequences would cause those sequences to function as a category.

In Table 2, three designs are shown that test for categorization when stimuli and responses both vary within categories, but each category has a common outcome. The first design, stimulus-response switch within versus between categories, is made possible by the fact that different responses are associated with each stimulus. In this design, responses and outcomes are kept intact and switched between stimuli. If a common outcome promotes categorization, subjects should learn the within-category switch faster than the between-category switch. The common outcome may serve as a mediator or common code between stimuli and responses within a category.

The second two tests are analogous to the instance to category generalization test and the total reversal versus partial reversal test shown in Table 1. In these designs, stimuli and responses remain intact, but outcome changes between stages. Experiments of these types should tell us if stimuli and responses can be categorized based on a common outcome. Some recent experiments in which rats were tested on a radial maze appear to fit these tests and will be discussed.

Evidence using the Stimulus-Response Switch Within Versus Between Categories Test

Evidence from an experiment performed by Edwards, Jagielo, Zentall, and Hogan (1982) indicates that a within-categories switch leads to positive transfer. Pigeons were used in a matching-to-sample experiment. Birds initially learned simultaneous matching problems in which the sample and comparison stimuli either were black and white patterns (plus sign and circle) or colors (red and green). A common reinforcer rewarded matching responses within each pattern and color pair of stimuli. In one training condition, for example, when plus and circle were the comparison stimuli, choice of plus led to a corn reinforcer when the sample was a plus sign, and choice of circle led to a wheat reinforcer when the sample was a circle; when the comparison stimuli were red and green, corn was delivered for choice of red when the sample was red, and

Table 2
Tests for Categorization performed when Stimuli (S) and Responses (R) differ with Categories, and each Category has a common Outcome (O)

Stimulus-Response Switch Within Versus Between Categories

Stage 1	Stage 2
	Within-Category Switch
$S_A \to R_1 \to O_1$	$S_A \to R_2 \to O_1$
$S_B \to R_2 \to O_1$	$S_B \to R_1 \to O_1$
	$S_C \to R_4 \to O_2$
$S_C \to R_3 \to O_2$	$S_D \to R_3 \to O_2$
$S_D \to R_4 \to O_2$	
	Between-Category Switch
	$S_A \to R_3 \to O_2$
	$S_B \to R_4 \to O_2$
	$S_C \to R_1 \to O_1$
	$S_D \to R_2 \to O_1$

Instance to Category Generalization Test (Comparison with Chance Baseline)

Stage 1	Stage 2	Stage 3
$S_A \to R_1 \to O_1$	$S_A \to R_1 \to O_2$	$S_B \to R_2$
$S_B \to R_2 \to O_1$		or
$S_C \to R_3 \to O_2$	$S_C \to R_3 \to O_1$	$S_D \to R_4?$
$S_D \to R_4 \to O_2$		

Total Reversal versus Partial Reversal Test

Stage 1	Stage 2
	Total Reversal Group
$S_A \to R_1 \to O_1$	$S_A \to R_1 \to O_2$
$S_B \to R_2 \to O_1$	$S_B \to R_2 \to O_2$
	$S_C \to R_3 \to O_1$
$S_C \to R_3 \to O_2$	$S_D \to R_4 \to O_1$
$S_D \to R_4 \to O_2$	
	Partial Reversal Group
	$S_A \to R_1 \to O_2$
	$S_B \to R_2 \to O_1$
	$S_C \to R_3 \to O_2$
	$S_D \to R_4 \to O_1$

wheat was delivered for choice of green when green was the sample.

In a transfer test, the pigeons learned new symbolic matching-to-sample problems. The sample stimuli and comparison responses were rearranged within food outcome categories. Thus, pigeons had to choose between red and green comparison stimuli when a plus-sign was the sample and between circle and plus-sign comparison stimuli when the red stimulus was the sample, with corn delivered as reward for choice of red and plus sign. When wheat was the reward outcome, birds had to choose between green and red comparison stimuli with a circle sample and between plus-sign and circle comparison stimuli with a green sample, with green and circle the correct choices. It was found that all four of the pigeons tested chose the correct comparison stimulus above the chance level of 50% on the first session of testing, with the average percent correct being about 64%. Although a negative transfer group also was tested in this study, it did not involve a complete between-category switch of stimuli and responses. The experiment then provides support for positive transfer when the within-category stimulus-response shift is performed.

Evidence using the Instance to Category Generalization Test

In an experiment carried out by Olthof, Macuda and Roberts (1995), rats were trained to run down the arms of a 12-arm radial maze with different outcomes (rewards) placed in food cups at the end of each arm. The arms on the maze were divided randomly into two sets of six arms each, Set A and Set B. On any given session, all of the arms in one set would contain a small piece of chocolate, and all of the arms in the other set would contain a Noyes pellet, a standard reward pellet for rats. Because each arm presents a different stimulus or location in space and entering each arm is a different response, the conditions for Stage 1 in Table 2 are met by the common reward outcomes found on the arms.

During testing over 30 sessions, the outcome placed on arms in Sets A and B changed randomly from session to session. Thus, the assignment on one session might be chocolate in Set A arms and Noyes pellets in Set B arms, and the assignment on the next session might be Noyes pellets in Set A arms and chocolate in Set B arms. This procedure is analogous to the picture-response-outcome reversal procedure used by Vaughan (1988) with pigeons. It is important to note that rats have a strong preference for chocolate over Noyes pellets and will enter arms containing chocolate before arms containing Noyes pellets if the same arms always contain these rewards (Macuda & Roberts, 1995). Figure 2 shows the results of this experiment. Preferences for arms containing chocolate and Noyes pellets are shown by plotting mean rank of entrance into arms containing each type of reward over sessions. A low mean rank means early entrance into arms of that type and a high mean rank means late entrance. The letters N and R along the abscissa indicate the initial assignment of reward types to sets of arms (Nonreversal = N) and the reversal of that initial assignment (Reversal = R). Through the first 15 sessions, little difference between the rewards appeared. Over Sessions 16-30, however, there emerged a clear preference for entering arms containing chocolate before arms containing Noyes pellets. Furthermore, this preference was equally strong on N and R sessions. These data indicate that rats only needed to sample the outcome on an initial arm or two of a session to find out which set contained chocolate and then entered the remaining chocolate arms before entering Noyes pellets arms. In terms of the design shown in Table 2, the initial arm or two visited represents Stage 2, in which the subject finds which outcome is associated with one member of a category. The remaining choices represent Stage 3, in which the subject's preference for the stimuli and responses (arm entries) of Set A or Set B indicate the generalization of the outcome

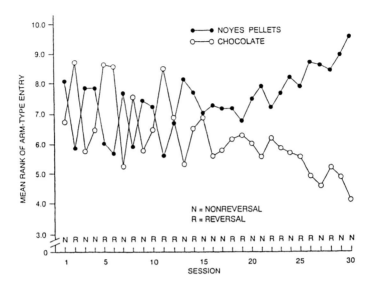

Figure 2. Mean rank of enterence into arms containing chocolate and arms containing Noyes pellets over 30 days of training with the locations of the two rewards randomly either nonreversed (N) or reversed (R).

experienced in Stage 2 to the remaining members of a category.

Evidence using the Total Reversal versus Partial Reversal Test

In an experiment performed by Macuda and Roberts (1995, Experiment 4), rats were trained for a number of sessions on a 12-arm radial maze with three different rewards placed in fixed arm locations. Four arms contained a piece of cheese, four contained a piece of chocolate, and four contained Noyes pellets. Rats developed a clear hierarchy of preferences among the arms and tended to enter cheese arms first, chocolate arms second, and Noyes pellets arms last. This behavior appears to be a form of behavioral chunking and is accompanied by a rapid rate of learning to eliminate errors or repetitions of arm entries (Dallal & Meck, 1990; Macuda & Roberts, 1995, Experiment 2). The stimulus-response sequences associated with entering arms with a common outcome may be categorized or chunked together. In the second stage of the experiment, a test of reference memory reorganization was given by changing the food outcomes located on each arm. The subjects were divided into two equivalent groups, a Chunk Maintained Group and a Chunk Compromised Group. In the Chunk Maintained Group, all of the arms that contained one type of food now had it replaced by another type of food. For example, all the arms that originally contained cheese now contained chocolate, all the arms that contained chocolate now contained Noyes pellets, and all the arms that contained Noyes pellets now contained cheese. This manipulation is equivalent to the total reversal procedure shown in Table

2. The Chunk Compromised Group was transferred to a maze in which the outcomes varied across arms that previously formed a chunk. For example, of the four arms that originally contained cheese, two now contained chocolate and the other two contained Noyes pellets. The arms that had contained chocolate and Noyes pellets similarly were divided between the remaining two rewards. This rearrangement of rewards is not exactly the same as a partial reversal, but, like a partial reversal, it forces the subject to form new categories.

The data presented in Figure 3 show the mean arm choices necessary to enter all 12 arms over sessions for the Chunk Maintained and Chunk Compromised Groups. During pretraining with the original food-type assignments, both groups showed nearly perfect performance, taking only slightly more than 12 choices to enter all 12 arms. With the introduction of new food locations, both groups showed disruption in performance, followed by improved accuracy. However, the Chunk Compromised Group required a significantly higher level of choices than the Chunk Maintained Group throughout testing. Thus, the total reversal condition adjusted significantly faster than the partial reversal condition. Animals had learned to treat arms with a common reward as a category or chunk and found it easier to reorganize reference memory by assigning new foods to existing chunks than by building new chunks.

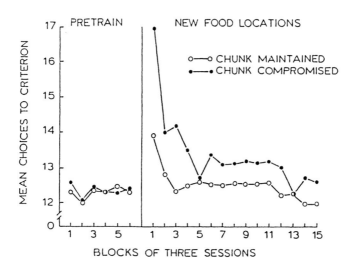

Figure 3. Mean are entries required to enter all 12 arms during pretraining and the placement of rewardsin new food locations (from Macuda & Roberts, 1995).

CONCLUSIONS AND SUGGESTIONS FOR FURTHER RESEARCH

The argument has been advanced that animals form complex S-R-O structures that link two or more stimuli together through common response or common outcome. Within such structures, categorization may be demonstrated in two ways. The first is through stimulus generalization. Stimuli that have not been responded to and yielded an outcome may still be classified as members of an S-R-O structure through their similarity to one or more of the stimuli in the structure. Substantial research summarized here can be accounted for by an exemplar theory that stresses the importance of stimulus similarity and generalization in animal concept learning studies. The possibility that animals use a higher-order category label to sort pictures from different natural categories cannot be ruled out, however, and studies which relate speed of categorization learning among pictures to their rate of response on generalization gradients might inform us further about the need or lack of need for a theory with higher-order representations. An important area for further research here is the development of methods for measuring the similarity of multidimensional stimuli in animals. Judgments of similarity among pictures used in animal categorization studies are based largely on human impressions. Although there appears to be considerable isomorphy between similarity and categorization in people and animals, some evidence of disagreement has been found (Roberts & Mazmanian, 1988). The establishment of a metric that would allow us to quantitatively specify a priori the degrees of similarity among different stimuli for a particular species then would make it possible to test more precisely theories of categorization based on stimulus generalization, such as Wasserman and Astley's (1994) recent extension of Spence's (1937) theory of discrimination learning.

The formation of categories among nonsimilar stimuli appears to occur through associative linkage with common responses or outcomes. Experiments with pigeons and rats using a variety of procedures, including visual discrimination, matching-to-sample, and spatial memory on the radial maze, all seem to support this conclusion. Most of these experiments used one of the transfer designs shown in Tables 1 and 2 and showed that stimuli linked together by a common response or outcome then functioned as a categorical unit. Thus, if some new response or outcome was associated with a subgroup of the stimuli in the category, the other members of the category also became associated with the new response or outcome. Associative linkage allows categories of nonsimilar stimuli to have an important property of concepts specified by Herrnstein (1990): Changes in response or outcome experienced with one or a few members of a category will rapidly propagate to other members of the category.

The specific mechanisms by which associative linkage within S-R-O structures might occur has not been specified and will not be gone into in detail. But, certainly some theorizing about such mechanisms can be found in the literature. In matching-to-sample experiments using two sample stimuli mapped onto a response to a single comparison stimulus, Urcuioli, et al. (1989) have speculated that pigeons learn a common code that mediates choice of the comparison stimulus. These samples often are vertical or horizontal lines and hues (red or green); more recently, it has been found that food and no-food sample stimuli may form common codes with color sample stimuli when they share a response to a common shape comparison stimulus (Zentall, Sherburne, & Urcuioli, 1995). Based on findings from their partial versus total reversal experiments, Zentall, et al. (1991) have suggested that the common code in this situation is the sample hue. For example, both red and vertical lines sample stimuli might elicit a representation of red which would then serve as a code for response to a dot comparison stimulus instead of a circle comparison stimulus. Hues may become the common code because they are more salient and memorable to pigeons than black-and-white patterns (Urcuioli & Zentall, 1986). However, in the more complex situation used by Vaughan (1988), it is not clear what the common codes would be for two sets of randomly chosen pictures of trees. A representation of a common response or outcome is one possibility for a common code (Edwards, et al., 1982), but that code would have to be constantly reversing to account for the Vaughan results. It may be that the common code will have to remain a hypothetical, but theoretically useful, entity to account for reversal effects when a large number of complex stimuli is used.

Another implication of S-R-O structures is that association occurs in a backward as well as a forward direction. That is, the delivery of a particular reinforcer outcome may activate members of the category that have that outcome in common. Recently, evidence for backward associations has been reported between red and green comparison stimuli and food and no-food outcomes (Zentall, Sherburne, & Steirn, 1992). Dallal and Meck (1990) and Macuda and Roberts (1995) have suggested that chunking on the radial maze may be controlled through higher-level food-representation nodes that access arm locations containing a particular food type.

One implication of complex S-R-O structures as categories is that it ought to be possible to alter response to stimuli within a category by modifying the outcome or response-outcome components of an S-R-O structure. As an example, let us take the procedure developed by Bhatt, et al. (1988), a central screen with pecking keys at each of the four corners. An additional modification is that there are two feeders, one to deliver wheat and the other to deliver corn. Suppose pigeons were shown pictures of 40 trees, randomly divided into two sets of 20 each, Set A and Set B. As pigeons are shown tree pictures, only the lower-left and upper-right keys are lit and record responses. When a Set A picture is shown, a peck on the lower-left key delivers wheat as a reward, and when a Set B picture is shown, a peck on the upper-right key delivers corn as reward. Once pigeons have learned to discriminate readily between Set A and Set B pictures, Stage 2 of the experiment is introduced. In Stage 2, the upper-left key and the lower-right key are alternately illuminated, with a peck on the upper-left key yielding wheat reward and a peck on the lower-right key yielding corn reward. After several sessions of this training, pigeons now would be returned to the Stage 1 task. However, on certain probe trials, tree pictures from Sets A and B would appear and only the upper-left and lower-right keys would be illuminated for choice, with response to either key providing reinforcement. The interesting prediction here is that pigeons should prefer to peck the upper-left key when Set A pictures are shown and to peck the lower-right key when Set B pictures are shown. If the delivery of corn and wheat in Stage 2 activated S-R-O structures in a backward fashion, then the stimuli or tree pictures associated with each outcome might also become associated with the new key- peck response that yielded that particular outcome.

Finally, an interesting possibility is that categories could be primed through the delivery of a particular outcome. For example, after Stage 1 in the hypothetical experiment just described, might it be possible to selectively enhance categorization of Set A or Set B pictures by prefeeding pigeons wheat or corn prior to the presentation of pictures on a daily session? On a radial maze in which animals had learned that different sets of arms contain cheese, chocolate, and Noyes pellets, could one selectively improve chunking of one set of arms by prefeeding rats the type of food contained in those arms? If the stimulus members of an S-R-O structure can be activated in memory by presentation of the outcome, these stimuli then might have an advantage over those in other structures which would be activated only later in a session.

Thinking of categories as S-R-O structures, with components that may be independently manipulable, seems to hold the possibility for exploring cognitive structure in animals. An understanding of how animals form groupings of stimuli into categories through association may begin to help us understand the similarities and differences between human and animal concepts. In some cases, we may find that the complexities of human concepts are only an extension of similar associative structures found in animals.

ACKNOWLEDGEMENTS

Preparation of this chapter was supported by a Research Grant from the National Sciences and Engineering Research Council of Canada to William A. Roberts.

REFERENCES

Bhatt, R. S., Wasserman, E. A., Reynolds, W. F., Jr., & Knauss, K. S. (1988). Conceptual behavior in pigeons: Categorization of both familiar and novel examples from four classes of natural and artificial stimuli. *Journal of Experimental Psychology: Animal Behavior Processes, 14*, 219-234.

Capaldi, E. J. (1992). Levels of organized behavior in rats. In W. K. Honig & J. G. Fetterman (Eds.), *Cognitive aspects of stimulus control* (pp. 385-404). Hillsdale, NJ: Erlbaum.

Cerella, J. (1979). Visual classes and natural categories in the pigeon. *Journal of Experimental Psychology: Human perception and performance, 5*, 68-77.

Dallal, N. L., & Meck, W. H. (1990). Hierarchical structures: Chunking by food type facilitates spatial memory. *Journal of Experimental Psychology: Animal Behavior Processes, 16*, 69-84.

Edwards, C. A., Jagielo, J. A., Zentall, T. R., & Hogan, D. E. (1982). Acquired equivalence and distinctiveness in matching to sample by pigeons: Mediation by reinforcer-specific extpectancies. *Journal of Experimental Psychology: Animal Behavior Processes, 8*, 244-259.

Herrnstein, R. J. (1984). Objects, categories, and discriminative stimuli. In H. L. Roitblat, T. G. Bever, & H. S. Terrace (Eds.), *Animal cognition* (pp. 233-261). Hillsdale, NJ: Erlbaum.

Herrnstein, R. J. (1990). Levels of stimulus control: A functional approach. *Cognition, 37*, 133-166.

Herrnstein, R. J., & de Villiers, P. A. (1980). Fish as a natural category for people and pigeons. In G. H. Bower (Ed.), *The psychology of learning and motivation* (Vol. 14, pp. 59-95). San Diego, Academic Press.

Herrnstein, R. J., & Loveland, D. H. (1964). Complex visual concept in the pigeon. *Science, 146*, 549-551.

Keller, F. S., & Schoenfeld, W. N. (1950). *Principles of psychology*. New York: Appleton-Century-Crofts.

Lea, S. E. G. (1984). In what sense do pigeons learn concepts? In H. L. Roitblat, T. G. Bever, & H. S. Terrace (Eds.), *Animal cognition* (pp. 263-276). Hillsdale, NJ: Erlbaum.

Macuda, T., & Roberts, W. A. (1995). Further evidence for hierarchical chunking in rat spatial memory. *Journal of Experimental Psychology: Animal Behavior Processes, 21*, 20-32.

Nakagawa, E. (1986). Overtraining, extinction and shift learning in a concurrent discrimination in rats. *Quarterly Journal of Experimental Psychology, 38B*, 313-326.

Olthof, A., Macuda, T., & Roberts, W. A. (1995, June). *Incentive effects on the radial maze and evidence for equivalence sets in rats*. Poster presented at the annual meeting of the Canadian Society for Brain, Behaviour, and Cognitive Science, Halifax, Nova Scotia.

Peterson, G. B. (1984). How expectancies guide behavior. In H. L. Roitblat, T. G. Bever, & H. S. Terrace (Eds.), *Animal cognition* (pp. 135-148). Hillsdale, NJ: Erlbaum.

Roberts, W. A., Cheng, K., & Cohen, J. S. (1989). Timing light and tone signals in pigeons. *Journal of Experimental Psychology: Animal Behavior Processes, 15*, 23-35.

Roberts, W. A., & Mazmanian, D. S. (1988). Concept learning at different levels of abstraction by pigeons, monkeys, and people. *Journal of Experimental Psychology: Animal Behavior Processes, 14*, 247-260.

Sands, S. F., Lincoln, C. E., & Wright, A. A. (1982). Pictorial similarity judgments and the organization of visual memory in the rhesus monkey. *Journal of Experimental Psychology: General, 111*, 369-389.

Spence, K. W. (1937). The differential response of animals to stimuli varying within a single dimension. *Psychological Review, 44*, 430-444.

Tolman, E. C. (1959). Principles of purposive behavior. In S. Koch (Ed.), *Psychology: A study of a science* (Vol. 2, pp. 92-157). New York: McGraw-Hill.

Trapold, M. A. (1970). Are expectancies based upon different positive reinforcing events discriminably different? *Learning and Motivation, 1*, 129-140.

Urcuioli, P. J., & Zentall, T. R. (1986). Retrospective coding in pigeons' delayed matching-to-sample. *Journal of Experimental Psychology: Animal Behavior Processes, 12*, 69-77.

Urcuioli, P. J., Zentall, T. R., Jackson-Smith, P., & Steirn, J. N. (1989). Evidence for common coding in many-to-one matching: Retention, intertrial interference, and transfer. *Journal of Experimental Psychology: Animal Behavior Processes, 15*, 264-273.

Vaughan, W., Jr. (1988). Formation of equivalence sets in pigeons. *Journal of Experimental Psychology: Animal Behavior Processes, 14*, 36-42.

Vaughan, W., Jr., & Greene, S. L. (1984). Pigeon visual memory capacity. *Journal of Experimental Psychology: Animal Behavior Processes, 10*, 256-271.

Wasserman, E. A. (1995). The conceptual abilities of pigeons. *American Scientist, 83*, 246-255.

Wasserman, E. A., & Astley, S. L. (1994). A behavioral analysis of concepts: Its application to pigeons and children. In D. L. Medin (Ed.), *The psychology of learning and motivation* (Vol. 31, pp. 73-132). San Diego, Academic Press.

Wasserman, E. A., & Bhatt, R. S. (1992). Conceptualization of natural and artificial stimuli by pigeons. In W. K. Honig & J. G. Fetterman (Eds.), *Cognitive apects of stimulus control* (pp. 203-223). Hillsdale, NJ: Erlbaum.

Wasserman, E. A., DeVolder, C. L., & Coppage, D. J. (1992). Non-similarity-based conceptualization in pigeons via secondary or mediated generalization. *Psychological Science, 3*, 374-379.

Wasserman, E. A., Kiedinger, R. E., & Bhatt, R. S. (1988). Conceptual behavior in pigeons: Categories, subcategories, and pseudocategories. *Journal of Experimental Psychology: Animal Behavior Processes, 14*, 235-246.

Wasserman, E. A., Kirkpatrick-Steger, K., Van Hamme, L. J., & Biederman, I. (1993). Pigeons are sensitive to the spatial organization of complex visual stimuli. *Psychological Science, 5*, 336-341.

Watanabe, S., Lea, S. E. G., & Dittrich, W. H. (1993). What can we learn from experiments on pigeon concept discrimination? In H. P. Zeigler & H.-J. Bischof (Eds.), *Vision, brain, and behavior in birds* (pp. 351-376). Cambridge, MA: MIT Press.

Zentall, T. R., Sherburne, L. M., & Steirn, J. N. (1992). Development of excitatory backward associations during the establishment of forward associations in a delayed conditional discrimination by pigeons. *Animal Learning and Behavior, 20*, 199-206.

Zentall, T.R., Sherburne, L.M., & Urcuioli, P.J. (1995). Coding of hedonic and nonhedonic samples by pigeons in many-to-one delayed matching. *Animal Learning and Behavior, 23*, 189-196.

Zentall, T. R., Steirn, J. N., Sherburne, L. M., & Urcuioli, P. J. (1991). Common coding in pigeons assessed through partial versus total reversals of many-to-one conditional and simple discriminations. *Journal of Experimental Psychology: Animal Behavior Processes, 17*, 194-201.

Stimulus Class Formation in Humans and Animals
T.R. Zentall and P.M. Smeets (Editors)
© 1996 Elsevier Science B.V. All rights reserved.

4

Acquired Equivalences and Mediated Generalization in Pigeon's Matching-to-Sample

Peter J. Urcuioli
Purdue University

Acquired equivalence refers to the finding that very different stimuli can sometimes produce the same behavior even though one of more of them has no direct reinforced connection with that behavior. It has long been regarded as one of more important psychological phenomena in need of explanation. The reason for its importance is that acquired equivalences appear to form one basis for what we loosely refer to as "novel behavior" - behavior which occurs appropriately in some situation despite never having been explicitly reinforced in that situation. Such an observation poses a challenge to traditional behavior analysis and behavior theory because such accounts usually appeal to explicit reinforcement or conditioning in the situation in question in order to explain the behavior's occurrence. The challenge to traditional explanatory ideas was recognized over 50 years ago by Hull (1939) who said that:

> "...the problem of stimulus equivalence is a fundamental one. This is true not only for behaviorism but for any psychology purporting to deal in a thorough-going manner with adaptive behavior....The problem...is essentially this: How can we account for the fact that a stimulus will sometimes evoke a reaction to which it has never been conditioned, i.e., with which it has never been associated?" (p. 9)

Hull's answer was essentially that the novel reaction could arise from the prior associative relations shared by that stimulus with others. Understanding what happens as a consequence of this prior conditioning history, an issue which Hull's (1939) paper addressed, thus provides a potential key to the explanation of novel behavior.

This chapter represents another attempt to understand acquired equivalences in animal learning, particularly those instances reported in pigeon's matching-to-sample (MTS). The attempt involves the resurrection of the explanatory ideas proposed by Hull (1939): namely, that physically unrelated stimuli come to control the same behavior because they produce some common reaction which then mediates generalization of subsequent performances from one stimulus to another. In a moment, I will explain this mediated generalization account of acquired equivalences more fully. First, however, I should say a few words about why I wish to resurrect this old explanatory idea but, at the same time, confine its application to the pigeon MTS literature.

"Resurrection" implies that something (i.e., the mediated generalization account) is dead. This is undoubtedly an overly harsh characterization. Nevertheless, judging from the broader literature, many researchers appear to regard mediated generalization as unable to provide either a comprehensive or desirable explanation of equivalence effects. Certainly, the human literature contains a number of findings which do not readily fit this conceptualization of acquired equivalences (Sidman, 1994). But rejecting this account as a viable explanation for some equivalence effects should not lead to its outright dismissal for all such effects. After all, there is no reason to suppose that multiple processes (mediated generalization being one) cannot contribute to this important behavioral phenomenon. Besides, the pigeon data which I will discuss in this chapter seem to naturally fit such a model.

Restricting my discussion to the pigeon MTS literature is both deliberate and conservative. I want readers to judge the merits of the mediated generalization argument within a limited domain first, one uncomplicated by diverse procedures, dependent measures, etc. If the analysis is unsuccessful or unconvincing here, then there will be greater justification in relegating it to a minor or inconsequential role overall. On the other hand, to the extent that it does successfully capture existing effects and predict new ones, then researchers might be wise to consider (or reconsider) its involvement elsewhere. Implicit in my treatment, of course, is the belief that mediated generalization does produce acquired equivalences in pigeon conditional discriminations and is probably involved in other paradigms and with other animals (including humans) as well.

To make my case, I will describe (after some general background material) three matching-to-sample tasks in which acquired sample equivalences have been demonstrated but which differ in the degree to which mediational processes are apparent. My description begins with a task involving an "obvious" (i.e., explicit) mediator, moves on to one with a less apparent or more elusive mediator, and ends with a task in which the mediator (if truly involved) is clearly implicit. The purpose of this organization is to shape a conceptual orientation in the reader - to make the point, in other words, that mediated generalization provides a good overall framework for understanding equivalence effects independently of how obvious the hypothesized mediator is. Like others before me (e.g., Jenkins, 1963; Peterson, 1984), I take the position that precise specification of the hypothesized mediator, although certainly desirable, is not crucial for evaluating the merits of the approach. Rather, it is theoretically more important to be able specify the conditions under which mediated generalization operates, and why.

THE PHENOMENON AND THE PROPOSED EXPLANATION

Stated in different terms, acquired stimulus equivalence generally refers to the finding that, as a result of training, stimuli become interchangeable with, or substitutable for, one another in their control over behavior (Dougher & Markham, 1994; Spradlin & Saunders, 1986). Furthermore, this interchangeability is not simply the result of perceptual similarity between stimuli - in other words, it is not just an instance of primary stimulus generalization (Honig & Urcuioli, 1981). Finally, acquired equivalences involve "emergent" relations: some of the stimuli in question, in other words, must be shown to control responding despite the absence of any explicit reinforcement history with respect to that responding.

A simple example will illustrate all of these points. Honey and Hall (1989) initially trained rats to obtain food in the presence of two different auditory stimuli. Subsequently, one stimulus was made aversive (i.e., it acquired conditioned suppressive properties) by pairing it with shock. After this "reassignment" training, Honey and Hall found that the remaining auditory stimulus also exhibited aversive properties despite never having itself been associated with shock. The two stimuli were thus *interchangeable* with, or substitutable for, one another not only in original learning (where they both received common treatment) but, more importantly, in new situations as well (where they did not). Another way to view Honey and

Hall's findings is that a new behavioral relation had emerged (viz., between the tested stimulus and its observed suppressive effects), ostensibly on the basis of the common associative history shared by the two auditory cues.

Although primary stimulus generalization would seem, at first glance, to readily explain the transfer of suppression between the explicitly conditioned and the tested stimulus (given that both were auditory), other conditions run by Honey and Hall (1989) showed that this explanation will not suffice. For example, aversive control did not transfer between the auditory stimuli unless they shared a common association with food during initial training. Thus, the acquired equivalence effect must have arisen via some "nonperceptual" route, one which apparently involved that shared food association.

An alternative, nonperceptual explanation which contains this sort of associative element is what Hull (1939) called secondary generalization, generalization between stimuli based upon their common relation to other events. Hull claimed that when two or more stimuli occasion the same response (e.g., appetitive behavior), they also acquire the capacity to produce implicit components of that response. These implicit responses were thought to have stimulus properties which could then serve as additional discriminative cues for other behavior. Consequently, if one of the original stimuli were explicitly conditioned to some new behavior, Hull proposed that a connection would also form between the implicit response to that stimulus and the new behavior. As a result of this additional connection, the new performance would then generalize to any other stimulus producing the same implicit response. Table 1 illustrates this how generalization from a directly trained to an "untrained" stimulus can be mediated in this fashion.

Table 1
A basic training and test sequence for demonstrating acquired stimulus equivalence (Actual/Observed) and a theoretical explanation in terms of secondary or mediated generalization (Theoretics).

	Training		Test
	Initial	Reassignment	
Actual/ Observed	S_X-R_A S_Y-R_A	S_X-R_B	S_Y-R_B
Theoretics		S_X $(r_A$-$s_A)$ R_B	S_Y $(r_A$-$s_A)$ R_B

Note. S_X and S_Y represent nominal discriminative stimuli, R_A and R_B are the reinforced responses. r_A and s_A represents an implicit response and its stimulus consequences.

The top portion of the table shows an actual training sequence involving two stimuli (S_X and S_Y), two responses (R_A and R_B), and the effect observed in testing. In terms of the Honey and Hall (1989) experiment, S_X and S_Y would be the auditory stimuli, R_A would represent appetitive behavior, and R_B would be the "new", aversive behavior. The bottom portion shows the theoretical mediating link developing between the implicit components $(r_A$-$s_A)$ of the originally trained response (R_A) and the new behavior (R_B) conditioned during reassignment training. It is this encircled link which permits S_Y to produce R_B in testing despite the absence of any explicit reinforcement history between the two. Thus, S_X and S_Y are interchangeable in their control over R_B because they access the same mediating process.

Although Hull thought the mediator was a fractional component of the originally conditioned response (R_A), a mediated generalization account of acquired stimulus equivalence does not require this. What *is* important for the analysis is that stimuli which initially have the same relation to some other event (e.g., a response or a reinforcer) will, as a consequence, produce some common reaction with stimulus properties capable of entering into other associative relations (see, for example, Hall, 1991, pp. 163-165). It is these hypothesized mediating relations, not the nature of the mediator, which permit predictions about generalization of performance, or lack thereof, to be derived. The next section describes an example of mediated generalization from the pigeon MTS literature in which the nature of the mediator (as well as predictions from the model) are obvious.

ACQUIRED SAMPLE EQUIVALENCES ARISING FROM AN OVERT MEDIATOR

In two-choice MTS with differential sample-response requirements, the samples used in training are readily interchangeable with other stimuli associated with those same differential requirements. A schematic of a design used by Urcuioli and Honig (1980, Exp. 3) to demonstrate this effect is shown in Table 2. The design shown here does not resemble in any immediately obvious way the schematics depicted in Table 1 given the more complicated, conditional discrimination procedure. Nevertheless, the similarities are there and should become at least conceptually clear in the forthcoming discussion.

Table 2
A design to show acquired sample equivalences in matching-to-sample with differential sample-response requirements.

Training		Testing
Phase 1	Phase 2	Phase 3
$S_1 \cdot$ DRL $\rightarrow C_1+$	$S_2 \cdot$ DRL	$S_3 \cdot$ DRL $\rightarrow C_1+$
$S_2 \cdot$ FR $\rightarrow C_2+$	$S_4 \cdot$ FR	$S_4 \cdot$ FR $\rightarrow C_2+$

Note. S_1-S_4 denote sample (or potential sample) stimuli; C_1 and C_2 denote comparison stimuli; (+) indicates correct comparison choice; DRL = differential-reinforcement-of -low-rates-of-responding schedule; FR = fixed-ratio schedule.

Pigeons were initially trained (in Phase 1) to high levels of matching accuracy on a task in which they produced the comparison alternatives (C_1 and C_2) by spacing two successive keypecks 3 sec apart to one sample (S_1) and by pecking 10 times with no temporal restrictions to the alternative sample (S_2). These differential-reinforcement-of-low-rates-of-responding (DRL) and fixed-ratio (FR) requirements, respectively, produced very different patterns of behavior: slow, spaced responding on DRL trials versus rapid, uninterrupted pecking on FR trials. Following MTS acquisition, these same response patterns were then conditioned off baseline (in Phase 2) to two novel center-key stimuli (S_3 and S_4). Finally, those stimuli were substituted for the samples in MTS in order to test their ability to immediately control comparison choice.

Urcuioli and Honig (1980, Exp. 3) found that, despite their very different physical characteristics, S_3 was interchangeable with S_1, as was S_4 with S_2. In other words, birds consistently chose C_1 following S_3 and C_2 following S_4 even though these particular relations had never been explicitly reinforced prior to testing (see also Urcuioli, 1984, Exp. 2; Hogan, Zentall, & Pace, 1983). Furthermore, this result could not be attributed to any inherent ability of pigeons to match S_3 to C_1 and S_4 to C_2 because those same relations produced *negative* transfer (i.e., below-chance levels of accuracy) when S_3 and S_4 were associated with the "opposite" pattern of responding than the samples they replaced.

This is a straightforward example of acquired sample equivalences via mediated generalization. First, S_3 and S_4 were shown to be functionally equivalent to S_1 and S_2, respectively, in the sense that they were interchangeable with, or substitutable for, one another in testing. Second, the equivalences were acquired, ostensibly via the samples' common association with DRL or FR response patterns. Third, generalization of matching performances across samples involved an explicit mediator, namely, the birds' differential sample behaviors (cf. Urcuioli, 1985). For example, successive sample keypecks on DRL trials showed characteristically long interresponse times (IRTs), whereas successive keypecks on FR trials were separated by relatively short IRTs. Observationally, too, birds behaved very differently on DRL and FR trials, often circling or moving away from the key between pecks on the former trials versus maintaining a steady pecking position on the latter.

Another way to conceptualize the transfer results is to consider S_1 and S_3, and S_2 and S_4, as members of different stimulus classes. The class concept (Goldiamond, 1962) means, first of all, that its members control the same behavior - in this case, either DRL or FR responding. More importantly however, operations applied to one stimulus in a class also affect other stimuli in the same class (Sidman, 1994). Thus, establishing one sample as a cue for choosing a particular comparison made the other sample in the DRL or FR class equally effective as a cue for that same choice. Here, then, is the connection to the operations and processes depicted in Table 1. Two samples occasion the same behavior (e.g., DRL) and one is then established as a cue for "new" or different behavior (comparison choice). Because of the common association to DRL (or FR) , the "new" performance then generalizes to the remaining sample. Granted, the differential sample-response design is unusual because S_3 and S_4 joined the DRL and FR class with S_1 and S_2, respectively, *after* conditional stimulus control had been established to S_1 and S_2. Nevertheless, this variation in the order in which the various controlling relations were established seems relatively minor and, quite obviously, inconsequential.

A stimulus-class view of these results raises some interesting questions. For example, would transfer still occur if differential responding were not required in testing or, indeed, in any phase in which conditional stimulus control was being established or reinforced? Stated otherwise, would the shared association of S_1 and S_3 (and of S_2 and S_4) to a particular response pattern *outside* of MTS be sufficient to produce transfer of conditional control between samples within MTS? Or does transfer require that differential sample responding continue throughout training and testing on MTS, as suggested by a mediated generalization analysis? The small amount of available evidence suggests that continued differential responding is required. For example, when Urcuioli and Honig (1980, Exp. 3) periodically removed the DRL versus FR contingencies during testing such that a single peck to either sample stimulus produced the comparisons, birds were much less likely to choose C_1 after S_3 and C_2 and S_4. Furthermore, the continued, albeit reduced, tendency to make "class-consistent" choices could reasonably be attributed to residual differential sample behavior occurring prior to the single sample keypeck on these probe trials.

Interestingly, this pattern of results resembles some earlier findings reported in the human mediated generalization literature. For example, Birge (1941; cited by Jenkins, 1963) and Kendler (1972) showed that stimuli with a common verbal association are much less effective substitutes for each other in new discriminations when the verbal labels are not explicitly required in those new discriminations. In the Kendler (1972) study, subjects showed excellent transfer of a spatial response across commonly named visual patterns if they said the names aloud. Transfer was greatly reduced, however, when subjects were not required to name each pattern during spatial-response conditioning and during testing. From a mediated generalization perspective, overt naming provides another discriminative cue for spatial performance, and this cue would be precluded (or at least weakened) when overt naming was not required during spatial-response acquisition and testing.

One final issue regarding the differential sample-response findings should be addressed. Does the observed transfer truly reflect emergent relations? "Emergent" implies that the relations in question have never been explicitly trained. Certainly, the S_3-C_1 and S_4-C_2 relations shown for testing in Table 2 were *not* explicitly trained. On the other hand, the DRL-C_1 and FR-C_2 relations also present in testing *were* explicitly reinforced during Phase 1. Thus, it is easy to reject these findings as instances of acquired equivalences because the DRL versus FR performances apparently provided a redundant conditional cue for choice during initial training. From this perspective, the observed "transfer" is nothing more than a continuation of prior reinforced training (i.e., there are no emergent relations). This same point was raised by Hayes (1989) and Saunders (1989) regarding a purported demonstration of stimulus equivalence by McIntire, Cleary, and Thompson (1987), who likewise trained and tested monkeys in MTS with differential sample-response contingencies.

The conflicting views here seem to boil down to what requires explanation versus the explanation itself. In the example, if the sample-comparison relations in testing are the focus of inquiry, then clearly new relations *have* emerged. Furthermore, those new relations are explicable by mediated generalization via the subjects' differential sample-response patterns. On the other hand, if that proposed mechanism itself is simply viewed as "part of training" (which indeed it is, according to a mediated generalization analysis), then nothing has really emerged and nothing seems in need of explanation. But the latter approach either begs the question of how acquired equivalences develop or categorizes these sorts of instances as "obvious" or "uninteresting". But "obvious" instances should not be ignored because they may very well provide valuable insights into what occurs when acquired equivalences develop by less noticeable means.

ACQUIRED SAMPLE EQUIVALENCES VIA COMMON REINFORCING OUTCOMES

The differential outcome literature provides another example of sample equivalences in pigeon's MTS. In a differential outcome task, the reinforcer for correct comparison choice on trials with one sample differs from the reinforcer for correct choice on trials with an alternative sample (Edwards, Jagielo, Zentall, & Hogan, 1982; Peterson, 1984; Urcuioli, 1990; Williams, Butler, & Overmier, 1990). The sample stimuli associated with unique outcomes (like those associated with differential sample responding) can be readily replaced by other stimuli with similar associations. Table 3 shows a design for demonstrating this transfer effect (cf. Peterson, 1984; Urcuioli, 1990, Exps. 3A and 3B).

Table 3
A design to show acquired sample equivalences in matching-to-sample with differential outcomes.

Training		Testing
Phase 1	Phase 2	Phase 3
$S_1 \rightarrow C_1 + (O_1)$	$S_3 \rightarrow (O_1)$	$S_3 \rightarrow C_1 + (O_1)$
$S_2 \rightarrow C_2 + (O_2)$	$S_4 \rightarrow (O_2)$	$S_4 \rightarrow C_2 + (O_2)$

Note. S_1-S_4 denote sample (or potential sample) stimuli; C_1 and C_2 denote comparison stimuli; (+) indicates correct comparison choice; O_1 and O_2 denote different reinforcing outcomes.

Pigeons initially learn a two-sample (S_1 and S_2), two-alternative (C_1 and C_2) matching task in which discriminably different outcomes (O_1 and O_2) are contingent upon the correct choices (Phase 1). Following acquisition, two new stimuli (S_3 and S_4) are paired (in Phase 2) with the same two outcomes used in initial training. Finally, those new stimuli are substituted for the samples in MTS. When the substitution involves the interchange of samples which are associated with the same outcome, positive transfer of performance is routinely observed (e.g., Peterson, 1984; Urcuioli, 1990). In other words, pigeons preferentially choose C_1 following S_3 and C_2 following S_4 despite never having been explicitly reinforced for responding in this fashion. This substitutability of S_3 for S_1, and S_4 for S_2, thus indicates an acquired sample equivalence based upon common reinforcing outcomes.

The typical explanation for this effect is that transfer is mediated by the subjects' differential outcome expectancies, as depicted in Table 4. According to this outcome-expectancy view (Honig & Dodd, 1986; Trapold, 1970), the unique sample-outcome relations in original training permit well-trained subjects to expect a particular outcome when a sample is presented (E_1 and E_2). Those expectancies have stimulus properties and thus can provide another cue for choice. Consequently, other stimuli (e.g., S_3 and S_4) generating those same, differential expectancies will support accurate matching performances. This can be appreciated by noting the common (highlighted) E_1-C_1 and E_2-C_2 relations in training and testing in Table 4.

Table 4
The outcome expectancy interpretation of acquired sample equivalences in differential-outcome matching-to-sample.

Training	Testing
$S_1 \cdot E_1 \rightarrow C_1 + (O_1)$	$S_3 \cdot E_1 \rightarrow C_1 + (O_1)$
$S_2 \cdot E_2 \rightarrow C_2 + (O_2)$	$S_4 \cdot E_2 \rightarrow C_2 + (O_2)$

Note. S_1-S_4 denote sample stimuli; C_1 and C_2 denote comparison stimuli; (+) indicates correct comparison choice; O_1 and O_2 denote different reinforcing outcomes; E_1 and E_2 represent expectancies of those outcomes.

    This, then, is another example of mediated generalization: generalization of matching performances based upon the common (expectancy) mediators conditioned to the sample stimuli. This conceptualization is supported by two additional findings. First, the pattern of comparison choice in testing corresponds precisely to the expectancy presumably elicited on a given trial by the sample. Thus, *negative* transfer can be obtained by substituting S_3 for S_2 rather than for S_1, and likewise substituting S_4 for S_1 rather than for S_2 (Edwards et al., 1982; Peterson & Trapold, 1980). Second, transfer of any kind requires that both the samples used in training and those substituted for them in testing be associated with differential outcomes. If not, there is no evidence for acquired sample equivalences - pigeons perform at chance levels of accuracy in testing (Peterson, 1984; Urcuioli, 1990).

    One recurring issue in the differential outcome literature concerns the nature of the hypothesized expectancies. With certain outcomes, the mediator may very well be differential responding which sometimes develops to the samples. For example, when the outcomes are food and the illumination of the food-hopper light with raising the hopper itself ("no food"), pigeons rapidly peck the food-associated sample but rarely peck the no-food-associated sample. Urcuioli and DeMarse (1994) recently showed that this peck versus no-peck sample-response pattern controls comparison choice in MTS with these outcomes. In short, differential sample behavior was a source of mediated generalization. It seems reasonable to suppose, then, that a similar acquired equivalence mechanism could be at work in any differential outcome task which promotes differential responding (e.g., Brodigan & Peterson, 1976). However, it is also important to recognize that sample substitutability, the index of acquired equivalences, does not require such differential responding. For example, transfer has also been observed in differential outcome tasks which do not yield overt differential sample responding (Edwards et al., 1982; Sherburne & Zentall, 1995).

    The point is that sample equivalences in the differential outcome paradigm easily fit a mediated generalization model independently of our ability to directly observe or specify the mediator. Similar differential outcome, transfer-of-control effects in the human stimulus equivalence literature (Dube, McIlvane, Mackay, & Stoddard, 1987; Dube, McIlvane, Maguire, Mackay, & Stoddard, 1989; Schenk, 1994) also follow at once from the model. Furthermore, the model makes clear, and sometimes rather unusual, predictions for performance during the critical substitution tests. For example, if the design shown in Table 3 is slightly modified such that, in testing, correct choices on S_3 trials yield O_2 (rather than O_1), and vice versa for correct choices on S_4 trials, pigeons' initial test performances are very accurate but then deteriorate to chance levels of accuracy (Peterson & Trapold, 1980; see also Urcuioli & Zentall, 1992, Exp. 3). Thus, even though birds begin testing by consistently choosing C_1 after S_3 and C_2 after S_4 and receiving reinforcement for those choices, these reinforced relations are not sufficient to maintain performance! A mediated generalization account makes sense of this peculiar finding. According to this account, the expectancies previously conditioned to S_3 and S_4 during Phase 2 training provide the "appropriate" mediating link to performance when testing begins (cf. Table 4). However, the reversal of the outcomes associated with S_3 and S_4 upon entering the test phase causes the original outcome expectancies conditioned to them to change and eventually be replaced by the opposite outcome expectancies. Those opposite expectancies then cue the opposite (incorrect) choice on each trial, causing the observed deterioration in performance.

THE MANY-TO-ONE PARADIGM: ACQUIRED SAMPLE EQUIVALENCES FROM COMMON COMPARISON-STIMULUS ASSOCIATIONS

Little effort seems needed to view the acquired equivalence effects described above as instances of mediated generalization because the mediating elements are either readily observed or easily appreciated. But what benefit is there to maintaining this conceptualization if the crucial mediator is either vague, unknown, or inaccessible? One possible benefit is the encouragement to analyze these ambiguous situations using the same reasoning and principles applied to the less ambiguous situations. For instance, the same manipulations used to detect acquired sample equivalences based upon explicit mediators ought to yield similar effects when the mediators are implicit.

A good example of this can be found in the recent literature on "many-to-one" MTS (Grant & Spetch, 1994; Urcuioli, DeMarse, & Zentall, 1994; Urcuioli, Zentall, Jackson-Smith, & Steirn, 1989; Urcuioli, Zentall, & DeMarse, 1995; see also Wasserman, DeVolder, & Coppage, 1992). In this task, multiple samples are initially associated with the same comparison choice response. If this shared association produces an acquired sample equivalence via the same mechanisms as do the shared associations in the differential sample-response and differential outcome paradigms, then we should be able to detect this fact using transfer-of-control manipulations of the sort already described. Specifically, establishing new relations to some of the samples with common comparison associations in many-to-one MTS should yield generalization of those new performances to the remaining samples. In fact, this prediction has been amply confirmed using the design shown in the top half of Table 5.

Pigeons initially learn to match physically unrelated sample stimuli to the same comparison alternatives (i.e., S_1 and S_3 to C_1, and S_2 and S_4 to C_2). There are no differential sample-response requirements and no differential outcomes, so observationally the birds' behavior in the presence of the various samples is indistinguishable. Nevertheless, at issue is whether or not this many-to-one mapping produces something other than a set of four independent sample-comparison relations. Transfer-of-control tests, like those depicted in Table 5 (see also Spradlin, Cotter, & Baxley, 1973) demonstrate that "something else" does emerge. For instance, after learning new comparison responses (C_3 and C_4) to two of the original samples, birds immediately generalize those newly learned comparison choices to the remaining, "untrained" samples (Urcuioli et al., 1989, Exp. 2). In short, the common

P.J. Urcuioli

comparison association in many-to-one MTS produces an acquired sample equivalence.

A mediated generalization explanation of these results would go as follows. As a result of many-to-one training, the presentation of S_1 and S_3 gives rise to the anticipation or memory of C_1 (i.e., these samples are "prospectively coded" as C_1 - cf. Honig & Dodd, 1986). Similarly, the presentation of S_2 and S_4 are prospectively coded as C_2. During subsequent reassignment training when one member of each sample pair is associated with a new comparison, the implicit coding responses for these samples become associated with (provide discriminative stimuli for) the new comparison choices. As a result, other samples yielding the same prospective codes will lead to those same choices even though the tested relations were never directly reinforced. Table 6 summarizes the theoretics of this mediational account. Interestingly, Spradlin and Saunders (1986, pp. 56-57) have suggested a conceptually similar account of human many-to-one performances.

Table 5
Testing acquired equivalences following many-to-one (MTO) and one-to-many (OTM) matching-to sample training.

Condition	Training		Testing
	Phase 1	Phase 2	Phase 3
MTO	$S_1 \rightarrow C_1+$ $S_2 \rightarrow C_2+$ $S_3 \rightarrow C_1+$ $S_4 \rightarrow C_2+$	$S_1 \rightarrow C_3+$ $S_2 \rightarrow C_4+$	$S_3 \rightarrow C_3+$ $S_4 \rightarrow C_4+$
OTM	$S_1 \rightarrow C_1+$ $S_2 \rightarrow C_2+$ $S_1 \rightarrow C_3+$ $S_2 \rightarrow C_4+$	$S_3 \rightarrow C_1+$ $S_4 \rightarrow C_2+$	$S_3 \rightarrow C_3+$ $S_4 \rightarrow C_4+$

Again, however, we might ask what is gained by inferring unobserved coding responses and their presumed "connection" to the comparison alternatives in testing. Isn't it sufficient to say that samples which are initially associated with the same comparison become members of the same stimulus class and that class membership, by definition, ensures between-member generalization of subsequent matching performances? Perhaps. But how this generalization occurs is left unspecified. Clearly, the samples in each class possess stimulus properties over and above their physical attributes, and those additional properties seem to arise in the same way as do explicit mediators (viz., from a particular, shared reinforcement history). Furthermore, a stimulus-class view devoid of mechanism will have some difficulty explaining why transfer does not occur when the same training relations in the many-to-one design are learned in a slightly different order as shown in the bottom half of Table 5.

In this sequence, birds initially learn (on different trials) to match each sample to two different comparisons (e.g., both C_1 and C_3 are correct after S_1 -- a "one-to-many" mapping).

Birds then learn to match new samples to two of the original comparisons, after which they are tested on the same emergent relations as birds in the many-to-one (MTO) sequence. The important thing to note is that at the point of testing, one-to many (OTM) birds have learned exactly the same sample-comparison relations as MTO birds: namely, S_1-C_1, S_2-C_2, S_3-C_1, S_4-C_2, S_1-C_3, and S_2-C_4. In each case, then, a many-to-one mapping is part of training: S_1 and S_3 both occasion the same comparison choice (C_1), as do S_2 and S_4 (viz., C_2). From an unembellished stimulus-class perspective, an acquired equivalence should develop between the members of these sample "pairs". Thus, given that the OTM birds also learn to match S_1 to C_3 and S_2 to C_4, they should then generalize these comparison choices to S_3 and S_4 in testing. In fact, they do not (Urcuioli et al., 1995).

Table 6
The theoretics of a mediated generalization account of acquired sample equivalences in many-to-one matching-to-sample.

Training		Testing
Phase 1	Phase 2	Phase 3
$\begin{array}{l} S_1 \rightarrow C_1+ \\ S_2 \rightarrow C_2+ \\ S_3 \rightarrow C_1+ \\ S_4 \rightarrow C_2+ \end{array}$	$\begin{array}{c} \qquad\quad "c_1" \\ S_1 \diagup \diagdown C_3+ \\ S_2 \diagdown \diagup C_4+ \\ \qquad\quad "c_2" \end{array}$	$\begin{array}{c} \qquad\quad "c_1" \\ S_3 \diagup \diagdown C_3+ \\ S_4 \diagdown \diagup C_4+ \\ \qquad\quad "c_2" \end{array}$

Note. "c_1" and "c_2" represent mediating responses to (prospective codes for) the samples (S_1-S_4). Lines connecting pairs of samples in Phase 1 indicate which samples have common comparison associations, the purported source of the c_1 and c_2 mediators.

The difference in the effectiveness of OTM versus MTO training sequences in producing acquired sample equivalences comes as no surprise to a mediated generalization view, however. Because the OTM training trials are randomized, even birds performing at high levels of accuracy cannot anticipate which correct comparison will appear following a sample. Thus, it is unlikely that those samples could generate the necessary prospective mediators to support transfer to the C_3 versus C_4 choices in testing. In other words, the sorts of linkages diagrammed in Table 6 to account for transfer following MTO training are not derivable in any straightforward way following OTM training. Without those common links, there should not be, and indeed there isn't any, transfer between samples.

SOME ADDITIONAL PREDICTIONS AND DERIVATIONS

In a recent paper (Urcuioli et al., 1995), I indicated that a mediated generalization model does predict the emergence of new relations following OTM matching providing that the two pairs of sample-comparison relations comprising the OTM task are trained in sequence (rather than concurrently) and that those relations are trained in a particular order. Specifically, if the S_1-C_1 and S_2-C_2 relations (cf. Table 5) are trained first, followed by S_1-C_3

and S_2-C_4, then the prospective codes for C_1 and C_2 purportedly generated by S_1 and S_2 via initial training should form links to the C_3 versus C_4 choices during subsequent training. Those links would then permit mediated transfer in testing. By contrast, if the training sequence is reversed (i.e., S_1-C_3 and S_2-C_4 are learned first), the necessary links will not form and transfer should not occur in testing. Thus, the order of training ought to matter greatly in producing acquired equivalences in sequential OTM matching.

By contrast, if the sample-comparison relations comprising MTO matching are "decomposed" and trained sequentially, transfer to derived relations in testing (cf. Table 5) should occur no matter what order the component training relations are learned. The reason is that in either case, the crucial mediating links necessary for subsequent transfer form after the two pairs of relations involved in MTO matching are learned. How well these predictions are borne out will certainly have an important bearing on the viability of the mediated generalization model.

This model also makes a noteworthy prediction regarding a phenomenon in the human equivalence literature which has yet to be convincingly demonstrated following standard (visual-visual) conditional discrimination training in other primates and in pigeons - symmetry (D'Amato, Salmon, Loukas, & Tomie, 1985; Hogan & Zentall, 1977; Lipkens, Kop, & Matthijs, 1988; Sidman, Rauzin, Lazar, Cunningham, Tailby, & Carrigan, 1982). Symmetry refers to the finding that the conditional relations learned between samples and comparisons also hold when the roles of those stimuli are reversed. Using capital letters to designate pairs of samples and pairs of comparisons, symmetry means that after subjects have learned A-B matching, they are immediately capable of B-A matching. However, because the samples and comparisons in typical MTS tasks appear in different locations, a failure to obtain symmetry in non-human animals might be a consequence of a disruptive shift in stimulus location during testing. To avoid this potential problem, Sidman et al. (1982, Experiment 1) arranged for subjects to have previous experience in which the samples and comparisons used in testing had already appeared (and were accurately discriminated) in their respective locations. This was accomplished by adding two identity matching tasks (A-A and B-B) in training to the task (A-B) used as the baseline for the symmetry tests (B-A). Nevertheless, symmetry still failed to emerge. The order in which the three training tasks were learned prior to testing in Sidman et al. (1982) is depicted on the left side of Table 7.

Note that A-A and B-B identity matching were learned first. Consequently, subsequent acquisition of A-B matching can be viewed either producing a one-to-many mapping (A-A and A-B) or a many-to-one mapping (B-B and A-B). If the behavioral result is more similar to the former than to the latter, then the failure to observe emergent B-A relations ("symmetry") is not surprising from a mediated generalization model. By this same account, a slight change in Sidman et al.'s training procedure ought to produce evidence for symmetry. This change, shown on the right side of Table 7, simply involves moving A-A identity matching to the end of training. By doing so, the first two phases of training (B-B and A-B) clearly represent many-to-one contingencies. These should produce acquired sample equivalences between the B and A samples such that when "new" comparison choices (A) are conditioned to one set of samples (A), those choices should immediately generalize to the remaining (B) set of samples. In other words, B-A matching ("symmetry") should emerge from the training sequence shown on the right.

One could contest, I suppose, whether or not such a finding would represent "real" symmetry. The argument would probably be that training the other, identity relations makes the symmetry test of the nonidentity relations less "pure". I would have two objections to this. First, considering that the identity tasks were included in Sidman et al.'s design to minimize stimulus location effects, had those results been different, I seriously doubt whether their data would have been dismissed as "not real symmetry". Second, such a dismissal in the context of the proposed experiment would miss the point entirely. The important thing would be that B-A relations indicative of symmetry can be made to emerge by training the baseline sample-comparison relations in a particular order. This would provide an especially impressive confirmation of the mediated generalization account of acquired sample equivalences.

Table 7
Testing for symmetrical sample-comparison relations following the training sequence used by Sidman et al. (1982) and an alternative sequence based mediated generalization principles.

	Sidman et al.	An alternative
Training	A-A	B-B
	B-B	A-B
	A-B	A-A
Testing	B-A	B-A

Note. A and B represent pairs of samples (to the left of the hyphens) and comparisons (to the right of the hyphens).

SUMMARY AND CONCLUSIONS

The proposal that acquired equivalences in pigeon's MTS, and perhaps in animal behavior more generally, are the consequence of mediated generalization processes is hardly novel. As a matter of fact, writing this chapter made me feel as though I was re-inventing the wheel given the long history and extensive literature on mediated generalization (e.g., Dugdale & Lowe, 1990; Hull, 1939; James & Hakes, 1965; Jeffrey, 1953; Jenkins, 1963; Kendall, 1983; Miller & Dollard, 1941). But this wheel may have gotten a flat in recent years. For example, in the human stimulus equivalence literature, the notion of mediated generalization as a way of explaining equivalence effects has fallen into disfavor (Sidman, 1994). In that literature, this issue translates into whether or not those effects are a consequence of names which subjects might provide to the various stimuli involved in training and testing (Dugdale & Lowe, 1990; Eikeseth & Smith, 1992; Sidman, Willson-Morris, & Kirk, 1986). As I indicated earlier, the human equivalence data suggest that naming is not necessary (i.e., is not a required "mediator") for transfer to derived relations.

But lack of necessity does not mean lack of involvement. It may be that naming, when available, contributes to the development of acquired equivalences, perhaps via the same processes discussed in this chapter. But independently of the resolution of this particular issue with regard to human equivalence class formation, we should seriously entertain mediated generalization as the primary process underlying acquired equivalences in non-human animals. After all, it may very well be that the inability of most animals to show the types of equivalence effects regarded as "standard" in the human literature (i.e., reflexivity, symmetry, and transitivity) arises precisely because the procedures used do not give rise to mediated generalization processes.

REFERENCES

Birge, J. S. (1941). *The role of verbal response in transfer.* Unpublished doctoral dissertation, Yale University.

Brodigan, D. L., & Peterson, G. B. (1976). Two-choice conditional discrimination performance of pigeons as a function of reward, expectancy, prechoice delay, and domesticity. *Animal Learning and Behavior, 4*, 121-124.

D'Amato, M. R., Salmon, D. P., Loukas, E., & Tomie, A. (1985). Symmetry and transitivity of conditional relations in monkeys (Cebus apella) and pigeons (Columba livia). *Journal of the Experimental Analysis of Behavior, 44*, 35-47.

Dougher, M. J., & Markham, M. R. (1994). Stimulus equivalence, functional equivalence, and the transfer of function. In S. C. Hayes, L. J. Hayes, M. Sato, & K. Ono (Eds.), *Behavior analysis of language and cognition (pp. 71-90).* Reno, NV: Context Press.

Dube, W. V., McIlvane, W. J., Mackay, H. A., & Stoddard, L. T. (1987). Stimulus class membership established via stimulus-reinforcer relations. *Journal of the Experimental Analysis of Behavior, 47*, 159-175.

Dube, W. V., McIlvane, W. J., Maguire, R. W., Mackay, H. A., & Stoddard, L. T. (1989). Stimulus class formation and stimulus-reinforcer relations. *Journal of the Experimental Analysis of Behavior, 51*, 65-76.

Dugdale, N., & Lowe, C. F. (1990). Naming and stimulus equivalence. In D. E. Blackman & H. Lejeune (Eds.), *Behaviour analysis in theory and practice: Contributions and controversies (pp. 115-138).* Hove, England: Erlbaum.

Edwards, C. A., Jagielo, J. A., Zentall, T. R., & Hogan, D. E. (1982). Acquired equivalence and distinctiveness in matching to sample by pigeons: Mediation by reinforcer-specific expectancies. *Journal of Experimental Psychology: Animal Behavior Processes, 8*, 244-259.

Eikeseth, S., & Smith, T. (1992). The development of functional and equivalence classes in high-functioning autistic children: The role of naming. *Journal of the Experimental Analysis of Behavior, 58*, 123-133.

Goldiamond, I. (1962). Perception. In A. J. Bachrach (Ed.), *Experimental foundations of clinical psychology* (pp. 280-340). NY: Basic Books.

Grant, D. S., & Spetch, M. L. (1994). Mediated transfer testing provides evidence for common coding of duration and line samples in many-to-one matching in pigeons. *Animal Learning and Behavior, 22*, 84-89.

Hall, G. (1991). *Perceptual and associative learning.* Oxford: Oxford University Press.

Hayes, S. C. (1989). Nonhumans have not yet shown stimulus equivalence. *Journal of the Experimental Analysis of Behavior, 51*, 385-392.

Hogan, D. E., & Zentall, T. R. (1977). Backward associations in the pigeon. *American Journal of Psychology, 90*, 3-15.

Hogan, D. E., Zentall, T. R., & Pace, G. (1983). Control of pigeons' matching-to-sample performances by differential sample-response requirements. *American Journal of Psychology, 96*, 37-49.

Honey, R. C., & Hall, G. (1989). The acquired equivalence and distinctiveness of cues. *Journal of Experimental Psychology: Animal Behavior Processes, 15*, 338-346.

Honig, W. K., & Dodd, P. W. D. (1986). Anticipation and intention in working memory. In D. F. Kendrick, M. E. Rilling, & M. R. Denny (Eds.), *Theories of animal memory (pp. 77-100)*. Hillsdale, NJ: Erlbaum.

Honig, W. K., & Urcuioli, P. J. (1981). The legacy of Guttman and Kalish (1956): Twenty-five years of research on stimulus generalization. *Journal of the Experimental Analysis of Behavior, 36*, 405-445.

Hull, C. L. (1939). The problem of stimulus equivalence in behavior theory. *Psychological Review, 46*, 9-30.

James, C. T., & Hakes, D. T. (1965). Mediated transfer in a four-stage stimulus-equivalence paradigm. *Journal of Verbal Learning and Verbal Behavior, 4*, 89-93.

Jeffrey, W. E. (1953). The effects of verbal and nonverbal responses in mediating an instrumental act. *Journal of Experimental Psychology, 45*, 327-333.

Jenkins, J. J. (1963). Mediated associations: Paradigms and situations. In C. N. Cofer & B. S. Musgrave (Eds.), Verbal behavior and learning (pp. 210-245). NY: McGraw-Hill.

Kendall, S. B. (1983). Tests for mediated transfer in pigeons. *Psychological Record, 33*, 245-256.

Kendler, T. S. (1972). An ontogeny of mediational deficiency. *Child Development, 43*, 1-17.

Lipkens, R., Kop, P. F. M., & Matthijs, W. (1988). A test of symmetry and transitivity in conditional discrimination performances of pigeons. *Journal of the Experimental Analysis of Behavior, 49*, 395-409.

McIntire, K. D., Cleary, J., & Thompson, T. (1987). Conditional relations by monkeys: Reflexivity, symmetry, and transitivity. *Journal of the Experimental Analysis of Behavior, 47*, 279-285.

Miller, N. E., & Dollard, J. (1941). *Social learning and imitation*. New Haven, CT: Yale University Press.

Peterson, G. B. (1984). How expectancies influence behavior. In H. L. Roitblat, T. G. Bever, & H. S. Terrace (Eds.), *Animal cognition (pp. 135-147)*. Hillsdale, NJ: Erlbaum.

Peterson, G. B., & Trapold, M. A. (1980). Effects of altering outcome expectancies on pigeons' delayed conditional discrimination performance. *Learning and Motivation, 11*, 267-288.

Saunders, K. J. (1989). Naming in conditional discrimination and stimulus equivalence. *Journal of the Experimental Analysis of Behavior, 51*, 379-384.

Schenk, J. J. (1994). Emergent relations of equivalence generated by outcome-specific consequences in conditional discrimination. *Psychological Record, 44*, 537-558.

Sherburne, L., & Zentall, T. R. (1995). Pigeons transfer between conditional discriminations with differential outcomes in the absence of differential-sample-responding cues. *Animal Learning and Behavior, 23*, 273-279.

Sidman, M. (1994). *Equivalence relations and behavior: A research story*. Boston: Authors Cooperative.

Sidman, M., Rauzin, R., Lazar, R., Cunningham, S., Tailby, W., & Carrigan, P. (1982). A search for symmetry in the conditional discriminations of rhesus monkeys, baboons, and children. *Journal of the Experimental Analysis of Behavior, 37*, 23-44.

Sidman, M., Willson-Morris, M., & Kirk, B. (1986). Matching-to-sample procedures and the development of equivalence relations: The role of naming. *Analysis and Intervention in Developmental Disabilities, 6,* 1-19.

Spradlin, J. E., Cotter, V. W., & Baxley, N. (1973). Establishing a conditional discrimination without direct training: A study of transfer with retarded adolescents. *American Journal of Mental Deficiency, 77,* 556-566.

Spradlin, J. E., & Saunders, R. R. (1984). Behaving appropriately in new situations: A stimulus class analysis. *American Journal of Mental Deficiency, 88,* 574-579.

Spradlin, J. E., & Saunders, R. R. (1986). The development of stimulus classes using match-to-sample procedures: Sample classification versus comparison classification. *Analysis and Intervention in Developmental Disabilities, 6,* 41-48.

Trapold, M. A. (1970). Are expectancies based upon different positive reinforcing events discriminably different? *Learning and Motivation, 1,* 129-140.

Urcuioli, P. J. (1984). Overshadowing in matching-to-sample: Reduction in sample-stimulus control by differential sample behaviors. *Animal Learning & Behavior, 12,* 256-264.

Urcuioli, P. J. (1985). On the role of differential sample behaviors in matching-to-sample. *Journal of Experimental Psychology: Animal Behavior Processes, 4,* 502-519.

Urcuioli, P. J. (1990). Some relationships between outcome expectancies and sample stimuli in pigeons' delayed matching. *Animal Learning and Behavior, 18,* 302-314.

Urcuioli, P. J., & DeMarse, T. (1994). On the relationship between differential outcomes and differential sample responding in matching-to-sample. *Journal of Experimental Psychology: Animal Behavior Processes, 20,* 249-263.

Urcuioli, P. J., DeMarse, T., & Zentall, T. R. (1994). Some properties of many-to-one matching with hue, response, and food samples: Retention and mediated transfer. *Learning and Motivation, 25,* 175-200.

Urcuioli, P. J., & Honig, W. K. (1980). Control of choice in conditional discriminations by sample-specific behaviors. *Journal of Experimental Psychology: Animal Behavior Processes, 6,* 251-277.

Urcuioli, P. J., & Zentall, T. R. (1992). Transfer across delayed discriminations: Evidence regarding the nature of prospective working memory. *Journal of Experimental Psychology: Animal Behavior Processes, 18,* 154-173.

Urcuioli, P. J., Zentall, T. R., & DeMarse, T. (1995). Transfer to derived sample-comparison relations by pigeons following many-to-one versus one-to-many matching with identical training relations. *Quarterly Journal of Experimental Psychology, 48B,* 158-178.

Urcuioli, P. J., Zentall, T. R., Jackson-Smith, P., & Steirn, J. N. (1989). Evidence for common coding in many-to-one matching: Retention, intertrial interference, and transfer. *Journal of Experimental Psychology: Animal Behavior Processes, 15,* 264-273.

Wasserman, E. A., DeVolder, C. L., & Coppage, D. J. (1992). Non-similarity-based conceptualization in pigeons via secondary or mediated generalization. *Psychological Science, 3,* 374-379.

Williams, D. A., Butler, M. M., & Overmier, J. B. (1990). Expectancies of reinforcer location and quality as cues for a conditional discrimination in pigeons. *Journal of Experimental Psychology: Animal Behavior Processes, 16,* 3-13.

Stimulus Class Formation in Humans and Animals
T.R. Zentall and P.M. Smeets (Editors)
© 1996 Elsevier Science B.V. All rights reserved.

5

Categorical Class Formation by an African Grey Parrot (*Psittacus erithacus*)

Irene Maxine Pepperberg

Department of Ecology & Evolutionary Biology
Department of Psychology
University of Arizona

Categorical class formation is considered to be distinct from stimulus generalization. Stimulus generalization "implies memorizing a specific reference stimulus or set of stimuli followed by responses to new stimuli based on a failure to discriminate between the reference stimuli and the new stimuli" (Thomas & Lorden, 1993, p. 132; see also Zentall, this volume). Categorical class formation, in contrast, "results in a distribution of affirming responses to exemplars of the concept that is essentially rectilinear" (Thomas & Lorden, 1993, p. 133; Zentall, this volume), or is the ability "to respond similarly to discriminated stimuli" (Zentall, Jackson-Smith, Jagielo, & Nallan, 1986, p. 153). The distinction between stimulus generalization and categorical class formation is clear for classes that are formed out of stimuli that are physically different, e.g., arbitrary classes formed by an experimenter. When stimuli are physically similar, e.g., for polymorphic classes such as fish, the distinction is less clear, particularly when we are asking an animal subject to form the class. In the case of fish, for example, the animal sorter might not use the same criteria as the experimenter to sort various stimuli into the designated class; responses might be based simply on the presence or absence of gills. Thus the animal sorter might not even be able to discriminate among the fish stimuli. New fish stimuli that differ considerably from the reference stimulus for humans thus might be indistinguishable to the animal sorter or not be distinguished; even if the animal were forced to make an identity/nonidentity judgement, that decision could be based, for example, merely on the size of the gills. Thus the extent to which animals can successfully form categorical classes is as yet unknown, although various approaches have been taken to examine this problem (for a review, see Zentall, this volume).

One approach is to examine a particular type of class formation, rarely studied in animals other than great apes and marine mammals, that involves verbal labels. Here, a subject does not simply create a class consisting of concrete items, but rather forms multiple abstract hierarchical classes. A subject learns, for example, to form classes (i.e., separate categories) of color labels and shape labels. These labels relate to actual physical attributes based on stimulus similarity (redness, triangularity, etc.), but are made of arbitrary sound patterns ("red", "blue", "3-corner") or arbitrary hand or pictorial signals. These labels, which represent distinct classes, are then grouped into higher-order abstract classes whose labels are also made of arbitrary patterns, i.e., "color" and "shape". I describe how an avian subject has learned to form such abstract classes.

Studying how these classes are formed, however, is not an end in itself; such classes can be used to examine additional cognitive capacities. In this chapter, therefore, I discuss how formation of these classes has enabled a Grey parrot (*Psittacus erithacus*) to categorize individual items in numerous ways, to demonstrate emergent relationships, to exhibit competence in understanding several unrelated concepts (same/different; bigger/smaller; quantification), and to form new arbitrary categories. I close by discussing why evolutionary pressures may have selected for such traits in this and other species.

CHOICE OF SUBJECT

The subject of these studies has been an African Grey parrot named Alex. He was approximately one year old when the project began. He resides in a laboratory (details in Pepperberg, 1981, 1994a) where he has been trained and tested by me and a number of undergraduate and graduate students since June, 1977. A Grey parrot was chosen as the subject because it was likely (a) to possesses cognitive capacities necessary for the tasks under investigation, and (b) be capable of functioning within the proposed paradigm. Specifically:

Grey parrots had already successfully solved discrimination problems (Koehler, 1943, 1972; Lögler, 1959; Thorpe, 1974), tests of numerical competency (Braun, 1952; Koehler, 1943, 1950; Lögler, 1959), associative labeling and other intermodal association tasks (Amsler, 1947; Boosey, 1947, 1956; Koehler, 1950, 1953, 1972; Lögler, 1959; Mowrer, 1950, 1954; Thorpe, 1974), and demonstrated simple forms of tool use (Boswall, 1977; Smith, 1971). Greys had also performed as accurately on new tasks as on training problems (Koehler, 1943, Lögler, 1959), suggesting flexibility in their response patterns (Koehler, 1953; Premack 1978; Rozin, 1976). Such success indicated cognitive abilities (Fodor, Bever, & Garrett, 1974; Geschwind, 1965; Lenneberg, 1964, 1967, 1976; Premack, 1978) that could be examined further--abilities, often already tested in apes and marine mammals, involving categorization, concepts of same/different, relative size, and quantification.

By the late 1970's, moreover, researchers had demonstrated the power of referential animal-human communication for examining cognitive abilities of chimpanzees (Gardner & Gardner, 1969, 1978; Premack, 1976; Rumbaugh, 1977) and dolphins (Herman, 1980); separate studies suggested that parrots might similarly be examined. Communication within psittacine communities seemed to be mediated by complex vocalizations, apparently learned through social interactions with conspecifics or other organisms (Busnel & Mebes, 1975; Nottebohm, 1970; Power, 1966a, 1966b; note Tenaza, 1976); laboratory data not only supported these observations, but also demonstrated that Greys' conspecific vocal interactions could be transferred to humans (Todt, 1975). Use of interspecies communication to examine Grey parrot cognition would also enable us to compare the bird's capacities directly to those of similarly-trained species. The Grey's vocal abilities, however, would allow use of a code based on human speech sounds. Unlike projects using American Sign Language, computer-based Yerkish, or artificial whistles and gestures, our study would require neither extensive training of the researchers nor complex equipment.

CLASS FORMATION: THE EFFECT OF MODELING PROCEDURES

We began by training our subject Alex to produce appropriate English labels to identify various objects (such as keys and pieces of paper and wood) and descriptors (such as redness, greenness, triangularity and squareness, etc.). Of particular interest was that the protocol used in Alex's training was, at the time, unique for a laboratory animal. He learned through a modeling technique called the Model/Rival or M/R procedure (Pepperberg, 1981) and our use of specific, physical items as intrinsic, referential rewards.

The M/R procedure was adapted from the work of Todt (1975) and Bandura (1971, 1977). M/R training involves three-way interactions between two competent human speakers and an avian student. M/R training primarily introduces new labels and concepts, but also aids in shaping correct pronunciation. Because this chapter is intended as a review, I describe the M/R procedure in some detail although the material has been published previously (Pepperberg, 1981, 1988b, 1990a, 1994a, 1994c).

During M/R training, humans demonstrate to a bird the targeted vocal behavior patterns. Sessions begin with a bird observing two humans handling an object; the item is one in which the bird has previously demonstrated interest. One human acts as a trainer of the second human. This trainer presents and asks questions about the item ("What's here?", "What matter [material]?", "What toy?"), giving praise and the object to the second human to reward correct answers. The technique thus demonstrates referential and contextual use of labels with respect to observable objects. A trainer shows disapproval for incorrect responses (errors similar to those made by a bird, such as partial identifications, unclear speech) by scolding and temporarily removing the object from sight. Thus the second human not only acts as a model for the bird's responses and a rival for the trainer's attention, but also illustrates the aversive consequences of errors. The model/rival is also asked to talk clearly or try again when responses are incorrect or garbled, thereby allowing the parrot to observe "corrective feedback" (see Goldstein, 1984; Vanayan, Robertson, & Biederman, 1985).

Unlike other modeling procedures (e.g., Todt, 1975; Goldstein, 1984), this protocol requires repeating an interaction while reversing roles of the human trainer and model/rival, and includes the parrot in the interactions. Thus, birds do not simply hear stepwise vocal duets, but observe and learn to engage in a communicative process (i.e., a process that involves reciprocity and that can be used by either party to request information or effect environmental change). Without role reversal, birds exhibit two behavior patterns (Todt, 1975) inconsistent with interactive, referential communication: They do not transfer responses to anyone other than the human who poses the questions, and they do not learn both parts of the interaction. Furthermore, because a bird is rewarded for successive approximations to a correct response, the protocol adjusts the level of training to the level of the bird. If a bird is inattentive or its accuracy regresses, trainers threaten to leave ("I'm gonna go away!"). Such a consequence is aversive, as our birds become agitated and will beckon a departing trainer ("Come here," "Want tickle").

The M/R technique specifically demonstrates the referent of the label to be learned and the rationale for learning by using intrinsic (referential) reinforcers: Reward for each correct identification is the item to which the label refers. Note that such a procedure is somewhat analogous to the differential outcome reward procedure occasionally used with pigeons (Edwards, Jagielo, Zentall, & Hogan, 1982; Peterson, 1984). In contrast, some programs designed to teach communication skills, for both humans and nonhumans, use extrinsic (nonreferential) rewards (see Pepperberg, 1990a). In these programs, all correct identifications of food or nonfood items or appropriate responses to various specific commands are rewarded with a single item (generally food) that neither directly relates to the skill being taught nor varies with respect to the specific task being targeted. Such extrinsic rewards may delay label acquisition by confounding the label or concept to be learned with some aspect of the reward item (Greenfield, 1978; Pepperberg, 1981; Miles, 1983). The M/R procedure, instead, provides the closest possible association of the label being taught and the item to which it refers (Pepperberg, 1981). The procedure also demonstrates that, at least initially, use of the label itself enables the subject to obtain the object in question (Pepperberg, 1988a).

My students and I have had considerable success using the M/R procedure. We showed Alex that "paper" was the answer to the question "What's here?" or "What's this?" for objects of a certain material and that "wood" was the answer for objects of different specific material, that the correct response was "rose" (red) plus the object label for a certain type of item (e.g., "rose wood") and "green" plus the object label for another (e.g., "green key"), that the answer was "3-corner" plus the object label for a different type of item (e.g., "3-corner key") and "4-corner" plus the object label for yet another (e.g., "4-corner paper") and so forth (Pepperberg, 1981, 1983). Alex thereby acquired functional use of these labels with respect to the specific training exemplars. My students and I then administered transfer tests with similar but nonidentical items to see the extent of his learning; i.e., to see the extent to which he could appropriately apply labels such as "paper" and "rose". Details of the test procedure are in Pepperberg (1981, 1983, 1990a, 1992a, 1994a).

Although Alex had been trained on a relatively small set of exemplars (e.g., different sized and shaped bits of index cards for "paper"), we found that he could respond with the appropriate label to *any* sample of the various materials (e.g., "paper" to all sorts of uncolored paper items) or to different examples of items (e.g., "nail" to any shape or size nail or screw) that he could name (a total of approximately 50 possibilities including foodstuffs; see Pepperberg, 1990a). His accuracy was approximately 80%. He would also combine one of seven relevant color or five relevant shape labels with the appropriate object label to identify fully (e.g., "green wood" or "3-corner paper") any given colored or shaped item when asked "What's this?" (Pepperberg, 1981, 1983; note that objects did not have both color and shape). Given that some exemplars were hand-dyed with food colors and others purchased in colored form and that the sizes of the objects were not uniform, the test items often varied considerably from the training exemplars. Alex's accuracy, however, did not differ significantly between test and training items (Pepperberg, 1981, 1983).

Of greater interest, however, was that we could now examine whether he had learned that there existed a set of responses--his color labels--that formed the class "color" and another set of responses--his shape labels--that formed the class "shape". Specifically, we wished to see if an avian subject could proceed from recognizing a particular instance of a category (e.g., labeling a particular object as "green") to recognizing that such labels represented a categorical class that also had a label. Success on such a task would show that the bird had a higher-order class concept, because the color labels have no intrinsic connection to the label "color" nor do the shape labels have an intrinsic connection to the label "shape".

My students and I examined this possibility with a combination of training and testing. We provided additional training through our modeling procedure so that Alex saw functional use of the questions "What color?" and "What shape?" with respect to items that were *either* colored *or* shaped. We then tested whether he had formed class categories of his labels by showing him objects that varied in both shape *and* color (e.g., a green wooden triangle) and querying him as to "What shape?" *or* "What color?"

Note that our tests (and all those discussed in subsequent sections) were designed to ensure against "expectation cuing" that may occur if a subject "expects" queries on a single topic. We intermingled different types of test questions (e.g. "What's here?", "What shape?", "What matter?") during training on other topics so that the only way that Alex could know the relevant class from which to chose answers was by interpreting the question appropriately. In contrast, contextual information in single-topic tests (the standard procedure in most laboratories) could be responsible for a better performance than would otherwise be justified by a subject's actual knowledge of a topic: A homogeneous set of questions might lead a subject to ignore all but a small subset of responses (see Terrace, 1979). Our birds, however, are never queried on a single topic (e.g., object labels) in a session, nor, more importantly, tested successively in one session on similar questions ("What's here?") or on more than three questions that have a particular correct response (e.g., "cork"). Moreover, only novel objects are used for testing, and identical exemplars are never used for identical questions (e.g., a bird is asked about material and colors of wool, paper and pieces of cork that differ from training exemplars and that differ from question to question). A question (with its exemplar) is repeated in a session only if the initial answer is incorrect (Pepperberg, 1981, 1983). Thus, even though the range of correct responses to questions (e.g., "What's here?", "What color?", "What shape?") was limited initially to just a relatively few labels, in any session a bird still had to choose from among the several possible responses to the object or color or shape questions to be correct (Pepperberg, 1981).

Alex's accuracy on the color/shape task was over 80% ($p<.0001$) and only a small number of errors (9 of 41 total mistakes in 270 trials) were of the wrong category (Pepperberg, 1983). Note that this study actually involved *reclassification* of many items: Alex could be asked the color of an item in one session and the shape of the same item in the next session. The data clearly showed that he could change the basis of classification given our vocal question and thus that he had formed at least two classes, one for color labels and one for shape labels. Once such classes were established, we could proceed to more complicated tasks.

CLASS FORMATION LEADS TO AN EMERGENT RELATIONSHIP: COMPREHENSION OF LABELS

Alex had shown that he knew how to respond to various questions by producing the appropriate color, shape, material, and object labels (e.g., "red", "4-corner", "wood", "key"), but none of the tasks to date had formally tested his comprehension of these labels. Specifically, he knew when to respond "key", but could he, on demand, appropriately choose a key from among a set of objects? Accurate comprehension in the absence of explicit training would demonstrate Alex's competence in an emergent relationship: symmetry. My students and I therefore tested him on a task (Pepperberg, 1990b), comparable to ones used with chimpanzees (Essock, Gill, & Rumbaugh, 1977) and marine mammals (Herman, 1987; Schusterman & Gisiner, 1988), that can be mastered only when a subject has full comprehension of the labels in its repertoire.

The test in question is a recursive task (Pepperberg, 1992a). A recursive task is hierarchical: The subject must divide the task into parts and apply the appropriate rule (the same one or a different one) first to determine how to solve each part and then, in turn, to the solutions of each part (see Premack, 1986). For example, a subject can be given several objects that each differ in color, shape and material and be asked "What material is the object of shape-W?", "What color is the object of material-X?", "What material is the object of color-Y?", *or* "What shape is the object of material-Z?" (see Pepperberg, 1990b, 1992a). To respond, the subject must (1) comprehend the symbols that represent all possible actions (e.g., "fetch" vs. "touch"; note Herman, 1987; Schusterman & Gisiner, 1988) or object attributes (e.g., "shape" vs. "number") that will guide its response; (2) comprehend additional symbols to determine the subset of information to which it will selectively attend (e.g., exemplars that are "blue") in the context of any possible collection of objects (Granier-Deferre & Kodratoff, 1986); and finally (3) determine its response and encode this response into an appropriate physical motion or verbal representation of an object or attribute. The subject demonstrates its competence by reporting on only a single aspect (e.g., color, shape, or material) of, or performing one of several possible actions (fetching, touching) on, the one designated object in the collection. The complexity of the question is determined by its context (the number of different possible objects from which to choose) and the number of its parts (e.g., the number of attributes used to specify the target and the number of actions from which to choose; Pepperberg, 1990b, 1992a).

Recursive tasks can also be evaluated by examining how they differ from other tasks (Pepperberg, 1990b, 1992a). Recursive tasks cannot be solved by responding with respect to a single set of criteria (e.g., match-to-sample based on color), nor by performing an action determined by a relatively simple 1:1 correlation ("Pick up X"). The tasks are not based on responses to single questions (e.g., "What's this?") for even a large number of different exemplars, nor to chaining two independent responses to different objects ("Do X to A and Y to B"; Premack, 1986). And, although recursive tasks are related to conditional tasks (e.g., "If tray is red, do match-to-sample; if tray is black, do oddity"), both the number of concepts involved and options for response are considerably greater; e.g., a recursive task requires the subject to process additional information as to whether the match is, for example, to be on the basis of color, shape *or* material (see Thomas, 1980).

Alex was thus shown trays of seven unique combinations of exemplars (out of 100 possible items) of varying colors, shapes, and materials and asked questions similar to those described above (e.g., "What color is the object of material-X?"). Thus he might be shown a collection consisting of a square purple key, a triangular yellow wood, a hexagonal green rawhide, a pentagonal blue paper, an orange clothespin, a gray box and a red truck and be asked "What color is key?" He did not receive any prior training before being asked such questions. His accuracy for all queries, which was better than 80% ($p<.0001$, Pepperberg, 1990b), was comparable to that of marine mammals and chimpanzees that had been tested on similar tasks.

Clearly, to achieve such accuracy, Alex not only had to comprehend the meaning of each of his labels, but also to understand the class into which each label fit. In the example given above, he had to understand not only that "key" referred to a particular set of objects and "purple" to a particular range of hues, but also that "purple" was part of the categorical class "color" rather than "shape". Moreover, he had to respond correctly with respect to novel collections and novel questions on each trial. Had he not formed the appropriate categorical classes, he could not have mastered the task.

I also administered a more difficult version of the test, by adding a conjunctive condition to the recursive task (Pepperberg, 1992a). Here Alex was again shown a 7-member collection but was now asked to provide information about the specific instance of one attribute of an item that was uniquely defined by the conjunction of two other attributes; e.g., "What object is color-A *and* shape-B?" Other objects on the tray exemplified one, but not both, of these defining attributes. The task thus requires that the subject process information about multiple categorical classes (see Thomas, 1980). Alex responded with an accuracy of 76.5%, which indicated that he understood all the elements in the three possible questions. For questions about color, material, and shape, respective scores were 7/11, 9/11, 10/12 (p between .04 and .0001, depending upon the question and how chance is defined; for details, see Pepperberg, 1992a). Again, his data were comparable to that of marine mammals that had similarly been tested (e.g., Herman, 1987; Schusterman & Gisiner, 1988), and provided further evidence of his comprehension of categorical classes and their elements.

CLASS FORMATION LEADS TO STUDIES OF "SAME/DIFFERENT" AND "NONE" (THE ABSENCE OF INFORMATION)

Could Alex also learn to use the labels for his categorical classes to describe abstract concepts of sameness and difference? According to Premack (1983), comprehension of these concepts is not the same as being able to respond appropriately to generalized match-to-sample and oddity-from-sample tasks, but rather involves the ability to use arbitrary symbols to represent the relationships of sameness and difference between sets of objects. Specifically, a subject that can demonstrate comprehension of "same" must be able to recognize (a) not only that two independent objects, A1 and A2, are both blue, but also (b) that there is only a single attribute, the category color, that is shared, and (c) that this attribute, or sameness, can be *immediately* extrapolated and *symbolically* represented not only for two other blue items, but also for two novel independent green items, B1 and B2, that have nothing in common with the original set of A's. The subject would likewise have to demonstrate a concept of difference that could also be extrapolated to two novel objects (see Pepperberg, 1987a). Such abilities, according to Premack (1978, 1983), should be restricted to the higher primates, and, because of the requirement for symbolization, are most likely to be exhibited by primates that have undergone some form of language-like training (i.e., humans and the great apes). Because Alex had already demonstrated an understanding of the categorical classes of color, shape, and material, I decided to investigate whether he could respond to questions of sameness and difference based on those classes (Pepperberg, 1987a).

We again used the M/R training procedure. Alex was shown pairs of objects that could differ with respect to three attributes: color, shape, or material (e.g., a blue rawhide square and a green wooden square; a green wooden triangle and a red wooden triangle). He would then see trainers query each other about "What's same?" or "What's different?" The correct response would be the label of the appropriate *class*, not the specific color, shape or material marker, that represented the correct response (e.g., the label "color", *not* the label "green"). Therefore, to be correct, Alex would have to learn to (1) attend to multiple aspects of two different objects; (2) determine, from a vocal question, whether the response was to be on the basis of "sameness" or "difference"; (3) determine, based on the exemplars, what exactly was "same" or "different" (e.g., were they both blue, or made of wood, or was one triangular and the other square?) and then (4) produce, vocally, the label for this particular class. The task thus required, at some level, that Alex perform a feature analysis based on the categorical classes he had learned: The responses could not be made on the basis of total physical similarity or difference (see Premack, 1983). In a subsequent study, we used the same techniques to train him to respond "none" if nothing was same or different (Pepperberg, 1988c).

Although Alex was trained on a small subset of items--objects that were red, green or blue; triangular or square; rawhide or wood--he was tested on a wide variety of objects. Thus Alex's responses on tests were unlikely to be made on the basis of absolute physical properties or by learning the answer to a given pair, as the number of possible permutations of question topic, correct response, and combination of exemplar attributes was very large. Moreover, because Alex's response would be a class label rather than a specific object or attribute label, we could also employ entirely novel objects whose color, shape, and material labels were unknown (e.g., pink plastic flamingos and pink plastic elephants). Thus, the parrot would have to be able to transfer between like and unlike pairs of colors, like and unlike pairs of shapes, and like and unlike pairs of materials, all of which would vary from the training exemplars.

Alex succeeded on this task. When presented with two objects that were identical or that varied with respect to some or all of the attributes of color, shape, and material, Alex responded with the appropriate class label as to which attribute was "same" or "different" for any combination (85%, all trials; 82.5%, first trials, $p<.0001$; Pepperberg, 1987a) and "none" if nothing was same or different (83.9%, all trials; 80.9%, first trials, $p<.0001$; Pepperberg, 1988c). He responded equally accurately to instances involving objects, colors, shapes, and materials not used in training, including those for which he had no labels.

Furthermore, Alex indeed responded to the specific questions, and not merely on the basis of his training and the physical attributes of the objects: His responses were still above chance levels when, for example, the question "What's same?" was posed with respect to a green wooden triangle and a blue wooden triangle. If he were ignoring the question and responding on the basis of his prior training, he would have determined, and responded with the label for, the one anomalous attribute (in this case, "color"). Instead, he responded with one of the two appropriate answers (in this case, "shape" or "mah-mah" [matter]; 90.2%, all trials; 89.1% first trials, $p<.0001$, Pepperberg, 1987a, 1988c).

Alex thus demonstrated transfer among categorical classes as well as among various instances of each class. According to Premack (1976, pp. 354-355) such transfers are crucial for determining that the behavior is not just stimulus generalization. Clearly, Alex could not have succeeded had he not formed categorical classes of color, shape, and material.

CLASS FORMATION LEADS TO THE STUDY OF NUMERICAL COMPETENCE

The question now arose as to whether Alex could form an entirely new categorical class consisting of labels for quantity. Could Alex be trained to reclassify a group of wooden objects known until now simply as "wood", or "green wood" so that he could identify them as "five wood"? To succeed on this task, he would have to understand that a new set of labels, "one", "two" "three", "four", "five", and "six" represented a novel class: a way to categorize objects based on a combination of physical similarity within a group and the group's quantity, rather than by the physical characteristics of the group members. He would also have to learn how to generalize this new class of numerical labels to sets of novel objects, to objects in random arrays, and to heterogeneous collections. The study would also provide information on a nonhuman's concept of number.

We again used our modeling procedure. A trainer would begin by holding up a number of objects and asking the human model "What's this?"; we later switched to "How many?" We used two different sets of objects (two keys or pieces of wood; five pieces of paper or wood) for training each quantity so that Alex would not associate the label with one particular set, but instead be encouraged to abstract the sole property--that of quantity--that the collections (the several pieces of wood or paper) had in common (Pepperberg, 1987b; see Premack, 1971 for the efficacy of such procedures in training labels for modifiers). Using a limited number of sets also enabled preliminary determination of Alex's ability to transfer to other sets of objects that had not been used in training but that consisted of familiar items; we thereby eliminated the possibility that fear of unfamiliar exemplars would bias the results (see Zentall & Hogan, 1974, Zentall, Edwards, Moore, & Hogan, 1981). Initially, Alex was trained to respond with the number tag and the object label (e.g., "five wood"); later, so that he could be tested on novel objects, he was retrained to produce only the number tag.

Alex's data suggest that he comprehended some concept of quantity and that he had formed an additional categorical class based on this concept (Pepperberg, 1987b). He recognized and labeled different quantities of simultaneously presented physical objects up to and including 6 (78.9%, all trials, $p<.0001$; Pepperberg, 1987b). Alex performed equally well on transfer sets as on training sets: The sets of objects did not have to be familiar nor placed in any particular pattern, such as a square or triangle. Furthermore, when presented with a heterogeneous collection--of X's and Y's--Alex responded appropriately to questions of either "How many X?" *or* "How many Y?" (62.5%, all trials; 70.0%, first trials, $p=.003$; Pepperberg, 1987b). Our findings on numerical concepts, however, did not demonstrate that Alex had an understanding of "number" comparable to that of a human child (e.g., Fuson, 1988): I have not yet examined, for example, the symmetrical relation by testing whether he can answer "What is the color of the three wool?" when given a collection of three green and five blue pompons. Nor have I conclusively shown that Alex can, for example, count sequential metronome clicks to tell us that he has heard "three"; such cross-modal transfer is critical for determining if an animal can "count" (e.g., Seibt, 1982).

Additional work with heterogeneous collections has nonetheless suggested some more advanced skills. Alex can be shown a "confounded number set" (collections of four groups of items that vary with respect to two color labels and two object labels--e.g., blue and red keys and cars) and be asked to label the number of items uniquely defined by the combination of one color and one object label (e.g., "How many blue key?"). His accuracy (overall, 83.3%, p varied between .03 and .0001 for the various numbers; Pepperberg, 1994a) replicates that of humans in a comparable study performed by Trick and Pylyshyn (1989).

Although I cannot claim that the mechanisms that Alex uses are identical to those of humans, the data suggest that a nonhuman, nonprimate, nonmammalian subject has succeeded to a degree that, in a great ape, would be taken to indicate a human level of competence. Specifically, he has shown flexibility not only in sorting with respect to abstract classes, but also in understanding the connection between different sets of labels and different categorical classes; i.e., he has the ability to reclassify objects with respect to a new class. Such a claim is supported by the error analysis: Although Alex occasionally made "generic errors"--i.e., provided solely the label of the material of the collection of objects (possibly as a consequence of his early training)--he only once responded with a shape label to a numerical question (Pepperberg, 1987b). Thus he was able to form a new set of categorical classes based on numbers of objects.

CLASS FORMATION LEADS TO STUDY OF RELATIVE SIZE

All of the research discussed up to this point involves the formation of categorical classes based at least indirectly on absolute physical criteria rather than relative concepts. Although items such as color and shape labels are symbolic and thus abstract, their references are to concrete entities. Demonstrating that animal subjects, and birds in particular, can respond to relative concepts is not a simple matter: Studies that did manage to demonstrate such behavior suggested that response on an absolute basis was always used in preference to response on a relative basis and that the latter response was often apparent only if the former was blocked in some manner (e.g., Hulse, Page, & Braaten, 1990; Page, Hulse, & Cynx, 1989; cf. Hurly, Ratcliffe, & Weisman, 1990; Weisman & Ratcliffe, 1989). Might Alex's training on categorical class formation enable him to learn to respond readily on a relative basis?

A student and I decided to investigate this possibility using the concept of relative size (Pepperberg & Brezinsky, 1991). Could Alex form classes based on bigger and smaller? These classes could not be based on any of the same criteria previously used or any common elements in the stimuli; what was "bigger" in one trial could be "smaller" in the next and vice versa. Such a task would not only enable us to obtain data that was directly comparable with work on marine mammals (Schusterman & Krieger, 1986), but Alex's use of a vocal code would enable us to demonstrate three types of flexibility in his cognitive capacities that could not be demonstrated within the design of other animal studies (Pepperberg & Brezinsky, 1991).

First, most previous studies used a simple direct form of response: The subject merely indicated through a single physical action (e.g., pointing) which object was bigger or smaller. The subject thus did not need to access or encode any additional information after the target object was identified (see Pepperberg, 1990a). In contrast, because Alex had previously learned to respond to and encode his responses as English vocalizations, we could require that he not only choose the correct exemplar based on the targeted dimension of size (larger or smaller), but also that he encode, as a vocal label, other information about a different dimension specific to that item. Thus Alex was to designate the appropriate exemplar not by pointing, but by labeling its color or material (see Premack, 1978 for discussion of the importance of such encoding when determining whether a subject has learned an abstract concept).

Second, most studies on relative concepts use transfer tests that involve only limited novelty: i.e., pairs of test exemplars that vary from the training exemplars with respect only to the single dimension that is being examined. In a study on relative size transposition, for example, a sea lion was given transfer tests on objects that were either smaller or larger than the training exemplars, but both sets of tests involved only balls (Schusterman & Krieger, 1986). Because our subject would be required to respond with the label for a category other than size (e.g., "What *color* smaller?" or "What *matter* bigger?" rather than "Go to the *smaller ball*"), we could test his ability to transfer to sets of physical objects that were entirely novel: objects he had never before seen, some of which were of materials, colors, or shapes he could not label. Reese (1968) has reviewed the literature that shows that the difficulty of a relational task increases with the number of dimensions that are varied.

Third, other protocols tested only for concepts of bigger or smaller; our task also examined how Alex would respond when test objects were of equal size. Because he had already learned to respond to the absence of similarity and difference between pairs of exemplars with respect to color, shape, and material by saying "none" (Pepperberg, 1988c), we could test if he would extend this knowledge, without specific training, to report on the *absence* of a difference in size. Evidence for his ability to respond not only to the positive instances of bigger and smaller but also to the absence of such information would strengthen the claim that he understood a relative concept (note Pepperberg, 1988c; see below).

After M/R training on "What color bigger?" and "What color smaller?" with a limited number of colors and objects (yellow, blue, green; cups, woolen felt circles, Playdoh rods), we tested Alex on a variety of familiar and unfamiliar items. Our data showed that Alex had indeed classified objects with respect to relative size; his overall test scores were 78.7% (see Pepperberg & Brezinsky, 1991). Although we did not examine whether he could (or would) transfer this concept to a different modality (such as amount of sound), whether the acquisition of this concept might help him learn a different relationship (e.g., relative darkness), or how close in size two objects must be before he could not discriminate a difference, our data suggested that Alex demonstrated a level of understanding at least equivalent to that of certain other animal subjects (e.g., Schusterman & Krieger, 1986). Not only did he transpose the size relationship to stimuli outside of the training domain with an accuracy of 80% (Pepperberg & Brezinsky) but because he was responding with the label for an attribute other than size (color), we could remove many absolute stimulus cues by working with objects that were entirely different from those used in training (see discussions in Pepperberg, 1987a, 1987b, 1990a, 1990c): He transferred his knowledge to objects of novel shapes and sizes, and colors not used in training, with an accuracy of 77.3% (Pepperberg & Brezinsky). These objects were often of shapes or materials that he could not label (e.g., hand-dyed styrofoam stars). Of particular interest were our findings that he could also, without training, indicate when the exemplars did not differ in size and answer questions based on object material rather than color (Pepperberg & Brezinsky, 1991). A detailed discussion of these points provides interesting examples of how Alex could generalize a previously learned concept to a new domain.

Probes Involving Exemplars of Equal Size (from Pepperberg & Brezinsky, 1991)

The first time that Alex was asked "What color smaller?" and shown a pair that did not differ in size, he responded with the query "What's same?" Such a response suggested that he had made some partial connection to the earlier study in which he was routinely shown two objects and asked "What's same?" or "What's different?" (Pepperberg, 1988c). We were careful not to answer his initial query with an appropriate class label; such a response, by association with this previous experiment, might have cued him to respond "none" (one of the four potentially correct responses in that study); we wanted to see if he could make the complete connection on his own. To our reply, "First you tell us what color smaller", he did indeed say "none".

Because Alex had not been trained on how to respond to pairs that were the same size--i.e., to an absence of difference in size--it would be easy to overemphasize the importance of these initial, spontaneous responses. Alex's first response was not a formal error. He did not, for example, respond with the color label of one of the two equally sized exemplars. Moreover, when unable to find a larger or smaller exemplar, he did not ignore our query and respond as if we had asked one of the other possible questions for which objects were also presented in pairs ("How many?", "What's different?"; that is, he did not reply "two" or "color", respectively). Alex, by asking "What's same?" (a query that he used on average less than once/day), was conceivably indicating an awareness of the similarity of size. And, because the number of possible vocalizations (~100) with which he could have responded suggests that his second answer of "none" was not a random reply, it is also tempting to claim that his initial responses were a demonstration of his understanding both of relative size and of the appropriate response to an absence of information.

But a behavior that is consistent with one hypothesis does not exclude other consistent hypotheses (see Kroodsma, 1989a, 1989b, 1990). For example, Alex will, on occasion, respond to any of our queries with requests for other information (Pepperberg, 1990c). We therefore believed that it was not Alex's specific initial responses but rather his overall behavior that would suggest a capacity for understanding a lack of difference in size. The only way to explore the extent of his understanding was to determine the extent to which he could replicate this behavior.

We therefore ran a number of subsequent trials to learn if Alex's initial responses had been a fortuitous accident. On these additional trials with equally sized exemplars, his first response was correct 9 of 10 times. If we count his response on the very first trial (his response of "What's same?") as an error, his score was 9/11. His overall score (all trials) was 11/13

(84.6%).
The overall accuracy of his responses thus suggested that he had a detailed understanding of the concepts of both relative size *and* absence of information. Even if his early answer of "none" had been a random reply and the subsequent, mostly correct, responses were the result of one-trial learning, the speed of such learning suggests that it was likely based on previous knowledge. Several researchers believe that learning is most efficient when new topics can be related to prior knowledge (e.g., Bruner, 1977; Piaget, 1954; see discussion in Pepperberg, 1990a), and there is some suggestion that efficient learning is thus a reflection of the ability--or intelligence--to recognize that information can be transferred between domains (note Rogoff, 1984, 1990). Whatever Alex's initial strategy, he did demonstrate the capacity to respond, with significant accuracy, on a problem that required not only understanding of a relative concept but also additional understanding of the absence of information.

Probes Involving Responses Based on Material Labels (from Pepperberg & Brezinsky, 1991)
Although Alex was trained to respond with the color of the appropriate exemplar, he was correct on his initial responses to "What matter bigger?" or "What matter smaller?" He responded correctly on all but two subsequent first trials for a total of 8/10 (80%) correct; his overall score was 10/12 (83.3%). One error was a response of the color of both objects; the other error was a response of "none". He did, however, correctly respond with the appropriate material label (and thus the label from the appropriate categorical class) on the two trials in which the exemplars' colors and materials both varied, and with "none" on the one trial in which the two objects were of identical size. Such data suggest that he was not limited to responding within a single dimension and that he was attending to our questions. He could have responded repeatedly with the color of the two exemplars or on the basis of, for example, "How many?" ("two") or "What's same?" ("color", "shape").

In sum, Alex had demonstrated that he could form classes based on a relative concept (bigger/smaller). He had also shown that he could use the labels that were previously associated with other categorical classes (both the category labels and the specific labels within each category) to answer questions in this set of relative classes. Such flexibility is not generally expected in a nonhuman, nonprimate, nonmammalian subject (Premack, 1978).

CLASS FORMATION AND TASK ERRORS

My students and I have recently realized that Alex is capable of forming a categorical class based on arbitrary criteria. Previously, we had noticed that his errors on any particular task were most often what we termed "in category"--e.g., when asked "How many?" the response, even if erroneous, was generally a number label, and, in contrast, errors on questions such as "What color bigger?" were generally color labels (Pepperberg, 1994a; Pepperberg & Brezinsky, 1991; L. Bolles, unpubl. data). Because all of Alex's tests included questions on a number of different topics, the results could not be a consequence of expectation cuing (see above; Pepperberg, 1981; Terrace, 1979). These data simply reinforced our findings that Alex uses our questions to access the appropriate category of answer. He also apparently formed two classes of labels based on obtainable objects versus locations: In his use of phrases "want X" and "wanna go Y", he never inserts a location label for X, nor an object label for Y. But a different study suggested that he was actually forming categories based on the way objects were presented in training.

As part of a study on Alex's capacity to recognize two-dimensional objects, a student began a study on our bird's ability to label items presented via a video display (Stanford, 1995). Previous studies had suggested that Alex could indeed respond to, for example, questions involving same/different about objects presented via a video display (Rutledge & Pepperberg, unpubl. data), but no formal study had been made of his ability to label two-dimensional televised objects. Of the dozens of training items that Alex is capable of identifying, the student chose eight physical items whose images would be transmitted onto a television monitor for Alex to identify. She chose keychain (a metal ring with multiple keys), chain (several linked paper clips), rock (pieces of dark porous lava), grate (a nutmeg grater), key (a metal house key), wood (tongue depressors), truck (a specific yellow metal toy car), and nail (a large metal screw). These specific items were chosen because Alex identifies the physical objects routinely with accuracy greater than 80%. The procedure was to place Alex in front of the television screen, project a live video image of the object, and ask him to identify the "picture toy"; the actual physical item was not in view.

Although Alex did not succeed on the video task for a number of behavioral reasons that will not be described here, his results were extremely interesting from the standpoint of class formation. Alex had apparently created a new class, "picture toy": Although his answers to the query "What picture toy?" were correct less than 20% of the time, 71%-88% of his responses (depending on the particular item) involved a label for one of the eight objects used in training. Thus Alex did not respond with a random error (e.g., any one of 40-plus other possible object labels, or 7 color labels, or 6 number labels, or 5 shape labels), but consistently responded "in category" for a class that was completely arbitrary with respect to the specific vocal labels and three-dimensional physical attributes of the objects. Apparently, Alex had created a categorical class based on the presence of the video system display, i.e., he formed a class of labels on the basis of properties such as "not touchable", "on a screen", "with a blue backdrop", etc. Why his answers were random within this category is not clear, although we suggest that he found the lack of interaction with the objects and student testers aversive, and possibly also learned that if he responded "in category" he obtained some minimal approbation from the students. In general however, because he did not succeed on the task, he received very few rewards (i.e., chances to interact with the actual physical objects). Interestingly, outside of these sessions, his accuracy at identifying the actual physical objects, their colors and quantities, remained at the usual >80%.

Clearly, Alex's history of categorical class formation influenced his behavior in this study. He had previously learned that specific questions and specific sets of answers (answers relating to some physical reality) formed a particular class; he then transferred that knowledge to the present case: He formed a class based upon only the information contained in the context of the training session. Such behavior suggests that the capacity for class formation may be basic to his learning abilities; i.e., to his capacity to "make sense" of his world. Such a suggestion raises the question of why class formation would be a basic skill.

ECOLOGICAL AND ETHOLOGICAL RELEVANCE OF THE ABILITY TO FORM CLASSES

Humans tend to view animal capacities in human terms. Most comparative studies use human abilities as the standard against which different species are judged, even though we know that in many cases such abilities are unnecessary for the survival of the species or that the animals excel in capacities that we lack: For some nonhumans, for example, discriminations based upon detecting the plane of polarized light may be more critical for survival than the ability to process certain abstract relations (Dyer & Gould, 1983; Dyer, Berry, & Richard, 1993). But the ability to categorize the world would seem to serve a true ecological need in a wide variety of species.

One would assume that a creature that can form certain basic categories (e.g., food or predator) with respect to items in its world that are not clearly physically identical is a creature that has a far better chance of survival. Learning to identify each individual food item or each individual predator would make little sense; most creatures should be able to identify, at the very least, categorical classes such as predator versus prey (e.g., food, whether animate or inanimate). Likewise, creatures would be expected to be able to form classes of edible versus nonedible items. At the simplest level, for example, such discriminations would be based on stimulus generalization; interestingly, such is the basis for the success of Batesian mimicry: a edible butterfly that mimics the physical patterning of an inedible species avoids being eaten by birds that have learned what is or is not edible. But an animal that forages on flowers, for example, likely forms a class for a wide range of edible flowers versus a class for a range of non-edible leaves; it would not necessarily learn to identify specific flowers or specific leaves. At only a slightly more sophisticated level would be classification of "danger from above" versus "danger from below" if different evasive tactics for each class are required (e.g., Seyfarth, Cheney, & Marler, 1980). Furthermore, so that other activities such as foraging or mating are not unduly interrupted, individuals should be able to separate such predator classes from similarly behaving nondangerous sympatric species (Seyfarth & Cheney, 1980). One would suppose that the widespread capacity across species for categorization would mean that even brains that are structured very differently (e.g., mammalian versus avian organization) provide similar solutions to the problems of dividing the world into meaningful classes.

Thus it is not the emergence of the ability to form categorical classes at some level that should surprise us; in fact, it would be the absence of such abilities that would prove notable: The need to extract regularity in the world would seem to be a basic capacity for survival. Of course, not all creatures might need (or possess) all the various levels of categorization, and determining the level at which an animal can form categorical classes is not a trivial matter.

The purpose and rationale for determining these levels are, however, often lost and the interpretation of data obtained in such studies often trivialized when the primary goal is to make comparisons between animals and humans. Studies on the formation of categorical classes must be designed to take into account the ecological and ethological framework of the creature that is being studied; i.e., a framework consisting of the niche in which the subject lives and its species-specific behavior patterns. The findings must be interpreted within this same framework (Pepperberg, 1994b). Of particular importance in this regard is that most studies to determine the abilities of animals to form various classes, my own included, often require that the subjects form classes that are outside of their natural domain. Alex, for example, can form some abstract classes related to human labels that refer to ecologically relevant aspects of his world (e.g., color), but he also forms some classes whose ecological relevance is not especially clear (e.g., picture toy). Interestingly, some researchers have demonstrated how learning can be greatly facilitated under ecologically and ethologically relevant conditions (Wright & Delius, 1994) and how learning that will not occur under traditional paradigms can be shown under ethologically relevant ones (reviews in Pepperberg, 1985, 1992b). Might Alex's success then be based less on the ecological relevance of the task, and more on the ethological relevance of his *training*?

I suggest that the training procedures that we use--specifically the M/R technique and intrinsic rewards--may be responsible for Alex's success because these procedures relate to how psittacine birds apparently learn from parents and peers (Todt, 1975; Pepperberg, 1981, 1990a, 1994b). These techniques differ dramatically from those used in standard experimental psychology laboratories (see Pepperberg, 1988b, 1990a, 1992b for detailed reviews and other chapters in this volume for examples), and I have also shown that less ethologically relevant variants of these techniques do not engender fully referential labeling in either psittacine birds or great apes (Pepperberg, in press). I have previously proposed that training techniques are especially critical in situations of *exceptional* learning: learning that is unlikely in the normal course of development but that can occur under certain conditions (Bandura, 1971, 1977; Pepperberg, 1985, 1988b, 1994a, 1994c). Forming categorical classes that are not ecologically relevant quite likely comes under this heading. Possibly what is of basic importance in some species is not the capacity for a particular task, but rather the capacity to learn a general type of task in a particular manner. Thus a parrot, or any other creature, can use its general capacity to form ecologically relevant classes and an ethologically based learning situation to acquire other, less relevant classes. Without the appropriate training situation, however, exceptional learning will not occur (see Pepperberg, 1994b, in press).

Note that such a proposal concerning Alex's capacities is particularly interesting because it does not relate his success to his training in a language-like code. Some researchers (e.g., Premack, 1983) have suggested that acquisition of a language-like code predisposes animals to acquire certain cognitive skills. I have, however, previously argued that Alex's labeling abilities are not isomorphic with those of humans and that labeling per se is unlikely to have enabled him to succeed on his various tasks (e.g., Pepperberg, 1987b, 1990a, 1990b, 1994a). I believe that his success is not a consequence of his use of a human-based code, but rather of the training techniques that enabled him to acquire this code.

In sum, one must be extremely careful about claims that a particular species does not form categorical classes or about the limitations of its class formation. The results of any particular study may be more a consequence of experimental conditions than the species' capacity. I suggest that at a certain level class formation is one of the most basic of capacities and that the level of such categorization is a consequence of the subject's general ecological and ethological circumstances. I furthermore hypothesize that an ethologically relevant training situation may engender the formation of various classes that themselves are not necessarily ecologically relevant.

REFERENCES

Amsler, M. (1947). An almost human Grey parrot. *Aviculture Magazine, 53*, 68-69.

Bandura, A. (1971). Analysis of modeling processes. In A. Bandura (Ed.), *Psychological modeling* (pp. 1-62). Chicago: Aldine-Atherton.

Bandura, A. (1977). *Social modeling theory*. Chicago: Aldine-Atherton.

Bolles, L. (1993). [Analysis of naming errors in a psittacine subject: What is right about what is wrong.] Unpublished raw data.

Boosey, E.J. (1947). The African Grey parrot. *Aviculture Magazine, 53*, 39-40.

Boosey, E.J. (1956). *Foreign bird keeping*. London: Illiffe Books, Ltd.

Boswall, J. (1977). Tool-using by birds and other behaviors. *Aviculture Magazine, 83*, 88-97; *84*, 162-166; *89*, 94-108.

Braun, H. (1952). Uber das Unterscheidungsvermögen unbenannter Anzahlen bei Papageien. *Zeitschrift für Tierpsychologie, 9,* 40-91. [Concerning the ability of parrots to distinguish unnamed numbers.]

Bruner, J.S. (1977). Early social interaction and language acquisition. In H.R. Schaffer (Ed.), *Studies in mother-infant interaction* (pp. 271-28). London: Academic Press.

Busnel, R.G., & Mebes, H.D. (1975). Hearing and communication in birds: the cocktail party effect in intraspecific communication of *Agapornis roseicollis. Life Science 17,* 1567-1569.

Dyer, F.C., & Gould, J.L. (1983). Honey bee navigation. *American Scientist, 71,* 587-597.

Dyer, F.C., Berry, N.A., & Richard, A.S. (1993). Honey bee spatial memory: use of route-based memories after displacement. *Animal Behaviour, 45,* 1028-1030.

Edwards, C.A., Jagielo, J.A., Zentall, T.R., & Hogan, D.E. (1982). Acquired equivalence and distinctiveness in matching to sample by pigeons: Mediation by reinforcer-specific expectancies. *Journal of Experimental Psychology: Animal Behavior Processes, 8,* 244-259.

Essock, S.M., Gill, T.V., & Rumbaugh, D.M. (1977). Language relevant object- and color-naming tasks. In D.M. Rumbaugh (Ed.), *Language learning by a chimpanzee* (pp. 193-206). New York: Academic Press.

Fodor, J.A., Bever, T., & Garret, M. (1974). *The psychology of language.* New York: McGraw-Hill.

Fuson, K.C. 1988. *Children's counting and concepts of number.* New York: Springer-Verlag.

Gardner, R.A., & Gardner, B.T. (1969). Teaching sign language to a chimpanzee. *Science, 165,* 664-672.

Gardner, R.A., & Gardner, B.T. (1978). Comparative psychology and language acquisition. In *Psychology: the State of the Art,* NYAS, *309,* 37-76.

Geschwind, N. (1965). Disconnexion syndromes in animals and man. Part I. *Brain, 88,* 237-294, 585-644.

Goldstein, H. (1984). The effects of modeling and corrected practice on generative language and learning of preschool children. *Journal of Speech and Hearing Disorders, 49,* 389-398.

Granier-Deferre, C., & Kodratoff, Y. (1986). Iterative and recursive behaviors in chimpanzees during problem solving: A new descriptive model inspired from the artificial intelligence approach. *Cahiers de Psychologie Cognitive, 6,* 483-500.

Greenfield, P.M. (1978). Developmental processes in the language learning of child and chimp. *Behavior and Brain Sciences, 4,* 573-574.

Herman, L.M. (1980). Cognitive characteristics of dolphins. In L.M. Herman (Ed.), *Cetacean behavior: Mechanisms and functions* (pp. 363-429). New York: Wiley & Sons.

Herman, L.M. (1987). Receptive competencies of language-trained animals. In J.S. Rosenblatt, C. Beer, M-C. Busnel, & P.J.B. Slater (Eds.), *Advances in the study of behavior, vol. 17* (pp. 1-60). Orlando, FL: Academic Press.

Hulse, S.H., Page, S.C., & Braaten, R.F. (1990). Frequency range size and the frequency range constraint in auditory perception by European starlings (*Sturnus vulgaris*). *Animal Learning & Behavior, 18,* 238-245.

Hurly, T.A., Ratcliffe, L., & Weisman, R. (1990). Relative pitch recognition in white-throated sparrows, *Zonotrichia albicollis. Animal Behaviour, 40,* 176-181.

Koehler, O. (1943). "Zähl"-Versuche an einem Kolkraben und Vergleichsversuche an Menschen. *Zeitschrift für Tierpsychologie, 5,* 575-712. ["Number" ability in a raven and comparative research with people.]

Koehler, O. (1950). The ability of birds to "count". *Bulletin of the Animal Behaviour Society,* *9*, 41-45.

Koehler, O. (1953). Thinking without words. *Proceedings of the XIVth International Congress of Zoology,* 75-88.

Koehler, O. (1972). Der Sprachebegabung der Papagein. In *Grzimek's Tierleben VIII,* Munich: Kindler-Verlag; Engl. trans., van Nostrand Reinhold. [The speaking abilities of parrots.]

Kroodsma, D.E. (1989a). Suggested experimental designs in song playbacks. *Animal Behaviour,* *37,* 600-609.

Kroodsma, D.E. (1989b). Inappropriate experimental designs impede progress in bioacoustic research. *Animal Behaviour, 38,* 717-719.

Kroodsma, D.E. (1990). How the mismatch between the experimental design and the intended hypothesis limits confidence in knowledge, as illustrated by an example from birdsong dialects. In M. Bekoff & D. Jamieson (Eds.), *Interpretation and explanation in the study of animal behavior: Comparative perspectives* (pp. 226-245). Boulder, CO: Westview Press.

Lenneberg, E.H. (1964). The capacity for language acquisition. In J.A. Fodor & J.J. Katz (Eds.), *The structure of language* (pp. 579-603). Englewood Cliffs, NJ: Prentice Hall.

Lenneberg, E.H. (1967). *Biological foundations of language.* New York: John Wiley and Sons.

Lenneberg, E.H. (1976). Problems in the comparative study of language. In R.B. Masterson, W. Hodos, & H. Jersion (Eds.), *Evolution, brain, and behavior: Persistent problems* (pp. 199-213). Hillsdale, NJ: Erlbaum.

Lögler, P. (1959). Versuche zur Frage des "Zähl"-Vermögens an einem Graupapagei und Vergleichsversuche an Menschen. *Zeitschrift für Tierpsychologie, 16,* 179-217. [Studies on the question of "number" sense in a Grey parrot and comparative studies on humans.]

Miles, H. L. (1983). Apes and language. In J. de Luce & H. T. Wilder (Eds.), *Language in primates* (pp. 43-61). New York: Springer-Verlag.

Mowrer, O.H. (1950). *Learning theory and personality dynamics.* New York: Ronald Press.

Mowrer, O.H. (1954). A psychologist looks at language. *American Psychologist, 9,* 660-694.

Nottebohm, F. (1970). Ontogeny of bird song. *Science, 167,* 950-956.

Page, S.C., Hulse, S.H., & Cynx, J. (1989). Relative pitch perception in the European starling (*Sturnus vulgaris*): Further evidence for an elusive phenomenon. *Journal of Experimental Psychology: Animal Behavior Processes, 15,* 137-146.

Pepperberg, I. M. (1981). Functional vocalizations by an African Grey Parrot (*Psittacus erithacus*). *Zeitschrift für Tierpsychologie, 55,* 139-160.

Pepperberg, I. M. (1983). Cognition in the African Grey Parrot: Preliminary evidence for auditory/vocal comprehension of the class concept. *Animal Learning & Behavior, 11,* 179-185.

Pepperberg, I.M. (1985). Social modeling theory: A possible framework for understanding avian vocal learning. *Auk, 102,* 854-864.

Pepperberg, I. M. (1987a). Acquisition of the same/different concept by an African Grey Parrot (*Psittacus erithacus*): Learning with respect to color, shape, and material. *Animal Learning & Behavior, 15,* 423-432.

Pepperberg, I. M. (1987b). Evidence for conceptual quantitative abilities in the African Grey Parrot: Labeling of cardinal sets. *Ethology, 75,* 37-61.

Pepperberg, I.M. (1988a). An interactive modeling technique for acquisition of communication skills: Separation of "labeling" and "requesting" in a psittacine subject. *Applied Psycholinguistics, 9*, 59-76.

Pepperberg, I.M. (1988b). The importance of social interaction and observation in the acquisition of communicative competence: Possible parallels between avian and human learning. In T.R. Zentall and B.G. Galef, Jr. (Eds.), *Social learning: Psychological and biological perspectives* (pp. 279-299). Hillsdale, NJ: Erlbaum.

Pepperberg, I. M. (1988c). Comprehension of "absence" by an African Grey Parrot: Learning with respect to questions of same/different. *Journal of the Experimental Analysis of Behavior, 50*, 553-564.

Pepperberg, I. M. (1990a). Some cognitive capacities of an African Grey Parrot (*Psittacus erithacus*). In P. J. B. Slater, J. S. Rosenblatt & C. Beer (Eds.), *Advances in the study of behavior, vol. 19* (pp. 357-409). New York: Academic Press.

Pepperberg, I. M. (1990b). Cognition in an African Grey Parrot (*Psittacus erithacus*): Further evidence for comprehension of categories and labels. *Journal of Comparative Psychology, 104*, 41-52.

Pepperberg, I. M. (1990c). Referential mapping: A technique for attaching functional significance to the innovative utterances of an African Grey Parrot (*Psittacus erithacus*). *Applied Psycholinguistics, 11*, 23-44.

Pepperberg, I. M. (1992a). Proficient performance of a conjunctive, recursive task by an African Grey parrot (*Psittacus erithacus*). *Journal of Comparative Psychology, 106*, 295-305.

Pepperberg, I.M. (1992b). Social interaction as a condition for learning in avian species: a synthesis of the disciplines of ethology and psychology. In H. Davis & D. Balfour (Eds.), *The inevitable bond* (pp. 178-204). Cambridge: Cambridge University Press.

Pepperberg, I.M. (1994a). Evidence for numerical competence in an African Grey parrot (*Psittacus erithacus*). *Journal of Comparative Psychology, 108*, 36-44.

Pepperberg, I.M. (April, 1994b). *The African Grey Parrot: How cognitive processing might affect allospecific vocal learning.* Paper presented at the Bielefeld Conference on Adaptive Behavior and Learning, Bielefeld, Germany.

Pepperberg, I.M. (1994c). Vocal learning in Grey parrots (*Psittacus erithacus*): Effects of social interaction, reference and context. *Auk, 111*, 300-313.

Pepperberg, I.M. (in press). Social influences on the acquisition of human-based codes in parrots and nonhuman primates. In C.T. Snowdon & M. Hausberger (Eds.), *Social influence on vocal development* (pp. xx-yy), New York: Cambridge Univ. Press.

Pepperberg, I.M., & Brezinsky, M.V. (1991). Acquisition of a relative class concept by an African Grey parrot (*Psittacus erithacus*): Discriminations based on relative size. *Journal of Comparative Psychology, 105*, 286-294.

Peterson, G.B. (1984). How expectancies guide behavior. In, H.L. Roitblat, T.G. Bever, & H.S. Terrace (Eds.), *Animal cognition* (pp. 135-148). Hillsdale, NJ: Erlbaum.

Piaget, J. (1952). *The origins of intelligence in children* (M. Cook, trans.). New York: International Universities Press.

Power, D.M. (1966a). Agnostic behavior and vocalizations of orange-chinned parakeets in captivity. *Condor, 68*, 562-581.

Power, D.M. (1966b). Antiphonal duetting and evidence for auditory reaction time in the orange-chinned parakeet. *Auk, 83*, 314-319.

Premack, D. (1971). On the assessment of language competence in the chimpanzee. In A. Schrier & F. Stollnitz (Eds.), *Behavior of nonhuman primates, vol. 4* (pp. 185-228), New

York: Academic Press.

Premack, D. (1976). *Intelligence in ape and man*. Hillsdale, NJ: Erlbaum.

Premack, D. (1978). On the abstractness of human concepts: why it would be difficult to talk to a pigeon. In S.H. Hulse, H. Fowler, & W.K. Honig (Eds.), *Cognitive processes in animal behavior* (pp. 421-451). Hillsdale, NJ: Erlbaum.

Premack, D. (1983). The codes of man and beast. *Behavioral and Brain Sciences, 6*, 125-167.

Premack, D. (1986). *Gavagai! or the future history of the animal language controversy*. Cambridge, MA: MIT Press.

Reese, H.W. (1968). *The perception of stimulus relations: Discrimination learning and transposition*. New York: Academic Press.

Rogoff, B. (1984). Introduction: thinking and learning in a social context. In B. Rogoff & J. Lave (Eds.), *Everyday cognition: Its development in social contexts* (pp. 1-8). Cambridge, MA: Harvard University Press.

Rogoff, B. (1990). *Apprenticeship in thinking: Cognitive development in a social context*. Oxford: Oxford University Press.

Rozin, P. (1976). The evolution of intelligence and access to the cognitive unconscious. In J.M. Sprague & A.N. Epstein (Eds.), *Progress in psychobiology and physiological psychology, vol. 6* (pp. 245-280). New York: Academic Press.

Rumbaugh, D.M. (Ed.). (1977). *Language learning by a chimpanzee*. New York: Academic Press.

Rutledge, D., & Pepperberg, I.M. (1988). [Video studies of same/different.] Unpublished raw data.

Schusterman, R.J., & Gisiner, R. (1988). Artificial language comprehension in dolphins and sea lions: the essential cognitive skills. *Psychological Record, 38*, 311-348.

Schusterman, R.J., & Krieger, K. (1986). Artificial language comprehension and size transposition by a California sea lion (*Zalophus californianus*). *Journal of Comparative Psychology, 100*, 348-355.

Seibt, U. (1982). Zahlbegriff und Zählverhalten bei Tieren: Neue Versuche und Deutungen. *Zeitschrift für Tierpsychologie, 60*, 325-341. [Numerical concepts and numerical behavior of animals: New studies and interpretations.]

Seyfarth, R.M., & Cheney, D.L. (1980). The ontogeny of vervet monkeys' alarm calling behavior: preliminary report. *Zeitschrift für Tierpsychologie, 54*, 37-56.

Seyfarth, R. M., Cheney, D.L, & Marler, P. (1980). Monkey responses to three different alarm calls: Evidence of predator classification and semantic communication. *Science, 210*, 801-803.

Smith, G.A. (1971). Tool use in parrots. *Aviculture Magazine, 77*, 47-48.

Stanford, K.N. (1995). *Studies on two-dimensional object identification in an African Grey parrot*. Unpublished BA honors thesis, University of Arizona.

Tenaza, R.R. (1976). Wild mynahs mimic wild primates. *Nature, 259*, 561.

Terrace, H.S. (1979). Is problem-solving language? *Journal of the Experimental Analysis of Behavior, 31*, 161-175.

Thomas, R.K. (1980). Evolution of intelligence: an approach to its assessment. *Brain, Behavior, and Evolution, 17*, 454-472.

Thomas, R.K., & Lorden, R.B. (1993). Numerical competence in animals: A conservative view. In S.T. Boysen & E.J. Capaldi (Eds.), *The development of numerical competence* (pp. 127-147). Hilldsale, NJ: Erlbaum.

Thorpe, W.H. (1974). *Animal and human nature*. New York: Doubleday.

Todt, D. (1975). Social learning of vocal patterns and modes of their applications in Grey Parrots. *Zeitschrift für Tierpsychologie, 39*, 178-188.

Trick, L., & Pylyshyn, Z. (1989). Subitizing and the FNST spatial index model. University of Ontario, COGMEM #44. [Based on paper presented at the 30th Psychonomic Society Meeting, Atlanta, GA.]

Vanayan, M., H., Robertson, A., & Biederman, G. B. (1985). Observational learning in pigeons: The effects of model proficiency on observer performance. *Journal of General Psychology, 112*, 349-357.

Weisman, R., & Ratcliffe, L. (1989). Absolute and relative pitch processing in black-capped chickadees, *Parus atricapillus. Animal Behaviour, 38*, 685-692.

Wright, A.A., & Delius, J.D. (1994). Scratch and match: Pigeons learn matching and oddity with gravel stimuli. *Journal of Experimental Psychology: Animal Behavior Processes, 20*, 108-112.

Zentall, T.R., Edwards, C.A., Moore, B.S., & Hogan, D.E. (1981). Identity: the basis for both matching and oddity learning in pigeons. *Journal of Experimental Psychology: Animal Behavior Processes, 7*, 70-86.

Zentall, T.R., & Hogan, D.E. (1974). Abstract concept learning in the pigeon. *Journal of Experimental Psychology, 102*, 393-398.

Zentall, T.R., Jackson-Smith, P., Jagielo, J.A., & Nallan, G.B. (1986). Categorical shape and color naming by pigeons. *Journal of Experimental Psychology: Animal Behavior Processes, 12*, 153-159.

III

FUNCTIONAL AND EQUIVALENCE CLASSES IN HUMANS

Stimulus Class Formation in Humans and Animals
T.R. Zentall and P.M. Smeets (Editors)
1996 Elsevier Science B.V.

6

Derived Stimulus Control: Are There Differences Among Procedures and Processes?

Kathryn J. Saunders, Dean C. Williams, and Joseph E. Spradlin

University of Kansas

New stimulus control that is predictable from a subject's training history, that is not based on primary stimulus generalization, and that has not been trained directly, has been demonstrated in numerous species. The processes by which stimulus control transfers among physically dissimilar stimuli are not well understood. Yet such transfer characterizes many important linguistic and cognitive behaviors. To cite one of the less understood examples, how is a child who learns to select the upper case letter "A" and the lower case letter "a", upon hearing the sound "A", later able to match the upper and lower case letters and to produce the sound "A" in response to both letters?

The term "stimulus class" has been used to label these and similar effects. Stimulus classes consisting of members without common defining features have been demonstrated under a number of different procedures. We will focus on demonstrations of stimulus classes involving instances of stimulus control that have not been shown previously by the organism, termed "derived stimulus control." As a way of distinguishing these classes from others, we note that one type of stimulus class, termed a "contingency class" (Sidman, Wynne, Maguire, & Barnes, 1989), does not involve new stimulus control (see Hayes, 1989). A prototypical contingency class demonstration begins with a group of stimuli that control the same response (Response A). Then, the contingencies change such that all of the stimuli come to control a different response (Response B). Ultimately, after repeated reversals of the contingencies across all of the stimuli, a contingency change in the presence of a subset of stimuli in the set results in corresponding stimulus control changes for all stimuli in the set (Sidman et al., 1989; Vaughan, 1988). The stimulus control changes, however, do not involve the demonstration of the first instance of a stimulus control relation, but rather the demonstration of a previously trained stimulus-response relation.

The procedures under which derived stimulus control has been demonstrated vary in structure and complexity. Moreover, it appears that some procedures more readily produce derived stimulus control in some populations. It is currently unclear whether performances produced by different procedures involve different processes.

Our goals here are to (1) review procedures for demonstrating derived stimulus control and to classify them based on structure, (2) explore the relationship between the various training structures and the likelihood of demonstrating stimulus classes in humans and animals, (3) note procedural differences that might affect the likelihood of demonstrating derived stimulus control within a particular training structure, and (4) consider whether or not the same processes are involved in stimulus class demonstration across procedures and subject populations.

Our structural classification will differentiate among procedures along two dimensions. First, we will differentiate procedures on the basis of whether the transfer is unidirectional, bidirectional, or both. If, for example, a study involves matching-to-sample procedures, and only the samples are shown to be substitutable for one another, we will refer to the transfer as unidirectional. In contrast, we will classify transfer in which sample and comparison stimuli are substitutable for one another as bidirectional (e.g., symmetry). Second, we will distinguish stimulus classes that are demonstrated within three-term contingencies (simple discrimination procedures, in which the discriminative stimulus is the first term) from those demonstrated within four-term contingencies (conditional discrimination or matching-to-sample procedures, in which the sample stimulus is the first term).

PROCEDURES AND OUTCOMES

Unidirectional Transfer

Response Mediated Transfer
    Pigeons, and presumably other species, demonstrate transfer when the procedures promote the development of a mediating response. There are two related strands of research that show response mediated transfer. In one strand, a different observing response is established in the presence of each sample stimulus within a matching-to-sample procedure (e.g., Urcuioli, 1985; Urcuioli & Honig, 1980). Then, the same two responses are established in the presence of two new samples. Following this training, test trials present the second pair of samples with the first pair of comparisons. The immediate accurate performance of the new conditional discrimination is mediated by the differential sample responses. Figure 1 shows that this transfer comes from the recombination of previously established stimulus-response and response-stimulus units. Our use of the term "mediation" will be limited to this form.

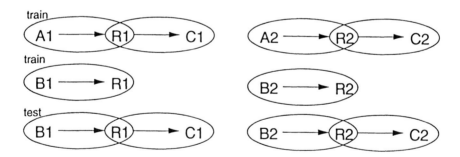

Figure 1. Prototypical training and testing procedures for studies showing transfer via trained differential sample responses. R1 and R2 are two different responses to the sample stimuli, for example, peck fast and peck slow. The other letters designate sample and comparison stimuli, with samples to the left of the array. First, both of the A-R-C relations are trained, then the B-R relations are trained. Test trials present B samples and C comparisons. The circles indicate the units developed through training and recombined in testing.

Performances involving differential sample responses may have different characteristics across humans and pigeons. For pigeons, differential responses come to control comparison selection, to the point of overshadowing control by the sample stimulus (Urcuioli, 1984). This is apparently not true for most humans. Although acquisition of arbitrary matching by humans with moderate mental retardation and by young, normally developing children is facilitated by differential sample responses, once arbitrary matching is established, comparison selection is not controlled by the differential response (Saunders & Spradlin, 1989, 1990, 1993; Sidman et al., 1982). For humans, then, differential responses facilitate matching accuracy by ensuring the successive discrimination between the sample stimuli. It remains to be seen whether this is true for more developmentally limited humans. An adult with severe mental retardation who communicates through gestures and a few one- or two-word utterances provides intriguing evidence to the contrary. Upon initially learning to match physically identical stimuli with the help of differential sample responses (two different vocalizations), accuracy decreased when the differential responses were not maintained (Saunders, Williams, & Spradlin, 1995). Should such findings be reproduced, they could help explain some of the perplexing performance deficits exhibited by some individuals with severe mental retardation.

In a second strand of research, the mediating behavior is established indirectly, by associating different stimuli with different reinforcers. For example, Peterson (1984) established delayed matching under a differential outcomes procedure. The sample-comparison relations A1-B1 and A2-B2 were trained; responding to comparison B1 produced food and responding to comparison B2 did not produce food. In other trials, food presentation followed the presentation of Stimulus C and no food followed Stimulus D. In tests, the C and D stimuli controlled the selection of B1 and B2, respectively. Presumably, A1 and C evoked very similar food-related pecking behaviors through an autoshaping process (Jenkins & Moore, 1973) and A2 and D did not, and these differential sample behaviors mediated comparison selection as described for differential sample responses that are trained directly.

Stimulus Classes Based on Many-to-One Training

When two or more stimuli control the same response or stimulus selection, which has been called many-to-one training (Urcuioli, Zentall, & DeMarse, 1995), a basis for the transfer of other responses across those stimuli has been established. When a new response or comparison selection is established to one of the stimuli, the remaining stimuli may control that response or comparison selection.

Stimulus classes or categories of essentially this form have been discussed by a range of theorists. Goldiamond (1962) referred to these as functional classes. Keller and Schoenfeld (1950) referred to mediated generalization and Hull (1943) to secondary generalization. These terms help to distinguish classes in which physically different stimuli control the same response from those based on primary stimulus generalization. Rosch and Mervis (1975) proposed three levels of categorization in human language. Their notion of superordinate concepts, those based on similar function rather than similar form, seems to fit here (see Wasserman, DeVolder, & Coppage, 1992). These stimulus classes have been demonstrated within simple discrimination procedures, within conditional discrimination of position procedures, and within conditional discrimination of stimulus procedures (matching to sample). We characterize the transfer as unidirectional. This is because, whether the stimulus class involves the substitutability of discriminative stimuli, as is the case in simple discriminations, or is based on substitutability of sample stimuli, the stimuli remain in their original positions. That is, in the transfer task the stimuli either control a specific response topography or selection of another stimulus.

   Stimulus classes based on control of common response.   Stimulus classes have been demonstrated within successive, simple discrimination procedures. The derived stimulus control is based on two or more stimuli controlling a common response topography. Such classes have been demonstrated with college students (Shipley, 1935), with normal children (Kendler, 1964; Reese, 1972), and with nonverbal children with severe and profound retardation (Spradlin & Dixon, 1995). The Spradlin and Dixon study (diagrammed in the top panel of Figure 2) will serve as a simple example.   Subjects learned to press a button when a tone was presented.

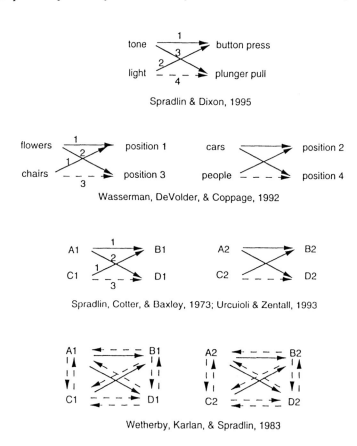

Figure 2. Four training procedures that are used to demonstrate derived stimulus control. Arrows point from discriminative stimuli to responses in the top panel, and from sample to comparison stimuli in the lower three panels. Solid arrows designate trained performances, and dashed arrows designate derived performances. Numerals next to the arrows indicate the order in which the relations were trained. Comparison stimuli with the same letter designation always appeared together.

Then, subjects were presented a light stimulus to determine whether the light also controlled button pressing. It did not. Next, subjects were trained to press the button when the light was presented. Thus, both the tone and the light independently controlled the button press. Next, subjects learned to pull a plunger when one of the two stimuli was presented. In tests without differential reinforcement, subjects pulled the plunger in response to the remaining stimulus. It is conceivable that the functional stimulus was actually stimulus onset. This seems unlikely, however, because the light did not control the button press after control of the button press by the tone had been established. The light and tone became members of the same stimulus class after both controlled the same response. Moreover, the light no longer controlled plunger responses after its control of the button response had been extinguished.

Stimulus classes based on a common position response in a conditional discrimination. In a conditional position discrimination, two or more sample stimuli are presented successively, and a response to a stimulus in a different position on the response panel is reinforced in the presence of each. For example, a response to a key on the right side of the panel might be reinforced in the presence of one sample, and a response to a key on the left in the presence of another sample. The conditional position discrimination procedure is a hybrid of successive simple discrimination (two or more successively presented stimuli each control a different response topography) and conditional discrimination (the conditional control of a simple discrimination--left key vs. right key).

A study by Wasserman et al. (1992) used four response keys, one in each of the four corners of the screen. Pigeons learned to respond to a key in one position when the sample was any member of two stimulus sets, flowers and chairs, and to respond to a second position when the sample was any member of two other stimulus sets, cars and people (details of counterbalancing have been omitted). Each stimulus set included 12 pictures. Next, subjects were taught to respond to a third position in the presence of flowers and to a fourth position in response to cars. Test trials with nondifferential reinforcement showed that chairs controlled responses to Position 3 and people controlled responses to Position 4 to a level significantly greater than would be expected by chance. Mean accuracy (for 8 pigeons) was 77% in the first test session conducted after high baseline accuracy was obtained. The procedure is shown in the second panel of Figure 2.

The conditional position discrimination may hasten the study of stimulus class relations among subjects in whom establishing matching to sample is difficult, such as humans with mental retardation (McIlvane, Dube, Kledaras, Iennaco, & Stoddard, 1990; Saunders & Spradlin, 1989) or young normal children (Smeets & Striefel, 1994). Carter and Eckerman (1975) showed that pigeons learned conditional position discriminations in substantially fewer sessions than were required for matching to sample.

Stimulus classes based on the selection of a common comparison stimulus in a conditional discrimination. This procedure, diagrammed in the third panel of Figure 2, is analogous to the previous one except that it involves the more typical arbitrary matching-to-sample procedure in which sample stimuli control choices that cannot be identified on the basis of their position. Subjects learn three conditional discriminations, AB, CB, and AD. (In this notation, the first letter designates the two sample stimuli [A1 and A2] and the second letter designates the two comparison stimuli [B1 and B2]; responses to B1 are reinforced in the presence of A1 and likewise for A2 and B2.) Two of the conditional discriminations have the same comparison stimuli. Tests determine whether the subject selects D1 when C1 is presented as the sample, and D2 when C2 is presented as the sample. Derived stimulus control resulting from this training and testing procedure has been demonstrated with both adolescent humans with mild mental retardation (Spradlin, Cotter, & Baxley, 1973) and pigeons (Urcuioli, Zentall, Jackson-Smith, & Steim, 1989).

Some differences in procedure and outcome bear mention. For the human subjects, test trial responses produced no feedback. For the pigeons, testing was conducted with differential reinforcement. The most important procedural difference became apparent in follow-up studies. With pigeon subjects, it is essential that the two conditional discriminations with the same comparison stimuli be established first, and perhaps simultaneously. Establishing AB and AD simultaneously (a one-to-many procedure), and then establishing CB does not result in derived CD relations even though the same three conditional discriminations are trained in both variations of the procedure (Urcuioli & Zentall, 1993; Urcuioli et al., 1995). In contrast, normally developing preschoolers have shown derived CD relations regardless of the order in which the conditional discriminations are trained and when the conditional discriminations are trained individually before being intermixed (Wetherby, Karlan, & Spradlin, 1983). Although the CD tests demonstrate only unidirectional transfer, the procedure makes possible tests for bidirectional transfer (shown in the bottom panel of Figure 2), which human subjects demonstrate under these procedures (Wetherby et al., 1983).

Multiple-Term Unidirectional Classes (Transitivity)

To test for transitivity, two conditional discriminations are taught, for example, AB and BC. Transitivity is demonstrated when the subject selects C1 when A1 is presented as the sample, and C2 when A2 is presented as the sample. Although stimuli retain their training function in the derived stimulus control relation (A stimuli are still samples and C stimuli are still comparisons), the derived stimulus control depends on the B stimuli having served both sample and a comparison function in the directly-trained relations. We distinguish between transitivity and many-to-one unidirectional classes because the latter involve stimuli that serve only in the first term of both the trained and derived stimulus control relations.

D'Amato, Salmon, Loukas, and Tomie (1985) found strong evidence of transitivity in primate subjects, although Sidman et al. (1982) did not. Some tests presented in chimpanzee language studies (Savage-Rumbaugh, 1981) provide evidence of transitivity, albeit with more complexity than the usual laboratory demonstration. Schusterman and Kastak (1993) demonstrated transitivity with a sea lion. Transitivity had not been demonstrated in pigeons (D'Amato et al., 1985; Lipkens, Kop, & Matthijs, 1988) until a recent study reported weak evidence (Kuno, Kitadate, & Iwamoto, 1994). In the Kuno et al. study, however, the A and B stimuli were much more similar within potential stimulus classes than across classes, which may have promoted transfer of control from the B to the A stimulus. Normal elementary school-aged children nearly always demonstrate transitivity. In our laboratory, three subjects with moderate mental retardation who initially had great difficulty learning arbitrary matching (although they learned rapidly at the time of testing) did not initially demonstrate transitivity within a completely visual arbitrary matching task. After training the transitivity test performances, one of the subjects subsequently came to demonstrate transitivity with new stimulus sets. The other two did not, despite "transitivity training," which involved reinforcing test-trial performances until high accuracy was achieved, across at least seven stimulus sets.

Although the differences observed across human subjects likely reflect subject characteristics, the literature as a whole includes many procedural differences that could affect outcome. As an example, consider the different outcomes of D'Amato et al. (1985) and Sidman et al. (1982). Although both studies involved monkeys, used automated matching-to-sample procedures, and either colors or abstract two-dimensional figures as stimuli, the studies differed in nearly every other procedural detail. Different species of monkeys were used, and D'Amato's monkeys apparently had more pre-experimental experience with matching-to-sample procedures. The specific stimuli differed (see D'Amato et al.). D'Amato et al. used subject-initiated trials and Sidman et al. (1982) did not. D'Amato et al. used a zero-delay matching procedure and Sidman et al. (1982) used simultaneous matching. D'Amato's intertrial interval was 20 s and Sidman's was 5 s. D'Amato presented massed test trials with differential reinforcement (tests in which the "incorrect" response was reinforced served as a control procedure); Sidman first presented unreinforced test trials that were interspersed in a baseline of three other conditional discriminations before differentially reinforcing test-trial selections. Finally, the subjects in Sidman's study had extensive previous exposure to the test trials with the same comparison stimuli (in the form of symmetry tests), during which interfering stimulus control may have developed.

Any of these factors could have played a role in the differences observed. For example, extensive laboratory experience might produce generalized conditional responding, facilitating test-trial accuracy (Saunders & Spradlin, 1990, 1993). A lengthier intertrial interval could reduce residual interfering stimulus control from previous trials (i.e., proactive interference). Perhaps most important, D'Amato et al. used differential reinforcement from the beginning of testing (with within-subject control procedures). There are no demonstrations of derived stimulus control in nonhumans without differential reinforcement on test trials, except in the ape language studies. Although the latter studies did not provide differential reinforcement on test trials, several derived stimulus control relations were reinforced prior to presenting unreinforced test trials for other derived relations (Savage-Rumbaugh, 1981). The virtually perfect test trial performance of the chimpanzees stands in contrast to other demonstrations in nonhuman subjects.

Response mediated transitivity. Derived performances that meet the definition of transitivity have also been demonstrated under both types of procedures that we discussed in the response mediated transfer section. Monkeys demonstrated virtually perfect accuracy on tests for symmetry and transitivity when differential sample responding mediated transfer test performance in the manner illustrated in Figure 1 (McIntire, Cleary, & Thompson, 1987; see Saunders, 1989 for an analysis).

Pigeons have shown positive outcomes on transitivity tests under differential outcomes procedures (Steirn, Jackson-Smith, & Zentall, 1991). In Experiment 2 of Steirn et al., different rates of sample pecking were established in the presence of two stimuli through an autoshaping procedure. Peas were presented after a red stimulus and the empty hopper was presented after a green stimulus. Next, the birds learned to select vertical and horizontal comparison stimuli after presentation of peas or the empty hopper, respectively. Presumably, the peas and the red sample evoked similar rates of pecking, as did the empty hopper and the green sample. Tests showed some control of vertical by the red sample and of horizontal by the green sample. Effects were small; group mean accuracy in the first 64-trial test session was 54% under differential reinforcement procedures. The difference between this accuracy level and the 45% accuracy level shown by a group trained with mediating responses that opposed the test trial contingencies was significant, however.

Symmetry or Bidirectional Transfer

Arbitrary matching to sample has been called *symbolic matching*. Some early studies of symmetry, or bidirectional transfer, were couched as minimal tests of the appropriateness of referring to arbitrary matching as symbolic matching. To test for symmetry, a subject is trained to select comparison B1 when A1 is presented as a sample and B2 when A2 is presented as a sample. Then, tests determine whether the subject selects A1 when A1 and A2 are presented as the comparisons and B1 is presented as the sample, and selects A2 when B2 is presented as the sample. This derived performance demonstrates symmetry or bidirectional transfer.

This form of transfer may seem less complex than those described above. It is not based on the linkage of two stimuli to a common third stimulus or response, as in our two previous examples. However, in several studies of primates, results are mostly negative (Dugdale & Lowe, 1990, chimpanzees; Sidman et al., 1982, rhesus monkeys, even with differential reinforcement throughout testing; D'Amato et al., 1985, cebus monkeys). (Note that both of the other studies cited used some differential reinforcement, but usually after exposure to unreinforced test trials.) The D'Amato et al. study is of special interest, as it found strong evidence of transitivity in monkeys under highly comparable test procedures (including differential reinforcement on test trials). In addition, unlike the unidirectional transfer discussed above, symmetry has not been demonstrated in pigeons (Lipkens et al., 1988; Rodewald, 1974; Sidman et al., 1982), even with differential reinforcement on test trials (D'Amato et al., 1985). Although positive symmetry test results were reported in a recent study of parakeets (Manabe, Kawashima, & Staddon, 1995, Experiment 3), the procedures used did not rule out the possibility of direct training of the putatively derived performances (Saunders & Williams, 1995).

The chimpanzee-language studies of Savage-Rumbaugh have not used the rather abstract arbitrary matching-to-sample procedures that are most common in the literature. Some of their tests, however, appear to demonstrate symmetry (Savage-Rumbaugh, Pate, Lawson, Smith, & Rosenbaum, 1983). In a study by Tomonaga, Matsuzawa, Fujita, and Yamamoto (1991), one of three chimpanzees showed 100% accuracy in the first test session, but decreased accuracy in two subsequent test sessions (each with 8 test trials). There was no programmed reinforcement on test trials, which could account for the diminishing accuracy across test sessions. The only nonhuman demonstration of highly accurate symmetry performance under abstract arbitrary matching procedures was by a sea lion (Schusterman & Kastak, 1993). Test-trial responses were differentially reinforced, but symmetry was concluded on the basis of performance on the first trial across a number of different stimulus sets.

Symmetry is typically shown in normal human adults and children (e.g., Sidman et al., 1982) and in adults with mild or moderate mental retardation (e.g., Saunders & Spradlin, 1990). Symmetry has also been demonstrated in subjects with severe retardation (e.g., Sidman, Willson-Morris, & Kirk, 1986). Symmetry appears to be less likely in subjects with severe-to-profound mental retardation and profoundly limited language skills, however (Saunders, Saunders, & Spradlin, 1989).

As with transitivity, the factors involved in apparent subject differences are unclear. A characteristic of symmetry tests that could diminish the likelihood of transfer in pigeons, for example, is that the test trial locations of the stimuli are different from training-trial locations (for related discussions see Iversen, Sidman, & Carrigan, 1986; Sidman et al., 1982; Zentall, Sherburne, Steirn, Randall, et al., 1992). There are two ways in which this might interfere with the demonstration of symmetry. First, if the stimuli that appear as samples in symmetry test trials have previously appeared only as comparisons, there is no evidence that they are discriminated when presented successively. Second, for pigeons, the location of a stimulus is one of the properties that acquires stimulus control, at least for horizontal and vertical line stimuli (Iversen et al., 1986). In a sense, for pigeons, a horizontal line presented on the middle of three response keys is not the same as a horizontal line presented on a side key. This would seem to be related to difficulties in demonstrating generalized identity matching in pigeons. Perhaps generalized identity matching is a prerequisite for symmetry. If so, current efforts to demonstrate symmetry should begin with efforts to demonstrate generalized identity matching.

Response mediated symmetry. Pigeons have also demonstrated performances that can be interpreted as meeting the definition of symmetry under differential outcomes procedures. In two experiments, pigeons learned to peck a red comparison when presented one sample and a green comparison when presented a different sample, but only the correct red comparison response produced food (Zentall, Sherburne, & Steirn, 1992). Tests presented food and no-food samples and red and green comparisons, with both positive and negative transfer arrangements across groups. In both experiments, the amount of sample pecking was much greater for the samples associated with food. This presumably established two units, "many pecks"--select red, and "few pecks"--select green. In the first 16 trials of the transfer test, the positive groups showed 56% and 54% accuracy and the negative groups showed 33% and 41% accuracy in Experiments 1 and 2, respectively. A third study minimized differential sample responding by presenting additional Phase 1 trials in which the no-food sample was followed by food. Group mean number of sample responses was not significantly different across samples. Transfer effects were very small, 53% and 48% for the positive and negative groups, respectively. The authors suggested that the latter study showed transfer without response mediation. The very small transfer effect suggests to us that further study is needed.

Equivalence Classes

Sidman and colleagues have offered an objective, more comprehensive definition of derived performances that are typically labeled as symbolic or representational. Their definition takes a large step towards filling a void eloquently described by Savage-Rumbaugh and colleagues, who noted that "no theoretical framework has been developed within the field of animal psychology to distinguish between conditioned discriminative responses and symbolic representational responses" (Savage-Rumbaugh, Rumbaugh, & Boysen, 1980, p. 51). These authors criticized early ape language research for assuming that symbolization is "inherent in the chimpanzee's capacity to select a symbol when presented with an object . . ." (p. 52). The studies of Savage-Rumbaugh and colleagues define symbolic behavior through tests for derived stimulus control.

Note the similarity of Sidman's concerns: "To determine whether a performance involves something more than conditional relations between sample and comparison stimuli," Sidman and Tailby (1982) noted, "requires additional tests." These are tests for symmetry, transitivity, and reflexivity (generalized identity matching of the stimuli involved in the trained relations). To Sidman, performances showing these three types of derived relations *together* defined symbolic behavior. Sidman called stimulus control relations with these three properties "equivalence relations." The development of this definition represents a major advance over relatively slippery terms that previously characterized attempts to define characteristics of symbolic behavior.

Normally developing human children and adults routinely demonstrate equivalence classes, as do individuals with mild mental retardation and some with moderate and severe mental retardation. Moreover, when one or more members of an equivalence class is given a new function through direct training, the remaining members of the class also demonstrate that function (Green, Sigurdardottir, & Saunders, 1991; Hayes, Kohlenberg, & Hayes, 1991). In that sense, an equivalence class is also a functional class, as defined by Goldiamond (1962).

The only formal demonstration of equivalence in a nonhuman animal is the previously discussed study of a sea lion by (Schusterman & Kastak, 1993). In addition, studies by Savage-Rumbaugh and colleagues contain evidence of the independent demonstration of symmetry or transitivity in tests that go beyond the basic demonstrations in their complexity (Savage-Rumbaugh, 1981; Savage-Rumbaugh et al., 1983).

We have previously mentioned the probable importance of differentially reinforced test-trial responses to Schusterman and Kastak's sea lion demonstration. The studies by Savage-Rumbaugh that have demonstrated equivalence-like performances also involve a potentially important procedural variation. All of the studied stimulus classes included at least one real object, and many of these objects had functions beyond the experimental context (some were foods). Thus, the chimpanzee language studies may have been building on existing stimulus classes rather than establishing classes "from scratch" in the laboratory. Once an equivalence class has been developed, it is easy to add new members to that class (Dixon & Spradlin, 1976; Saunders, Wachter, & Spradlin, 1988). This is in no sense a criticism, but rather another example of potentially illuminating procedural differences that have not yet been analyzed. Interestingly, some of the same chimpanzees who demonstrated emergent performances involving familiar objects (Savage-Rumbaugh, 1981) did not demonstrate symmetry with matching-to-sample procedures that incorporated stimuli that did not participate in extra-experimental contingencies (Dugdale & Lowe, 1990). In fact, one of the chimps who had previously demonstrated stimulus classes involving real objects did not even learn the abstract arbitrary matching baseline in the study by Dugdale and Lowe.

Some studies involving individuals with moderate and severe mental retardation also started with existing classes. For example, the five subjects in Sidman's first three studies demonstrated from 50% to 75% accuracy in matching pictures (or, for one subject, letters) to their spoken names (20 different pictures were presented in an 8-choice task) prior to establishing the other performances that were prerequisite to emergent behavior (Sidman, 1971; Sidman & Cresson, 1973; Sidman, Cresson, & Willson-Morris, 1974; diagnoses ranged from high moderate to severe mental retardation). The classes of pictures and spoken words were expanded to include written words. A study by Mackay and Ratti (1990) involved subjects with severe retardation who could already name numerals and who rapidly learned to select numerals in the presence of spoken words. The classes of spoken words and numerals were expanded to include positions on a recognition span test board. These observations also apply to some other studies involving subjects with severe mental retardation (Mackay, 1985; Mackay & Sidman, 1984).

IS THERE EMPIRICAL EVIDENCE FOR ACROSS SPECIES DIFFERENCES

One must walk a fine line in coming to conclusions about across-species differences. It is important to explore a range of procedural adaptations before concluding that differences exist (Sidman, 1960). It seems clear that there is much work to do along these lines. It is equally important, however, not to overlook the possibility that procedural changes that produce similar performances do so through different behavioral mechanisms (Skinner, 1966) or even that the same procedures might promote similar performances through different mechanisms. As

Mackintosh (1988) noted, "the discovery of a pattern of differences can give valuable clues to the nature of those mechanisms."

The evidence currently available suggests a pattern of performance differences across species, however, we do not yet have the whole picture. Moreover, the pattern might change as more studies are conducted, especially studies designed explicitly to compare performance across procedures in the same species. We think a close look at the pattern of results is timely, however, as it may help guide research that either confirms or disconfirms the pattern. For the sake of providing maximum contrast, we focus primarily on differences between human and pigeon stimulus control processes.

Pigeons more readily demonstrate unidirectional transfer (including response mediated transfer) than they demonstrate symmetry. Especially noteworthy are failures to demonstrate symmetry with differential reinforcement throughout testing (D'Amato et al., 1985). Yet pigeons have shown strong evidence of unidirectional transfer after many-to-one training and under response mediated transfer procedures. In contrast, human subjects (including most with mental retardation) nearly always demonstrate symmetry.

An argument against the conclusion that pigeons have not demonstrated symmetry comes from an early discussion of the definition of equivalence. The argument can be applied to the demonstration of unidirectional transfer after many-to-one training, as reported by Urcuioli et al., 1989 (see third panel of Figure 2). According to Sidman and Tailby's (1982) analysis, the CD test does not simply reflect unidirectional transfer, it is a combined test for symmetry and transitivity. It demonstrates symmetry for the AB relation and transitivity across the C, B, A, and D stimuli. Moreover, given these properties, one would expect the demonstration of CA if tested. Unfortunately, no published study has conducted tests for all of these relations after a many-to-one training procedure in pigeons. This would seem to be an important question for future research. Some evidence can be drawn, however, from studies using other procedures. If the CD test is a combined test for symmetry and transitivity, one would expect pigeons to demonstrate symmetry. As of yet, pigeons have not demonstrated symmetry. Thus, the logical argument that the many-to-one transfer shown by pigeons is indicative of symmetry does not have empirical support.

Another striking difference between human and pigeon performance is in the role that differential sample responses can play. The two species are similar in that establishing differential sample responses can speed acquisition of matching to sample. For pigeons, however, this procedure apparently establishes a chain; the sample controls the differential response and the differential response controls comparison selection. Moreover, the stimulus control by the differential response can overshadow control by the sample. That is, disrupting the differential response decreases matching accuracy. In general, for humans, differential sample responding is not part of an invariant chain. It does not interfere with the development of direct control by the sample stimuli, but presumably facilitates matching accuracy by ensuring the discrimination between the sample stimuli.

Is it possible that pigeons' tendency towards response mediation and the relative ease with which unidirectional transfer is demonstrated under many-to-one procedures are related? One possibility is that pigeons are limited to forms of transfer that occur via the recombination of chains. What follows is admittedly speculative, but it fits the pattern of results observed thus far. It is similar to the mediation account that Urcuioli presents in this volume. It seems possible, however, that the form of mediating behaviors is arbitrarily related to both the sample and comparison stimuli, as it is in studies in which the mediating response is directly trained.

How do the mediating responses get there? Our tentative proposal is that they are adventitiously selected from behavior emitted between sample presentation and the comparison response, as has been suggested for time-based reinforcement schedules (e.g., Laties, Weiss, Clark, & Reynolds, 1965; Laties, Weiss, & Weiss, 1969; Nevin & Berryman, 1963; Schwartz & Williams, 1971). The responses could take a number of forms; varying force, duration, topography, or location on the key are possibilities. In addition, mediating responses may not be directed at the sample key, as Blough (1959) reported. Presumably, these responses are maintained because their occurrence makes subsequent reinforcement of the measured response more likely.

How could different mediating responses develop in the presence of each sample stimulus? This is the most speculative part of the account. Although different mediating responses were observed in some early studies of pigeons' delayed matching-to-sample performance, these behaviors were observed with delays longer than 0 s (Berryman, Cumming, & Nevin, 1963; Blough, 1959). Blough's (1959) classic account of the development of mediating behavior under delayed matching procedures may apply here even though the studies currently under discussion used only 0-delay procedures. Pigeons may be likely to emit some initially irrelevant behavior prior to responding to the comparison stimulus, and this behavior may be reinforced adventitiously. Given pigeons' tendency for responses to gain control of comparison selection, however, when this behavior is the same across samples, acquisition of arbitrary matching may be slowed. Thus, different behaviors are selected by the contingencies and pigeons may learn stimulus - response - stimulus chains. That is, in learning the AB and CB conditional discriminations shown in the third panel of Figure 2, pigeons may actually learn A1-R1-B1, A2-R2-B2, C1-R1-B1, C2-R2-B2 (R1 and R2 refer to different responses). Each of these chains can be broken into two overlapping units (e.g., A1-R1 and R1-B1). Thus, when A1-D1 is trained, A1-R1-D1 is established. Now we have both the C1-R1 unit and the R1-D1 unit. There is ample evidence that such units can recombine to form the C1-R1-D1 chain.

There is a large amount of evidence that affirms consequents of a mediating response account. In addition to what we have covered, failures to demonstrate symmetry are consistent with this account, because the test-trial sample stimulus, formerly a comparison, would not control a mediating response. Moreover, pigeons would not be expected to match stimuli that controlled the same comparison selection (i.e., the AC and CA tests shown in the bottom panel of Figure 2) because responses to these stimuli had never been controlled by a mediating response.

Findings that responses are sufficient to mediate derived matching performances do not prove that they are necessary. If findings of sufficiency fit into a pattern of convergent findings, however, they provide a piece of the puzzle. It remains to be seen whether untrained mediating responses can be studied through other than inferential means. The problem is similar to that of whether self-instruction or stimulus naming is necessary for the demonstration of equivalence relations, in which the most convincing evidence would be consistent failure in the absence of naming (e.g., in animals).

Regardless of the mediating response issue, it seems essential to take a single-subject approach. Data from one of the strongest demonstrations of many-to-one transfer in pigeons provides a case in point. Urcuioli et al. (1989) showed the data for each of six subjects. Across the first 16 test trials, accuracy was 50% for one subject, 95% for another, and intermediate for the other four subjects. Clearly, something very different is happening across the subjects. The situation seems ripe for experimental analysis.

CONCLUSIONS

We suggest that there is more than one type of transfer involved in the stimulus class literature, and that some species may be limited to unidirectional transfer that essentially involves the recombination of chains. The bases for this suggestion are as follows. Pigeons demonstrate unidirectional transfer that may not involve symmetry or transitivity. They also demonstrate transfer that can be mediated by behaviors that occur between the presentation of the sample stimulus and the response to the comparison stimulus (Urcuioli & Honig, 1980). Moreover, such intervening behaviors may play different roles for pigeons than for human subjects. Finally, pigeons have yet to demonstrate nonmediated symmetry or equivalence. Furthermore, our own research indicates that some people with retardation do not readily demonstrate equivalence relations. Yet individuals with severe and profound retardation and with little or no conventional verbal behavior demonstrate unidirectional transfer. Finally, equivalence requires both symmetry and transitivity, neither of which seems required for first-term, unidirectional transfer.

The literature contains much speculation as to the conditions that are necessary for the demonstration of derived stimulus control in humans (e.g., Horne & Lowe, 1996, and accompanying commentary). We will not add to that discussion here. The present account suggests only what humans are *not* doing. In contrast to pigeons and perhaps other species, the way that humans acquire stimulus control relations allows numerous forms of derived stimulus control, including symmetry. We have not said, however, what determines derived stimulus control in human subjects.

AUTHOR NOTES

Preparation was supported by National Institute of Child Health and Human Development Grants No. R29-HD27314, PO1-HD18955, and P30-HD02528 to the Schiefelbusch Institute for Life Span Studies, University of Kansas. We thank our colleagues on the Program Project Grant, Communication of People with Mental Retardation, for their helpful comments and Donna Dutcher and Pat White for editorial assistance. Correspondence address: Parsons Research Center, P.O. Box 738, Parsons, KS 67357. email: ksaunders@parsons.lsi.ukans.edu

REFERENCES

Berryman, R., Cumming, W. W., & Nevin, J. A. (1963). Acquisition of delayed matching in the pigeon. *Journal of the Experimental Analysis of Behavior, 6*, 101-107.

Blough, D. S. (1959). Delayed matching in the pigeon. *Journal of the Experimental Analysis of Behavior, 2*, 151-160.

Carter, D. E., & Eckerman, D. A. (1975). Symbolic matching by pigeons: Rate of learning complex discriminations predicted from simple discriminations. *Science, 187*, 662-664.

D'Amato, M. R., Salmon, D. P., Loukas, E., & Tomie, A. (1985). Symmetry and transitivity of conditional relations in monkeys (*Cebus apella*) and pigeons (*Columba livia*). *Journal of the Experimental Analysis of Behavior, 44*, 35-47.

Dixon, M. H., & Spradlin, J. E. (1976). Establishing stimulus equivalence among retarded adolescents. *Journal of Experimental Psychology, 21*, 144-164.

Dugdale, N., & Lowe, C. F. (1990). Naming and stimulus equivalence. In D. E. Blackman & H. Lejeune (Eds.), *Behavior analysis in theory and practice: Contributions and controversies* (pp. 115-138). Hillsdale, NJ: Erlbaum.

Goldiamond, I. (1962). Perception. In A. J. Bachrach (Ed.), *Experimental foundations of clinical psychology* (pp. 280-340). New York: Basic Books.

Green, G., Sigurdardottir, Z. G., & Saunders, R. R. (1991). The role of instructions in the transfer of ordinal functions through equivalence classes. *Journal of the Experimental Analysis of Behavior, 55,* 287-304.

Hayes, S. C. (1989). Nonhumans have not yet shown stimulus equivalence. *Journal of the Experimental Analysis of Behavior, 51,* 385-392.

Hayes, S. C., Kohlenberg, B. S., & Hayes, L. J. (1991). The transfer of specific and general consequential functions through simple and conditional equivalence relations. *Journal of the Experimental Analysis of Behavior, 56,* 119-137.

Horne, P. J., & Lowe, C. F. (1996). On the origins of naming and other symbolic behavior. *Journal of the Experimental Analysis of Behavior, 65,* 185-241.

Hull, C. E. (1943). *Principles of behavior: An introduction to behavior theory.* New York: Appleton-Century-Crofts.

Iversen, I. H., Sidman, M., & Carrigan, P. (1986). Stimulus definition in conditional discriminations. *Journal of the Experimental Analysis of Behavior, 45,* 297-304.

Jenkins, H. M., & Moore, B. R. (1973). The form of the auto-shaped response with food or water reinforcers. *Journal of the Experimental Analysis of Behavior, 20,* 163-181.

Keller, F. S., & Schoenfeld, W. S. (1950). *Principles of psychology.* New York: Appleton-Century-Crofts.

Kendler, H. H. (1964). Concept of the concept. In A. W. Melton (Ed.), *Categories of human learning* (pp. 212-336). New York: Academic Press.

Kuno, H., Kitadate, T., & Iwamoto, T. (1994). Formation of transitivity in conditional matching to sample by pigeons. *Journal of the Experimental Analysis of Behavior, 62,* 399-408.

Laties, V. G., Weiss, B., Clark, R. L., & Reynolds, M. D. (1965). Overt "mediating" behavior during temporally spaced responding. *Journal of the Experimental Analysis of Behavior, 8,* 107-116.

Laties, V. G., Weiss, B., & Weiss, A. B. (1969). Further observations on overt "mediating" behavior and the discrimination of time. *Journal of the Experimental Analysis of Behavior, 12,* 43-57.

Lipkens, R., Kop, P. F. M., & Matthijs, W. (1988). A test of symmetry and transitivity in the conditional discrimination performances of pigeons. *Journal of the Experimental Analysis of Behavior, 49,* 395-409.

Mackay, H. A. (1985). Stimulus equivalence in rudimentary reading and spelling. *Analysis and Intervention in Developmental Disabilities, 5,* 373-387.

Mackay, H. A., & Ratti, C. A. (1990). Position-numeral equivalences and delayed position recognition span. *American Journal on Mental Retardation, 95,* 271-282.

Mackay, H. A., & Sidman, M. (1984). Teaching new behavior via equivalence relations. In P. H. Brooks, B. Sperber, & C. MacCauley (Eds.), *Learning and cognition in the mentally retarded* (pp. 493-513). Hillsdale, NJ: Erlbaum.

Mackintosh, N. J. (1988). Approaches to the study of animal intelligence. *British Journal of Psychology, 79,* 509-525.

Manabe, K., Kawashima, T., & Staddon, J. E. R. (1995). Differential vocalization in budgerigars: Towards an experimental analysis of naming. *Journal of the Experimental Analysis of Behavior, 63,* 111-126.

McIlvane, W. J., Dube, W. V., Kledaras, J. B., Iennaco, F. M., & Stoddard, L. T. (1990). Teaching relational discrimination to individuals with mental retardation: Some problems and possible solutions. *American Journal on Mental Retardation, 95*, 283-296.

McIntire, K. D., Cleary, J., & Thompson, T. (1987). Conditional relations by monkeys: Reflexivity, symmetry, and transitivity. *Journal of the Experimental Analysis of Behavior, 47*, 279-285.

Nevin, J. A., & Berryman, R. (1963). A note on chaining and temporal discrimination. *Journal of the Experimental Analysis of Behavior, 6*, 109-113.

Peterson, G. B. (1984). How expectancies guide behavior. In H. L. Roitblat, T. G. Bever, & H. S. Terrace (Eds.), *Animal cognition* (pp. 135-148). Hillsdale, NJ: Erlbaum.

Reese, H. W. (1972). Acquired distinctiveness and equivalence of cues in young children. *Journal of Experimental Child Psychology, 13*, 171-182.

Rodewald, H. K. (1974). Symbolic matching-to-sample by pigeons. *Psychological Reports, 34*, 987-990.

Rosch, E., & Mervis, C. B. (1975). Family resemblances: Studies in the internal structure of categories. *Cognitive Psychology, 7*, 573-605.

Saunders, K. J. (1989). Naming in conditional discrimination and stimulus equivalence. *Journal of the Experimental Analysis of Behavior, 51*, 379-384.

Saunders, K. J., & Spradlin, J. E. (1989). Conditional discrimination in mentally retarded adults: The effect of training the component simple discriminations. *Journal of the Experimental Analysis of Behavior, 52*, 1-12.

Saunders, K. J., & Spradlin, J. E. (1990). Conditional discrimination in mentally retarded adults: The development of generalized skills. *Journal of the Experimental Analysis of Behavior, 54*, 239-250.

Saunders, K. J., & Spradlin, J. E. (1993). Conditional discrimination in mentally retarded subjects: Programming acquisition and learning set. *Journal of the Experimental Analysis of Behavior, 60*, 571-585.

Saunders, K. J., & Williams, D. C. (1995). *A study of bidirectional transfer in parakeets: An alternative interpretation with suggested control procedures.* Manuscript submitted for publication.

Saunders, K. J., Williams, D. C., & Spradlin, J. E. (1995). Conditional discrimination by adults with mental retardation: Establishing relations between physically identical stimuli. *American Journal on Mental Retardation, 99*, 558-563.

Saunders, M. D., Saunders, R. R., & Spradlin, J. E. (1989, May). *Tests for symmetry and equivalence in nonverbal adolescents with severe handicaps.* Paper presented at the 15th annual meeting of the Association for Behavior Analysis, Milwaukee, WI.

Saunders, R. R., Wachter, J., & Spradlin, J. E. (1988). Establishing auditory stimulus control over an eight-member equivalence class via conditional discrimination procedures. *Journal of the Experimental Analysis of Behavior, 49*, 95-115.

Savage-Rumbaugh, E. S. (1981). Can apes use symbols to represent their world? *Annals of the New York Academy of Science, 364*, 35-59.

Savage-Rumbaugh, E. S., Pate, J. L., Lawson, J., Smith, S. T., & Rosenbaum, S. (1983). Can a chimpanzee make a statement? *Journal of Experimental Psychology: General, 112*, 457-492.

Savage-Rumbaugh, E. S., Rumbaugh, D. M., & Boysen, S. (1980). Do apes use language? *American Scientist, 68*, 49-61.

Schusterman, R. J., & Kastak, D. (1993). A California sea lion (*Zalophus Californianus*) is capable of forming equivalence relations. *Psychological Record, 43*, 823-839.

Schwartz, B., & Williams, D. R. (1971). Discrete-trials spaced responding in the pigeon: The dependence of efficient performance on the availability of a stimulus for collateral pecking. *Journal of the Experimental Analysis of Behavior, 16*, 155-160.

Shipley, W. C. (1935). Indirect conditioning. *Journal of General Psychology, 12*, 337-357.

Sidman, M. (1960). *Tactics of scientific research: Evaluating experimental data in psychology.* New York: Basic Books.

Sidman, M. (1971). Reading and auditory-visual equivalences. *Journal of Speech and Hearing Research, 14*, 5-13.

Sidman, M., & Cresson, O., Jr. (1973). Reading and crossmodal transfer of stimulus equivalences in severe retardation. *American Journal of Mental Deficiency, 77*, 515-523.

Sidman, M., Cresson, O., Jr., & Willson-Morris, M. (1974). Acquisition of matching to sample via mediated transfer. *Journal of the Experimental Analysis of Behavior, 22*, 261-273.

Sidman, M., Rauzin, R., Lazar, R., Cunningham, S., Tailby, W., & Carrigan, P. (1982). A search for symmetry in the conditional discriminations of rhesus monkeys, baboons, and children. *Journal of the Experimental Analysis of Behavior, 37*, 23-44.

Sidman, M., & Tailby, W. (1982). Conditional discrimination vs. matching-to-sample: An expansion of the testing paradigm. *Journal of the Experimental Analysis of Behavior, 37*, 5-22.

Sidman, M., Willson-Morris, M., & Kirk, B. (1986). Matching-to-sample procedures and the development of equivalence relations: The role of naming. *Analysis and Intervention in Developmental Disabilities, 6*, 1-19.

Sidman, M., Wynne, C. K., Maguire, R. W., & Barnes, T. (1989). Functional classes and equivalence relations. *Journal of the Experimental Analysis of Behavior, 52*, 261-274.

Skinner, B. F. (1966). Operant behavior. In W. K. Honig (Ed.), *Operant behavior: Areas of research and application* (pp. 12-32)

Smeets, P. M., & Striefel , S. (1994). A revised blocked-trial procedure for establishing arbitrary matching in children. *Quarterly Journal of Experimental Psychology, 47B*, 241-261.

Spradlin, J. E., Cotter, V. W., & Baxley, N. (1973). Establishing a conditional discrimination without direct training: A study of transfer with retarded adolescents. *American Journal of Mental Deficiency, 77*, 556-566.

Spradlin, J. E., & Dixon, M. H. (1995). Emergent stimulus--Response relations in children with severe, mental retardation. *American Journal on Mental Retardation, 100*, 313-322.

Steirn, J. N., Jackson-Smith, P., & Zentall, T. R. (1991). Mediational use of internal representations of food and no-food events by pigeons. *Learning and Motivation, 22*, 353-365.

Tomonaga, M., Matsuzawa, T., Fujita, K., & Yamamoto, J. (1991). Emergence of symmetry in a visual conditional discrimination by chimpanzees (Pan Troglodytes). *Psychological Reports, 68*, 51-60.

Urcuioli, P. J. (1984). Overshadowing in matching-to-sample: Reduction in sample-stimulus control by differential sample behaviors. *Animal Learning and Behavior, 12*, 256-264.

Urcuioli, P. J. (1985). On the role of differential sample behaviors in matching-to-sample. *Journal of Experimental Psychology: Animal Behavior Processes, 11*, 502-519.

Urcuioli, P. J., & Honig, W. K. (1980). Control of choice in conditional discriminations by sample-specific behaviors. *Journal of Experimental Psychology: Animal Behavior*

Processes, 6, 251-277.

Urcuioli, P. J., & Zentall, T. R. (1993). A test of comparison-stimulus substitutability following one-to-many matching by pigeons. *Psychological Record, 43*, 745-759.

Urcuioli, P. J., Zentall, T. R., & DeMarse, T. (1995). Transfer to derived sample-comparison relations by pigeons following many-to-one versus one-to-many matching with identical training relations. *Quarterly Journal of Experimental Psychology, 48B*, 158-178.

Urcuioli, P. J., Zentall, T. R., Jackson-Smith, P., & Steirn, J. N. (1989). Evidence for common coding in many-to-one matching: Retention, intertrial interference, and transfer. *Journal of Experimental Psychology: Animal Behavior Processes, 15*, 264-273.

Vaughan, W., Jr. (1988). Formation of equivalence sets in pigeons. *Journal of Experimental Psychology: Animal Behavior Processes, 14*, 36-42.

Wasserman, E. A., DeVolder, C. L., & Coppage, D. J. (1992). Non-similarity-based conceptualization in pigeons via secondary or mediated generalization. *Psychological Science, 3*, 374-379.

Wetherby, B., Karlan, G. R., & Spradlin, J. E. (1983). The development of derived stimulus relations through training in arbitrary-matching sequences. *Journal of the Experimental Analysis of Behavior, 40*, 69-78.

Zentall, T. R., Sherburne, L. M., & Steirn, J. N. (1992). Development of excitatory backward associations during the establishment of forward associations in a delayed conditional discrimination by pigeons. *Animal Learning and Behavior, 20*, 199-206.

Zentall, T. R., Sherburne, L. M., Steirn, J. N., Randall, C. K., Roper, K. L., & Urcuioli, P. J. (1992). Common coding in pigeons: Partial versus total reversals of one-to-many conditional discriminations. *Animal Learning and Behavior, 20*, 373-381.

Stimulus Class Formation in Humans and Animals
T.R. Zentall and P.M. Smeets (Editors)

7

Mediating Associations, Essentialism, and Nonsimilarity-based Categorization

Suzette L. Astley and Edward A. Wasserman

Cornell College and The University of Iowa

There has been great interest in categorization over the past 30 years. A computer search of nearly any psychology database using the keyword "categorization" is likely to net several hundred references published in the last 5 years alone. It is a topic of strong and immediate concern to philosophers, linguists, and computer scientists as well as psychologists.

Why has categorization received this interest? What about this capability requires such a high degree of empirical and theoretical scrutiny? One reason for this interest and scrutiny may be the cognitive efficiency categorization permits. Younger and Cohen (1985) write,

> Imagine for a moment an organism faced with a novel environment without the benefit of concepts and categories. Imagine the tasks of perceiving, remembering, thinking, and talking without the ability to organize incoming information into existing category structures. Each percept, object, or event would be perceived as unique. Each would have to be remembered as different from all others, a different label applied to each object and event. The sheer diversity would prove overwhelming (p. 211).

Others, like Thelen and Smith (1994), treat categorization as a core capacity on which other psychological processes critically depend: "Category formation is the primitive of mental life; the ontogeny of category formation is the basis for behavioral development (p. 162)." In her book reviewing the literature on children's categorization, Ellen Markman (1989) also comments on these notions: "Categorization, then, is a means of simplifying the environment, of reducing the load on memory, and of helping us to store and retrieve information effectively (p. 11)."

Another reason for the booming interest in categorization may be that there is little agreement on the processes that create adult human categorization behavior. Widely divergent theories have been devised to account for this capacity. Family resemblance and prototype models formed the basis for a substantial amount of research in the 1970s and 1980s. Exemplar and connectionist models gained popularity during the 1980s. Since the early- to mid-1980s, an essentialist approach has been prominent in the developmental literature. This diversity of theoretical approaches to categorization continues apace in the current literature; there is no commonly agreed on approach to explaining this ubiquitous and fundamental psychological process.

One difficulty in devising a single coherent theoretical approach to categorization may be that researchers and theorists make fundamentally different assumptions about the processes that may be involved in categorization and about the best way to examine them. The editor of an earlier work of ours (Wasserman & Astley, 1994) urged us to examine evidence concerning the notion that human conceptual categories are fundamentally based on abstract theories humans have about the nature of objects -- an approach radically different from our own preferences for a focus on perceptual similarity and associational processes. If psychologists are ever to come to to a more comprehensive and coherent view of how categorization works, it will be necessary for us to at least consider assumptions and research approaches which may be widely divergent from our own. The first portion of this paper represents such an attempt.

We begin by describing a type of theory-based model (the essentialist view) that is currently dominant in the developmental literature, and we then critically evaluate research adduced to support the essentialist model. In later portions of the chapter, however, we elaborate a mediational model in an attempt to account for nonsimilarity-based categorization. We describe research with humans and with nonhuman animals that documents the effectiveness of common experience in creating classes which go beyond perceptual resemblance. We also describe the results of new research on response mediation as a basis for categorization behavior in children. In the concluding section of the chapter, we return to a discussion of the role of perceptual and nonperceptual processes in categorization and describe our plans for future research.

THE ESSENTIALIST APPROACH TO CATEGORIZATION

The essentialist approach to categorization downplays the importance of perceptual similarity. It posits that people are most likely to categorize an object based on a theory they have about the object's essential nature (Medin & Ortony, 1989). Thus, people act as if objects and living things have a core essence that constrains and generates the superficial features on which perceptual similarity may be based. Perceptual similarity may guide categorization if theory-relevant information is unavailable; but, the assumed essence is hypothesized to be a more powerful determinant of categorization and of inferences about objects and living things than is perceptual similarity (Keil, 1989).

According to Medin and Ortony (1989), knowledge representations of object concepts have an "essence placeholder," the contents of which may change over time. This essence placeholder provides a fundamental basis for categorization, one that has a causal relationship to other attributes of an object or a living thing, even while other aspects of its content may change over time or vary between specific instances or types of objects or living things. As an example, Medin and Ortony cite the concept of *boy* and say that its core essence placeholder might contain "properties such as *male*, *young*, and *human* that could be used to understand its relation to other concepts like *girl*, *colt*, and *man* (p. 185)."

Gelman, Coley, and Gottfried (1994) view commonsense theories of the sort referred to by Medin and Ortony (1989) as like scientific theories, in that they posit unobservable constructs that have a lawful and causal relationship to events in the world. These constructs are domain specific; they differ depending on the type of events that are to be explained or categorized. These abstract commonsense theories provide, as do scientific theories, a basis for categorization. "People's tendency to create explanatory constructs can lead us to classify together entities that have salient differences but share *theory-relevant properties* (Gelman et al., 1994, p. 343, emphasis in the original)."

Gelman et al. also see differences between scientific theories and commonsense theories. Scientific theories are considered to be more explicit and formal than commonsense theories. A goal of scientific theory-building is to create a clearly and explicitly stated set of principles for testing. Gelman et al., however, say that nonscientists are frequently unable to state *explicitly* the principles of their commonsense theories even when they may understand them *implicitly*. Gelman et al. believe, further, that nonscientists do not engage in the sort of vigorous hypothesis testing of their commonsense theories that is characteristic of science.

As mentioned above, to date, empirical support in the developmental literature for essentialist theories has come from studies of two fundamental types -- transformation and induction studies. In the first type of study, natural kind entities are physically transformed and research participants are asked whether the "kind" of the entity has changed. In one of the scenarios used by Keil (1989), for example, children were asked to indicate whether a raccoon modified to resemble and smell like a skunk was a raccoon or a skunk. Children's general tendency to resist changes in biological kind despite surface changes was seen as evidence for the operation of theories rather than perceptual similarity in categorization.

The other type of study examines inductive inferences from one entity to another. A series of studies by Gelman and Markman (1986, 1987) are often cited in this regard. In the 1986 studies, for example, Gelman and Markman presented two standard stimuli and described one unseen attribute on which the standard stimuli differed. They then presented a target stimulus which perceptually resembled one of the standard stimuli but was of the same ontological category as the other standard stimulus. Children were significantly more likely to say that the target stimulus shared the unseen attribute of the standard stimulus of the same ontological category than they were to say the target shared the unseen attribute of the standard stimulus which perceptually resembled the target. Gelman and Markman and other essentialist theorists cite this study and others like it as evidence against perceptual similarity as a strong determinant of categorization in children and as support for the essentialist model.

Many writers have postulated that some aspects of the tendency to form theories is innate. After describing the essence placeholder as a part of an object concept and elaborating its causal nature, Medin and Ortony (1989) write, "Our third tenet is that organisms have evolved in such a way that their perceptual (and conceptual) systems are sensitive to just those kinds of similarity that lead them toward the deeper and more central properties (p. 186)." Keil (1994) refers to the tendencies to form theories as "modes of construal." To date, Keil (1994) reports observing three modes of construal: mechanical, intentional, and teleological. Keil grants that these modes of construal may be initially acquired through general learning processes, but he believes this possibility to be highly unlikely given their early emergence in children. Keil (1994) rejects the notion that attention to nonperceptual attributes of living things might come about in older children because of general associative or inductive processes, an approach that he refers to as the empiricist view. In support of this argument, he cites demonstrations that children, "have been shown not to be seduced by surface similarity and instead rely on deeper relations and principles ... (p. 239)." In addition, he claims that empiricist accounts are fundamentally unable to account for such changes:

> empiricist accounts have great difficulty demonstrating how an interconnected set of explanatory beliefs, or an intuitive theory, could ever emerge. There is no known route from association to domain-specific theories or belief clusters that does not build in preexisting biases to construct certain classes of theories over others; and those biases cannot simply be perceptually driven. For centuries, empiricists have claimed that all knowledge could be bootstrapped out of

constraints laid down by a set of sensory and perceptual primitives, but we have yet to see any such model work even for a notion as apparently simple as causation (p. 238).

Keil concludes that we are left with no alternative but to posit primal theories:

> Rather than being the more parsimonious view, the empiricist account has to explain how a set of properties and relations becomes differentially salient for picking out and thinking about living things, especially when many of those properties are not obvious in immediate experience. I therefore move on to the primal theories view, under the assumption that there is no positive evidence that even very young children structure their concepts in terms of raw similarity spaces constrained only by perceptual principles and associativelike laws (p. 240).

Carey and Spelke (1994) similarly argue that the simple fact that conceptual change occurs argues against its basis in perceptual experience. They write, "If the development of domain-specific reasoning is constrained by domain-specific perception, and if the same system of knowledge underlies both reasoning and perception, then no person at any level of expertise is in a position to learn that his or her initial system of knowledge is false (p. 179)."

A CRITIQUE OF ESSENTIALIST THEORIES

The work discussed above strongly suggests that perceptual similarity has limitations as the sole explanation of categorization behavior. Resemblance models that rely solely on perceptual similarity are therefore inadequate. Does the work mentioned above, however, incontestably point to essentialist theories as the source of categorization behavior in young children? We think not.

As mentioned above, transformation and induction studies such as those of Gelman and Markman (1986, 1987) and Keil (1989) have often been cited as strong support for the essentialist model. These studies show that children may sometimes rely strongly on nonperceptual factors in categorizing objects or extending attributes to new exemplars. It is not clear, however, how this reliance on nonperceptual processes has come about. Has it come about through childrens' use of theories about the essences of natural kinds or has it come about through direct experience with the entities or instruction about them from adults? Gelman and Markman (1986), for example, studied the induction of what they classed as "category-relevant" and "perceptually-relevant" properties to new exemplars. They found that when the attributes were category relevant, the children were likely to assume that the target shared the attribute of the standard stimulus of the same ontological category. When the attributes were perceptually relevant, however, the children were likely to assume that the target shared the attribute of the standard stimulus which resembled the target. Gelman and Markman, however, provided few examples of the category-relevant and perceptually-relevant attributes nor did they provide much information about the participants' responses to individual attributes. It may be that children had already learned about some of these attributes and that this past learning guided their choices. Without more information about the attributes and the children's responses to them we cannot judge whether past experience or essentialist theories are most likely to have guided the children's choices.

Gelman and Markman do list the attributes in their 1987 study, but they provide no information about the participants' responses to individual attributes. In neither set of studies, did Gelman and Markman assess the children's understanding of the attributes before their exposure to the experimental paradigm. In the 1987 study, the set of attributes relevant for biological categories included type of food, means of reproduction, type of respiration, and ability to see in the dark. For the nonbiological categories, the category-relevant attributes included whether the substance melts snow, is smooth inside, melts or floats in water, or melts in a hot environment. We think it is likely that children as young as 3 may have already learned the category relevance of some of these attributes through experience or instruction and that this learning -- not a theory of essences of living things -- guided their responses to the target items.

In addition, the mechanisms that might produce essentialist theories and guide their use in categorization seem rather poorly specified at this point. In agreement with this sentiment, Gelman and Kalish (1993) write, "Researchers who study the role theories play in categorization have generally accepted causality as a primitive notion and have not analyzed how causality works within theories (p. 13)." It may be that some essentialist theorists are actually referring to a complex mediator composed of associated attributes learned through experience when they talk about a child's theory. If so, then one might legitimately ask why it is necessary to postulate essentialist theories at all. Why not simply talk about mediators and their formation?

Gelman and Kalish (1993) do develop some principles that provide greater specificity in essentialist theory, but their own evidence addresses them very indirectly. In addition, several works in a recent book edited by Hirschfeld and Gelman (1994) on essentialist theory fail to provide a clear empirical test of the way relationships develop between causal notions and the features used for categorization (Carey & Spelke, 1994; Gopnik & Wellman, 1994; Keil, 1994). The mechanisms by which attributes are derived from or connected with theories must be given a more thorough examination before essentialist theory can be considered to have passed a strong empirical test.

As noted earlier, many essentialist theorists assume an innate basis for theories or for the tendency to form theories. These writers, however, advance arguments that are not altogether convincing and that are bolstered by little empirical evidence. Keil (1994) writes that he works under, "the assumption that there is no positive evidence (p. 240)" favoring perceptual and associative laws in children's structuring of categories. He believes that, "... we have yet to see any such model actually work even for a notion as apparently simple as causation (p. 238)." He implies that attempts at this sort of "empiricist" account have failed, but he cites no failed attempts. Keil's assumption that perceptual and associative processes cannot account for children's categories (or can only account for them with great difficulty) seems to be the main basis on which he adheres to the primal theories view; he cites little evidence or persuasive argument for this view.

In summary, we find attempts at explicating categorization behavior via essentialist accounts to be limited in three major respects. First, there seems to be very little indication that a tendency to form theories about the essences of natural kinds is innate, although innateness seems to be assumed by many of those working in this area. Second, empirical work appears only indirectly to address the specific mechanisms by which causally relevant theories about essences might affect categorization; even if the nativists are right and there is a core essentialist theory or tendency to form theories present at birth, then the mechanism by which experience affects it and the way it is elaborated during development need to be studied. Finally, we believe that much of the evidence adduced to support essentialist theory seems easily explainable by different, more extensively researched mechanisms, like mediation and selective attention. In the sections of this chapter to follow, we will outline a preliminary model of how mediational processes might account for evidence like that discussed above, and detail research with nonhuman animals and human children on associational processes in the formation of nonsimlarity-based classes.

MEDIATION AND NONSIMILARITY-BASED CATEGORIZATION

Clearly, there is a need for a deeper examination of the basic processes that might contribute to the formation of stimulus classes not based on perceptual similarity. Unfortunately, research examining natural concepts in children may not be ideally suited to this examination. First, as noted above, looking at the structure of already-formed classes may tell us very little about the processes that led to their formation. Second, in natural categories, the essential nature of the objects in a category is confounded with their functional associations. Is the grouping of different-appearing dogs by humans, for example, due a theory we have about to their essential natures or simply due to the fact that we have learned many common associates to them. Dogs share essential factors such as DNA and also may be hypothesized to share many common associates in the experience of a human, so it is difficult to disentangle the role of these two factors in category formation. The research described below entails experimentally-created groupings of stimuli so that we may more intensively examine the basic process that might contribute to category formation.

In the remainder of this paper, we will consider an approach that relies on mediation via learned associations. According to classic models of mediation, internal stimulus and response cues become associated with particular external objects or events (e.g., Kendler & Kendler, 1975; Osgood, 1953; Underwood, 1966; see also Urcuioli's contribution to this volume). These mediating cues may then guide later behavior. According to this approach, exemplars from the same ontogenetic category might come to be classified together because they share many common associates.

As we examine the potential role of mediating associations in category formation we will look more closely at superordinate categories. Superordinate categories, like furniture, are classes of objects or events whose grouping cannot be based on perceptual similarity (e.g., Rosch, Mervis, Gray, Johnson, & Boyes-Braem, 1976). Lamps and chairs, for example, are perceptually quite dissimilar; however, they are both considered to be members of the superordinate category "furniture." Lamps and chairs might come to belong to this common superordinate category in part because they are found together (e.g., in furniture stores and in our living rooms), because they are used together (one often sits in a chair in order to read by lamplight), or because they are called by a common name ("furniture"). These common experiences may provide mediating cues that guide the common classification of perceptually dissimilar lamps and chairs. These mediating cues are not present in the immediate perceptual experience of the objects, but they do depend on past experience with them.

A fuller consideration of the category "animal" may make the explanation we are proposing clearer. We might propose that constellations of attributes are learned through experience with or instruction about items in the domain of "animal." Thus, children may learn through experience that organisms that generate self-directed motion also breathe in a particular way, reproduce, and metamorphose over time. Even children as young as 3 years old are likely to have repeatedly seen birds, insects, or pet animals move without apparent outside intervention and to have observed different kinds of respiration in different sorts of animals like fish and mammals. They are likely to have seen both young and old animals of the same species. They are likely also to have noticed that a change in the perceptual attributes of a living thing through maturation or other mechanisms like disguise does not change the identity of the individual organism. Through experience or instruction, these attributes are likely to have become associated with one another, and a whole constellation of expectations about living things may arise when any one of the attributes is encountered. These expectations may then mediate inductive inferences about new and related attributes of natural kind entities.

It is conceivable that children may learn very early in development that cues that relate to ontogenetic categories are more important determiners of some aspects of natural kind entities than is perceptual similarity. The reliance on category-based cues may not be due to any innate tendency to believe in essences or to theorize about the nature of objects and living things, but may instead simply reflect learned tendencies to direct attention to ontogenetic category information because it has been predictive of important outcomes in the past. So, if a child wishes to avoid being licked, bitten, or knocked down, it may be important for her to determine whether the dog in front of her is a living organism or a stuffed toy. She may need to use what she has learned in the past about the types of movement typical of living dogs more than she uses the overall shape of the dog or its color to make such a determination. Thus, the child's desire to determine the identity of the furry entity in front of her may lead her to weigh information that is diagnostic of ontogenetic category more heavily than configural cues like color or shape. The failure of perceptual aspects of objects to guide behavior in the work of Keil (1989) and Gelman and Markman (1986) may therefore not uniquely implicate theories as the basis for categorization.

RELEVANT EXPERIMENTS WITH ANIMALS AND HUMANS

One of the goals of this book is to bring together related research with animals and with humans. We will therefore begin with a review of research with animal subjects, from our own laboratory and those of others, and will then move to research that we have conducted with children.

A note about terminology and methodology is in order here. Stimuli that have come to be treated as equivalent due to common associates have sometimes been referred to as a functional stimulus class and the demonstration that such a class exists has been referred to as functional equivalence (Goldiamond, 1966; Sidman, 1990). We will use this terminology in our discussion of research below. The demonstration of functional equivalence requires a transfer test where common associations determine responding more than can be accounted for by perceptual similarity alone. The experiments described below share this feature. A substantial number of studies have been conducted on this problem with animal subjects in the last several years. We present only a sampling of these studies here. Interested readers should consult Urcuioli's contribution to this volume for a description of additional work in this area.

Some of our own work with animal subjects failed to find evidence of learning of functional stimulus equivalence (Bhatt & Wasserman, 1989). Other work, however, has shown that pigeons can form nonsimilarity-based functional equivalence sets. Vaughan (1988) found that, after several discrimination reversals, pigeons came to treat members of each of two 20-items slide sets as functional equivalents of one another. Importantly, all 40 slides depicted trees; thus, the 20 items in each set were random assortments, with no obvious perceptual "glue" to bind them together.

Hall (1990) described a study with rat subjects conducted with R. C. Honey. This study, as well, succeeded in demonstrating that association with a common outcome can produce functional stimulus equivalence. Preliminary training was given with a noise, a tone, and a clicker, each presented an equal number of times. Assignment of the tone and clicker to the designations "A" and "B" were counterbalanced across subjects. Stimulus B was always follwed by food and Stimulus A was not. Treatment of the noise stimulus (N) differed across groups. For half of the subjects (Group A-B+N+), the noise was followed by food during preliminary training and for the other half of the subjects (Group A-B+N-) the noise was not followed by food. Then the noise was associated with shock, and conditioned suppression to the noise, tone, and clicker was assessed in a test session. Tests showed the greatest generalized suppression to the signal which had received the same outcome as the noise did in preliminary training. That is, subjects in A-B+N- suppressed significantly more to Stimulus A and those in A-B+N+ spppressed significantly more to Stimulus B. This study established that association with a common consequence is sufficient to create functional equivalence, and it did so with generalization between stimuli on a new task. (Vaughan studied generalization on a task the subjects had performed before.) A later study using a similar procedure (Hall, Ray, and Bonardi, 1993) showed functional equivalence when food served as an antecedent for two stimuli and not for two others. Thus, association with a common antecedent is also sufficient to produce functional stimulus equivalence.

Urcuioli, Zentall, Jackson-Smith, and Steirn (1989) provided additional evidence of functional stimulus equivalence. Their Experiment 2 also used a three-phase design. Pigeons first learned a many-to-one matching-to-sample task, in which a vertically striped comparison key was correct when the sample was red (R) or vertically striped (V) and a horizontally striped comparison key was correct when the sample was green (G) or horizontally striped (H). Then the R and G samples were associated with circle (C) and dot (D) comparison stimuli. Finally, transfer of training for the remaining samples to the new comparison stimuli was assessed. For half of the pigeons (the consistent group) the V sample had the same new correct comparison stimulus as the R sample and the H sample had the same new correct comparison stimulus as the G sample. For the other half of the pigeons (the inconsistent group) the V sample had a different new correct comparison stimulus than the R sample and the H sample had a different new correct comparison than the G sample. If association with a response to a common stimulus in Phase 1 established functional stimulus equivalence in the R/V and G/H combinations, then the consistent group should have learned the Phase 3 discrimination significantly faster than the inconsistent group. The data supported this prediction. Studies described by Zentall, Steirn, Sherburne, and Urcuioli (1991) reported similar results.

A later study (Urcuioli & Zentall, 1993) using a one-to-many procedure attempted to establish whether association with a common antecedent could create a functional stimulus class in a procedure like that of the Urcuioli et al. (1989) study. In Phase 1, vertical (V) and red (R) stimuli were the correct alternatives when the sample was a plus (P), and horizontal

(H) and green (G) stimuli were the correct alternatives when the sample was a square (S). All subjects received Phase 2 training in which V was now correct following a blue (B) sample and H was now correct following a white (W) sample. Test sessions examined transfer of Phase 2 training to the R and G comparisons when the associations with common antecedents was either congruent or incongruent with Phase 1 training. For the congruent group, pecks to R were correct when the sample was B and pecks to G were correct when the sample was W. For the incongruent group, pecks to R were correct when the sample was W and pecks to G were correct when the sample was B. This experiment found only weak evidence for transfer of Phase 1 training. Only one of six congruent birds and one of six incongruent birds showed significant evidence of transfer. This result contrasts with the significant effects of association with a common antecedent in the Hall et al. (1993) study. It may be that food as an antecedent provides a more salient mediating cue than does a less biologically significant stimulus, and that this factor accounts for the divergent results in the two studies. The divergence may also be due, however, to a difference in the procedures or species used in the two studies. Further research is needed to determine the source of the different results in these studies.

The work described above provides evidence that even pigeons and rats can learn to treat perceptually dissimilar stimuli as though they are the same when the stimuli are associated with common antecedents or consequences. The Urcuioli et al. (1989) and Zentall et al. (1991) work, however, used simple geometric stimuli and the Hall (1990) and Hall et al. (1993) experiments used simple sounds. A study by Wasserman, DeVolder, and Coppage (1992) extended the three-phase many-to-one procedure to photographic stimuli in three categories: people, flowers, cars, and chairs. Figure 1 schematically depicts the to two of the categories (C1 and C2) and a different response (R2) to the other two categories (C3 and C4). In Reassignment Training, new responses were learned to two of design of this experiment. In Original Training, the participants learned one response (R1)the categories; R3 was associated with C1 and R4 was associated with C3. In Test, transfer of the new responses to the nonreassigned members (C2 and C4) of each pair joined in Original Training was examined. The results demonstrated that animals can treat stimuli in perceptually dissimilar categories in a similar fashion when a common mediating response has joined them; the pigeons showed a significant tendency to choose R3 in the presence of C2 exemplars and to choose R4 in the presence of C4 exemplars. A study by DeVolder and Lohman (reported in Wasserman & DeVolder, 1993) replicated this effect with preschool children.

If the classes of stimuli created by the three-phase many-to-one procedure are to parallel human superordinate conceptual categories even more closely, however, then we must establish that the classes that are formed by this procedure are open-ended. Human superordinate categories like furniture encompass diverse basic-level categories which themselves have open and, at least theoretically, infinite membership. The name "furniture" is not reserved for the familiar lamps and chairs of our own homes, but is also applied to lamps and chairs we see for the first time. To establish that experimentally created classes are open sets requires tests with novel stimuli from the categories of stimuli joined in the first phase of training. The use of photographs of stimuli in basic-level categories with the three-phase many-to-one procedure allows for just such tests. The experiments described below include novel stimulus tests.

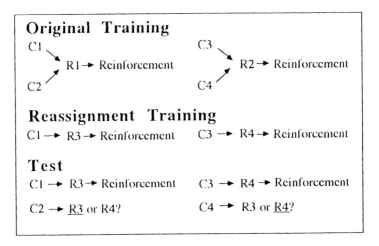

Figure 1. A schematic diagram of the design of the Wasserman, DeVolder and Coppage (1992) study and the two experiments reported here. The designations C1, C2, C3, and C4 represent separate classes of stimuli, and R1, R2, R3, and R4 represent different responses. Outcomes consistent with a mediational outcome in Test sessions are indicated by underlining.

Experiment 1

This study used the the three-phase many-to-one procedure to examine transfer of discriminative responding to novel exemplars. We also sought to replicate the DeVolder and Lohman study with different experimental stimuli. We wanted the images to be naturalistic, but also to vary from one another in systematic ways. So, we chose to study simulated human faces. This study was conducted by the first author and Paul Norwood.

The stimuli were 20 simulated human faces created with Mac-a-Mug software (Shaherazam Software, Kalamazoo, MI). The faces were black line drawings on a white background and were approximately 2 in wide and 3 in high. There were six faces in each of four "families," which corresponded with C1, C2, C3, and C4 of Figure 1. The members of each family had the same hair and chin, but the individuals had unique eyebrows, eyes, noses, and mouths; no other face shared those specific features. All of the faces had the same ears. The four faces used in Pretraining and in Original and Reassignment Training are shown in the leftmost four columns of Figure 2. The two novel faces used in Test are shown in the rightmost two columns of Figure 2. Like the family members used in Original and Reassignment Training, the novel faces had the family-characteristic hair and chin, but they had unique eyebrows, eyes, noses, and mouths.

As mentioned earlier, this study used the three-phase procedure described in Figure 1. Briefly, Original Training was intended to create the mediating responses. Reassignment Training sought to teach new responses to some of the members of the pairs of classes joined in Original Training. The Test phase aimed to examine transfer of the new responses to the two categories that were withheld during Reassignment Training. During Test, training with

Exemplars used in Original and Reassignment   Novel Exemplars

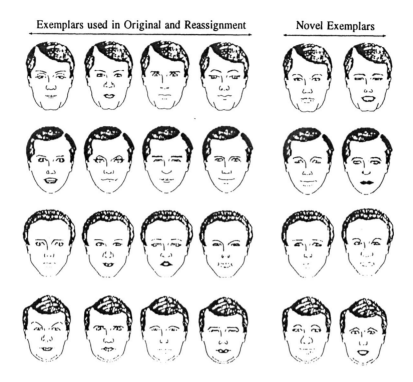

Figure 2. The stimuli used in Experiment 1. The rows represent the four different "families". The four leftmost columns contain the exemplars used in Original and Reassignment Training and the two rightmost columns contain the novel exemplars introduced in the Test.

C1 and C3 continued with reinforcement contingencies as they were in Reassignment Training. Responses during the Test phase were nondifferentially reinforced to stimuli from C2 and C4 as well as to novel exemplars from the four categories. If association with a common response in Original Training created a mediating response, then one would expect participants predominantly to choose R3 in the presence of C2 stimuli and to choose R4 in the presence of C4 stimuli during test sessions.

The participants were 32 children between the ages of 5 and 7, who were individually tested at several day care centers; an additional 5 children began the study, but they decided to end their participation before the test phase. The data from four participants were discarded because the experimental setting was too noisy for concentration or because of procedural errors. There were an equal number of boys and girls in the study, and equal number of boys and girls of each age served in each of the counterbalanced conditions of the study.

The stimuli were presented on an 11-in black-and-white computer monitor. The children were asked to respond to the faces by pointing directly at a location on the screen. The children's responses were followed by the experimenter's manipulation of the computer mouse to indicate the location to which the child had pointed. As pilot testing had found this joint category task to be hard for children of these ages to learn, we preceded Original Training with special Pretraining (described in the next paragraph) and with exposure to the Reassignment training procedure. We suspected that these measures might aid learning in Original Training. Other measures we took to facilitate learning were to give two exposures each to Original Training and to Reassignment Training, and to prompt correct responses on the first four trials of the first exposures to Original Training and Reassignment Training.

In Pretraining, the children were first shown the hair and chin attributes (with no interior features) characteristic of each of the four families; they were told that they would see "boys" from each of these families. Then, the children were shown each of the faces, one at a time, at the top of the screen and the four family outlines (hair and chin) at the bottom of the screen. The children were told to match (by pointing) the face at the top of the screen with the correct family below. The children responded at a very high level of accuracy in this task.

Before starting the main portion of the experiment, the children were informed that they would be playing a new game in which their job was to help the boys whom they had seen earlier get home for dinner. Each trial in Original Training began with the presentation of 1 of the 16 faces in the middle of the computer screen. After 1 sec, line drawings of two houses appeared as well, one in the upper left corner of the screen and the other in the lower right corner. One of the houses was correct for two of the families and the other was correct for the other two families. The joint categories of families were counterbalanced, so that the combination of families associated with a common response was varied across participants. Correct pointing responses were followed by auditory feedback from the computer: a cartoon-like voice said, "I'm home, what's for dinner?" Incorrect choices were also followed by auditory feedback from the computer: the computer voice said, "Oh-oh, this isn't my home." The experimenter also verbally emphasized the correctness or incorrectness of the children's choices.

In Reassignment Training, only faces from C1 and C3 were shown, this time in conjunction with two houses that were *not* available in Original Training. One house appeared in the upper right corner of the computer screen and the other appeared in the lower left corner. One of the houses was designated as correct for faces from C1 and the other house was designated as correct for faces from C3. The reinforcement contingencies were arranged so that for half of the children correct C1 and C3 responses were shifted in a horizontal direction (e.g., from the upper left house to the upper right house) and for the other half they were shifted in a vertical direction (e.g., from the upper left house to the lower left house). Correct choices were followed by the same computer and experimenter feedback as in Original Training.

At the beginning of the Test, the children were told that they would be playing a game like the one that they had just played (in Reassignment Training), but that they would now see boys from all four of the families and some new boys too. In the 56-trial Test period, there were four presentations of each of the four familiar faces from C1 and C3, with correct responses and consequences arranged as in Reassignment Training. There were also two presentations of each of the four familiar faces from C2 and C4, and participants received positive feedback after choices in the presence of these stimuli no matter which house they selected. Also in the Test period was a single presentation of each of the two novel faces from each of the four families, again with choices nondifferentially reinforced by computer and experimenter feedback. Test trials were organized in blocks of seven, with each block comprising four trials with two different faces from each of C1 and C3, two trials with one face from each of C2 and C4, and one trial with a novel face from one of the four different families.

The order of phases was: Reassignment Training 1, Original Training 1, Original Training 2, Reassignment Training 2, and Test. Correct responding was prompted on the first four trials of Reassignment Training 1 and Original Training 1. There was no prompting during Original Training 2, Reassignment Training 2, or Test. Pretraining and all other phases of the experiment were completed within a single session, which lasted from 45 to 90 min.

The primary group of interest in our assessment of the role of mediation in joint category formation comprises those children who performed at a high level of accuracy in Original and Reassignment Training; only the participants who performed at a consistently high level have a good chance of having learned the mediating response and of demonstrating the new response in the Test session. Thus, the results reported here are for only those subjects whose performance on the last exposure to Original and Reassignment Training significantly exceeded chance (50%) on the binomial test at $p < .05$. To meet these criteria, the participants had to achieve at least 75.0% correct in Original Training and at least 81.2% correct in Reassignment Training. For ease of explaining the results, responding to C2, C4, and novel exemplars that accorded with the expectations of a mediational analysis will be called correct, even though all responses in the presence of those stimuli were reinforced.

A total of nine participants met criterion in both Original and Reassignment training: none of the 4-year-olds, one of the 5-year-olds, four of the 6-year-olds, and four of the 7-year-olds. These subjects averaged 100% correct in Original Training 2 and 98.6% correct in Reassignment Training 2. Test session results for the participants who met the criteria on both Original and Reassignment Training are shown in Figure 3. On the Test trials, they averaged 99.6% correct to the C1 and C3 exemplars and 93.8% to the C2 and C4 exemplars. Responding on trials with novel exemplars was similar to that on trials with familiar exemplars. The participants averaged 100% correct to novel exemplars from C1 and C3 and 88.9% correct to novel exemplars from C2 and C4. These effects were all significantly different from chance (50%) on the binomial test at $p < .001$. Thus, responding to the familiar and reassigned C1 and C3 exemplars accorded with the reinforcement contingencies. In addition, responding to the familiar and nonreassigned C2 and C4 stimuli was appropriate to the category with which they were linked in Original Training for both familiar and novel exemplars.

We conducted an analysis of variance (ANOVA) on the Test data of those subjects who met criterion in Original and Reassignment Training to examine further the effects of novelty and category. The category variable reflected whether the stimuli were in the reassigned (C1 and C3) or the nonreassigned categories (C2 and C4). A 2 (category) x 2 (novelty) repeated-measures ANOVA produced a significant main effect of category [$F(1,8)$ = 28.08, $p < .001$], but no significant main effect of novelty [$F(1, 8) = 1.98, p > .10$] nor a significant category x novelty interaction [$F(1, 8) = 2.63, p > .10$]. Thus, the subjects performed significantly better on the exemplars from the categories that had been reassigned ($M = 99.8\%$) than on the exemplars from the categories that had not been reassigned ($M = 91.3\%$). The novelty of the exemplars had no statistically significant effect on responding.

These results again provide evidence that response mediation can produce similar behavior to perceptually distinct exemplars. It extends our understanding in demonstrating that mediation will also guide responding to novel exemplars from the component categories

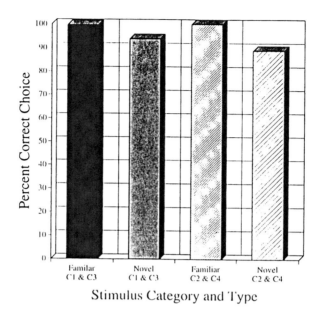

Stimulus Category and Type

Figure 3. The percent correct choice to familiar and novel exemplars from the classes reassigned (C1 and C3) and not reassigned (C2 and C4) in the Test of Experiment 1. The data were averaged over subjects who met criterion in both Original and Reassignment Training.

joined by a common response. This study, however, leaves several issues open for further exploration. First, human faces have unique attributes as stimuli for human participants (see Johnson & Morton, 1991), and some aspect of this uniqueness may have contributed to the effects seen in Experiment 1. Thus, we need to know whether we can replicate this effect with a different sort of stimulus.

We also were unable to study nonsimilarity-based categorization in 4-year-olds, as none of them learned the Original and Reassignment Training tasks sufficiently well to proceed to Test. The 4-year-olds took longer to complete each phase of training and we frequently seemed to lose their full attention before the test phase of the study. In addition, only one 5-year-old met the criteria, so we know little about the possibility of response-mediated nonsimilarity-based categorization in 5-year-olds. Overall, only 28% of all participants met or exceeded criterion in both Original and Reassignment Training. We do know that the older children who met criterion generalized to novel exemplars, but we wished to see whether this result might also be typical of a higher percentage of our participants. We therefore attempted in Experiment 2 to devise a training and testing procedure that some 4-year-olds and a higher percentage of all participants might be able to complete.

Finally, if participants did not recognize the novelty of the new exemplars, then it would be trivial to show that they categorized them with the familiar ones. So, in Experiment 2, after the participants had made their choices on some Test trials, we asked them whether they had seen the exemplar earlier in the experiment.

Experiment 2

This study, completed by the first author and Brent Finger, used silhouettes of leaves and needles from trees as stimuli. The images were scanned from nature guides used for tree identification. The on-screen size of the individual images varied; the widths ranged from 1.2 to 3.6 in and the heights ranged from 1.0 to 2.5 in. Exemplars of maple, pine, willow, and nut trees were used. We will refer to the tree types as C1, C2, C3, and C4. Four exemplars from each type of tree (depicted in the leftmost four columns of Figure 4) were used in Original and Reassignment Training, and two novel exemplars (depicted in the rightmost two columns of Figure 4) from each tree type were introduced during the Test phase.

The participants were 48 children between the ages of 4 and 6 who were individually tested at several day care centers. Mean ages were 4:5 (years:months), 5:6, and 6:6. An additional three children began the study, but they decided to end their participation before the Test phase. The data from six subjects were discarded because the testing situation was too noisy for an accurate test or there was a procedural error during the experiment. An equal number of boys and girls served at each age level in each counterbalanced condition of the study.

The stimuli were presented on an 11-in black-and-white computer monitor. The children were asked to respond by pointing directly at a location on the screen. The children's responses were followed by the experimenter's manipulation of the computer mouse to indicate the location to which the child had pointed. Trials in this experiment were like those of Experiment 1. A trial began when a silhouette appeared in a box in the center of the computer screen. One sec later, two differently patterned squares appeared at two diagonally opposite corners of the center box. During Original Training, these squares were at the upper left and lower right corners of the box. During Reassignment, two new squares were at the lower left and upper right corners of the box. When the squares appeared, the experimenter asked, "Where do these kind go?" or "Which box do these kind go with?" Each child was asked to point to one of the two squares. Correct choices were followed by an ascending series of bell-like tones and praise from the experimenter; incorrect choices were followed by a descending series of tones and confirmation from the experimenter that the child's choice was incorrect. A practice trial with a silhouette of an oak leaf was used to give instructions and to allow the child to hear the tones indicating correct and incorrect choices. The experimenter maintained a friendly and encouraging demeanor throughout the experiment to sustain the child's attention. Training and testing were conducted over 2 consecutive days. A performance criterion was set for each phase of Original and Reassignment Training as indicated below, and children who did not meet or exceed criterion within six blocks in any phase of the experiment were thanked for their assistance and dismissed from the study.

Original Training in this experiment was conducted over several phases to make the task somewhat easier for the children to finish. In the first phase of Original Training, children saw exemplars from C1 and C3. For C1 a response to the upper left square (R1) was correct and for C3 a response to the lower right square (R2) was correct. Trials were organized in blocks of eight, one with each exemplar from each of C1 and C3. Performance was averaged over each block of trials and a child continued until he or she exceeded 85% correct. Phase 2 of Original Training was conducted exactly like Phase 1, except that exemplars from C2 and C4 were used. For C2 a response to the upper left square (R1) was correct and for C4 a response to the lower right square (R2) was correct. Phase 3 of Original

Exemplars used in Original and Reassignment Training   Novel Exemplars

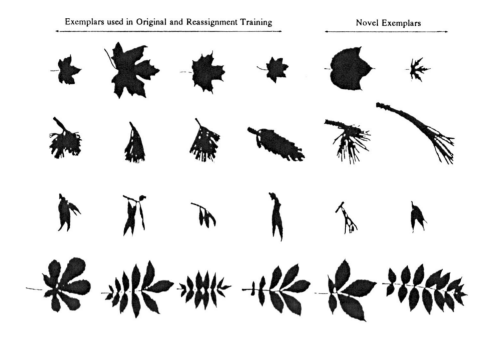

Figure 4. The stimuli used in Experiment 2. The rows represent the four different types of trees: maples, pines, willows, and nut trees, in order from top to bottom. The four leftmost columns contain the exemplars used in Original and Reassignment Training and the two rightmost columns contain the novel exemplars introduced in the Test.

Training included exemplars from C1, C2, C3, and C4. Trials were organized in blocks of 16, with one exemplar from each of the four categories. As before, each child continued until he or she exceeded 85% correct on a block of trials. Assignment of tree types to C1, C2, C3, and C4 was counterbalanced, so that the combination of tree types associated with a common response was varied systematically across participants. This much of the experiment was completed on the first day of the study, and it took about 30 to 40 min for children who met criterion on each of the three phases. As thanks and encouragement to return on the following day, each child was given his or her choice from among a set of stickers.

On the second day, each child was given a second exposure to Phase 3 of Original Training, this time to a criterion of 90% correct. Immediately following this phase was Reassignment Training, during which the children saw only exemplars from C1 and C3. Only the lower left and upper right squares (corresponding to the locations for R3 and R4) were available during Reassignment Training, and reinforcement contingencies were arranged so that for half of the children correct C1 and C3 responses were shifted in a horizontal direction (e.g., from upper left square to upper right square) and for the other half they were shifted in a vertical direction (e.g., from upper left square to lower left square). Participants completed this phase of training when they achieved a criterion of 85% correct.

The Test phase immediately followed completion of Reassignment Training. During the Test, only the lower left and upper right response alternatives (i.e., R3 and R4) were available, as they were in Reassignment Training. Trials were given with both familiar and novel exemplars from C1, C2, C3, and C4. Responses to familiar C1 and C3 exemplars were differentially reinforced as in Reassignment Training. Responses to familiar stimuli from C2 and C4 and to all novel exemplars were nondifferentially reinforced; the child heard the ascending tones and was praised no matter which response alternative he or she chose. Trials were organized in blocks of seven, with each block containing two trials with exemplars each from C1 and C3, two trials each with a single exemplar from C2 and C4, and one trial with a novel exemplar from one of the four categories. There were eight blocks of trials in the Test phase. This distribution was needed to maintain a moderate level of differential reinforcement to help keep each child focused on correct responding.

On six Test trials, the participant was asked whether or not he or she had seen that type of tree earlier in the experiment. To avoid biasing responses, on three of the trials the child was asked "Is this a new one or one you saw before?" and on the other three the child was asked "Is this one you saw before or a new one?" A predetermined list of exemplar types was created, so that the experimenter asked about one familiar exemplar from each of the four categories and one novel exemplar from two different categories with each participant. The lists were systematically varied so that, over participants, all exemplars were tested. The experimenter asked the question on the first trial on which a particular exemplar appeared.

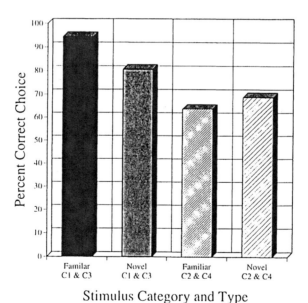

Figure 5. The percent correct choice to familiar and novel exemplars from the classes reassigned (C1 and C3) and not reassigned (C2 and C4) in the Test of Experiment 2. The data were averaged over subjects who met criterion in both Original and Reassignment Training.

Even though the performance criteria were higher in this study than in Experiment 1, a higher overall percentage of participants (42.6%) met the criteria in both Original and Reassignment Training. Of the 20 participants meeting the criteria, 3 were 4-year-olds, 4 were 5-year-olds, and 13 were 6-year-olds. These subjects averaged 97.8% correct on their last block of Original Training and 95.6% correct on their last block of Reassignment Training.

The overall results (depicted in Figure 5) for those children meeting the criteria were as predicted by the mediation hypothesis. Whether these results significantly differed from chance (50%) was evaluated with the binomial test; as before, responding to the nondifferentially reinforced C2, C4, and novel exemplars was called correct if it accorded with the reinforcement contingencies to the appropriate C1 and C3 exemplars. Responding to the familiar C1 and C3 stimuli averaged 94.4% correct (significantly different from chance at $p < .001$). The means for the 4-, 5-, and 6-year-olds were 91.3%, 90.6%, and 97.1%, respectively. Responding to the C2 and C4 exemplars averaged 80.6% correct (significantly different from chance at $p < .001$). The averages for the 4-, 5-, and 6-year-olds were 79.2%, 78.1%, and 81.7%, respectively.

Responding to the novel C2 and C4 exemplars resembled that to the C1 and C3 exemplars. Responding to the novel C1 and C3 exemplars averaged 63.8% correct (significantly different from chance, $p < .05$). The means for the 4- through 6-year-old groups were 66.7%, 62.5%, and 63.5%, respectively. Responding to the novel C2 and C4 exemplars averaged 68.8% correct (significantly different from chance at $p < .05$). The means for the 4- through 6-year old groups were 91.7%, 62.5%, and 65.3%, respectively.

We computed an ANOVA on the Test data of those subjects who met criterion in Original and Reassignment Training to examine further the effects of novelty and category. A 2 (category) X 2 (novelty) repeated-measures ANOVA revealed a significant main effect of novelty [$F(1,19) = 35.19, p < .001$], and a significant category x novelty interaction [$F(1, 19) = 6.86, p < .05$], but no significant main effect of category [$F(1,19) = 1.50, p > .10$]. Analyses of the simple main effects revealed a marginally significant difference between the reassigned and nonreassigned categories when the exemplars were familiar [$F(1,19) = 3.80, p < .10$], but not when the exemplars were novel ($F < 1$).

The participants were, in general, highly accurate in their determination of which of the exemplars they had seen earlier in the experiment and which exemplars were novel. The mean percentage of correct identifications was 89.6% for the familiar exemplars and 87.8% for the novel exemplars. These effects are significantly different from chance on the binomial test at $p < .01$. A one-way between-subjects ANOVA found a significant main effect of age on the identification accuracy measure [$F(2,17) = 21.77, p < .001$]. Accuracy of identification means for the 4-, 5-, and 6-year-olds were 55.7%, 100.0%, and 92.9%, respectively. Pairwise comparisons revealed a significant difference between 4- and 5-year-olds [$F(1,5) = 87.44, p < .001$] and a significant difference between 4- and 6-year-olds [$F(1,14) = 30.22, p < .001$], but no difference between 5- and 6-year olds [$F(1,15) = 1.66, p > .10$]. The 4-year-olds' overall percent correct identification was 66.7% for the familiar exemplars but only 33.3% for the novel exemplars. One of the four-year-olds said that all of the tested exemplars were ones she had seen before and the other two children were correct 50% of the time on both familiar and novel exemplars. Only three 4-year-olds met criterion on Original and Reassignment Training; so, it is difficult to examine further the potential reasons for this difference between the 4-year-olds and the older children. We can conclude, however, that the three 4-year-olds tested in this study may not have distinguished the novel exemplars from the familiar ones, but that the older participants surely did.

This study essentially replicated the overall findings of Experiment 1; participants demonstrated response-mediated categorization and generalized their responding to novel exemplars from the component categories. It expands on those findings in three significant ways. First, it demonstrates these two effects with stimuli other than computer generated line drawings of faces. The leaf/needle silhouettes we used were representations of natural stimuli and thus differed from one another in potentially complex and not-easily-definable ways. Nevertheless, we obtained response-mediated responding and generalization to novel exemplars with these stimuli.

Second, we succeeded in increasing the overall percentage of participants who met criterion in both Original and Reassignment Training, even though the criteria themselves were raised. In addition, the procedural modifications allowed the testing of at least a few 4-year-olds. However, the relatively low percentage of children who learned the Original Training and Reassignment tasks well enough to proceed to the Test phase is of continuing concern. The responses that constitute our data are from a selected sample, as they include only those subjects who performed well on the earlier phases of training, and our standards were relatively high. We might wonder whether the processes that led to our findings might be found also in those children who performed more poorly on Original Training and Reassignment. It may be that the latter children were approaching the task in a fundamentally different way and might have shown very different results if they had been able to proceed to test. One fact which argues against this possibility, however, is that the results of Experiment 2, in which a substantially higher percentage of participants proceeded to the test phase, were very much like those of Experiment 1. Thus, when the procedure was modified by reducing the session length and gradually introducing stimuli during Original training, a higher percentage of participants proceeded to the test phase, but the overall results remained essentially the same. In spite of our best efforts, inattention and eventual boredom with the task over the 30-60 min required in each session must have contributed to the tendency of our youngest participants to do poorly on Original and Reassignment Training. Indeed, given that the stimuli in Experiment 2 were black silhouttes of leaves and needles from trees it may be impressive that as many as 42% of the children (who are likely to be accustomed to color cartoons) were able to perform at above-chance levels. We suspect that our tests are tapping into processes that contribute to learning in all of our subjects, not just those who proceed to the Test phase. We must further modify our procedure to achieve an even higher percentage who proceed to the Test phase, however, before we know whether we are correct in our suspicions.

Finally, we found that most of the children recognized that the novel exemplars were ones they had not seen before. Thus, at least for the older children, we are confident that the participants generalized responding to novel exemplars for reasons other than the trivial one that they did not distinguish these stimuli from the training exemplars.

SUMMARY AND CONCLUSION

Essentialist theories of categorization are currently popular within developmental and cognitive psychology. These theories posit that individuals assume that natural kind entities have an essence that determines their surface features. This essence more strongly affects the way that people categorize objects than does perceptual similarity. One sort of evidence that is offered in support of essentialist theory is that people resist inferring changes in kind unless modifications over time in a natural entity are internally and naturally produced. Also cited in support of essentialist theories is the finding that children will use category-relevant information more than perceptual similarity in inferring unseen, internal attributes of natural kind entities. The tendency to form essentialist theories is often assumed to be innate.

Our critical review found research on essentialist theory to be deficient in several regards. The assumption of an innate basis for individuals' theories or for their tendency to form theories seems unsupported by evidence or persuasive argument. In addition, essentialist theorists have only recently begun to elaborate more specifically the testable extensions of their theory, and, to date, very little research has been done on these more testable aspects of the theory.

An additional model that is considered to be a type of theory-based approach to categorization hypothesizes that prior knowledge affects categorization (e.g., Heit, 1992; Wisniewski, 1995; Wisniewski & Medin, 1992). The basic notion is that human subjects bring prior knowledge about objects to categorization tasks. This prior knowledge interacts with the attributes of the stimuli and affects the research participants' tendencies to categorize the stimuli. The prior knowledge theory seems to allow for experience with objects in the world to play a role in creating the knowledge base, and thus, may be more compatible with our approach than is the essentialist model. Greater specificity concerning what "knowledge" is and what experiences create it are necessary, however, before we can truly assess the parallels between the knowledge-based approach and our own.

It is clear, however, that perceptual similarity has real limitations as an explanation for human categorization behavior. Other mechanisms must come into play. We chose to explore a mediational model, which hypothesizes learned associations between stimuli and responses. We described experiments with animals and children that support the usefulness of mediating associations as a potential bridge between perceptually distinct stimuli. Two new studies with young children found evidence of transfer to novel exemplars from categories joined by a common response.

Although the work cited here indicates that factors other than perceptual similarity can play an important role in the ability of both humans and nonhuman animals to group stimuli, the door is not yet closed on perceptual similarity as a factor in the formation of object concepts in humans (see, e.g., Barsalou, 1993; Gelman & Medin, 1993; Jones & Smith, 1993; Mandler, 1993). Future research should examine further the ways that perceptual and nonperceptual factors might interact in producing object categories. We believe that the technique used in our latest research, described above, provides one approach to integrating perceptual and nonperceptual factors. In that research, nonperceptual factors (secondary or mediated generalization) led to the grouping of discriminatively distinct classes (e.g., C1 with C2, and C3 with C4) and perceptual factors (primary stimulus generalization) presumably led to transfer of training to novel exemplars within each of these classes. Research in our laboratory that examines such transfer in pigeons is currently underway.

Our plans for the future include an examination of other sorts of procedures that might be effective in creating a nonsimilarity-based class in pigeon subjects when the stimuli are photographs of objects and living things. We have already shown that association with a common response will support such class formation. Will association with a common delay of reinforcement, a distinctive schedule of reinforcement, a common contextual cue, or mere temporal or spatial contiguity also support nonsimilarity-based class formation with photographic stimuli in pigeons? We hope our research over the next few years will begin to answer these questions.

AUTHOR NOTES

The preparation of this manuscript was supported by National Institute of Mental Health Grant MH51562. Experiments 1 and 2 were partially funded by a Faculty Development Grant from Cornell College to the first author. A preliminary report of the results of Experiment 1 was presented at the 1993 meeting of the Midwestern Psychological Association and is also discussed in Wasserman and Astley (1994). The authors would like to thank Tom Spalding for helpful comments on an early draft of the manuscript for this paper.

Correspondence concerning this article should be addressed to Suzette L. Astley, Psychology Department, Cornell College, 600 First St. W., Mt. Vernon, IA 52314-1098.

REFERENCES

Barsalou, L. W. (1993). Challenging assumptions about concepts. *Cognitive Development, 8,* 169-180.

Bhatt, R. S. & Wasserman, E. A. (1989). Secondary generalization and categorization in pigeons. *Journal of the Experimental Analysis of Behavior (Special Issue on the Experimental Analysis of Cognition), 52,* 213-224.

Carey, S., & Spelke, E. (1994). Domain-specific knowledge and conceptual change. In L. A. Hirschfeld & S. A. Gelman (Eds.), *Mapping the mind: Domain specificity in cognition and culture.* New York: Cambridge University Press.

Gelman, S., Coley, J. D., & Gottfried, G. M. (1994). Essentialist beliefs in children: The acquisition of concepts and theories. L. A. Hirschfeld & S. A. Gelman (Eds.), *Mapping the mind: Domain specificity in cognition and culture.* New York: Cambridge University Press.

Gelman, S. A., & Kalish, C. W. (1993). Categories and causality. In R. Pasnak & M. L. Howe (Eds.), *Emerging themes in cognitive development.* New York: Springer Verlag.

Gelman, S. A., & Markman, E. M. (1986). Categories and induction in young children. *Cognition, 23,* 183-209.

Gelman, S. A., & Markman, E. M. (1987). Young children's inductions from natural kinds: The role of categories and appearances. *Child Development, 58,* 1532-1541.

Gelman, S. A., & Medin, D. L. (1993). What's so essential about essentialism? A different perspective on the interaction between perception, language, and conceptual knowledge. *Cognitive Development, 8,* 157-167.

Goldiamond, I. (1966). Perception, language, and conceptualization rules. In B. Kleinmutz (Eds.), *Problem Solving: Research, Method, and Theory* (pp. 183-224). New York: John Wiley and Sons.

Gopnik, A., & Wellman, H. M. (1994). The theory theory. In L. A. Hirschfeld & S. A. Gelman (Eds.), *Mapping the mind: Domain specificity in cognition and culture.* New York: Cambridge University Press.

Hall, G. (1990). Reasoning and associative learning. In H. LeJeune & D. E. Blackman
    (Eds.), *Behavior analysis in theory and practice: Contributions and controversies.*
    Hillsdale, NJ: Lawrence Erlbaum Associates.
Hall, G., Ray, E., & Bonardi, C. (1993). Acquired equivalence between cues trained with
    a common antecedent. *Journal of Experimental Psychology: Animal Behavior
    Processes, 19,* 391-399.
Heit, E. (1992). Categorization using chains of examples. *Cognitive Psychology, 24,*
    341-380.
Hirschfeld L. A. & Gelman, S. A. (Eds.), *Mapping the mind: Domain specificity in
    cognition and culture.* New York: Cambridge University Press.
Johnson, M. H., & Morton, J. (1991). *Biology and cognitive development: The case of
    face recognition.* Oxford: Blackwell.
Jones, S. S., & Smith, L. B. (1993). The place of perception in children's concepts.
    Cognitive Development, 8, 113-119.
Keil, F. C. (1989). *Concepts, kinds, and conceptual development.* Cambridge, MA: MIT
    Press.
Keil, F. C. (1994). The birth and nurturance of concepts by domains: The origins of
    concepts of living things. In L. A. Hirschfeld & S. A. Gelman (Eds.), *Mapping the
    mind: Domain specificity in cognition and culture.* New York: Cambridge University
    Press.
Kendler, H. H., & Kendler, T. S. (1975). From discrimination learning to cognitive
    development: A neobehavioristic odyssey. In W. K. Estes (Ed.), *Handbook of
    learning and cognitive processes.* Hillsdale, NJ: Erlbaum.
Mandler, J. (1993). On concepts. *Cognitive Development, 8,* 141-148.
Markman, E. M. (1989). *Categorization and naming in children.* Cambridge, MA: MIT
    Press.
Medin, D., & Ortony, A. (1989). Psychological Essentialism. In S. Vosniadou & A.
    Ortony (Eds.), *Similarity and analogical reasoning.* Cambridge: Cambridge
    University Press.
Osgood, C. E. (1953). *Method and theory in experimental psychology.* New York:
    Oxford University Press.
Rosch, E., Mervis, C. B., Gray, W. D., Johnson, D. M., & Boyes-Braem, P. (1976). Basic
    objects in natural categories. *Cognitive Psychology, 8,* 382-439.
Sidman, M. (1990). Equivalence relations: Where do they come from? In H. LeJeune &
    D. E. Blackman (Eds.), *Behavior analysis in theory and practice: Contributions and
    controversies.* Hillsdale, NJ: Lawrence Erlbaum Associates.
Thelen, E., & Smith, L. B. (1994). *A dynamic systems approach to the development of
    cognition and action.* Cambridge, MA: MIT Press.
Underwood, B. J. (1966). *Experimental psychology.* New York: Appleton-Century-
    Crofts.
Urcuioli, P. & Zentall, T. E. (1993). A test of comparison-stimulus substitutability
    following one-to-many matching by pigeons. *The Psychological Record, 43,* 745-760.
Urcuioli, P. J., Zentall, T. R., Jackson-Smith, P., & Steirn, J. N. (1989). Evidence for
    common coding in many-to-one matching: Retention, intertrial interference, and
    transfer. *Journal of Experimental Psychology: Animal Behavior Processes, 15,* 264-
    273.

Vaughn, W., Jr. (1988). Formation of equivalence sets in pigeons. *Journal of Experimental Psychology: Animal Behavior Processes, 14,* 36-42.

Wasserman, E. A., & Astley, S. L. (1994). A behavioral analysis of concepts: Its application to pigeons and children. In D. L. Medin (Ed.), *The psychology of learning and motivation.* New York: Academic Press.

Wasserman, E. A., & DeVolder, C. L. (1993). Similarity- and nonsimilarity-based conceptualization in children and pigeons. *Psychological Record, 43,* 779-793.

Wasserman, E. A., DeVolder, C. L., & Coppage, D. J. (1992). Nonsimilarity-based conceptualization in pigeons via secondary or mediated generalization. *Psychological Science, 3,* 374-379.

Wisniewski, E. J. (1995). Prior knowledge and functionally relevant features in concept learning. *Journal of Experimental Psychology: Learning, Memory, and Cognition, 21,* 449-468.

Wisniewski, E. J. & Medin, D. L. (1994). On the interaction of theory and data in concept learning. *Cognitive Science, 18,* 221-281.

Younger, B. A. & Cohen, L. B. (1985). How infants form categories. In G. H. Bower (Ed.), *The psychology of learning and motivation* (pp. 211-247). New York: Academic Press.

Zentall, T. R., Steirn, J. N., Sherburne, L. M., & Urcuioli, P. J. (1991). Common coding in pigeons assessed through partial versus total reversals of many-to-one conditional and simple discriminations. *Journal of Experimental Psychology: Animal Behavior Processes, 17,* 194-201.

IV

EQUIVALENCE CLASSES: STIMULUS CONTROL VARIABLES

Stimulus Class Formation in Humans and Animals
T.R. Zentall and P.M. Smeets (Editors)
© 1996 Elsevier Science B.V. All rights reserved.

8

Stimulus Classes and the Untrained Acquisition of Stimulus Functions

Michael J. Dougher and Michael R. Markham

University of New Mexico and Florida International University

Identifying the conditions under which stimuli acquire their functions is a primary focus of research in the field of learning. By stimulus functions we are referring here to all of the various effects that antecedent and consequential stimuli have on behavior. Included are conditional, discriminative and eliciting functions, motivation, reinforcement, and punishment. Although the term stimulus function appears here to refer only to the role of the stimulus, it is important to note that stimulus functions specify relations between stimuli and behavior. One obvious way that stimuli acquire these function is through direct conditioning. There is, however, increasing evidence that stimuli can also acquire these functions in the absence of direct training. Of course, stimulus functions can be indirectly acquired via primary generalization, but the phenomena of interest here does not appear related to the formal features of the relevant stimuli. This untrained acquisition of stimulus function is one of the most interesting findings to emerge from the recent and growing body of research on stimulus classes, and it is the primary topic of this paper.

STIMULUS CLASSES AND EMERGENT STIMULUS FUNCTION

Terminology

Functional Equivalence Classes
The relation between stimulus classes and the untrained acquisition or emergence of stimulus function is interesting and complex. However, one of the problems in interpreting and integrating the stimulus class literature is that there is an inconsistent terminology for talking about stimulus classes. Investigators often use different names for the same types of classes and the same names for different types of classes. For example, in a recent text on the psychology of learning, Donahoe and Palmer (1994) define a functional class as a "a range of stimuli that may differ physically but have similar uses and control common responses" (p. 357). These authors also distinguish among functional classes, stimulus classes, discriminative stimulus classes, and equivalence classes. These distinctions and the respective definitions of the various types of classes are quite different from those offered by Catania (1992) in another learning text. Dube, McDonald, and McIlvane (1991) and Dube, McIlvane, Callahan and Stoddard (1993) adopt Goldiamond's (1962; 1966) terminology and use the term functional stimulus classes to refer to a set of stimuli where, 1) all of the members of the class share a common stimulus function; and 2) variables (contingencies) applied to a subset of the class tend to affect the remaining members without explicit training. Sets of stimuli that meet this definition have also been called stimulus classes (Goldiamond, 1962, 1966; Skinner, 1935), contingency classes (Sidman, Wynne, Maguire & Barnes, 1989), functional classes (Sidman et al, 1989), functional equivalence classes (de Rose, McIlvane, Dube, Galpin & Stoddard, 1988; Dougher & Markham,

1994), stimulus equivalence classes (McIntire, Cleary, & Thompson, 1987), equivalence sets (Vaughan, 1988), conceptual categories (Bhatt & Wasserman, 1989; Lea, 1984), and concepts (Wasserman, DeVolder, & Coppage, 1992; Wasserman & DeVolder, 1993).

In an earlier attempt to achieve some consistency in terminology, we offered a classification of stimulus classes that distinguished among three types of classes: stimulus classes, functional equivalence classes, and stimulus equivalence classes (Dougher and Markham, 1994). Stimulus classes were defined simply as sets of stimuli that share a common stimulus function. For example, a set of stimuli that share a discriminative function over some behavior would be considered a stimulus class. Functional equivalence classes were reserved for sets of stimuli that met both criterion of Goldiamond's definition. Stimulus equivalence classes were defined according to Sidman's definition, which is described in greater detail below.

Unfortunately, these distinctions are too vague and the proposed typology is problematic.. For example, with respect to the definition of stimulus classes, it is not clear what is meant by "share a common stimulus function." Would we say, for example, that four physically dissimilar stimuli that exerted discriminative control over a topographically similar response (e.g., pecking for grain) constitute a stimulus class? What these stimuli have in common is that they all evoke a formally similar behavior that produces the same reinforcer. But, as Dube (personal communication, November 23, 1993) points out, this is analogous to defining response classes on the basis of the form or physical features of a response. As Skinner (1935) argued, there are clear advantages to defining stimuli and responses in terms of their function rather than their form or topography. If we take Skinner's approach, then shared function is not defined in terms of the specific relation between a stimulus and some topographically defined response, but between a stimulus and a class of behaviors defined by their relation to a class of consequences. Thus, shared function is defined in terms of contingencies of reinforcement. As this definition of shared function is applied to stimulus classes, a set of stimuli can be said to share a function only to the extent that the members of the set are similarly affected by variables applied to a subset of its members. Thus, the application of a variable to a subset of a collection of stimuli *is* the test for determining whether the stimuli share a stimulus function and can, therefore, be called a class. For present purposes a set of stimuli will be considered a class only if it has been shown that they are all similarly affected by the application of some variable to a subset of its members. According to this definition, functional equivalence classes are sets of stimuli that are functionally substitutable. Otherwise, the stimuli will be considered functionally independent, even though they may control topographically similar responses.

Stimulus Equivalence Classes

Applying Goldiamond's criterion to functional equivalence classes obviates the need for our previous distinction between a stimulus class and a functional equivalence class. However, we still need to address the distinction between functional equivalence classes and stimulus equivalence classes. As defined by Sidman and Tailby (1982) and more recently endorsed by Sidman (1995), stimulus equivalence classes are sets of stimuli among whose members emergent reflexivity, symmetry, and transitivity have been demonstrated. These relations are demonstrated in conditional discrimination arrangements. By this definition, stimulus equivalence itself is characterized by functional substitutability. What distinguishes stimulus equivalence classes from functional equivalence classes are the specific functions that are shared by the members of stimulus equivalence classes.

While many researchers distinguish between stimulus equivalence classes and other types of stimulus classes, the question is whether this is a useful distinction. We would argue that it is useful only to the extent that it facilitates communication among researchers, describes different behavioral phenomena, and facilitates research that attempts to identify the determinants of and the relation between the two types of classes. There is some evidence that, at least with respect to non-biologically relevant stimuli, symmetry is not readily demonstrated by non-humans (e.g., Dube et al, 1993; c.f. Schusterman & Kastak, 1993; Zentall, Sherburne & Steirn, 1992). The relative ease with which it appears in language able humans may be related to certain biological capacities and early training histories that are unique or at least more common to humans (e.g., Hayes, 1991, 1994). It is precisely the differential ease with which humans demonstrate symmetry relative to non humans and the apparent similarity between these relations and symbolic behavior that has led many investigators to suggest that stimulus equivalence may underlie language (Hayes, 1994; Sidman, 1995, especially pp. 1-18). Because of the definitional distinction between stimulus equivalence and functional equivalence, a good deal of research attempted to identify the relevant variables involved in stimulus class formation in general, and the distinction between stimulus equivalence and functional equivalence classes, in particular. Even if the distinction does not prove to be useful in the long run, it does appear to be serving a useful function now.

Transfer of function
By transfer of function, we are referring to the untrained acquisition or emergence of stimulus functions among members of stimulus classes. Given the definition of stimulus classes we have adopted in this paper, it may seem redundant to talk about stimulus classes and the transfer of function; stimulus classes are defined at least in part by the transfer of function. But, at least with respect to the stimulus equivalence literature, the term transfer of function typically refers to a function that is independent of the shared functions that define the class.

Although the term transfer of function is used by many investigators, Sidman (1995, e.g., pp. 392-393; 448; 463) objects to it. His primary concern is that it is unnecessary to appeal to an additional process called transfer to account for the observations of untrained acquisition of functions. Relying on mathematical set theory, Sidman argues that these observations are accounted for more parsimoniously as the merger or union of overlapping stimulus classes (sets). That is, members of one stimulus class may also belong to other classes, defined by different stimulus functions. When a stimulus is a member of more than one class, the classes can be said to be overlapping, and, unless other factors come into play, the overlapping classes will merge, (there will be a union of the sets) and the members of both classes will acquire the functions of each. Although Sidman is concerned about the implications of accounting for emergent stimulus functions by appeal to a transfer process, many investigators use the term only as a label or a description in the same way that the union or merger of classes is a description. Regardless of the label used, it is clear that the transfer of function or the union of stimulus classes is not an inevitable or automatic result of a stimulus being a member of more than one stimulus class. In Sidman's terminology, rather than a union of classes, an intersection of classes may occur when there are overlapping stimulus classes, at least with respect to certain functions. What is critical at this point is to identify the conditions under which transfer of function or the union of classes occurs.

Stimulus Equivalence Classes and Emergent Stimulus Functions
As was stated previously, stimulus equivalence classes are characterized by the emergence

of stimulus function. The stimulus functions to be discussed here, however, are those that accrue to all of the members of a class after stimulus equivalence classes are established and a novel function is subsequently trained for just one or a subset of the members of the class. Taken as a whole, the relevant studies have shown that virtually any behavioral function that is trained for one member of a stimulus equivalence class will automatically be acquired by, or, as many investigators have described it, will transfer to the other members of that class.

The typical procedures used in these studies are as follows. First, some number of equivalence classes are trained and tested using conditional discrimination procedures. Then, one member or a subset of class members from one of the classes is selected and given some behavioral function. Following this, the remaining members of all of the classes are tested to see if they have acquired the function. If the function is acquired by the other members of the class from which the subset of stimuli was selected and trained, but not by members of the other classes, the function is said to have transferred or to have been acquired in the absence of direct training.

Using similar procedures, investigators have demonstrated the transfer of simple discriminative control (de Rose et al, 1988), ordinal functions (Green, Sigurdardottir, & Saunders, 1991; Lazar, 1977; Lazar & Kotlarchyk, 1986) conditional control (Wulfert & Hayes, 1988), contextual control (Gatch & Osborne, 1989; Hayes, Kohlenberg, & Hayes; 1991), and conditioned reinforcement and punishment (Greenway, Dougher, & Wulfert, 1966; Hayes, Kohlenberg, & Hayes, 1991). In addition to these operant functions, respondent or classically conditioned functions have also been shown to transfer among members of stimulus equivalence classes. Dougher, Augustson, Markham, Greenway and Wulfert (1994) demonstrated the transfer of both conditioned fear elicitation (as measured by changes in skin conductance) and extinction of fear elicitation. Similarly, Barnes and Roche (in press) have shown the transfer of conditioned sexual arousal.

Functional equivalence classes and emergent stimulus functions

One of the difficulties in interpreting this literature is that there is such a variety of procedures that researchers have used to create functional equivalence classes. What they appear to have in common is the association of a set of stimuli with similar contingencies of reinforcement. One obvious example of this is a study by Vaughan who presented pigeons with 40 different slides of trees that were randomly assigned to two sets of 20 slides each. At the beginning of the experiment an S+ function was assigned to the first set of slides and an S- function to the second set. A successive discrimination procedure was used wherein key pecks within 2 sec. of the presentation of S+ slides resulted in access to grain. Following presentations of S- slides, the absence of pecking for 2 sec. terminated the slides and started a new trial. When the pigeons reliably discriminated the sets of slides, the contingencies were reversed so that the S+ slides became S-, and vice versa. This reversal procedure was repeated a number of times until the birds made only one or two errors after a contingency reversal. That is, once a response to a previous S+ was extinguished, the other slides in that set functioned as S-, while the slides in the other set functioned as S+. The contingency reversals established a transfer of the discriminative function of the slides that was trained in the early trials (see Dube et al, 1993, and Sidman, 1995 pp. 448-463, for a further discussion of repeated reversal procedures and the appropriate tests for whether they result in functional stimulus classes).

Vaughan simply correlated sets of stimuli with the presence or absence of a contingent relation between a particular behavior and the presentation of food. That is, the stimuli were associated with what behavior analysts call a two-term reinforcement contingency. The two-term contingency is the basic unit of analysis in behavior analysis and is comprised of behavior, the first term, its consequence, the second term, and the contingent relation between them (For a detailed description of basic and complex contingencies of reinforcement as they pertain to the units of analysis in behavior analysis, see Sidman, 1986). In the Vaughan study the sets of slides were correlated with a two-term contingency unit consisting of the same topographical response (key pecks) and the same type of reinforcer (food). In this way, the respective sets of slides functioned as discriminative stimuli. Which of the two sets of slides functioned as S+ or S- on any given trial was conditional upon whether reinforcement was delivered on the previous trial for key pecks to a slide from one of the sets.

The Vaughan study used a very basic experimental procedure, and there are other more complex procedures that can and have been used to investigate stimulus classes. For example sets of stimuli may be differentially associated with three-term contingencies. A three-term contingency consists of a two-term contingency plus a discriminative stimulus. Through its correlation with the two-term contingency, the discriminative stimulus functions to increase the probability of the operant response. As Sidman (1986) points out, match-to-sample arrangements essentially entail the differential association of a stimulus or sets of stimuli with three-term contingencies.

Conditional discrimination arrangements can be conceptualized either as examples of four-term contingencies (e.g., Sidman & Tailby) or three-term contingencies consisting of separable compound discriminative stimuli (Dougher, & Markham, 1994; Stromer, McIlvane & Serna, 1993). Regardless of the perspective one takes on this issue, the sample stimuli in such arrangements are seen to exert conditional control over some aspect of a three-term operant contingency. If multiple stimuli are associated with such a three-term contingency, these stimuli may form a functional equivalence class. For example, using a many-to-one training procedure, Spradlin, Cotter, and Baxley (1973) reported a study where developmentally delayed children were first trained to match each of two comparison stimuli to a different set of sample stimuli (e.g., A1-X, A2-X,; B1-Y, B2-Y). Then a subset of each set of samples was selected, and subjects were trained to match each of two new comparisons to one of the subsets (e.g., A1-Z;) When tested with the remaining samples, the subjects reliably matched the new comparisons to the appropriate sample stimuli (e.g., A2-Z). By virtue of their common association with the original comparison stimuli (actually with the three-term contingencies consisting of the comparisons as discriminative stimuli, the selection response and the reinforcing consequence), the samples had become interchangeable with each other with respect to their functional relation to the new comparison stimuli. In a later study, Spradlin and Saunders (1986) used similar training procedures then tested to see what subjects would do when a subset of the previously trained samples were presented as comparisons in a match-to-sample arrangement (e.g., A1 as sample and A2 and B2 as comparisons). They found that subjects were immediately able to match the samples that had been previously related to the same comparisons.

Similar results have been obtained with non-human subjects. Over a series of studies, Urcuioli, Zentall and colleagues (e.g., Urcuioli, Zentall, Jackson-Smith, & Steirn, 1989; Urcuioli and Zentall, 1993; Urcuioli, Zentall & DeMarse, 1995), have trained pigeons using a variety of procedures. Some subjects were taught multiple sample-single comparison discriminations (many-to-one) and others were taught single sample-multiple comparison discriminations (one-to-many). Then, a second set of conditional discriminations was trained, depending upon the type of initial training. If the original training was many-to-one, then subjects were trained to match novel comparisons to some of the original samples. If the original training was one-to-many, then subjects were trained to match some of the original comparisons to novel samples. Test trials were then conducted to see if emergent matching occurred. After many-to-one training, emergent matching would entail the matching of novel comparisons to the appropriate original samples that were not used in the second training phase. After one-to-many training, emergent matching would entail matching the original comparisons that were not used in the second training phase to the appropriate novel samples. The results of these experiments suggest that emergent matching did occur, i.e., there was a transfer of function, following many-to-one training but not following one-to-many training. The authors attribute these differences to what they term the "directionality" of training (but see Sidman, 1995, pp 525-528, for a discussion of the possible implications of the differences in the types of discrimination learning entailed by the two types of procedures.

Wasserman et al (1992) also demonstrated the formation of functional equivalence classes with pigeons by associating sets of stimuli with different three-term contingencies. The investigators used four categories of stimuli (people, flowers, chairs, and cars), each consisting of 12 examples. Slides of the individual examples from the four categories, C1, C2, C3, and C4 were projected on a screen in the experimental chamber, and the birds were trained to peck report key, R1, if the slide was from C1 or C2, and to peck report key R2 if the slide was from C3 or C4. Once the birds reliably discriminated the categories in this way, they were then trained to peck two new report keys, R3 and R4, in the presence of C1 and C3, respectively. In the test phase, the birds were presented with R3 and R4 and samples from C2 and C4. The pigeons reliably chose R3 in response to slides from C2 and R4 in response to C4. That is, the newly trained conditional functions of C1 and C3 transferred to C2 and C4, respectively. Wasserman and DeVolder (1993) report similar results with children except that the human subjects achieved higher levels of accuracy with less training.

Associations with respondent contingencies

Emergent stimulus functions have also been reported when stimuli are commonly associated with respondent or Pavlovian contingencies. For example, Honey & Hall (1989) presented rats with two different auditory stimuli, each of which was followed by food. Then, one of the stimuli was repeatedly paired with shock so that it acquired a conditioned suppressive effect on ongoing appetitive behavior. When the other auditory stimulus was presented, it also disrupted appetitive behavior although it had never been paired with shock. A subsequent experiment revealed that the transfer of conditioned suppression did not occur if the auditory stimuli did not share a common association with food in the original training.

Functional equivalence classes and the emergence of novel functions

In addition to its reliance on respondent procedures to create functional stimulus classes, the Honey and Hall study differs from most of the other studies investigating functional equivalence classes in that it examined an emergent function that differed from the function used to establish stimulus classes during training. Honey and Hall established a stimulus class by commonly associating two stimuli with food, but the emergent function that was investigated was conditioned suppression. In this respect, this study is similar to the stimulus equivalence and transfer of function studies described earlier in the paper. In those studies, the stimulus functions that transferred (e.g., sequencing, reinforcement, respondent elicitation) were different from that (conditional discrimination) used to establish the classes during baseline training. In contrast, the emergent functions that have been demonstrated with functional stimulus classes largely have been restricted to those functions trained during baseline to establish the functional classes. By function, we are referring to the general type of relations between a stimulus and a class of behavior or a class of stimuli and not to any specific relations between stimuli and a given response or a given stimulus. For instance, the studies described earlier by Wasserman et al. and Urcuioli, Zentall and colleagues demonstrated the transfer of conditional stimulus control over arbitrary matching responses from a set of trained stimuli to a set of untrained stimuli. The function that transferred, conditional control of arbitrary matching, was the same one used to establish the functional classes, even though the specific stimuli involved differed. There are very few studies that have investigated the relation between functional stimulus classes and the transfer of a novel function, i.e., a function that is different from that used in training to establish the classes.

Sidman, et al (1989) used a variation of Vaughan's repeated reversal procedures to establish two functional stimulus classes with one normal and two developmentally delayed humans. They then tested for the emergence of stimulus equivalence relations among the functional class members. Two of the three subjects demonstrated equivalence relations (see Sidman, 1995, Chapter 11 for a detailed discussion of the implications of these results for understanding the relation between functional stimulus classes and stimulus equivalence).

Greenway, Dougher, and Markham (1995) also used repeated reversal procedures to establish two functional equivalence classes, and then investigated the transfer of a conditional stimulus function among the members of the classes. Ten undergraduates were presented with a two-choice simple, simultaneous discrimination procedure which required that they select one of two arbitrary visual symbols presented on a computer monitor. Pressing the "1" key on the computer keyboard selected the left symbol, and pressing "2" selected the symbol on the right. One of three different pairs of stimuli, arbitrarily designated as A1-A2, B1-B2, and C1-C2, were presented on each trial. Selections of A1, B1, and C1 were followed by the word "correct,", and selections of A2, B2 and C2 were followed by the word "wrong." When subjects were able to complete 24 consecutive trials with two or fewer errors, the contingencies were reversed so that selections of A2, B2 and C2 were now considered correct, and selections of A1, B1, and C1 were now wrong. When the criterion of two or fewer errors in 24 consecutive trials was attained, the contingencies were reversed again. This continued until subjects were able to complete five consecutive 24-trial blocks with two or fewer errors. The number of 24-trial blocks necessary to meet criterion varied between six and 26, but all subjects eventually met criterion. Once this criterion was met, a novel discrimination function was trained for A1 and A2. Subjects were instructed to press either the letter "Q" or "P" when a symbol appeared on the screen. A1 and A2 were then randomly presented. When A1 was present, selections of "Q" produced the word "correct," and selections of "P" produced the word "wrong." When A2 was present, selections of "P" produced the word "correct," and sections of "Q" produced the word "wrong." Pressing any other key during training was ignored. Training continued until subjects completed two consecutive 24-trial blocks with no errors. To test for a transfer of function, five six-trial blocks were presented in extinction where each symbol was presented once in random order within each block. Transfer was said to occur if the subjects selected "Q" to all presentations of A1, B1, and C1, and "P" to all presentations of A2, B2, C2. Six of the 10 subjects demonstrated immediate transfer of the novel function from the A to the corresponding B and C stimuli. The four remaining subjects repeated the training and testing procedures. Two subjects demonstrated transfer after one retraining session, one subject required two retraining sessions, and the fourth declined further participation after one retraining session. What is interesting about these findings is that even though the repeated reversal data showed that all of the subjects evidenced the formation of two functional equivalence classes, only six of the subjects showed evidence of the transfer of the novel conditional function to the other members of the classes. Thus, it appears that novel functions will sometimes, but not always, transfer among members of functional equivalence classes.

In discussing these results, we considered the possibility that the reversal training might have actually interfered with the later tests for transfer of the novel function for some subjects. Learning to reverse or alternate the way they responded to stimuli whenever there was a change in the training contingencies may have generalized to changes in the testing situation. Thus, for some of the subjects, the appearance of new stimuli may have signaled a reversal of contingencies to the subjects, and they behaved accordingly. The data for some of the subjects suggested that this was a possibility, but a direct test has not been conducted. The data do suggest, however, that the relation between the training and testing contexts may be an important variable in the formation of stimulus classes.

Emergent functions resulting from the pairing of stimuli with elements of a contingency

While emergent stimulus functions may result from procedures that create functional equivalence classes, emergent functions can also arise from other procedures. In particular, they seem to arise from the association of stimuli with elements of contingencies that are used to train particular stimulus functions. For example, Kruse, Overmier, Konz, and Rokke (1983) found that response-independent pairings of a stimulus and reinforcer facilitated the subsequent untrained acquisition of conditional discriminative control by that stimulus. In a conditional discrimination arrangement, rats were trained to press one of two levers, L1 or L2, conditional upon the presentation of one of two auditory stimuli. In the presence of auditory stimulus A1, responses to L1 were reinforced with food. In the presence of auditory stimulus A2, responses to L2 were reinforced with a sucrose solution. The rats were then exposed to response-independent pairings of a new auditory stimulus, A3, with either food or sucrose. Finally, conditional discrimination tests were given with A3 as the conditional stimulus to see whether the common association of A1 and A3 with food for some rats and A2 and A3 with sucrose for others would facilitate stimulus control by A3 over responses to L1 and L2, respectively. Although A3 did not control responding to the same extent as either A1 or A2, it did exert significant control over the rats' lever pressing (see also Peterson & Trapold, 1980). In this case, the emergent function of A3 occurred not because it was a member of a functional equivalence class with either A1 or A2, but because it was associated with a common reinforcer. Before this pairing, neither A1 nor A2 shared any function with A3. The pairing seems to have created a shared function between A1 and A3 for some rats and A2 and A3 for others, but before it can be said that a functional equivalence class had been formed, it must be demonstrated that a variable applied to either A1 or A2, depending upon the experimental condition, similarly affects A3.

McIlvane, Dube, Klendaras, de Rose, and Stoddard (1992) report the development of emergent conditional stimulus control by differentially relating samples and comparisons in an identity matching task to a common reinforcer. These investigators first trained autistic children in a two-comparison identity matching task where selections of comparison A1 in the presence of sample A1 and selections of comparison B1 in the presence of sample B1 resulted in the same reinforcer, SR1. Selections of A2 in the presence of sample A2 and selections of B2 in the presence of sample B2 were followed by SR2. Thus, A1 and B1 were commonly related to one reinforcer, and A2 and B2 were commonly related to a different reinforcer. Probe trails consisted of the presentation of either A1 or A2 as samples with comparisons B1 and B2, or B1 and B2 as samples with comparisons A1 and A2. On these trials, subjects reliably chose the comparisons that had been related to the samples via the common reinforcer. That is, samples A1 and A2 had indirectly acquired a conditional function for the selection of comparisons B1 and B2, respectively, and samples B1 and B2 had acquired a conditional function for selections of A1 and A2, respectively. The investigators then reversed the relation between the reinforcers and the A and B stimuli, such that SR1 now followed correct identity matches for both A2 and B1, and SR2 followed correct identity matches for both A1 and B2. The effect of this reversal was to alter the relation between the A and B stimuli such that two of the subjects selected comparisons that were related to the same reinforcers as were the samples. Thus, A1 and A2 evoked selections of B2 and B1, respectively, while B1 and B2 evoked selections of A2 and A1, respectively.

Zentall et al (1992) reported what they described as emergent symmetry in pigeons when biologically relevant stimuli (food) were used in training and testing. In this study, pigeons were first trained with identity matching procedures where correct responses to a red comparison were followed by food, and correct responses to a green comparison were followed by a no-food outcome. In subsequent tests for symmetry, red and green samples were replaced by food and no-food samples, and red and green served as comparisons. The results indicated that food samples were associated with a preference for the red comparison, and no-food samples were associated with a preference for green comparisons (See also Sherburne & Zentall, 1995, for similar results using delayed matching procedures, and Steirn, Jackson-Smith & Zentall, 1991, for the emergence of conditional stimulus control via transitive associations with food).

Smeets, Barnes and Luciano (in press) report several studies that have shown the transfer of a discriminative function when established discriminative stimuli are paired with novel stimuli. For instance, Boelens and Smeets (1990, Experiment 1) established S+ and S- functions for two stimuli, A1 and A2, respectively, on a simultaneous discrimination task. Then the A stimuli were associated with respective B stimuli through match-to-sample training, such that responding to B1 in the presence of A1 and to B2 in the presence of A2 was reinforced. To determine whether the discriminative functions of the A stimuli had transferred to the B stimuli, the B stimuli were presented in the simultaneous discrimination task. Most subjects consistently selected B1 (see also, de Rose et al, 1988; Smeets, 1994, Experiment 2). Similar results obtain when the A and B stimuli are associated through procedures other than match-to-sample. For example, Boelens & Smeets, 1990, Experiment 2 associated the A and B stimuli through a procedures they called reinforced and non-reinforced contiguity. In reinforced contiguity, the A and B stimuli were presented as complex stimuli in a simultaneous discrimination task involving two simple discriminations. Either A1B1 or A2B2 were presented with A3B3. Responses to A1B1 and A2B2 were reinforced. In non-reinforced contiguity, (Smeets, 1994, Experiment 2; Smeets et al, in press), A1B1 and A2B2 were presented in a simple discrimination task with no programmed consequences. Both procedures resulted in most subjects selecting B1 in the subsequent B1/B2 probes. Although the A and B stimuli appeared to share a function in these studies, it is premature to conclude that they were members of a stimulus class. It still must be demonstrated that both stimuli are similarly affected by variables applied to either one. An interesting and important question arises in this regard, however, and that concerns the conditions under which stimulus classes are formed. This issue is addressed below.

Variables relevant to the formation of stimulus classes
The prerequisites for the formation of stimulus equivalence classes has received a good deal of attention. Sidman (e.g., 1990; 1995 pp. 512-524) has argued that stimulus equivalence is a primitive result in some organisms of certain contingency arrangements. Dugdale and Lowe (1990) contend that equivalence classes arise from the common naming of a set of stimuli, and Hayes (1991; 1994) has explained equivalence as an instance of a more general operant class called relational responding. Less attention has been paid to the prerequisites for the formation of functional stimulus classes and the conditions under which different stimulus classes merge.
If we define functional equivalence classes as a set of stimuli that are correlated with the same contingencies of reinforcement and affected similarly by variables applied to a subset of the class, then the formation of stimulus classes ought to be a function of at least four specific variables: 1) The extent to which the components of the contingency with which the stimuli are correlated are specific or exclusive to that contingency; 2) The extent to which the members of a stimulus class are exclusively members of that class and not others; 3) The tests used to ascertain whether a set of stimuli meet the definitional criteria for a functional equivalence class; and 4) The contexts in which the tests are applied. These are discussed separately below.

The extent to which the components of a contingency are specific to that contingency
Stimulus classes sometimes form when a group of stimuli are associated with specific contingencies of reinforcement. Thus, stimuli A and B might form a class because of their common association with reinforcement for a particular response. Similar responses in the absence of A and B are extinguished. It seems reasonable, however, that if one wanted to create more than one stimulus class, the formation of the classes would be facilitated if the respective contingencies to which the two sets of stimuli were related were as distinct as possible. For example, relating sets of samples to three-term contingencies in conditional discrimination arrangements may result more readily in the formation of separate stimulus classes if the respective contingencies not only have distinct comparison stimuli but topographically distinct behaviors and reinforcers. Most of the studies concerned with stimulus equivalence classes have associated distinct samples with distinct comparison stimuli, but the responses (stimulus selection) and reinforcers for correct responses (verbal feedback, candy, etc.) are identical regardless of class. It may be that the formation of the distinct classes would be facilitated if all of the response requirements and the reinforcers associated with the respective contingencies were also distinct.
We are unaware of direct evidence pertaining to this suggestion, but indirect support comes from a number of studies that have investigated emergent conditional discriminations where the training stimuli were differentially associated with different types of reinforcers. These procedures have been referred to as outcome-specific. In outcome-specific procedures, there is a consistent relation between type of reinforcement and the specific conditional and discriminative stimuli (samples and comparisons) presented on the various trials. For example, selections of B1 conditional upon the presentation of A1 are consistently reinforced with food, while selections of B2 in the conditional upon the presentation of A2 are consistently reinforced with water. Thus, A1 and B1 are commonly associated with food while A2 and B2 are commonly associated with water.
Outcome-specific studies can be contrasted with those that use outcome varied procedures. In outcome varied procedures, the relation between type of reinforcement and the specific stimuli presented on various trials is varied. On any given trial, selections of B1 in the presence of A1

may be reinforced with either food or water. McIlvane et al. (1992) reviewed several studies that investigated the relative effects of outcome-specific vs. outcome-varied reinforcement on performance in conditional discrimination arrangements. In sum, outcome-specific procedures have been shown to enhance the acquisition of conditional discriminations (e.g., Brodigan & Peterson, 1976; Edwards, Jagielo, Zentall, & Hogan, 1982) and facilitate delayed matching-to-sample performance (Edwards, et al., 1982). Moreover, Edwards et al. (1982) have shown that conditional discrimination performance in pigeons can be seriously disrupted when the relations between the reinforcers and the specific conditional discrimination arrangements used in training are reversed. These studies suggest that there would be a relation between the formation of stimulus classes and the distinctiveness of the contingencies with which they are associated, but it is still an empirical question.

Exclusivity of class membership
When the elements of a stimulus class are also members of other classes, variables applied to a subset of the class may not have similar affects on all of the other members. Take the example offered by Goldiamond (1966) to illustrate the concept of stimulus classes. A red light, a stop sign, and a policeman's raised hand are a class of stimuli, all of which control stepping on the brake pedal to stop a car (we are grateful to W. V. Dube for suggesting this example). If a variable relevant to this three-term contingency is applied to one member of the class, e.g., the brake pedal fails at a stop sign, that change is likely to affect the control exerted by all of the other members of the class. For example, in the presence of all three stimuli, the driver may use the handbrake to stop the car. However, the policeman is also a member of a class of stimuli discriminative for immediate punishment. Therefore, a variable that may affect the control exerted by the stop sign and red light, such as driving late at night on a deserted street, would not affect the control exerted by the policeman. While this is an obvious example of stimuli having multiple class membership, problems can arise in both experimental and applied situations when it is unclear that stimuli are members of more than one stimulus class.

The tests for stimulus classes
As we have seen, there are a variety of ways of testing for the formation of stimulus classes, and the determination of whether a set of stimuli can be called a stimulus class depends to some extent on the procedures used to test for class formation. For example, using similar training procedures but different testing procedures from those in the Wasserman and DeVolder study described earlier, Bhatt and Wasserman reported two experiments where functional equivalence classes (categories) failed to emerge. In both experiments, the investigators initially trained pigeons to peck one of four different keys conditional upon the presentation of slides from one of four categories (cat, flower, car, and chair). After reaching the training criterion in Experiment 1, the pigeons received training that rendered one stimulus from each category discriminative for one of four different FR reinforcement schedules. Then the other 44 slides were presented to see if they also had acquired discriminative control over the birds' pecking in line with the training given to the sample from each category. The findings were negative.

A similar training procedure was used in Experiment 2 of this series. Once the birds met the training criteria, one stimulus from each of the four categories was selected for "reassignment" training. During reassignment training, the birds were presented with the same four keys used in training, but they were trained to peck a different key from the one originally trained for that category. Once they reached criterion in this retraining phase, the remaining slides from each category were presented to see if the birds would classify them according to the original training or according to the reassignment training. The pigeons classified according to the original training. The results of these experiments led the authors to conclude that functional equivalence classes (conceptual categories) had not formed. Instead, the authors contended that it was more parsimonious to conclude that the categorization training led to the formation of stimulus-response connections between individual stimuli and responses.

Although there were a number of procedural differences between the Bhatt and Wasserman and the Wasserman and De Volder studies that makes direct comparison difficult (including the number of reassignment training trials), it is possible that the differences in outcome were related to differences in the procedures used to test for the formation of functional equivalence classes. In the Bhatt and Wasserman studies, the tests for the formation of classes involved functions that were very different from those trained in baseline or directly competed with the original training. Reassignment training in the Wasserman and DeVolder study involved a stimulus function that was identical to that trained in baseline, and subjects were trained to peck a new response key rather than one that had been associated with a competing contingency. In fact, the retraining procedures in the Bhatt and Wasserman study may have functioned to remove the selected stimuli from their originally trained classes. This, of course, could be tested directly.

Other testing procedures might also have produced different results and led to different conclusions about whether the training procedures had resulted in the formation of functional equivalence classes. Suppose, for example, that after obtaining their negative results, Bhatt & Wasserman had taken a sample from each of the four categories used in their study, extinguished responding to each, and then found responding had extinguished to the other stimuli in each of the four categories? These hypothetical findings would be similar to those of some of the subjects in the Greenway et al (1995) study described earlier where subjects showed behavior in reversal training that satisfied the definition of a stimulus class, but when a new function was trained to one of the members of the class, the new function did not always transfer to the other members.

As we suggested earlier in regard to this study, the reversal training may have produced a generalized tendency for subjects to alternate their responses to stimuli which may have actually interfered with the demonstration of functional equivalence among the members of the class. At the least, these data suggest that the relation between the training and testing contexts may be critical to the demonstration of stimulus classes.

A critical question at this point is this: If we take Goldiamond's definition of a functional class must we require that *any* variable applied to one member of a set of stimuli affect the other members before we are justified in calling the collection of stimuli a class? If different types of tests yield different results then the task is to identify the variables that determine whether a variable applied to a subset of a class will affect the other members. One variable that seems relevant in this regard is the context in which the tests for the formation of stimulus classes are conducted.

The testing context
        A number of studies have demonstrated that the formation of stimulus equivalence classes can be brought under contextual control (e.g., Bush, Sidman & de Rose, 1989; Gatch & Osborn; Hayes et al, 1991; Lynch & Green, 1991; Wulfert & Hayes). Less attention has been given to the contextual control over the transfer of function or the merger of stimulus classes after stimulus classes are formed. Clearly, some form of contextual control over class merger must

exist, or, as Hayes (1991) points out "nothing would prevent all types of relational responding from occuring with regard to all events" (p. 27). As well, there are obvious examples where stimuli are clearly in equivalence relations with each other, but not all of their functions are shared. Snakes, the printed word, S N A K E, and the spoken word, "snake" are clearly members of a stimulus equivalence class, but while one may run from a snake in the desert, one does not generally run in fear from a biology lecture when the word "snake" is uttered. Obviously, the contexts are very different, and it may be that some element of the context determines which functions of a stimulus are shared with the other members of a stimulus class. Yet, to our knowledge, there have been no published studies that have conclusively demonstrated contextual control of the union of stimulus classes or the transfer of function among stimuli in a class. Indirect evidence is suggested by the results of a study by Greenway et al (1996). After training three stimulus equivalence classes, we conditioned one member of one class to function as a conditioned reinforcer and one member of another class to function as a conditioned punisher in a simultaneous simple discrimination task (letter choice). These functions clearly transferred to the other members of the respective classes for most subjects, but when the task was altered, the transferred function did not maintain for several of the subjects. We considered it possible that the tasks themselves functioned as contextual stimuli for some of the subjects, and, in the context of the new task, the functions did not transfer. Clearly more research is needed to address the important issue of contextual control over the transfer of function.

SUMMARY AND CONCLUSIONS

Research in the area of stimulus classes and the untrained acquisition of stimulus functions is both interesting in its own right and theoretically important for our understanding of complex behavior. However, there are many issues that need to be addressed in this field. Among these is the identification of the prerequisites for the formation of stimulus classes and the variables that control their union. The present paper attempted to provide a conceptual scheme for integrating the various findings from the stimulus class literature and to identify classes of variables that may shed light on the relevant issues in the field.

REFERENCES

Barnes, D. & Roche, B. (in press). A transfer of respondently conditioned sexual arousal through derived arbitrary relations. *Journal of the Experimental Analysis of Behavior.*
Bhatt, R. S., & Wasserman, E. A. (1989). Secondary generalization and categorization in pigeons. *Journal of the Experimental Analysis of Behavior, 52*, 213-225.
Boelens, H., & Smeets, P. (1990). An analysis of emergent simple discriminations in children. *Quarterly Journal of Experimental Psychology, 42B*, 135-152.
Brodigan, D. A., & Peterson, G. B. (1976). Two-choice conditional discrimination performance of pigeons as a function of reward expectancy, pre-choice delay, and domesticity. *Animal Learning and Behavior, 4*, 121-124.
Bush, K. M., Sidman, M., & de Rose, T. (1993). Contextual control of emergent equivalence relations. *Journal of the Experimental Analysis of Behavior, 43*, 567-584.
Catania, A. C. (1992). *Learning* (3rd ed.). Englewood Cliffs, NJ: Prentice Hall.
de Rose, J. C., McIlvane, W. J., Dube, W. V., Galpin, V. C., & Stoddard, L. T. (1988). Emergent simple discriminations established by indirect relations to differential

consequences. *Journal of the Experimental Analysis of Behavior, 50*, 1-20.

Donahoe, J. W., & Palmer, D. C. (1994). *Learning and Complex Behavior*. Needham Heights, MA: Allyn and Bacon.

Dougher, M. J., Augustson, E. M., Markham, M. R., Greenway, D., & Wulfert, E. (1994). The transfer of respondent eliciting and extinction functions through stimulus equivalence classes. *Journal of the Experimental Analysis of Behavior, 50*, 125-144.

Dougher, M. J., & Markham, M. R. (1994). Stimulus equivalence, functional equivalence, and the transfer of function. In Hayes, S. C., Hayes, L. J., Sato, M., & Oko, K. (Eds.), *Behavior analysis of language and cognition* (pp. 71-90). Reno, NV: Context Press.

Dube, W. V., McDonald, S. J., & McIlvane, W. J. (1991). A note on the relationship between equivalence classes and functional stimulus classes. *Experimental Analysis of Human Behavior Bulletin, 9*, 7-11.

Dube, W. V., McIlvane, W. J., Callahan, T. D., & Stoddard, L. T. (1993). The search for stimulus equivalence in nonverbal organisms. *Psychological Record, 43*, 761-778.

Dugdale, N. A. & Lowe, C. F. (1990). Naming and stimulus equivalence. In D. E. Blackman & H. Lejeune (Eds.), *Behavior analysis and contemporary psychology*, vol 2 (pp. 115-138). London: Lawrence Erlbaum.

Edwards, C. A., Jagielo, J. A., Zentall, T. R., & Hogan, D. E. (1982). Acquired equivalence and distinctiveness in matching to sample by pigeons: Mediation by reinforcer-specific expectancies. *Journal of the Experimental Psychology: Animal Behavior Processes, 8*, 344-259.

Gatch, M. B., & Osborne, J. G. (1989). Transfer of contextual stimulus function via equivalence class development. *Journal of the Experimental Analysis of Behavior, 51*, 369-378.

Goldiamond, I. (1962). Perception. In A. J. Bacharach (Ed.), *Experimental foundations of clinical psychology* (pp. 280-340). New York: Basic Books.

Goldiamond, I. (1966). Perception, language, and conceptualization rules. In B. Kleinmuntz (Ed.) *Problem solving* (pp. 280-340). New York: Wiley.

Green, G., Sigurdardottir, Z. G., & Saunders, R. R. (1991). The role of instructions in the transfer of ordinal functions through equivalence classes. *Journal of the Experimental Analysis of Behavior, 55*, 287-304.

Greenway, D. E., Dougher, M. J., & Markham, M. R. (1995). S+/S- reversal procedures may not result in functional equivalence. *Experimental Analysis of Human Behavior Bulletin, 13*, 16-18.

Greenway, D. E., Dougher, M. J. & Wulfert, E. (1996). The transfer of conditioned reinforcement and punishment functions through stimulus equivalence classes. *Psychological Record, 46*, 131-144.

Hayes, S. C. (1991). A relational control theory of stimulus equivalence. In L. J. Hayes & P. N. Chase (Eds.), *Dialogues on verbal behavior* (pp. 19-40). Reno, NV: Context Press.

Hayes, S. C., Kohlenberg, B. S., & Hayes, L. J. (1991). The transfer of general and specific consequential functions through simple and conditional equivalence relations. *Journal of the Experimental Analysis of Behavior, 56*, 119-137.

Hayes, S. C. (1994). Relational Frame Theory: A functional approach to verbal behavior. In S. C. Hayes, L. J Hayes, M Sato, & K Ono (Eds.), *Behavior analysis of language and cognition* (pp. 11-30). Reno, NV: Context Press.

Honey, R. C., & Hall, G. (1989). The acquired equivalence and distinctiveness of cues. *Journal of Experimental Psychology: Animal Behavior Processes, 15*, 338-346.

Kruse, J. M., Overmier, J. B., Konz, W. A., & Rokke, E. (1983). Pavlovian conditioned stimulus effects upon instrumental choice behavior are reinforcer specific. *Learning and Motivation, 14*, 165-181.

Lazar, R. (1977). Extending sequence-class membership with matching to sample. *Journal of the Experimental Analysis of Behavior, 27*, 381-392.

Lazar, R. M., & Kotlarchyck, B. J. (1986). Second-order control of sequence class equivalence in children. *Behavioral Processes, 13*, 205-215.

Lea, S. E. G. (1984). In what sense do pigeons learn concepts? In H. L. Roitblat, T. G. Bever, & H. S. Terrace (Eds.), *Animal cognition* (pp. 263-276). Hillsdale, NJ: Erlbaum.

Lynch, D. C. , & Green, G. (1991). Development of cross modal transfer of contextual control of emergent stimulus relations. *Journal of the Experimental Analysis of Behavior, 56*, 139-154.

McIlvane, W. J., Dube, W. V., Klendaras, J. B., de Rose, J. C., & Stoddard, L. T. (1992). Stimulus reinforcer relations and conditional discriminations. In S. C. Hayes, & L. J. Hayes (Eds.), *Understanding verbal relations* (pp 43-67). Reno, NV: Context Press.

McIntire, K. D., Cleary, J., & Thompson, T. (1987). Conditional relations by monkeys: Reflexivity, symmetry,,and transitivity. *Journal of the Experimental Analysis of Behavior, 47*, 279-285.

Peterson, G. B., & Trapold, M. A. (1980). Effects of altering outcome expectancies on pigeons' delayed conditional discrimination performance. *Learning and Motivation, 11*, 267-288.

Schusterman, R. J. & Kastak, D. (1993). A California Sea Lion (Zalophus californianus) is capable of forming equivalence relations. *Psychological Record, 43*, 823-839.

Sherburne, L. M., & Zentall, T. R. (1995). Delayed matching in pigeons with food and no-food samples: Further evidence of backward associations. *Animal Learning and Behavior, 23*, 177-181.

Sidman, M. (1990). Equivalence relations: Where do they come from? In D. E. Blackman & H. Lejeune (Eds.), *Behavior analysis in theory and practice: Contributions and controversies* (pp. 93-114). Hillsdale, NJ: Erlbaum.

Sidman, M. (1995). *Equivalence relations and behavior: A research story.* Boston, MA: Authors Cooperative Publishers.

Sidman, M., & Tailby, W. (1982). Conditional discrimination vs. matching to sample: An expansion of the testing paradigm. *Journal of the Experimental Analysis of Behavior, 37*, 5-22.

Sidman, M., Wynne, C. K., Maguire, R. W., & Barnes, T. (1989). Functional classes and equivalence relations. *Journal of the Experimental Analysis of Behavior, 52*, 261-274.

Skinner, B. F. (1935). The generic nature of the concepts of stimulus and response. *Journal of General Psychology, 5*, 427-458.

Smeets, P. M. (1994). Stability of emergent simple discriminations in young children. *Journal of Experimental Child Psychology, 57*, 397-417.

Smeets, P. M., Barnes, D., & Luciano, M., C. (in press). Reversal of emergent simple discrimination in children: A component analysis. *Journal of Experimental Child Psychology.*

Spradlin, J. E., Cotter, V. W., & Baxley, N. (1973). Establishing a conditional discrimination without direct training: A study of transfer with retarded adolescents. *American Journal of Mental Deficiency, 77*, 556-566.

Spradlin, J. E., & Saunders, R. R. (1986). The development of stimulus classes using match-to-sample procedures: Sample classification vs. Comparison classification. *Analysis and Intervention in Developmental Disabilities, 6*, 41-58.

Steirn, J. N., Jackson-Smith, P., & Zentall, T. R. (1991). Mediational use of internal representations of food and no-food events by pigeons. *Learning and Motivation, 22*, 353-365.

Stromer, R., McIlvane, W. J., & Serna, R. W. (1993). Complex stimulus control and equivalence. *Psychological Record, 43*, 585-598.

Urcuioli, P. J. & Zentall, T. R. (1993). A test of comparison-stimulus substitutability following one-to-many matching by pigeons. *Psychological Record, 434*, 745-759.

Urcuioli, P. J., Zentall, T. R. & DeMarse, T. (1993). Transfer to derived sample-comparison relations by pigeons following many-to-one versus one-to-many matching with identical training relations. *Quarterly Journal of Experimental Psychology, 48B*, 158-178.

Urcuioli, P. J., Zentall, T. R., Jackson-Smith, P., & Steirn, J. N. (1989). Evidence for common coding in many-to-one matching: Retention, intertrial interference, and transfer. *Journal of Experimental Psychology: Animal Behavior Processes, 15*, 264-273.

Vaughan, W. (1988). Formation of equivalence sets in pigeons. *Journal of the Experimental Analysis of Behavior, 14*, 36-42.

Wasserman, E. A., & DeVolder, C. L. (1993). Similarity- and nonsimilarity-based conceptualization in children and pigeons. *Psychological Record, 43*, 779-794.

Wasserman, E. A., DeVolder, C. L., & Coppage, D. J. (1992). Non-similarity based conceptualization in pigeons via secondary or mediated generalization. *Psychological Science, 3*, 374-379.

Wulfert, E., & Hayes, S. C. (1988). Transfer of a conditioned ordering response through conditional equivalence classes. *Journal of the Experimental Analysis of Behavior, 50*, 125-144.

Zentall, T. R., Sherburne, L. M., & Steirn, J. N. (1992). Development of excitatory backward associations during the establishment of forward associations in delayed conditional discriminations by pigeons. *Animal Learning and Behavior, 20*, 199-206.

Zentall, T. R., Steirn, J. N., Sherburne, L. M., & Urcuioli, P. J. (1991). Common coding in pigeons assessed through partial vs. total reversals of many-to-one conditional discriminations. *Journal of Experimental Psychology: Animal Behavioral Processes, 17*, 194-201.

Stimulus Class Formation in Humans and Animals
T.R. Zentall and P.M. Smeets (Editors)
© 1996 Elsevier Science B.V. All rights reserved.

153

9

New Procedures for Establishing Emergent Matching Performances in Children and Adults: Implications for Stimulus Equivalence

Dermot Barnes, Paul M. Smeets, and Geraldine Leader

University College Cork, Ireland and University of Leiden, The Netherlands

The training procedures employed in the investigation of stimulus equivalence often involve relatively straight-forward conditional discrimination training (e.g., Barnes, McCullagh, & Keenan, 1990; Devany, Hayes, & Nelson, 1986; Saunders, Wachter, & Spradlin, 1988; Sidman & Tailby, 1982; Smeets, Schenk, & Barnes, 1995; Spradlin & Saunders, 1986; Wulfert, Dougher, & Greenway, 1991). During such training, for example, selecting stimulus B in the presence of stimulus A is reinforced, and selecting stimulus C in the presence of B is reinforced (i.e., see A pick B, and see B pick C). During a subsequent test, subjects may select A in the presence of B, B in the presence of C (B-A and C-B are symmetry relations), and C in the presence of A (C-A is a combined symmetry and transitivity, or equivalence relation) (see Barnes, 1994; Barnes & Holmes, 1991; Fields & Verhave, 1987; Hayes, 1991; Sidman, 1990). Although conditional discrimination training is normally employed in equivalence studies, there are a number of exceptions to this general rule, and two of these exceptions are directly relevant to the current chapter.

The first of these involves using simple, rather than conditional, discrimination training to generate emergent matching performances. In one study, for example, three adult humans (two mentally handicapped and one normal) were trained in a series of simple discrimination reversals and they were then tested for equivalence responding (Sidman, Wynne, McGuire, & Barnes, 1989; see also Vaughan, 1988). The basic procedure was as follows. The subjects were presented with a number of two-choice simultaneous simple discriminations, in which choosing one stimulus was reinforced but choosing the other was not (A1+/A2-, B1+/B2-, C1+/C2-). After these discriminations had been mastered all of the stimulus functions were reversed (A1-/A2+, B1-/B2+, C1-/C2+), and when the reversed discriminations were mastered, the functions were again reversed. This reversal procedure was continued until a subject made only one error (i.e., picked an S- stimulus) on the first trial after a reversal had occurred. When a subject met this criterion he or she was exposed to a standard matching-to-sample test for equivalence responding (e.g., A1-B1, B1-A1). In effect, this test determined whether the simple discrimination reversal training was sufficient to generate equivalence relations among each of the two groups of stimuli that had always functioned together as either positive or negative discriminative stimuli. (Parenthetically, Sidman [1994, pp. 450-453] has recently suggested that the reversal procedure employed in the 1989 study may have inadvertently trained the to-be-tested equivalence responding. This issue need not concern us here, however, because Sidman and his colleagues have recently developed a type of reversal procedure that circumvents this problem [Sidman, 1994, pp. 453-463]).

The second way in which researchers have departed from straight-forward conditional discrimination training is in the use of multi-element or compound stimuli (Maguire, Stromer,

Mackay, & Demis, 1994; Markham & Dougher, 1993; Schenk, 1993; Stromer & Mackay, 1993; Stromer, McIlvane, & Serna, 1993; Stromer & Stromer, 1990a, 1990b). In one of the studies by Stromer and Stromer (1990a), for example, subjects were trained on arbitrary conditional discrimination tasks with two-element complex samples: A1B1-D1, A2B2-D2, A1C1-E1, A2C2-E2. Subsequent probes revealed that most subjects related all "1" and "2" single-element stimuli conditionally to one another. Similar findings have been reported when stimuli are added to stimuli of identity matching tasks under nonreinforced conditions (Smeets, Schenk, & Barnes, 1994, 1995; Smeets & Striefel, 1994). For example, in the study by Smeets, et al. (1995), preschool children received training on two identity matching tasks with A stimuli (A1-A1, A2-A2) followed by a series of conditional discrimination probes (no programmed consequences) with complex AB and AC stimuli (AB-A, B-AB; AC-A, C-AC). These tasks were designed to facilitate responding to both elements of the complex stimuli. Subsequent probes (A-B, A-C, B-C, and vice versa) demonstrated that all children conditionally related the single element A, B, and C stimuli to one another in a class consistent fashion (A1-B1-C1, A2-B2-C2). These studies did not demonstrate, however, how compound stimulus control contributed to the formation of conditional relations. For example, after being trained on the A-A identity matching tasks in the Smeets, et al. study (1995), the subjects could, when exposed to the A-AB tasks, initially have matched the A sample with the A element of the AB comparison (A-A matching); subsequently, however, the compounding of the B and A elements in the comparison stimulus may have facilitated a shift from identity matching to arbitrary matching (i.e., across trials, subjects began matching A to B rather than A to A). Thus the A-B relations were between the samples and comparison elements. If so, the arbitrary relations could only emerge when complex stimuli are used in the context of a conditional discrimination task. On the other hand, the conditional A-B relations (A1-B1, A2-B2) may have come about independently of the samples. Perhaps, simply responding to both elements of the AB stimulus was sufficient for conditional relations between compound elements to emerge. If so, the conditional A-B relations simply emerged from the presentation of compound stimuli. Thus, similar findings should also be obtained if the complex stimuli were used in simple discrimination tasks. Suppose that after being trained to point (or not to point) to A, subjects receive a series of probes, one with a complex AB stimulus and one with B. Will subjects who point to A, AB and B, relate the A and B stimuli conditionally to one another in subsequent A-B and B-A probes?

In the present chapter we describe a series of studies showing that conditional relations between stimuli may arise as a function of spatial contiguity (compounded stimuli) and temporal contiguity (sequential presentations of individual stimuli). In the first half of the chapter we will describe two studies showing how emergent matching performances can be established via compound stimulus control and simple discriminations. As indicated previously, both types of behavioral control have been utilized separately in equivalence studies. The type of procedure outlined above (Train A1+/A2-; Test A1B1+/A2B2-, B1+/B2- and the conditional A-B), however, is the first to combine both simple discriminations and compound stimulus control as a means of generating emergent matching behaviors. In the latter half of the chapter we will describe experiments showing novel conditional stimulus relations emanating from temporal contiguity, and we will consider how these experiments may help us to identify and analyze at least some of the important variables that generate responding in accordance with equivalence relations.

GENERATING EMERGENT CONDITIONAL DISCRIMINATIONS VIA SIMPLE DISCRIMINATIONS AND STIMULUS COMPOUNDING

In the initial study (Schenk, 1995), eight 5-year-old preschool children received training on identity matching-to-sample tasks (A-A) and on two simple discrimination tasks (A1+/A2- and A3+/A4-) followed by a series of simple discrimination probes (no programmed consequences). Two of the probes presented complex AB stimuli (A1B1/A2B2, A3B3/A4B4) and two presented the B stimuli alone (B1/B2, B3/B4). Subjects (N=6) who showed transfer from A to B via AB (A1B1+/A2B2-, A3B3+/A4B4-, B1+/B2-, B3+/B4-) also received conditional discrimination probes with A+ and B+ stimuli (B1-A1, B3-A3, and vice versa) or with A- and B- stimuli (B2-A2, B4-A4, and vice versa, see Table 1). Four of these subjects (67%) related the paired A and B stimuli conditionally to one another. The other two subjects treated the conditional discrimination probes as simple discrimination tasks and systematically responded to one comparison irrespective of the sample.

The second study (Smeets, Barnes, Schenk, & Darcheville, in press) examined to what extent Schenk's (1995) findings were a function of the fact that, in the conditional discrimination probes, (a) all stimuli (samples and comparisons) had the same S+ or S- functions, and (b) the comparisons (e.g., A1 vs A3) were different from those used in the simple discrimination tasks (A1 vs A2). In effect, during the conditional discrimination probes the subjects could not respond in accordance with the previously obtained simple discriminations (e.g., A1 and A3 were both correct choices during the simple discrimination training), and thus responding to the sample and the comparisons may have been facilitated (i.e., more informally, subjects were prevented from treating the conditional discrimination as a simple discrimination, and thus they chose between the comparisons based on the sample stimulus). The question we asked at this point was as follows: Would young children also relate the paired A and B stimuli conditionally to one another if the conditional discrimination probes incorporated the same comparisons as the simple discrimination tasks (A1+ vs A2-, B1+ vs B2-), and if not, would older and more intellectually advanced persons demonstrate this emergent discrimination? Preschool children (N=24) were used in Experiments 1-3 (eight in each experiment), high functioning mentally retarded adults (N=4) were used in Experiment 4, and normal adults (N=4) were used in Experiment 5. Figure 1 illustrates the stimuli that were used in Experiment 1. In the first three experiments, the subjects received pretraining (see Table 1) on one or two unrelated conditional discrimination tasks (Experiment 1: X-YZ; Experiment 2: A-A, B-B; Experiment 3: X-A, B-Y). These tasks provided the subjects with a history of conditional discrimination, so that any possible failures on the critical conditional discrimination probes (B-A, A-B) could not be attributed simply to unfamiliarity with the task. The subjects then received training on a two-choice discrimination task with A1 and A2. Pointing to A1 was reinforced, pointing to A2 was not reinforced (A1+/A2-). Then they received four discrimination probes. Two were simple discrimination probes, one with complex AB stimuli (A1B1/A2B2) and one with B stimuli (B1/B2); and two were conditional discrimination probes (A-B and B-A). In Experiment 3, subjects who responded accurately on the A-B and B-A probes received additional tests that incorporated the X and Y stimuli used during the pretraining (A-X, Y-B, X-B, B-X, Y-A, A-Y, X-Y, Y-X, X1+/X2-, Y1+/Y2-). Experiments 4 and 5 were basically the same except that subjects, who responded accurately on the A-B and B-A tests, were also given the opportunity to demonstrate transfer from B to C via BC (B1C1/B2C2 and C1/C2 tests) and to relate all other directly and indirectly linked stimuli of the same functions conditionally to one another (B-C, C-A, and vice versa).

Table 1
Experimental Designs of Schenk (1995) and Smeets et al. (in press) experiments.

Schenk (1995)	Smeets et al.(in press)	
Pretraining	Pretraining	
	Experiments 1-3	Experiments 4-5
1. Trn A1-A1, A2-A2	1. Trn X1-Y1Z1, X2-Y2Z2 (E1) Trn A1-A1, A2-A2 (E2) B1-B1, B2-B2 Trn X1-A1, X2-A2 (E3) B1-Y1, B2-Y2	1. Trn B1-B1, B2-B2
Training and Tests	Training and Tests	

2. Trn A1+/A2-
3. Tst A1B1+/A2B2-
4. Tst B1+/B2-
5. Trn A3+/A4-
6. Tst A3B3+/A4B4-
7. Tst B3+/B4-
8. Tst B1-A1, B3-A3
  A1-B1, A3-B3
9. Tst B2-A2, B4-A4
  A2-B2, A4-B4
	2. Trn A1+/A2-
	3. Tst A1B1+/A2B2-
	4. Tst B1+/B2-
	5. Tst B1-A1, B2-A2
	  A1-B1, A2-B2
	  Exp. 3 only
	6. Tst A1-X1, A2-X2
	7. Tst Y1-B1, Y2-B2
	8. Tst X1-B1, X2-B2
	  B1-X1, B2-X2
	9. Tst A1-Y1, A2-Y2
	  Y1-A1, Y2-A2
	10. Tst X1-Y1, X2-Y2
	  Y1-X1, Y2-X2
	11. Tst X1+/X2-
	12. Tst Y1+/Y2-
		2. Trn A1+/A2-
		3. Trn A1B1+/A2B2-
		4. Tst B1+/B2-
		5. Tst A1-B1, A2-B2
		  B1-A1, B2-A2
		6. Trn C1-C1, C2-C2
		7. Tst B1C1+/B2C2-
		8. Tst C1+/C2-
		9. Tst B1-C1, B2-C2
		  C1-B1, C2-B2
		10. Tst C1-A1, C2-A2
		  A1-C1, A2-C2

Note: The numbers indicate the sequence in which the tasks were presented.

The performances on the conditional discrimination probes differed markedly across populations. Only six (25%) children (four in Experiment 1, none in Experiment 2, and two in Experiment 3) systematically related the paired A and B stimuli of the same functions conditionally to one another (A1-B1, A2-B2, and vice versa). When given the opportunity (Experiment 3), two of these children also related the indirectly linked stimuli to one another (B1-X1, B2-X2; A1-Y1, A2-Y2; X1-Y1, X2-Y2; and vice versa) and responded to the X and Y stimuli in the same way as to the A and B stimuli (X1+/X2-, Y1+/Y2-). Thus, for both these subjects, two four-member stimulus classes had been established (A1-B1-X1-Y1, A2-B2-X2-Y2)

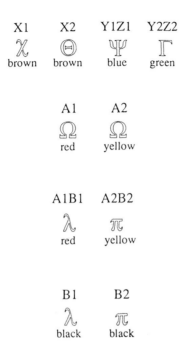

Figure 1. Stimuli used in Experiment 1 of the study by Smeets, et al. (in press).

that can be defined by stimulus and functional equivalence. The other children (N=18) typically treated the conditional discrimination probes as simple discrimination tasks and frequently, if not always, selected the trained or derived S+ stimuli, irrespective of the samples. The performances of the mentally retarded adults (Experiment 4) were very similar. One subject (25%) related all directly and indirectly paired stimuli of the same functions (S+, S-) conditionally to one another (A1-B1-C1, A2-B2-C2). The other three subjects systematically responded to the S+ stimuli. By contrast, all four (100%) normal adults in Experiment 5 completed the entire training and test sequence in a (near) errorless fashion (i.e., they responded in accordance with stimulus and functional equivalence classes).

For the two subjects in Experiment 3 who conditionally matched the X and Y stimuli to one another, the emergent conditional relations could be seen as responding in accordance with equivalence relations with the complex AB stimuli functioning as mediating nodes between the X and Y stimuli (i.e., X1-A1 and B1-Y1 pretraining followed by A1B1 compounding produces X1-Y1, and vice versa). For the other subjects who showed conditional A-B and B-A discriminations (four in Experiment 1, one in Experiment 4, and four in Experiment 5), these discriminations could be based strictly on the discriminative (S+, S-) functions of the stimuli. For example, after obtaining transfer from A to B via AB and from B to C via BC (A1+/A2-,

A1B1+/A2B2-, B1+/B2-, B1C1+/B2C2-, C1+/C2-) in Experiment 5, the adults could have related the A, B, and C stimuli to one another on the basis of their corresponding S+ and S- functions. If we follow a recent suggestion by Sidman (1994, pp. 463-474) to include responses as well as stimuli in equivalence relations, this performance might also be considered equivalence responding. From this perspective, during the initial simple discrimination training (A1+/A2-) two equivalence relations were formed: A1-pointing, A2-no pointing. Furthermore, when the A stimuli were superimposed on the B stimuli and the B stimuli on the C stimuli, two four-member equivalence relations emerged based on the relation between each stimulus and the pointing/no pointing responses (i.e., B1-pointing and C1-pointing produced B1-C1 and C1-B1 matching; B2-no pointing and C2-no pointing produced B2-C2 and C2-B2 matching). At the present time therefore, these findings do not clearly show whether the emergent conditional discriminations resulted from: (a) spatial contiguity or compounding (A1B1, therefore A1-B1 and B1-A1), or (b) from discriminative stimuli controlling the same responses (A1-point, B1-point, therefore A1-B1 and B1-A1). Nevertheless, it is important to remember that two subjects in Experiment 3 conditionally matched the X and Y stimuli to one another, and thus it appears that differential response functions do not have to be established for all "class 1" and "class 2" stimuli.

The simple discrimination performance of most children and adults with mental retardation on the conditional discrimination probes suggested that their responses were exclusively controlled by the S+ and S- functions of the comparison stimuli. One possible explanation for this outcome is that the apparent similarity between the simple and conditional discrimination probes (all tasks used the same comparisons [A1 vs A2, B1 vs B2]), together with the absence of corrective feedback (possibly functioning as nonverbal approval), may have encouraged these subjects to "ignore" the samples and respond as before (i.e., select the S+ stimuli; see also Sidman, 1994, pp. 419-421). If this interpretation is correct, then this problem might be remedied in future studies by incorporating additional cues to respond appropriately on both types of discrimination tasks (e.g., simple discrimination tasks with green backgrounds and conditional discrimination tasks, pretraining tasks and probes on white backgrounds).

A second explanation for the current data is that the performances of most of the children and mentally retarded adults were controlled by the contrasting functions (S+, S-) of the comparisons used in the conditional discrimination probes. This could be assessed by repeating Schenk's study but with different probes. After training A1+/A2- and A3+/A4- and obtaining transfer from A to B via AB (A1B1+/A2B2-, A3B3+/A4B4-, B1+/B2-, B3+/B4-), conditional discrimination probes could be presented with B1+ and B4- as samples and with A1+ and A4- as comparisons. Note that, as in Schenk's study, the choice stimuli (A1+ and A4-) would be different from those used in the simple discrimination tasks (A1+ and A2-, A3+ and A4-) but, in contrast to Schenk's study, they would possess contrasting functions.

A third possible explanation might be that the simple discrimination performance on the conditional discrimination probes was a function of the S+ and S- comparisons being associated with differential *reinforcement* rather than with the differential responding. The stimuli to which the subjects responded were directly (A1+) or indirectly associated with reinforcement (B1+). The stimuli to which they did not respond were not associated with reinforcement (A2-, B2-). To test this account children could be trained on a successive discrimination task during which responding to A1 is reinforced and not responding to A2 is also reinforced (i.e., reinforcers are paired with both stimuli). After showing transfer from A to B via AB, would these subjects relate B1 to A1 and B2 to A2 (and vice versa) in conditional discrimination probes?

It is also important to note, however, that in the conditional discrimination probes, these subjects' responses may not have been exclusively controlled by the S+ stimuli. In effect, subjects' responses may have been under perfect though inappropriate sample control. For example, during the B-A tests, the subjects could have responded to A1 (S+) in the presence of B1 (S+) and responded away from A2 (S-) in the presence of B2 (S-). Thus what seemed like a simple discrimination performance may have been a conditional discrimination performance. This is an interesting possibility and certainly warrants further study.

Although both studies outlined thus far leave many questions unanswered, the obtained findings add to the body of knowledge on the conditions that lead to novel conditional relations. Existing research has shown that, after being trained on arbitrary conditional discriminations, children much younger and persons more seriously handicapped than those used in our studies (Barnes, McCullagh, & Keenan, 1990; Devany, Hayes, & Nelson, 1986; de Rose, McIlvane, Dube, Galpin, & Stoddard, 1988; Lipkens, Hayes, & Hayes, 1993; Saunders, Saunders, Kirby, & Spradlin, 1988; Spradlin, Cotter, & Baxley, 1973) and even nonhumans (Schusterman & Kastak, 1993; Tomanoga, Matsuzawa, Fujita, & Yamamoto, 1991; Yamamoto & Asano, 1995; Urcuioli & Zentall, 1993) will demonstrate novel conditional stimulus relations (not always reliable and not always equivalence) that are consistent with those that were explicitly trained. In this light, the efficacy of simple discriminations with compound stimuli in producing conditional discriminations in mentally young populations is modest (Schenk, 1995) if not very low (Smeets, et al., in press). By contrast, compounding in simple discriminations produced conditional discriminations in all normal adults. These findings indicate that arbitrary conditional discriminations may be the most effective but certainly not the only condition leading to novel and untrained conditional stimulus relations. Furthermore, the data suggest that as verbal humans develop (see also below), novel conditional stimulus relations may emerge rather easily from tasks and stimulus configurations increasingly remote from standard conditional discrimination tasks.

GENERATING EMERGENT CONDITIONAL DISCRIMINATIONS USING A RESPONDENT TRAINING PROCEDURE

The first half of this chapter reviewed two studies that used simple discrimination training and the subsequent presentation of stimulus compounds to produce untrained conditional discriminations in a range of human subjects. We have recently developed another procedure that also appears to generate emergent matching performances in adult humans (Leader, Barnes, & Smeets, in press). The basic procedure involves presenting an arbitrary stimulus A that reliably predicts the appearance of a second arbitrary stimulus B (i.e., A->B; note A and B are never presented simultaneously). Following sufficient exposure to this respondent training procedure, a subject is given the opportunity to pick stimulus A (as a comparison) in the presence of stimulus B (as a sample) on a matching-to-sample task. In effect, having been exposed to A->B respondent training will the subject respond in accordance with the B-A symmetry relation? Furthermore, if stimulus A always precedes B and B always precedes C in a respondent training procedure (A->B->C), a subject can also be given the opportunity to choose A in the presence of C on a subsequent matching-to-sample task. In other words, having been exposed to A->B->C respondent training will the subject respond in accordance with the C-A equivalence relation? The second half of this chapter will focus on the data that we have gathered using the respondent training procedure (all subjects were experimentally naive, undergraduates attending University College Cork, and the stimuli were three-letter nonsense syllables).

Experiment 1

The first study we conducted, using the respondent training procedure, involved three conditions. In Condition 1, five subjects were provided with detailed instructions that specified that the first part of the experiment (the respondent training) was related to the second part (the equivalence test): "During the first stage of this experiment you will be presented with nonsense syllables on the computer screen. You should pay close attention to this first stage because it is relevant to the second stage of the experiment." The five subjects were exposed to a respondent training procedure in which six stimulus pairs (A1->B1, B1->C1, A2->B2, B2->C2, A3->B3, B3->C3) were presented on a computer screen (i.e., no overt observing responses were required, and no measures were taken to ensure that the subjects attended to the stimuli). A 0.5 s interstimulus interval separated the stimuli each pair, and a 3 s interpair interval separated the presentation of stimulus pairs (see Figure 2). All six stimulus pairs were presented in this fashion, in a quasi-random order for sixty trials, the only constraint being that each stimulus pair was presented once in each successive block of six trials (i.e., each stimulus pair was presented

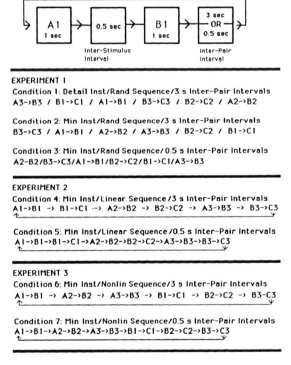

Figure 2. Diagrammatic representation of the respondent training procedure (top panel). Lower panels indicate the instructions (Detailed or Minimal), the sequences (Random, Linear, and Nonlinear), and the inter-pair intervals (0.5 s or 3 s) used across the seven conditions in the three Experiments. Note that the sequences shown for Experiment 1 are just three examples of the many quasi-random sequences that could occur within any six-trial block (see text for details). For Experiments 2 and 3, however, the stimuli were always presented in the same sequence shown in the diagram.

10 times).

Following the respondent training, the subjects were exposed to a three-choice matching-to-sample procedure that tested for the six symmetry relations (i.e., B1-A1, B2-A2, B3-A3, C1-B1, C2-B2, C3-B3) and the three equivalence relations (C1-A1, C2-A2, C3-A3). The computer presented the nine matching-to-sample tasks and recorded the subjects' responses; no feedback was presented during the equivalence test. The nine relations were tested in a quasi-random order for 90 trials, the only constraint being that each of the nine tasks occurred once within each block of nine trials. A consistency criterion was used that required each subject to choose the same but not necessarily correct comparison at least 9 times out of 10 on each of the 9 tasks ("correct" will be used to describe responses that are in accordance with the symmetry and equivalence relations). This consistency criterion was used to control for the effects of inadvertent feedback provided by repeated training and testing (see Barnes & Keenan, 1993, p. 63, for rationale), and has been used successfully in a number of previous studies (e.g., Dymond & Barnes, 1995; in press; Roche & Barnes, in press). If a subject produced an inconsistent performance (i.e., less than 9 out of 10 "same responses" on any of the tasks) they were immediately reexposed to the entire experimental procedure again (i.e., respondent training and equivalence testing). Due to time constraints, Subjects' 6 and 14 were allowed a 24 hr break between sessions 4 and 5. If a subject did not produce a consistent performance by their fourth exposure to the entire experimental sequence, and their performance was less than 50 percent correct (i.e., the subject produced fewer than 45 correct responses), the performance was classified as inconsistent and the subject's participation in the study was terminated. If, however, a subject produced more than 50 percent correct responding on a fourth exposure to the equivalence test, additional exposures to the training and testing were provided until he or she either produced fewer than 50 percent correct responses or produced a consistent performance. This criterion thereby ensured that a subject who produced an inconsistent performance, that was considerably higher than chance (i.e., 33% correct), would not be prevented from retraining and retesting.

In Condition 2, an additional five subjects were exposed to the same procedures, except that they were given minimal instructions at the beginning of the respondent training (i.e., "Look at the screen") that did not specify a relationship between the first and second parts of the experiment (all remaining conditions also used minimal instructions). This condition allowed us to assess whether specifying a link between respondent training and testing, facilitates, suppresses, or does not effect the emergence of equivalence responding (cf. Green, Sigurdardottir, & Saunders, 1991; Sigurdardottir, Green, & Saunders, 1990; Saunders, Saunders, Williams, & Spradlin, 1993).

Finally, in Condition 3 another five subjects were exposed to the same procedures employed in Condition 2 (minimal instructions), except that the 3 s inter-pair interval was reduced to 0.5 s (i.e., all stimuli were separated by 0.5 s). This final "control" condition was designed simply to test our assumption that shorter inter-stimulus intervals, relative to inter-pair intervals, was necessary for equivalence responding to emerge (i.e., we assumed that obscuring the temporal boundary between stimulus pairs would prevent the formation of the predicted equivalence relations) . As outlined below, however, this assumption proved to be false.

The total percentage of correct responses across the 90 test trials (i.e., 60 symmetry and 30 equivalence) for each subject's final exposure to the equivalence test is shown in Figure 3. All but two subjects across Conditions 1, 2, and 3 produced almost perfect equivalence responding. Two subjects showed a consistently incorrect performance on their third and second exposures respectively, and thus their participation in the study was terminated. Six exposures was the maximum required (Subject 1) and two was the minimum (Subjects 4, 8, and 15). These data clearly show that the respondent training procedure, combined with either detailed or minimal instructions, can reliably generate equivalence responding in the absence of explicit conditional discrimination training in the experimental context. Interestingly, in Condition 3 four subjects produced almost perfect equivalence responding. This outcome was unexpected; it was assumed that reducing the 3 s inter-pair intervals to 0.5 s (i.e., to the same value as the inter-stimulus intervals) would prevent subjects from discriminating the six separate stimulus pairs, and thus prevent the formation of equivalence relations. Imagine, for example, that a subject is presented with the following stimuli A3->B3->B1->C1 during the first block of six respondent training trials; how might this subject discriminate the A3->B3 pairing from the B1->C1 pairing

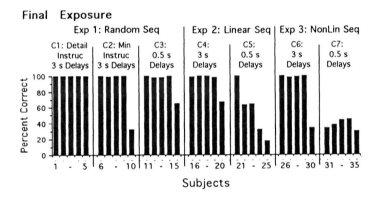

Figure 3. Summary of results for all subjects across the seven conditions from the three experiments. Each bar on the graph shows percent correct across the ninety symmetry and equivalence test trials for each subject's final exposure to the equivalence test.

if each stimulus is separated by the same time interval of 0.5 s (i.e., from the subject's perspective, is B3 paired with A3 or B1)? To answer this question we considered the consistency versus inconsistency of the stimulus pairings across the entire respondent training procedure. In effect, although a subject might not discriminate the A3->B3 pairing from the B1->C1 pairing across the first block of six respondent training trials, in the next block of six trials (and every block thereafter) A3->B3 may be followed by any of the other stimulus pairs (e.g., B2->C2), and thus across blocks of six trials A3->B3 and B1->C1 are paired consistently whereas B3->B1 are not. The second experiment we conducted was designed to examine this issue.

Experiment 2

The second study involved two conditions (4 & 5), and an additional 10 subjects numbered 16 to 25. All other aspects of this experiment were identical to Experiment 1, except for the following differences.

Condition 4 was identical to Condition 2 in Experiment 1, except that the stimulus pairs were always presented in the same, fixed (rather than random) sequence during the respondent training phase (A1->B1, B1->C1, A2->B2, B2->C2, A3->B3, B3->C3; see Figure 2, Panel 4). The term "linear" is used to describe this sequence because the stimuli participating in each predicted equivalence relation were presented in the same A-B-C, linear-like sequence. Presenting the stimuli in this way ensured that each stimulus always appeared in a consistent position in the sequence relative to the others; subjects could not, therefore, discriminate the six stimulus pairs based on the fact that only some pairs remained together consistently. In this condition, however, it was predicted that the 3 s inter-pair intervals, relative to the 0.5 s inter-stimulus intervals, would allow the subjects to discriminate among the six pairs of stimuli and therefore demonstrate equivalence responding.

Condition 5 was identical to Condition 4, except that the 3 s inter-pair intervals were reduced to 0.5 s (Figure 2, panel 5). It was predicted that the inter-pair intervals of 0.5 s, combined with the fixed linear sequence, would prevent reliable discrimination among the six stimulus pairs. For example, how might subjects discriminate reliably the B1->C1 pairing from the C1->A2 pairing if each stimulus presentation is separated by 0.5 s and the stimuli are always presented in the same fixed order (i.e., from the subjects' perspective, is C1 paired with B1 or A2)? Furthermore, if the subjects fail to discriminate reliably the six stimulus pairs, it is also likely that they will fail to demonstrate reliably the formation of the predicted equivalence relations. For example, when C1 is presented as a sample with A1, A2, and A3 as comparisons, will subjects select; A1 based on the A1->B1->C1 stimulus pairings, A2 based on the C1->A2 stimulus pairings, or A3 based on the C1->A2->B2->C2->A3 stimulus pairings?

The percentage of correct responses on the final equivalence test for Subjects 16 to 25 is presented in Figure 3. In Condition 4 (Linear Sequence/3 s Inter-pair intervals), Subjects 16, 17, 18 and 19 produced near perfect equivalence responding on either the first, second, or third exposure to the test. Subject 20 produced consistently incorrect responding on the first exposure. In Condition 5 (Linear Sequence/0.5 s Inter-pair intervals), Subject 21 was the only one of the five subjects to demonstrate equivalence responding (on the second exposure to the test). Subjects 22 and 23 produced near perfect symmetry responding (see Table 2), but did not produce equivalence responding on their second and third exposures, respectively (i.e., consistently incorrect performances). Subject 24 was consistently incorrect on the first exposure. Subject 25 produced inconsistent responding across 4 exposures to the test, and failed to exceed 50 percent correct responding, and thus the subject's participation in the study was terminated.

The results indicate that in the Linear/0.5 s Inter-pair intervals Condition, the stimulus pairings during respondent training may sometimes facilitate the formation of symmetry but not equivalence relations (see Table 2). Inspection of Figure 2 (Condition 5) allows us to see how this might have happened. Consider, for example, the first five stimuli in the respondent training (A1->B1->B1->C1->A2). In this sequence, B1 is always paired with A1 and C1, and C1 is always paired with B1 and A2. Consequently, during a symmetry test, in which B1 is presented as a sample and A1, A2, and A3 are presented as comparisons, A1 is the only stimulus that has been paired with the sample B1. Similarly, on a symmetry test in which C1 is presented with B1, B2, and B3, B1 is the only comparison that has been paired with the with the sample during the respondent training, symmetry responding may sometimes emerge following this procedure. Consider now, the equivalence test trial where C1 (the sample) is presented with A1, A2, and A3 (the comparisons). During the sequence training, C1 has been paired directly with A2 but not

Table 2
Detailed results of Experiment 2 for those subjects who produced a consistently incorrect performance on their final exposure to the equivalence tests

S 10 (Random Seq Min Instruc)	S 15 (Random Seq 0.5 s Delays)	S 20 (Linear Seq 3 s Delays)	S 22 (Linear Seq 0.5 s Delays)	S 23 (Linear Seq 0.5 s Delays)
		Symmetry Trials		
B1->A3	B1->A1	B1->A1	B1->A1	B1->A1
B2->A3	B2->A2	B2->A2	B2->A2	B2->A2
B3->A3	B3->A3	B3->A3	B3->A3	B3->A3
C1->B3	C1->B1	C1->B1	C1->B1	C1->B1
C2->B3	C2->B2	C2->B2	C2->B2	C2->B2
C3->B3	C3->B3	C3->B3	C3->B3	C3->B3
		Equivalence Trials		
C1->A3	C1->A2	C1->A2	C1->A2	C1->A2
C2->A3	C2->A3	C2->A3	C2->A3	C2->A3
C3->A3	C3->A1	C3->A1	C3->A1	C3->A1

S 24 (Linear Seq 0.5 s Delays)	S 30 (Nonlinear 3 s Delays)	S 33 (Nonlinear 0.5 s Delays)	S 34 (Nonlinear 0.5 s Delays)
		Symmetry Trials	
B1->A3	B1->A2	B1->A2	B1->A1
B2->A3	B2->A3	B2->A3	B2->A3
B3->A3	B3->A3	B3->A3	B3->A3
C1->B2	C1->B1	C1->B1	C1->B1
C2->B3	C2->B3	C2->B3	C2->B3
C3->B1	C3->B3	C3->B3	C3->B3
		Equivalence Trials	
C1->A2	C1->A3	C1->A2	C1->A3
C2->A3	C2->A3	C2->A2	C2->A1
C3->A1	C3->A1	C3->A1	C3->A2

A1 (i.e., it is removed from A1 by B1). Thus, subjects may be more likely to choose the directly paired A2 comparison, rather than the A1 comparison that is paired indirectly to C1 through the B1 stimulus (i.e., A1-B1-C1). (Note, however, that the symmetry and equivalence responding produced by Subject 21 suggests that in some instances the symmetry-facilitating effect of the linear sequence may also produce equivalence responding). In summary, therefore, symmetry responding in the absence of equivalence responding may be predicted for the Linear/0.5 s Interpair intervals Condition, if we accept that some subjects are likely to match comparisons to samples that were directly paired during the respondent training. Experiment 3 was designed to examine this issue.

Experiment 3

Experiment 3 consisted of Conditions 6 and 7. In both of these conditions, the fixed linear sequence employed in Experiment 2 was modified so that the stimuli were presented in a fixed nonlinear sequence (i.e., A1->B1, A2->B2, A3->B3, B1->C1, B2->C2, B3->C3). The term "nonlinear" is used to describe this sequence because the A and B stimuli participating in each of the predicted equivalence relations were presented before the B and C stimuli from each of the predicted relations. The nonlinear sequence ensured that on four of the six tasks that tested for symmetry responding, two of the comparison stimuli (one "correct" and the other "incorrect") had been directly paired, during training, with the sample stimulus (e.g., B1 was directly paired with A1 and A2). In effect, either comparison was equally correct based on direct pairing. It was predicted, therefore, that reliable symmetry responding, in the absence of equivalence responding, should not occur with any subject using the nonlinear respondent training procedure.

Condition 6 was identical to Condition 4, except that the stimulus pairs were always presented in the same nonlinear sequence during the respondent training procedure (i.e., A1->B1, A2->B2, A3->B3, B1->C1, B2->C2, B3->C3; see Figure 2, panel 6). Presenting the stimuli in this way ensured that each stimulus always appeared in a consistent position in the sequence relative to the others, and thus, as in the previous Experiment, the subjects could not discriminate the six stimulus pairs based on the consistency versus inconsistency of the stimulus pairings. Although Condition 6 employed a fixed, nonlinear sequence, it also used 3 s inter-pair intervals. Consequently, it was predicted that these delays, relative to the 0.5 s inter-stimulus intervals, would allow the subjects to discriminate the six stimulus pairs and therefore demonstrate equivalence responding.

Condition 7 was identical to Condition 6, except that the inter-pair intervals of 3 s were reduced to 0.5 s (Figure 2, panel 7). It was predicted that the 0.5 s inter-pair intervals combined with the nonlinear sequence would prevent the "symmetry facilitating effect" of Condition 5. Consider, for example, the first five stimuli in the nonlinear sequence (i.e., A1->B1->A2->B2->A3). In this sequence, B1 is directly paired with both A1 and A2, and thus during a symmetry test in which B1 is presented as a sample with A1, A2, and A3 as comparisons, both A1 and A2 are equally likely choices if a subject simply selects the comparison that was directly paired with the sample during the respondent training.

Four subjects in Condition 6 (26, 27, 28, 29) produced near perfect equivalence responding on either their second exposures (26 and 29) or on their third exposures (27 and 28) to the test. Subject 30 produced a consistently incorrect performance on the third exposure (see Figure 3). In Condition 7, Subjects 31, 32, and 35 produced inconsistent (and below 50 percent correct) responding on their fourth exposures, and in accordance with the consistency criterion their participation was terminated. Subjects 33 and 34 were consistently incorrect on their third and second exposures respectively (see Figure 3), and neither of these subjects produced symmetrical responding (see Table 2). As predicted, therefore, the "symmetry generating effect" of the Linear/0.5 s Inter-pair intervals Condition was absent in the Nonlinear/0.5 s Inter-pair intervals Condition.

Discussion

These three experiments clearly demonstrate that it is possible to produce equivalence responding in adult human subjects using a respondent training procedure. Furthermore, it was shown that the effectiveness of the respondent procedure in producing equivalence is dependant upon; (i) the presence of longer inter-pair intervals relative to the inter-stimulus intervals, and (ii) the sequence in which the stimulus pairs are presented. Subjects produced equivalence responding after the random sequencing of stimulus pairs, both with and without detailed instructions (Conditions 1 and 2). Interestingly, when the 3 s inter-pair interval was reduced to 0.5 s, subjects continued to produce equivalence. This finding suggested that the consistency versus inconsistency of stimulus pairing during the random sequencing produced the appropriate discriminations between stimulus pairs (in the absence of the 3 s inter-pair intervals) necessary for the formation of equivalence relations. Evidence for this was produced in the linear and nonlinear conditions in which most subjects formed equivalence relations when provided with 3 s inter-pair intervals, but failed when these delays were reduced to 0.5 s (i.e., the fixed linear and nonlinear sequences prevented the appropriate discriminations between stimulus pairs and thus the formation of equivalence relations observed in the random sequencing conditions).

Perhaps the most remarkable general finding from these experiments is that subjects were not explicitly trained to select any of the stimuli in a matching-to-sample context before the equivalence test was administered. Previous research with mentally retarded humans has shown the merger and development of equivalence relations by unreinforced conditional selection of comparison stimuli following a history of matching-to-sample training and equivalence testing (Saunders, Saunders, Kirby, & Spradlin, 1988). In effect, after the subjects had demonstrated the formation of equivalence relations in the Saunders et al. study they were then allowed to choose (in the absence of differential reinforcement) which novel comparisons "went with" the previously trained samples, and having done so they related these novel comparisons in a 'relation-consistent-manner' to the remaining stimuli participating in the previously established equivalence relations. In contrast, the current procedures produced reliable equivalence responding in the absence of any prior matching-to-sample training or successful equivalence testing.

The fact that the respondent procedure successfully lead to equivalence responding indicates that this procedure may help us to explore further the stimulus equivalence effect. For example, it remains uncertain as to whether the respondent training will lead to equivalence responding in young or verbally disabled human subjects. Of course, the current procedure would most likely have to be 'simplified' for these populations. For instance, a subject could be respondently trained with just one stimulus pair, A1-B1, and then tested repeatedly using a single matching-to-sample task (i.e., present B1 as sample with A1, A2, and A3 as comparisons); the next stimulus pair could then be trained and tested in a similar manner, and so on, until all equivalence relations had been formed. If young or verbally disabled individuals demonstrate equivalence using this simplified respondent training, it could be argued that the standard conditional discrimination training is perhaps an "overly complicated" procedure for generating equivalence responding in human populations. On balance, imagine that young, verbally-able children, who would be expected to show equivalence responding using the typical matching-to-sample preparation (e.g., Barnes, et al., 1990; Barnes, Browne, Smeets, & Roche, 1995; Devany, et al., 1986; Eikeseth & Smith, 1992), failed to demonstrate equivalence using the simplified respondent method. Such an outcome would indicate that certain features of the matching-to-sample format itself provide important controlling variables over the emergence of equivalence relations (see Barnes, 1994, p. 110). Further research that modified the respondent procedure (e.g., by introducing an observation response, or an operant requirement similar to that used in configural conditioning experiments; see Sutherland & Rudy, 1989) might then identify exactly what properties of the matching-to-sample training help determine equivalence responding in young, human populations. In summary, by developing a range of procedures that either produce, or fail to produce, equivalence in different subject populations it should be possible to identify the important controlling variables involved in equivalence responding. The three experiments outlined above (and the studies described in the first half of the chapter) represent an important step in this direction.

THEORETICAL IMPLICATIONS FOR STIMULUS EQUIVALENCE

The data from all of the studies presented in this chapter raise some interesting theoretical issues concerning the nature of stimulus equivalence itself. Stimulus equivalence was originally seen as the exclusive product of a four-term contingency (i.e., equivalence emerged only from differentially reinforced conditional discriminations; see Sidman, 1994, pp. 378-379). More recent formulations, however, have moved away from this view (Barnes, 1994; Hayes, 1991; Sidman, 1994; Stromer, McIlvane, & Serna, 1993). For example, Sidman (1994) has suggested that; (i) equivalence responding may emerge from three-term contingencies (e.g., from differentially reinforced simple discriminations), (ii) responses as well as stimuli may participate in equivalence relations, and (iii) respondent conditioning may also result in the establishment of equivalence relations. The studies presented in this chapter showed that (i) simple discrimination training and testing with compound stimuli (three-term contingencies) sometimes produce equivalence responding, (ii) some of the emergent matching performances obtained using such procedures suggest that it may be useful to include stimuli and responses in equivalence relations, and (iii) respondent training reliably produced equivalence responding in adult humans. These data therefore appear to be consistent with Sidman's revised, formal definition of stimulus equivalence.

The current data, however, are also consistent with the relational-frame account of stimulus equivalence (Barnes, 1994; Hayes, 1991). From this perspective, if a subject is provided with an appropriate history of reinforcement, in the relevant context, equivalence responding may emerge from a three-term contingency (Barnes & Roche, in press), responses as well as stimuli may participate in equivalence relations (see Dymond & Barnes, 1994, 263-264), and respondent contingencies may produce equivalence responding (see Leader, et al., in press, for a detailed discussion of this issue). Furthermore, the emphasis relational frame theory places on reinforcement history may help to explain why the mental age of a subject population appears to predict, to some extent, whether equivalence responding will emerge from training procedures that are formally quite different from the traditional matching-to-sample equivalence test. In effect, mentally older subjects are more likely to pass an equivalence test than are younger subjects, after non-matching-to-sample training, because the older participants usually have relatively extended and varied histories of reinforcement for responding in accordance with equivalence relations across a wide range of social and problem-solving contexts. More informally, the relatively extended and varied histories of the mentally older subjects employed in the current series of experiments allowed them to discriminate quite easily that the simple discrimination or respondent training was being used to "inform them which stimuli go together", and the matching-to-sample tasks were being used to determine whether they had "learned which stimuli go together."

At the present time, it is not clear whether Sidman's "new" formulation of stimulus equivalence or relational frame theory (or a third alternative) will provide the most adequate account of emergent matching performances. Whatever the outcome, the procedures outlined in the current chapter will likely play an important role in establishing the relative strengths and weaknesses of these and perhaps other accounts of stimulus equivalence.

SUMMARY AND CONCLUSION

The experiments reported in this chapter focused on the effects of spatial and temporal contiguity on emergent matching performances in human subjects. The first two studies (Schenk, 1995; Smeets et al., in press) demonstrated that when stimulus compounds are used in simple discrimination tasks (spatial contiguity), the various elements may subsequently enter into emergent conditional discriminations. These emergent performances appear to depend; (i) on the mental age of the subjects, and (ii) on whether the conditional discrimination probes permit subjects to continue responding as they did during the simple discrimination training and testing. The next study (Leader, et al., in press) showed that when individual stimuli are presented one at a time in various sequences (temporal contiguity) matching performances consistent with the training often emerge for human adults. The emergent performances were shown to depend upon; (i) the presence of longer inter-pair intervals relative to the inter-stimulus intervals, and/or (ii) the use of a quasi-random sequence for presenting the stimulus pairs. The procedures of all three studies therefore allowed us to identify and systematically analyze the effects of spatial and temporal contiguity on emergent matching performances in various human populations.

REFERENCES

Barnes, D. (1994). Stimulus equivalence and relational frame theory. *Psychological Record, 44*, 91-124.

Barnes, D., Browne, M., Smeets, P.M., & Roche, B. (1995). A transfer of functions and a conditional transfer of functions through equivalence relations in three to six year old children. *Psychological Record, 45*, 405-430.

Barnes, D. & Holmes, Y. (1991). Radical behaviorism, stimulus equivalence, and human cognition. *Psychological Record, 41*, 19-31.

Barnes, D., & Keenan, M. (1993). The transfer of functions through arbitrary and nonarbitrary stimulus relations. *Journal of the Experimental Analysis of Behavior, 5*, 61-81.

Barnes, D., McCullagh, P.D., & Keenan, M. (1990). Equivalence class formation in non-hearing impaired children and hearing impaired children. *The Analysis of Verbal Behavior, 8*, 19-30.

Barnes, D., & Roche, B. (in press). Relational frame theory and stimulus equivalence are fundamentally different: A reply to Saunders. *Psychological Record.*

de Rose, J.C., McIlvane, W.J., Dube, W.V., Galpin, V.C., & Stoddard, L.T. (1988). Emergent simple discrimination established by indirect relation to differential consequences. *Journal of the Experimental Analysis of Behavior, 50*, 1-20.

Devany, J.M., Hayes, S.C., & Nelson, R.O. (1986). Equivalence class formation in language-able and language-disabled children. *Journal of the Experimental Analysis of Behavior, 46*,

243-257.

Dymond, S., & Barnes, D. (1994). A transfer of self-discrimination response functions through equivalence relations. *Journal of the Experimental Analysis of Behavior, 62,* 251-267.

Dymond, S., & Barnes, D. (1995). A transformation of self-discrimination response functions in accordance with the arbitrarily applicable relations of sameness, more-than, and less-than. *Journal of the Experimental Analysis of Behavior, 64,* 163-184.

Dymond, S., & Barnes, D. (in press). A transformation of self-discrimination response functions in accordance with the arbitrarily applicable relations of sameness and opposition. *Psychological Record.*

Eikeseth, S., & Smith, T. (1992). The development of functional and equivalence classes in high functioning autistic children: The role of naming. *Journal of the Experimental Analysis of Behavior, 58,* 123-133.

Fields, L., & Verhave, T. (1987). The structure of equivalence classes. *Journal of the Experimental Analysis of Behavior, 48,* 317-332.

Green, G., Sigurdardottir, Z.G., & Saunders, R.R. (1991). The role of instructions in the transfer of ordinal functions through equivalence classes. *Journal of the Experimental Analysis of Behavior, 5,* 287-304.

Hayes, S. C. (1991). A relational control theory of stimulus equivalence. In L. J. Hayes and P. N. Chase (Eds.), *Dialogues on Verbal Behavior,* (pp. 19-40). Reno NV: Context Press.

Leader, G., Barnes, D., & Smeets, P.M. (in press). Establishing equivalence relations using a respondent-type training procedure. *Psychological Record.*

Lipkins, R., Hayes, S.C., & Hayes, L.J. (1993). Longitudinal study of the development of derived relations in an infant. *Journal of Experimental Child Psychology, 56,* 201-239.

Maguire, R.W., Stromer, R., Mackay, H.A., & Demis, C.A. (1994). Matching to complex samples and stimulus class formation in adults with autism and young children. *Journal of Autism and Developmental Disabilities, 24,* 753-772.

Markham, M.R., & Dougher, M.J. (1993). Compound stimuli in emergent stimulus relations: Extending the scope of stimulus equivalence. *Journal of the Experimental Analysis of Behavior, 60,* 529-542.

Roche, B., & Barnes, D. (in press). Sexual categorization and arbitrarily applicable relational responding: A critical test of the derived difference relation. *Psychological Record.*

Saunders, K.J., Saunders, R.R., Williams, D.C., & Spradlin, J.E. (1993). An interaction of instructions and training design on stimulus class formation: Extending the analysis of equivalence. *Psychological Record, 43,* 725-744.

Saunders, R.R., Saunders, K.J., Kirby., K.C., & Spradlin, J.E. (1988). The merger and development of equivalence classes by unreinforced conditional selection of comparison stimuli. *Journal of the Experimental Analysis of Behavior, 50,* 145-162.

Saunders, R.R., Wachter, J., & Spradlin, J.E. (1988). Establishing auditory stimulus control over an eight-member equivalence class via conditional discrimination procedures. *Journal of the Experimental Analysis of Behavior, 49,* 95-115.

Schenk, J.J. (1993). Emergent conditional discrimination in children: Matching to compound stimuli. *Quarterly Journal of Experimental Psychology, 46B,* 345-365.

Schenk, J.J. (1995). Complex stimuli in nonreinforced simple discrimination tasks: Emergent simple and conditional discriminations. *Psychological Record, 45,* 477-494.

Schusterman, R.J., & Kastak, D. (1993). A California sea lion (Zalophus Californianus) is capable of forming equivalence relations. *Psychological Record, 43*, 823-839.

Sidman, M. (1990). Equivalence relations: Where do they come from? In Blackman and H. L. Lejeune (Eds.). *Behaviour analysis in theory and practice: Contributions and Controversies*, (pp. 93-114). Hove, England: Erlbaum.

Sidman, M. (1994). *Equivalence relations and behavior: A research story.* Boston, Authors Cooperative.

Sidman, M., & Tailby, W. (1982). Conditional discrimination vs. matching-to-sample: An expansion of the testing paradigm. *Journal of the Experimental Analysis of Behavior, 37*, 5-22.

Sidman, M., Wynne, C.K., McGuire, R.W., & Barnes, T. (1989). Functional classes and equivalence relations. *Journal of the Experimental Analysis of Behavior, 52*, 261-274.

Sigurdardottir, Z.G., Green, G., & Saunders, R.R. (1990). Equivalence classes generated by sequence training. *Journal of the Experimental Analysis of Behavior, 53*, 47-63.

Smeets, P.M., Barnes, D, Schenk, J.J., Darcheville, J.C. (in press). Emergent simple discriminations and conditional relations in children, adults with mental retardation, and normal adults. *Quarterly Journal of Experimental Psychology*.

Smeets, P.M., Schenk, J.J., & Barnes, D. (1994). Establishing transfer from identity to arbitrary matching tasks via complex stimuli under testing conditions. *Psychological Record, 44*, 521-536.

Smeets, P.M., Schenk, J.J., & Barnes, D. (1995). Establishing arbitrary stimulus classes via identity-matching training and non-reinforced matching with complex stimuli. *Quarterly Journal of Experimental Psychology, 48B*, 311-328.

Smeets, P.M., & Striefel, S. (1994). Matching to complex stimuli under nonreinforced conditions: Errorless transfer from identity to arbitrary matching tasks. *Quarterly Journal of Experimental Psychology, 47B*, 39-62.

Spradlin, J.E., Cotter, V.W., & Baxley, N. (1973). Establishing a conditional discrimination without direct training: A study of transfer with retarded adolescents. *American Journal of Mental Deficiency, 53*, 47-63.

Spradlin, J.E., & Saunders, R.R. (1986). The development of stimulus classes using matching-to-sample procedures: Sample classification versus comparison classification. *Analysis and Intervention in Developmental Disabilities, 6*, 41-58.

Stromer, R., & Mackay, H.A. (1993). Delayed identity matching to complex samples: Teaching students with mental retardation spelling and the prerequisites for equivalence classes. *Research in Developmental Disabilities, 14*, 19-38.

Stromer, R., McIlvane, W.J., & Serna, R.W. (1993). Complex stimulus control and equivalence. *Psychological Record, 43*, 585-598.

Stromer, R., & Stromer, J.B. (1990a). The formation of arbitrary stimulus classes in matching to complex samples. *Psychological Record, 40*, 51-66.

Stromer, R., & Stromer, J.B. (1990b). Matching-to-complex samples: Further study of arbitrary stimulus classes. *Psychological Record, 40*, 505-516.

Sutherland, R.J., Rudy, J.W. (1989). Configural association theory: The role of the hippocampal formation in learning, memory and amnesia. *Psychobiology, 17*, 129-144.

Tomonaga, M., Matsuzawa, T., Fujita, K., & Yamamoto, J. (1991). Emergence of symmetry in visual conditional discrimination by chimpanzees (*Pan Troglodytes*). *Psychological Reports, 68*, 51-60.

Urcuioli, P.J., & Zentall, T.R. (1993). A test of comparison-stimulus substitutability following one-to-many matching by pigeons. *Psychological Record, 43*, 745-759.

Vaughan, W., Jr. (1988). Formation of equivalence sets in pigeons. *Journal of the Experimental Psychology: Animal Behavior Processes, 14*, 36-42.

Wulfert, E., Dougher, M. J., & Greenway, D. E. (1991). Protocol analysis of the correspondence of verbal behavior and equivalence class formation. *Journal of the Experimental Analysis of Behavior, 56*, 486-504.

Yamamoto, J., & Asano, T. (1995). Stimulus equivalence in a chimpanzee (*Pan troglodytes*). *Psychological Record, 45*, 3-21.

Stimulus Class Formation in Humans and Animals
T.R. Zentall and P.M. Smeets (Editors)
© 1996 Elsevier Science B.V. All rights reserved.

10

Stimulus Equivalence: A Class of Correlations, or a Correlation of Classes?

Carol Pilgrim & Mark Galizio

University of North Carolina at Wilmington

The defining properties of equivalence relations (i.e., reflexivity, symmetry, and transitivity) have been operationalized in terms of the conditional discrimination procedures generally used to study and elaborate them (Saunders & Green, 1992; Sidman, 1986; Sidman & Tailby, 1982). Thus, stimulus classes are typically established through arbitrary match-to-sample procedures. However, accurate choices on trained conditional discriminations are not considered sufficient to demonstrate that the performances represent symbolic matching processes. Further proof in the form of unreinforced probe performances demonstrating generalized matching (reflexivity), reversibility of sample and comparison stimulus functions (symmetry), and stimulus control involving novel stimulus combinations (transitivity), is required before stimulus equivalence is inferred (Sidman & Tailby, 1982).

We believe that the tight linkage between the mathematical set theory definition of equivalence relations and the training and testing procedures used to demonstrate them has been responsible in part for the attractiveness of this important experimental approach. Some of the problems addressed by equivalence researchers have long histories of study with less rigorous methodologies (e.g., Lakoff, 1987). While the precision of set theory criteria brought focus to the study of many traditional issues within psychology, it has also led to some questions about the nature of the phenomena under study. In this chapter, we will first describe experiments in which reversals of baseline conditional discriminations appeared to have different effects across probe trial types (i.e., reflexivity, symmetry, and transitivity/equivalence). We then examine other empirical evidence that performances on the various probe trial types may differ in potentially important ways. Finally, we review studies that use measures other than probe trials to assess equivalence-like phenomena. The theme considered throughout is a fundamental one for even the simplest of analytic units. Skinner (1935/1972) originally prompted our consideration of the nature of stimulus (and response) classes by asking whether the reflex was best considered "a correlation of classes or a class of correlations" (p. 461). Continued exploration of the same question may be of value in helping to guide our analysis of complex phenomena such as those involved in stimulus equivalence. We believe that caution may be indicated with respect to assumptions about equivalence as a necessarily cohesive behavioral unit, and that this point carries implications for the research strategies used to study stimulus equivalence.

BASELINE CONTINGENCY REVERSALS AND STIMULUS EQUIVALENCE

A puzzling effect of contingency reversals

In the experiments to be described here the apparatus was a modified Wisconsin General Test Apparatus much like those traditionally used to study non-human discrimination learning.

Stimuli were three-dimensional objects that could be displaced by the subject to reveal either a token exchangeable for money (in studies with adult subjects) or a piece of fruit or candy (in studies with children). In a preliminary study from our laboratory (Pilgrim & Galizio, 1990), experimental manipulations were designed to bring about a modification or disruption of equivalence patterns. After learning baseline AB and AC conditional discriminations and showing the emergence of two three-member equivalence classes (i.e., A1B1C1 and A2B2C2), college student subjects were exposed to a reversal of the AC conditional discrimination. In the reversal condition, choosing comparison stimulus C2 was reinforced given A1 as a sample stimulus; choosing C1 was reinforced given sample A2. This manipulation might have been expected to produce a re-organization of the classes (i.e., A1B1C2 and A2B2C1). The surprising results were that while symmetry performances were immediately controlled by the reversed baseline contingencies for 3 of 4 subjects (i.e., comparison A1 was chosen given a C2 sample, and A2 was chosen given a C1 sample), reflexivity and transitivity performances remained consistent with the original equivalence classes. Figure 1 follows one representative subject (PJ) through the experimental conditions. The top panels show performances on the baseline AC trials by trial block (6 trials/block). Each data point represents the percentage of trials on which

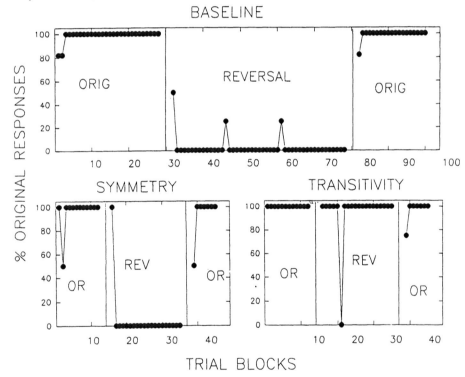

Figure 1. Performances of one subject (PJ) from Pilgrim and Galizio (1990) on AC baseline (top panel), CA symmetry (bottom left) and transitivity probe trials across the conditions of the experiment. The vertical axis represents, for each trial block, the percentage of trials on which responses were consistent with the original training contingencies or the equivalence classes established by them.

responding was consistent with the original conditional discrimination training contingencies. The baseline conditional discriminations were readily acquired and maintained at or near 100% accuracy for PJ, and for the other subjects as well. When the reinforcement contingencies were reversed, choices on AC trials also changed in a manner that directly reflected the new contingencies. Thus, choices approached near-zero "percent original" responding (that is, C2 was correctly chosen given A1, and so on).

Figure 1 also shows performance on CA symmetry probe trials. The vertical axis represents the percentage of CA trials on which responses were consistent with the equivalence classes established by the original training contingencies. During the original training condition, almost 100% of the choices made were consistent with the predicted equivalence classes. Following the AC reversal (REV), CA choice patterns also reversed in keeping with the changed contingency. Compare this with performances on transitivity probe trials shown in Figure 1. For Subject PJ and the other subjects, transitivity was clearly demonstrated during the original training conditions. Notably, these original patterns persisted even after the AC reversal, and despite the fact that symmetry patterns were consistent with the new baseline.

The inconsistencies between transitivity and baseline performances were interesting because baseline relations are commonly held to be the basis for equivalence class performances. Even more striking was the contrast between transitivity and symmetry test performances, because equivalence classes are defined by congruent patterns of responding on all tests of equivalence properties (Sidman & Tailby, 1982). Thus, it seemed that the experimental strategy of attempting to disrupt equivalence classes might be useful in testing the nature and integrity of these emergent performances, and we have conducted several additional experiments to assess the generality of the preliminary findings just described.

Replication and extension of the effect

In one study (Pilgrim & Galizio, 1995) we tested college students and one high school student with procedural variations that allowed a greater number and variety of class challenges and more refined tests of class reorganization, and that addressed the possibility of extraneous sources of control in the previous procedures. Compared to our earlier work, a greater number of baseline conditional discriminations were trained (i.e., AC, BC, and AD), and therefore larger equivalence classes (four-member classes) were tested, prior to any baseline modifications. The structure of this training arrangement replicated that of a study in which transitivity patterns did change in keeping with baseline manipulations (Spradlin, Cotter, & Baxley, 1973). It also provided for a comparison of transitivity probes involving stimuli separated by one versus two training steps (or nodes; see Fields, Adams, Verhave, & Newman, 1990; Fields, Verhave, & Fath, 1984), thus providing a test for alternative forms of stimulus control that may have been induced by the reversal manipulations (see Carrigan & Sidman, 1992). In addition, the relation between probe practice and performance modification following reversal was assessed, because repeated practice of an emergent conditional discrimination prior to reversal might influence its probability following reversal. One transitivity probe type (CD/DC probes) was presented for the first time after the reversed baseline had been mastered, in order to test whether novel probes would be more likely than previously-presented ones to generate responses in keeping with the modified baseline.

An additional test for assessing the impact of baseline reversal on equivalence class reorganization was also studied. Following the AD reversal, a new, DE conditional discrimination was trained. The question of interest here involved how E stimuli would be

176 C. Pilgrim and M. Galizio

treated on transitivity probe trials. Given that E stimuli could only become class members via their relation to D stimuli, and given that the original AD relations had been reversed, performances on transitivity trials involving E stimuli provided an independent index of the relations between D stimuli and other class members. Finally, the larger classes established in this study allowed for a second baseline conditional discrimination (BC) to be reversed, and for probe trial arrangements that unambiguously distinguished between baseline-consistent class reorganization and simple disruption or reversal of all relations. Thus, the impact of a more extensively modified baseline on equivalence performances was assessed.

Results of Pilgrim and Galizio (1995) closely paralleled those of our first study. Trained conditional discriminations and symmetry-probe performances were extremely sensitive to reinforcement modifications, changing when, and only when, contingencies for the related baseline relations did. In contrast, patterns on transitivity probes showed little or no impact of baseline reversals and instead remained predominantly consistent with the originally established equivalence classes. Thus, the stability of transitivity patterns reported in our 1990 study could not be attributed to a particular training arrangement or class size, the ratio of changed to unchanged baseline relations that served as the context for testing, or practice on particular probe types prior to reversal manipulations.

In addition, Pilgrim and Galizio (1995) provided evidence that certain alternative forms of stimulus control were unlikely explanations for the effect. Carrigan and Sidman (1992) proposed an account of results like those from our reversal manipulation based on the fact that subjects can solve a two-choice match-to-sample problem by either *selecting* the correct comparison stimulus when presented with a sample (Type S or select relation) or by *rejecting* the incorrect comparison stimulus (Type R or reject). The two types of stimulus control would be indistinguishable for baseline or symmetry probe performances, but choices on reflexivity probe trials should differ, with Type S control generating identity matching performance (given A, choose A) and Type R generating a "non-match" pattern (given A, choose not-A). In the Pilgrim and Galizio (1990) study, reflexivity tests were given before and after the baseline reversal. The standard reflexivity pattern (identity matching) was observed in all conditions, so there was nothing to suggest that the reversal manipulations produced an overall switch to Type R control. However, interpretation of reflexivity performances can be ambiguous because differing stimulus control topographies can result in similar choice patterns (e.g., Saunders & Green, 1992).

Findings from Pilgrim and Galizio (1995) offer additional complications for an account of reversal effects based on a shift to Type R control. As with reflexivity tests, transitivity/ equivalence performances can also differentiate Type S from Type R control if the number of required nodes, or training stages, is odd (see Carrigan & Sidman, 1992; Johnson & Sidman, 1993). In the Pilgrim and Galizio study both 1- and 2-node transitivity probes were presented and there were no differences in performance between them either before or after baseline reversal. The absence of a "toggling" back and forth between original and reorganized transitivity performances with even and odd nodal distances is evidence against the notion that Type R stimulus control patterns of the sort proposed by Carrigan and Sidman (1992) emerged after baseline reversals. However, Carrigan and Sidman point out that because the reversal involved only one of the baseline conditional discriminations (AC relations in our studies), Type R control may have developed in that relation alone. In a case involving mixed stimulus control patterns, tests across the two types would be invalid indicators of transitivity/equivalence, and choice patterns would necessarily be determined by factors other than equivalence relations.

Interestingly, the results obtained here across subjects and studies were rather consistent for patterns that should be unrelated to equivalence. Although an a priori Type R account of these results is not easily specifiable, the possibility that baseline reversals generated a complex mixture of Type R and Type S control cannot be ruled out (Carrigan & Sidman, 1992; McIlvane, Kledaras, Munson, King, de Rose, & Sidman, 1987).

Taken together, these reversal data can and have been viewed as a potentially significant challenge to current theoretical formulations of equivalence (Carrigan & Sidman, 1992). More specifically, the dissociation between symmetry and transitivity patterns raises questions about the integrity of the equivalence phenomenon, as defined by cohesiveness among the properties of reflexivity, symmetry, and transitivity. How and why baseline reversals should impact equivalence properties differentially has yet to be satisfactorily explained, but the reported independence of symmetry and transitivity patterns under some conditions might signal caution in interpreting different probe performances as necessarily indicative of a single underlying, fundamental, or unified relation (i.e., equivalence). Similarly, the practice of inferring multiple equivalence properties (e.g., symmetry and transitivity) from performance on a single probe trial type (e.g., the combined test for equivalence) must be viewed with caution.

Other studies of baseline reversals

Reversal manipulations have been investigated by other equivalence researchers, with mixed results (see Spradlin, Saunders, & Saunders, 1992, for a review). In these studies, however, symmetry tests were either not presented (Saunders, Saunders, Kirby, and Spradlin, 1988; Spradlin, et al., 1973; Spradlin, et al., 1992) or not possible given the baseline (Dube, McIlvane, Maguire, Mackay, & Stoddard, 1989), so there are no other mentions in the literature of probe pattern dissociations such as those we reported. While a similar lack of correspondence between equivalence probe performances and reversed baseline relations has been described using somewhat different baseline procedures (Saunders, et al., 1988; Spradlin, et al., 1992), modified transitivity/equivalence patterns, in keeping with reversed baseline relations, have also been reported (Dube, et al., 1989; Saunders, et al., 1988; Spradlin, et al., 1973; Spradlin, et al., 1992).

These mixed findings suggest the need for research programs aimed at identifying the variables related to convergence versus dissociation between probe and baseline choice patterns.

Under what conditions are congruent choice patterns controlled? What sorts of variables give rise to the dissociation effect? We are currently conducting experiments designed to evaluate the impact of various subject and training variables on probe performances during reversal conditions. Pilot data and theoretical considerations have directed our initial efforts to examination of duration of exposure to original reinforcement contingencies, number of comparison stimuli presented per trial, magnitude of reinforcement for correct responses on baseline trials, and subject age.

Because reports of modified transitivity performances in reversal studies to date have all involved subject populations other than college students, we wondered whether young normally-capable children would show more or less sensitivity to the reversal of baseline discriminations (Pilgrim, Chambers, & Galizio, 1995). In a relatively straightforward systematic replication of Pilgrim & Galizio (1990), children (5-7 years old) learned two conditional discriminations (i.e., AB and AC) and showed the emergence of two three-member equivalence classes (A1B1C1 and A2B2C2). Figure 2 shows baseline performances for four of the children. The leftmost panels show the final sessions of the original training which were marked by stable, accurate performances. Because preliminary studies showed that children had difficultly mastering

178

C. Pilgrim and M. Galizio

reversals in the context of intermixed baseline and probe trial types, AC reversals were trained in a restricted context of only AC trials. Accurate baseline responding persisted when the unchanged AB trial types and probe trials were added to the sessions (AB/AC MIX; REV-FULL). Note that in the full reversal conditions (REV-FULL) all four children were responding with the original pattern on AB trials and in accord with the reversed AC contingencies on virtually 100% of the AC trials. When original reinforcement contingencies were reinstated (OR-Full, rightmost panels), original response patterns were re-established in all cases. Thus, baseline performances were sensitive to reversals of the AC contingencies when the reversals were introduced in restricted baselines (i.e., AC trials only).

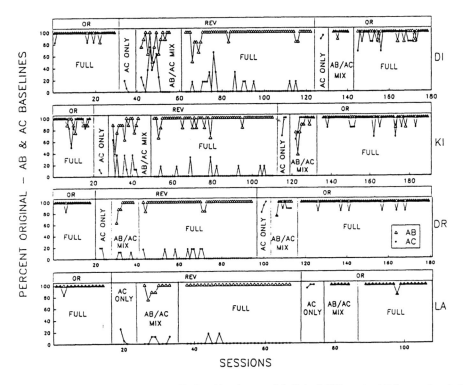

Figure 2. Children's performances from Pilgrim, Chambers, and Galizio (1995) on the AB (open triangles) and AC (filled circles) baseline conditional discrimination trials of each session. Consecutive sessions are represented on the horizontal axis. The vertical axis represents the percentage of 6 AB or AC baseline trials on which responses were consistent with the original training contingencies.

On reflexivity, symmetry, and transitivity probes following the reversal, the predominant pattern across probe trials was one of inconsistent conditional control (i.e., choice of comparison stimulus was no longer controlled by the sample stimulus). Figure 3 shows CA symmetry performances for the five children. Note that symmetry patterns emerged for each subject during the original reinforcement condition (OR). After reversal (REV), responding became inconsistent

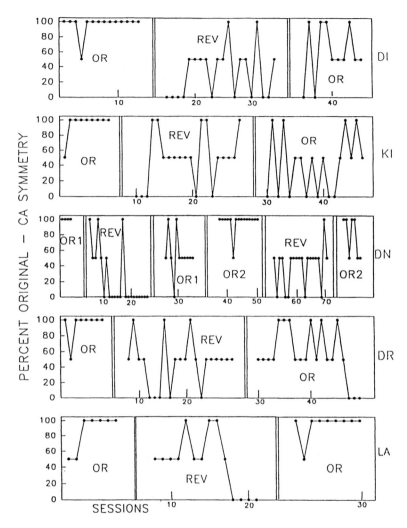

Figure 3. Children's performances on the two CA symmetry probe trials of every symmetry test session. Consecutive symmetry test sessions are represented on the horizontal axis. The vertical axis represents the percentage of CA probe trials on which responses were consistent with the equivalence classes established by the original training contingencies. Double vertical lines indicate intervening training sessions that did not include probe trials.

and in some cases, remained inconsistent when original contingencies were reinstated. Importantly, responding on BA symmetry trials was also disrupted after reversals for 3 of 5 subjects even though the trained (and stable) AB discriminations were unchanged, and reflexivity probe performances were also disrupted for 3 of the subjects. Figure 4 shows responding on transitivity probe trials. Again, the expected emergent patterns were seen with all 5 subjects

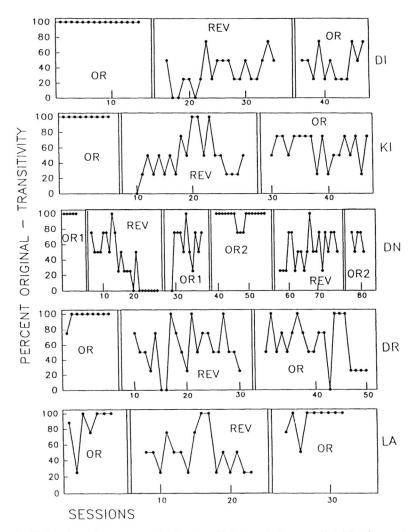

Figure 4. Children's performances on the four transitivity/ equivalence probe trials of every transitivity test session. Consecutive transitivity test sessions are represented on the horizontal axis. The vertical axis represents the percentage of transitivity/equivalence probe trials on which responses were consistent with the equivalence classes established by the original training contingencies. Double vertical lines indicate intervening training sessions that did not include probe trials.

during original conditions, but responding became inconsistent after the reversal. Thus, while baseline discriminations came under the control of reversed contingencies, children's probe trial performances generally became erratic across all probe trial types. There was some limited indication of equivalence class reorganization in keeping with the new baseline for two of the subjects: LA and DN. Because these were two of the older subjects in the sample, the possibility of developmental trends is suggested.

These findings suggest that, given similar challenges, equivalence class performances may be more easily disrupted in young children than in adults, and that the study of young children may provide a promising opportunity for empirical evaluation of variables that contribute to the stability of probe performances. However, these results were similar to those of the adults (Pilgrim & Galizio, 1990; 1995) in demonstrating a discrepancy between the choice patterns shown on probe trials and those performed concurrently on the prerequisite baseline conditional discriminations.

Other studies of the variables that may influence baseline reversal effects are underway. Although these experiments are not complete, we have obtained some intriguing preliminary findings. Figure 5 shows transitivity/equivalence performances of four subjects, chosen to illustrate the point that several different patterns of responding are possible after reversals. The top left panels show data from Subject 1 after a relatively brief exposure to original reinforcement conditions (12 baseline trial blocks with probes as compared to the typical 40 or more in our earlier work). After AB and AC discrimination training, BC and CB transitivity/equivalence patterns emerged rapidly and became stable until the AC reversal was performed. At that time, Subject 1 showed an immediate change in transitivity performance that stabilized with virtually no "original" responding. Baseline, symmetry and transitivity performances were all consistent with reorganized classes, A1B1C2 and A2B2C1. This subject thus represents the first adult from our laboratory with postreversal performances suggesting class reorganization. We suspect that the abbreviated training phase was important in this case,

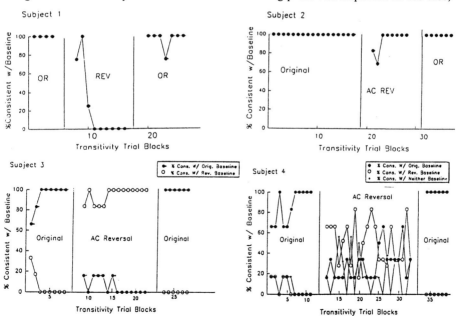

Figure 5. Performances of four subjects on transitivity probe trial blocks. The vertical axis represents, for each trial block, the percentage of trials on which responses were consistent with the equivalence classes established by the original training contingencies. For Subject 1 original training involved two, three member classes (2-choice), while Subjects 2-4 were trained on three, three-member classes (3-choice).

because other experimental conditions closely replicated those of our earlier work (e.g., 2 comparison choices, $.01 per token payoff, etc.).

The next panels of Figure 5 show performances from three subjects whose training followed the general outlines described above but involved three, three-member classes (A1B1C1, A2B2C2, A3B3C3). Subject 2 was exposed to the original training conditions for an amount of time more analogous to that arranged in our earlier studies (i.e., 45 trial blocks), while Subjects 3 and 4 received relatively brief exposure (approximately 20 trial blocks). In addition, reinforcer magnitude was increased (from $.01 to $.02) for Subject 3. Once the baselines were mastered and equivalence classes demonstrated, reinforcement contingencies were modified for one of the baseline conditional discriminations (i.e., from A1-C1, A2-C2, A3-C3 to A1-C2, A2-C3, A3-C1).

As in our previous work, baseline and symmetry performances for these subjects changed rapidly and in keeping with the contingency manipulation. However, responses on transitivity probes were interesting and varied. Figure 5 shows the data of one subject (S2) whose performance following extended exposure to original conditions reproduced that noted in our earlier work with two comparison stimuli; stable transitivity patterns were consistent with those exhibited prior to the contingency change. Subject S3, however, for whom reinforcer magnitude had been increased and exposure to original conditions shortened, showed a reorganization of transitivity patterns like those shown by S1. Finally, after brief exposure to original conditions, Subject S4 showed a disruption of responding with no consistent pattern emerging even after extended testing. Although this subject's performance is similar in some ways to that of the children during reversal conditions, it should be noted that choice patterns became stable and consistent with the baseline relations upon return to original conditions. While a Type R influence cannot be completely ruled out by these data (Reject relations might still be possible, if unlikely, with 3 comparison choices), other training parameters (e.g., duration of exposure to original conditions) certainly take on weight as possible contributors to the variability in reversal condition patterns.

These preliminary findings suggest to us that the determinants of probe patterns following the modification of baseline conditional discriminations will prove to be multiple and complex. On the one hand, this conclusion may be self-evident; performances established and maintained under extinction conditions seem likely to be under weak control and subject to many influences. Still, this same point must be true of probe patterns as they emerge initially, and when contingencies are returned to their original condition, yet the patterns there are orderly, and consistent with available accounts of equivalence in a straightforward way. Thus, a continued search for order in the workings of reversal patterns seems prudent.

At the present though, a point to be reckoned with is that baseline, reflexivity, symmetry, and transitivity/equivalence probe patterns can become inconsistent with each other under some conditions. One possibility worth consideration is that, given the right circumstances (i.e., baseline reversals), these operationally distinct stimulus-control relations may have the capacity to become independent units. Certainly, it would seem that variables other than the current baseline conditional discriminations help to determine probe trial patterns under reversal conditions. Other authors have noted that probe patterns may become independent of the baselines from which they emerge (e.g., Saunders, et al., 1988; Spradlin, et al., 1992). The dissociation of baseline/symmetry and transitivity/equivalence seen in some of our studies may suggest that the independence can go a step further. When the integrity of one component of a behavioral complex is unaffected by alterations in another, we often conclude that the complex consisted of a correspondence between multiple, smaller behavioral units (e.g., Catania, 1992).

OTHER COMPARISONS OF PROBE TRIAL TYPES

The discrepancies noted between choice patterns on the various probe and baseline trial types following conditional discrimination reversals appeared to have some generality. In this context, it also seems interesting to consider cases in which different probe trial types give rise to reliable performance differences under non-reversal conditions. While the comparison selections on probe trial types typically co-vary in non-reversal conditions, thus providing the defining measure of equivalence, there are indications that the different tests may reveal unique response characteristics.

Delayed emergence

One example is provided by the frequently reported finding of delayed emergence (e.g, Spradlin, Cotter, & Baxley, 1973); that is, for many subjects in equivalence experiments, performances on probe trials do not become consistent with the predicted equivalence classes without repeated probe testing. For present purposes, the relation of interest lies in the fact that when delayed emergence is reported, the temporal order in which class-consistent patterns emerge for different probe trial types is often very predictable, with symmetry patterns emerging before transitivity or equivalence patterns (e.g., Bush, Sidman, & de Rose, 1989; Dube, Green, & Serna, 1993; Fields, et al., 1990; Kennedy, 1991; Sidman, Kirk, & Willson-Morris, 1985; Sidman, Willson-Morris, & Kirk, 1986), and transitivity/equivalence relations involving a small number of nodal stimuli emerging prior to those involving a greater number (e.g., Dube, et al., 1993; Fields, et al., 1990; Kennedy, 1991).

In some cases, symmetry patterns have been repeatedly demonstrated with no evidence of transitivity/equivalence until many trials of those test types are presented (e.g., Bush, et al., 1989). In our laboratory over the past two years, we have seen 7 subjects who failed to show evidence of transitivity/equivalence even after extended exposure to those probe trials (10 - 27 trial blocks with 6-8 probe trials per block), despite consistently demonstrating symmetry patterns. While it could not be safely argued that these subjects would never have shown equivalence, their performances suggest an independence of symmetry and transitivity patterns. Collectively, these data might be interpreted as indicative of differential emergence of equivalence-defining properties. Descriptions (e.g., Sidman, et al., 1985; Sidman, et al., 1986) of certain emergent performances (e.g., symmetry) as "prerequisite" to the demonstration of others (e.g., equivalence) also imply that these properties may not emerge as an integrated unit.

Reaction time measures

A second measure revealing of performance differences across probe trial types is reaction time or latency to make a comparison choice. Although training, testing, and measurement procedures have varied, latencies to respond on trained discriminations or symmetry trials have reliably proven to be shorter than the latencies shown on transitivity and equivalence trials, at least during initial testing (Bentall, Dickins, & Fox, 1993) and in some cases, even after class-consistent response patterns had been well-demonstrated on all probe types (Spencer & Chase, in press; Wulfert & Hayes, 1988). Across studies, mean latencies on symmetry tests trials have been consistently longer than those for trained relations (at least with unfamiliar stimuli), although these differences were significant only in the Spencer and Chase study (in press). A number of theorists have noted the relation between fluency, or response speed, and the long-term maintenance of behaviors established in educational settings (e.g., Johnson & Layng, 1992;

Spencer & Chase, in press). Thus, these reaction time data might be seen as indicating that the trial types typically used to define equivalence can give rise to performances that differ in potentially important ways.

Reinforcer estimation

Another interesting example of differences in performance across probe trial types comes from a novel procedure that we have been exploring. As the final step of their experimental participation, we asked subjects from our research on equivalence class formation to provide retrospective reinforcer frequency estimates for each of the trial types that had been presented. Subjects were instructed to: "Look at each {stimulus} arrangement and make an estimate of the percentage of times a white token would be available for each of the choices. Your estimate could range from 0% if you think that a white token was never available, up to 100% if you think that a white token was always available." The experimenter then presented an intermixed succession of each of the trial types that had been programmed during training and testing. A frequency estimation was recorded for each possible choice on each trial type.

We have collected reinforcer estimation data from 30 subjects. Fourteen subjects were exposed to a single set of baseline relations and probe trials prior to the estimation task. The other 16 subjects completed the task at the conclusion of experiments involving reversals and return to baseline contingencies. On both baseline and probe trial types, these subjects based estimations on the original baseline conditions, which were also the conditions encountered immediately before the estimation session. Figure 6 shows mean estimates for all subjects for correct or class-consistent relations, and Table 1 summarizes individual subject data on all relations.

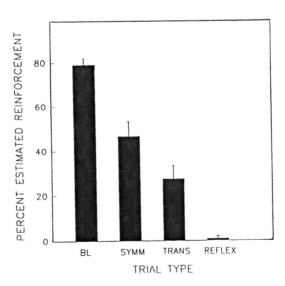

Figure 6. Mean percent estimated reinforcement for all subjects plotted as a function of trial type (baseline-BL, symmetry-symm, transitivity-trans, and reflexivity-reflex).

Table 1
Percentage Reinforcement Estimated for Various Trial Types in Subjects With and Without Reversals.

Subject	Correct/Class Consistent Choice				Incorrect/Class Inconsistent Choice			
	BL	Sym	Trans	Reflex	BL	Sym	Trans	Reflex
No Reversal Subjects								
1	56	54	21	*	6	0	0	*
2	90	90	90	*	0	0	0	*
3	69	59	2	*	0	0	0	*
4	100	100	100	*	0	0	0	*
5	100	100	100	*	0	0	0	*
6	68	35	0	*	3	0	0	*
7	75	71	50	*	0	0	0	*
8	83	83	26	*	0	0	0	*
9	98	99	0	*	0	0	0	*
10	84	0	0	0	0	0	0	0
11	71	20	59	13	0	0	0	0
12	79	0	0	0	0	0	0	0
13	94	95	50	*	6	0	9	*
14	95	82	0	0	0	0	0	0
Reversal Subjects								
15	75	79	80	0	0	0	0	0
16	100	17	50	0	0	0	0	0
17	67	8	5	*	0	0	0	*
18	80	0	0	*	0	0	0	*
19	78	63	29	*	17	8	0	*
20	53	0	0	0	25	0	0	0
21	50	75	38	0	0	0	0	0
22	68	25	0	0	13	6	0	0
23	65	73	23	0	23	0	0	0
24	75	43	14	0	0	0	0	0
25	75	0	0	0	0	0	0	0
26	88	0	0	0	0	0	0	0
27	100	80	50	0	0	0	0	0
28	85	0	0	0	0	0	0	0
29	53	43	36	*	0	0	0	*
30	100	0	0	0	25	0	0	0

* No reflexivity probes administered

Not surprisingly, the highest estimates were given on baseline trial presentations, with the mean of about 80% only slightly above the actual experiment-wise reinforcer probability (approximately 75%) for those trials. A striking feature of the results was that subjects estimated frequent reinforcement for class-consistent symmetry and transitivity/equivalence probe trial choices. Despite the fact that reinforcers were never available on probe trials, estimates ranged as high as 100% on both symmetry and transitivity probe trial presentations. In contrast, 12 of the 14 subjects who received reflexivity trials discriminated them (i.e., gave estimates of 0%). Repeated measures ANOVA and Tukey's post hoc tests revealed significant differences overall and between all pairs of baseline, symmetry and transitivity trial types (F (2, 56)= 37.8, p < .01). Higher estimates were given for baseline trial types than for symmetry trials, which in turn generated higher estimates than transitivity/equivalence trials. (Reflexivity trial types were excluded from the statistical analysis because all but 2 subjects gave estimates of zero.) This same pattern was evident in the estimates given by 18 of the 22 individual subjects who did not give uniformly low (0% - 8 subjects) or high (90% or greater - 4 subjects) estimates on every probe trial.

Table 1 presents individual subject estimates and shows that subjects rarely estimated reinforcement for incorrect or class-inconsistent comparison choices. That most subjects assigned non-zero values to class-consistent choices on symmetry and transitivity probes raises questions about the control of responding on probe trials. However, an important point with regard to equivalence theory is that baseline, symmetry, transitivity, and reflexivity trial arrangements generated clearly differentiated responses for most subjects. Thus these data provide another instance of "non-equivalence" across the trial types that define equivalence classes.

It has been argued that effects like those just described (sometimes termed nodal distance; e.g., Fields, Adams, & Verhave, 1993; Fields, et al., 1990; Fields, Newman, Adams, & Verhave, 1993; Fields, et al., 1984; or nodal number effects; e.g, Sidman, 1994) imply limits to the substitutability, or differences in the relatedness of stimuli comprising an equivalence class. One possibility that we would like to consider is that such arguments may be confusing substitutability of stimuli within a class and the substitutability of the tests used to evaluate equivalence. Perhaps what these data offer is confirmation that reflexivity, symmetry, and transitivity/equivalence tests are different from each other. Even when these performances are viewed as indicative of a single, more general, and integrated relation (e.g., equivalence), the properties being evaluated are distinct, both conceptually and operationally. (If they were not, multiple test types would be unnecessary.) Thus, the test types are not all "equivalent" to one another, and the various performances that these test types control illustrate that point.

More challenging for current views of equivalence are the indications that probe performances, ostensibly indicative of a single equivalence class, may participate in very different functional relations, and that they may sometimes vary independently. A number of theorists (e.g., Hayes, 1991; Sidman, 1994) have emphasized that members of an equivalence class need not, and perhaps cannot be equivalent along every dimension. Rather, they need only be equivalent in terms of the dimension that defines the class, the basis for the class partition, and context determines when functions will be shared. However, it remains unclear how this feature of class membership might be immediately applicable to the orderly differences that occur within a single context for delayed emergence, latency, or estimation. These cases are particularly interesting because the defining requirements for a given equivalence relation can be satisfied, yet response functions vary with probe type. Again, it seems useful to consider whether such findings may not be indicative of independent stimulus-control relations.

The data reviewed to this point have been focused on comparing performances across the different probe trial types used to measure equivalence. We have argued that such comparisons raise some important issues for a view of the equivalence relation as an integrated behavioral unit. To be explained are the observations that the defining components of a single unit can function independently in some circumstances. There is another case in which it seems important to examine closely the correspondence between measures of equivalence. This second and complementary approach to the study of equivalence will take the form of comparing probe trial performances with different measures of "equivalence-like" phenomena.

CONVERGENT VALIDITY WITH RESPECT TO MEASURE OF EQUIVALENCE

Most theoretical interpretations of stimulus equivalence emphasize that equivalence classes formed in the laboratory provide a useful model of natural language categories. In fact, many features of natural language classes do seem nicely modeled by findings from equivalence studies. Particularly important examples are provided by research emphasizing the impressive generative nature of equivalence classes (e.g., Dube, et al., 1989; Saunders, et al., 1988; Saunders, Wachter, & Spradlin, 1988; Sidman, et al., 1985; Sidman & Tailby, 1982), their capacity for contextual control (e.g., Bush, et al., 1989; Kennedy & Laitinen, 1988; Lynch & Green, 1991; Wulfert, Greenway, & Dougher, 1994), their approximation of syntactic relations (e.g., Green, Sigurdardottir, & Saunders, 1991; Lazar, 1977; Sidman, 1992; Sigurdardottir, Green, & Saunders, 1990), and their characteristic transfer of function, whereby new functions established for one member of a class emerge for all members of the class (e.g., Barnes & Keenan, 1993; Dougher & Markam, 1994; Hayes, Kohlenberg, & Hayes, 1991). Indeed, analogies drawn between stimulus equivalence and other complex human abilities more traditionally called cognitive have become increasingly common. Examples include equivalence as a model for categorization (e.g., Bush, et al., 1989, Wulfert & Hayes, 1988), rule following (Hayes, Thompson, & Hayes, 1989), social stereotyping (e.g., Kohlenberg, Hayes, & Hayes, 1991), and the spread of conditioned emotional responses (Dougher, Augustson, Markham, Greenway, & Wulfert, 1994).

However, it seems likely that researchers from disciplines outside of behavior analysis might find our analogies between equivalence and language or other cognitive abilities unconvincing. Although arbitrary match-to-sample procedures are commonly used in the laboratory, their immediate application to many important naturally-occurring behavior patterns that might involve equivalence-like processes is sometimes strained. Further, very different strategies have been used by cognitive and developmental psychologists to make inferences about the phenomena that equivalence has been said to "explain." Direct comparisons between the primary literatures are difficult and infrequent. It seems possible that empirical work on equivalence would enjoy broader attention if the relations between our literature and that of more traditional psychological approaches were clarified.

For example, the reinforcer estimation measures described earlier might be seen as consistent with classic studies of semantic memory (e.g., Bransford & Franks, 1971). In studies of incidental learning, sentence recognition was determined more by whether a given sentence was consistent with the derived theme of a story, than whether it had, in fact, been presented. In the same sense, our subjects' reinforcer estimations were controlled more by equivalence-class consistency than by whether reinforcers had actually been presented. Comparison choices on probe trials that had never been reinforced were likely to occasion non-zero reinforcement estimates if they were class-consistent. These sorts of similarities have led us to further analysis of techniques outside the traditions of behavior analysis.

In order to provide more direct comparison with other literatures, our laboratory has begun to collect one or more "nontraditional" measures in addition to the standard tests of equivalence classes as part of our ongoing work on class formation and modification. In some cases, these measures are taken during the subject's exit session, as a final step in their experimental participation. In other cases, these measures have been the focus of experimental inquiry in their own right.

Stimulus sorting

One commonly used measure of categorization or concept formation involves the simple sorting of objects or pictures (e.g., Ludvigson & Caul, 1964; Rosch & Mervis, 1977), but this assessment technique has received little attention in studies of stimulus equivalence (cf., Green, 1990). Because some of our work has been conducted with abstract 3-dimensional objects, we were able to use this feature to obtain measures of stimulus sorting. Forty-seven college students were randomly assigned to one of two experimental groups (n = 16 in each) or a control group (n = 15). Subjects in the control group received no training. Subjects in the experimental groups learned 3 two-choice conditional discriminations (AB, BC, and AD) to mastery (14 of 16 trials correct for two consecutive trial blocks, with no more than one error on any trial type). No probe trials were presented. All subjects were given the Stimulus Sorting Task. One experimental group and the control group sorted all 8 of the stimuli presented during training. The second experimental group sorted only 6 of the stimuli (B, C, and D stimuli; the "nodal" A stimuli were omitted). Subjects were instructed to: "Please place these objects into groups, whatever groups you think are most appropriate." An experimenter recorded the groupings when the subject indicated that they had finished.

Nine of the 16 subjects in each of the experimental conditions sorted stimuli into groupings consistent with the equivalence classes that would be predicted, given the trained baseline relations (Figure 7); that is, all stimuli from each class were physically placed together and distanced from the stimuli in each of the other classes. None of the 15 control subjects sorted stimuli into class-consistent groupings (Figure 7). A 2 x 3 chi square analysis revealed significant differences between experimental and control conditions (p < .01).

With respect to measures of sorting then, performances following conditional discrimination training appeared to be consistent with the formation of equivalence classes, and with data from studies of categorization and concept formation. These data also indicate that exposure to probe trials was not required in order to see evidence of class formation as measured by sorting, although it may help. In a recently completed study, a greater percentage of subjects (32 of 37) demonstrated class-consistent groupings after, as compared to before, experience with probe trials. Still, sorting might prove a useful alternative to consider when questions arise concerning an active or instructive role for probe trials in the emergence of equivalence relations (e.g., Sidman, 1990). Importantly, class-consistent sorting in the absence of nodal stimuli supports the possibility that the sorting measure can reveal derived relations (i.e., BD/DB relations in this case), and not just directly trained stimulus pairs.

Stimulus recall

Bousfield (1953) showed that when subjects were presented with words belonging to separate semantic categories prior to a free recall task, the words were recalled in clusters reflecting category membership regardless of the order of their original presentation. Category

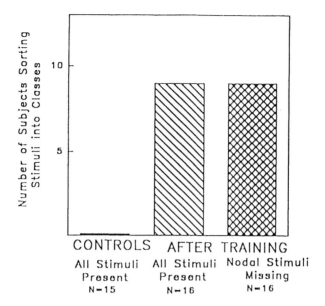

Figure 7. Number of subjects from each group who sorted stimuli in class-consistent groupings.

clustering in free recall has proven to be a highly robust effect, typically interpreted as a reflection of semantic organization in retrieval (e.g., Broadbent, Cooper, & Broadbent, 1978; Bower, Clark, Lesgold, & Winzenz, 1969). If equivalence classes function similarly to natural language categories, one might expect to observe class clustering in the free recall of equivalence class members. We tested this possibility by including recall tests in our studies of equivalence class formation.

In a preliminary study similar in design to the sorting experiment described above, 18 experimental subjects (college students) were taught 3 conditional discriminations (AB, BC, and AD) with abstract stimuli on a two-choice match-to-sample task, in order to establish the basis for two four-member equivalence classes. A test for stimulus recall immediately followed mastery of the baseline training. For the Recall Task, subjects were told, "Now we would like to see how well you can remember the objects that have been used in this experiment. Please tell me all of the objects that you can remember." No mention of a recall test had been made prior to these instructions. The experimenter recorded each stimulus description in order. Fifteen control subjects received the recall test after being exposed to the same conditional discrimination "training" procedures, except that no feedback of any type was provided. This control condition was designed to equate exposure to stimuli, without providing a basis for the acquisition of conditional discriminations.

Recall data are described as the number of changes from one class to another in the sequence of recalled stimuli (i.e., number of changeovers). The minimum number of changeovers for a sequence showing perfect clustering, as described by Bousfield and others, would be one for this training arrangement (e.g., recall of all 4 Class 1 stimuli, followed by recall of all 4 Class

2 stimuli). The mean number of changeovers for these control subjects was 3.6 (see Table 2). Two subjects in the experimental group recalled stimuli with the minimum number of changeovers possible, thus showing perfect clustering for all stimuli that were recalled (6 and 7 stimuli out of 8 for the 2 subjects). However, mean number of changeovers for the experimental subjects was exactly that of the controls, 3.6.

Table 2
Means and Ranges of Changeovers and Number of Stimuli Recalled for Control and Experimental Subjects.

	Mean # of Changeovers	Range	Mean # of Stimuli Recalled	Range
Control Subjects	3.6	2-6	7.3	5-8
Experimental Subjects	3.6	1-5	7.0	3-8

Thus, where stimulus sorting was generally consistent with conditional discrimination training and probe performances, this was true only infrequently for stimulus recall, and may stand in contrast to classic recall findings involving verbal categories (e.g., Bousfield, 1953). While equivalence clustering might be obtained given different testing conditions or contextual cues, it occurred only rarely under conditions analogous to those used during tests of verbal recall. Although no consistent, competing pattern (e.g., clustering by contiguously-presented comparison arrays) was evident across subjects, it is possible that recall was influenced by stimulus dimensions extraneous to class membership. It is interesting and worthy of further investigation that this should be the case for recall and not for the other equivalence measures, even for the same subject. Of course, an alternative interpretation is that the classic clustering phenomenon is influenced by variables other than category membership and worthy of further analysis in its own right.

Thus, we have seen that the measures typically used by behavior analysts to make inferences about equivalence relations are usually, but not always, internally consistent. Similarly, comparison of our standard equivalence measures and those preferred in other disciplines can often, but not always, provide good face validity. It seems important to recognize and deal with these complexities, in order to advance our own understanding and to reach audiences outside of behavior analysis.

SUMMARY AND CONCLUSIONS

This chapter has encouraged consideration of the possibility that the three defining properties of equivalence, reflexivity, symmetry, and transitivity, may represent independent stimulus-control relations (or stimulus control topographies; McIlvane & Dube, 1992). At first glance this suggestion might seem a somewhat radical departure from current views of equivalence, but after careful consideration, we will argue here that it is not. In fact, the mathematical definition of equivalence specifies only required test outcomes, not the make-up of the behavioral unit(s) that include these outcomes. The predictive value of the set theory framework is undeniable, and the structured approach that this framework has provided for study and training of complex behavioral repertoires (often termed cognitive) has yielded impressive results. Rather than reject this framework, we have explored a possible friendly amendment based on recognition of the limiting cases for which set theory does not provide clear predictions. A definition of equivalence that allowed for correspondence among three independent stimulus-control relations might provide even greater generality, while maintaining the precision and rigor of the set theory framework.

Such a conceptual modification might also provide for new focus on empirical avenues that have received little emphasis to date. Most importantly, the view described here would command attention to issues of why independent stimulus-control relations should show such remarkable consistency in so many contexts with human subjects. Behavior analysts have emphasized close correspondence between other types of operant classes (e.g., the correspondence between what we say and what we do; Catania, 1992; Catania, Lowe, & Horne, 1990), with important implications for both practical (e.g., Risley & Hart, 1968; Rogers-Warren & Baer, 1976) and theoretical (e.g., Catania, Matthews, & Shimoff, 1982; Matthews, Shimoff, & Catania, 1987; Matthews, Shimoff, Catania, & Sagvolden, 1977) enterprises. Interestingly, renewed attempts to identify the histories and current variables necessary for consistency across relations would help to address an issue that often seems neglected or avoided with respect to equivalence performances. Although the properties of equivalence specified by set theory must be congruent by definition, few accounts have made explicit statements about why or how that consistency comes to be. Where the equivalence relation is seen as a unified, integrated given, whether a frame or a fundamental stimulus function, the properties of reflexivity, symmetry, and transitivity are sometimes treated as logical necessities of that relation, rather than as discriminated operants requiring explanation in their own right. Consistency across performances on the now-standard test trial types would appear to be an appropriate target for increased empirical attention.

Other interesting implications follow from the view that equivalence involves correspondence among independent stimulus-control relations. Notably, a number of studies of non-human species and derived stimulus relations have revealed suggestive evidence for some subset of the defining equivalence properties (e.g., transitivity but not symmetry; D'Amato & Colombo, 1986; D'Amato, Salmon, Loukas, & Tomie, 1985; reflexivity - e.g., Pack, Herman, & Roitblat, 1991; Zentall & Hogan, 1974; symmetry - e.g., Tomonaga, Matsuzawa, Fujita, & Yamamoto, 1991; Zentall, Sherburne, & Steirn, 1992; transitivity - e.g., Steirn, Jackson-Smith & Zentall, 1991) or for other signs of emergent stimulus relations (e.g., Fersen, Wynn, Delius, & Staddon, 1991; McGonigle & Chalmers, 1977). If equivalence properties are separable relations, it may be unwise to consider these findings from animal subjects as extraneous to equivalence processes. Indeed, investigations involving cases where equivalence properties are not all consistent may be the most likely to reveal variables critical for equivalence-defining correspondences.

A second important caution also follows from our analysis. At least one reason that behavior analysts have found equivalence research attractive lies in the experimental approach it affords the study of complex behavioral repertoires traditionally placed within the cognitive domain. Despite the many advantages of this approach, the findings reviewed here suggest that we not become overzealous in attempts to account for complex human skills and abilities in terms of any single process. Still, successes to date warrant continued experimental analysis of the fit between the laboratory model of equivalence and important psychological functions. Investigating the multiple determinants of probe trial correspondences may very well shed light on the phenomena studied by our cognitive colleagues.

REFERENCES

Barnes, D., & Keenan, M. (1993). A transfer of functions through derived arbitrary and nonarbitrary stimulus relations. *Journal of the Experimental Analysis of Behavior, 59*, 61-81.

Bentall, R.P., Dickins, D.W., & Fox, S.R.A. (1993). Naming and equivalence: Response latencies for emergent relations. *Quarterly Journal of Experimental Psychology, 46B*, (May), 187-214.

Bousfield, W.A. (1953). The occurrence of clustering in recall of randomly arranged associates. *Journal of General Psychology, 49*, 229-240.

Bower, G.H., Clark, M.C., Lesgold, A.M., & Winzenz, D. (1969). Hierarchical retrieval schemes in recall of categorized word lists. *Journal of Verbal Learning and Verbal Behavior, 8*, 323-343.

Bransford, J.D., & Franks, J.J. (1971). Abstraction of linguistic ideas. *Cognitive Psychology, 2*, 331-350.

Broadbent, D.E., Cooper, P.J., & Broadbent, M.H.P. (1978). A comparison of hierarchical and matrix retrieval schemes in recall. *Journal of Experimental Psychology: Human Learning and Memory, 4*, 486-497.

Bush, K.M., Sidman, M., & de Rose, T. (1989). Contextual control of emergent equivalence relations. *Journal of the Experimental Analysis of Behavior, 51*, 29-45.

Carrigan, P.F., Jr., & Sidman, M. (1992). Conditional discrimination and equivalence relations: A theoretical analysis of control by negative stimuli. *Journal of the Experimental Analysis of Behavior, 58*, 459-504.

Catania, A.C. (1992). *Learning* (3rd ed.). Englewood Cliffs, NJ: Prentice Hall, Inc.

Catania, A.C., Lowe, C.F., & Horne, P. (1990). Nonverbal behavior correlated with the shaped verbal behavior of children. *Analysis of Verbal Behavior, 8*, 43-55.

Catania, A.C., Matthews, B.A., & Shimoff, E. (1982). Instructed versus shaped human verbal behavior: Interactions with nonverbal responding. *Journal of the Experimental Analysis of Behavior, 38*, 233-248.

D'Amato, M.R., & Colombo, M. (1985). Auditory matching-to-sample in monkeys (*Cebus apella*). *Animal Learning and Behavior, 13*, 375-382.

D'Amato, M.R., Salmon, D., Loukas, E., & Tomie, A. (1985). Symmetry and transitivity of conditional relations in monkeys (*Cebus apella*) and pigeons (*Columba livia*). *Journal of the Experimental Analysis of Behavior, 44*, 35-47.

Dougher, M.J., Augustson, E.M., Markham, M.R., Wulfert, E., & Greenway, D.E. (1994). The transfer of respondent eliciting and extinction functions through stimulus equivalence classes. *Journal of the Experimental Analysis of Behavior, 62*, 331-351.

Dougher, M.J., & Markham, M.R. (1994). Stimulus equivalence, functional equivalence, and the transfer of function. In Hayes, S.C., Hayes, L.J., Sato, M., & Ono, K. (Eds.), *Behavior analysis of language and cognition* (pp. 71-90). Reno, NV: Context Press.

Dube, W.V., Green, G., & Serna, R.W. (1993). Auditory successive conditional discrimination and auditory stimulus equivalence classes. *Journal of the Experimental Analysis of Behavior, 59,* 103-114.

Dube, W.V., McIlvane, W.J., Maguire, R.W., Mackay, H.A., & Stoddard, L.T. (1989). Stimulus class formation and stimulus-reinforcer relations. *Journal of the Experimental Analysis of Behavior, 47,* 159-175

Fersen, L. von, Wynne, C.D.L., Delius, J.D., & Staddon, J.E.R. (1991). Transitive inference formation in pigeons. *Journal of Experimental Psychology: Animal Behavior Processes, 17,* 334-341.

Fields, L., Adams, B.J., & Verhave, T. (1993). The effects of equivalence class structure on test performances. *Psychological Record,* 43, 697-712.

Fields, L., Adams, B.J., Verhave, T., & Newman, S. (1990). The effects of nodality on the formation of equivalence classes. *Journal of the Experimental Analysis of Behavior, 53,* 345-358.

Fields, L., Newman, S., Adams, B.J., & Verhave, T. (1993). Are stimuli in equivalence classes equally related? *Psychological Record, 43,* 85-106.

Fields, L., Verhave, T., & Fath, S. (1984). Stimulus equivalence and transitive associations: A methodological analysis. *Journal of the Experimental Analysis of Behavior, 42,* 143-157.

Green, G. (1990). Differences in development of visual and auditory-visual equivalence relations. *American Journal on Mental Retardation, 95,* 260-270.

Green, G., Sigurdardottir, Z.G., & Saunders, R.R. (1991). The role of instructions in the transfer of ordinal functions through equivalence classes. *Journal of the Experimental Analysis of Behavior, 55,* 287-304.

Hayes, L.J., Thompson, S., & Hayes, S.C. (1989). Stimulus equivalence and rule following. *Journal of the Experimental Analysis of Behavior, 52,* 369-378.

Hayes, S.C. (1991). A relational control theory of stimulus equivalence. In L.J. Hayes & P.N. Chase (Eds.), *Dialogues on verbal behavior* (pp. 19-40). Reno, NV: Context Press.

Hayes, S.C., Kohlenberg, B.S., & Hayes, L.J. (1991). The transfer of specific and general consequential functions through simple and conditional equivalence relations. *Journal of the Experimental Analysis of Behavior, 56,* 119-137.

Johnson, K.R., & Layng, T.V.J. (1992). Breaking the structuralist barrier: Literacy and numeracy with fluency. *American Psychologist, 47,* 1475-1490.

Johnson, C., & Sidman, M. (1993). Conditional discrimination and equivalence relations: Control by negative stimuli. *Journal of the Experimental Analysis of Behavior, 59,* 333-347.

Kennedy, C.H. (1991). Equivalence class formation influenced by the number of nodes separating stimuli. *Behavioural Processes, 24,* 219-245.

Kennedy, C.H., & Laitinen, R. (1988). Second-order conditional control of symmetric and transitive stimulus relations: The influence of order effect. *Psychological Record, 38,* 437-446.

Kohlenberg, B.S., Hayes, S.C., & Hayes, L.J. (1991). The transfer of contextual control over equivalence classes through equivalence classes: A possible model of social stereotyping. *Journal of the Experimental Analysis of Behavior, 56,* 505-518.

Lakoff, G. (1987). *Women, fire, and dangerous things.* Chicago: University of Chicago Press.

Lazar, R. (1977). Extending sequence-class membership with matching to sample. *Journal of the Experimental Analysis of Behavior, 27,* 381-392.

Ludvigson, H.W., & Caul, W.F. (1964). Relative effect of overlearning on reversal and nonreversal shifts with two and four sorting categories. *Journal of Experimental Psychology, 68,* 301-306.

Lynch, D.C., & Green, G. (1991). Development and crossmodal transfer of contextual control of emergent stimulus relations. *Journal of the Experimental Analysis of Behavior, 56,* 139-154.

Matthews, B.A., Shimoff, E.H., & Catania, A.C., (1987). Saying and doing: A contingency-space analysis. *Journal of Applied Behavior Analysis, 20,* 69-74.

Matthews, B.A., Shimoff, E., Catania, A.C., & Sagvolden, T. (1977). Uninstructed human responding: Sensitivity to ratio and interval contingencies. *Journal of the Experimental Analysis of Behavior, 27,* 453-467.

McGonigle, B.O., & Chalmers, M. (1977). Are monkeys logical? *Nature, 267,* 694-696.

McIlvane, W.J., & Dube, W.V. (1992). Stimulus control shaping and stimulus control topographies. *The Behavior Analyst, 15,* 89-94.

McIlvane, W.J., Kledaras, J.B., Munson, L.C., King, K.A.J., de Rose, J.C., & Stoddard, L.T. (1987). Controlling relations in conditional discrimination and matching by exclusion. *Journal of the Experimental Analysis of Behavior, 48,* 187-208.

Pack, A.A., Herman, L.M., & Roitblat, H.L. (1991). Generalization of visual matching and delayed matching by a California sea line (*Zalophus californianus*). *Animal Learning and Behavior, 19,* 37-48.

Pilgrim, C., Chambers, L., & Galizio, M. (1995). Reversal of baseline relations and stimulus equivalence: II. Children. *Journal of the Experimental Analysis of Behavior, 63,* 239-254.

Pilgrim, C., & Galizio, M. (1990). Relations between baseline contingencies and equivalence probe performances. *Journal of the Experimental Analysis of Behavior, 54,* 213-224.

Pilgrim, C., & Galizio, M. (1995). Reversal of baseline relations and stimulus equivalence: I. Adults. *Journal of the Experimental Analysis of Behavior, 63,* 225-238.

Risley, T.R., & Hart, B. (1968). Developing correspondence between the nonverbal and verbal behavior of preschool children. *Journal of Applied Behavior Analysis, 1,* 267-281.

Rogers-Warren, A.R., & Baer, D.M. (1976). Correspondence between saying and doing: Teaching children to share and praise. *Journal of Applied Behavior Analysis, 9,* 335-354.

Rosch, E., & Mervis, C.B. (1977). Children's sorting: A reinterpretation based on the nature of abstraction in natural categories. In R.C. Smart & M.S. Smart (Eds.), *Readings in Child Development and Relationships* (2nd ed). New York: Macmillan.

Saunders, R.R., & Green, G. (1992). The nonequivalence of behavioral and mathematical equivalence. *Journal of the Experimental Analysis of Behavior, 57,* 227-241.

Saunders, R.R., Saunders, K.J., Kirby, K.C., & Spradlin, J.E. (1988). The merger and development of equivalence classes by unreinforced conditional selection of comparison stimuli. *Journal of the Experimental Analysis of Behavior, 50,* 145-162.

Saunders, R.R. Wachter, J.A., & Spradlin, J.E. (1988). Establishing auditory stimulus control over an eight-member equivalence class via conditional discrimination procedures. *Journal of the Experimental Analysis of Behavior, 49,* 95-115.

Sidman, M. (1986). Functional analysis of emergent verbal classes. In T. Thompson & M.D. Zeiler (Eds.), *Analysis and integration of behavioral units* (pp. 213-245). Hillsdale, NJ: Lawrence Erlbaum Associates.

Sidman, M. (1990). Equivalence relations: Where do they come? In D.E. Blackman & H. Lejeune (Eds.), *Behaviour analysis in theory and practice: Contributions and controversies* (pp. 93-114). Hillsdale, NJ: Erlbaum.

Sidman, M. (1992). Equivalence relations: Some basic considerations. In S.C. Hayes & L.J. Hayes (Eds.), *Understanding verbal relations* (pp. 15-27). Reno, NV: Context Press.

Sidman, M. (1994). *Equivalence relations and behavior: A research story.* Boston, MA: Authors Cooperative, Inc.

Sidman, M., Kirk, B., & Willson-Morris, M. (1985). Six-member stimulus classes generated by conditional-discrimination procedures. *Journal of the Experimental Analysis of Behavior, 43,* 21-42.

Sidman, M., Willson-Morris, M., & Kirk, B. (1986). Matching-to-sample procedures and the development of equivalence relations: The role of naming. *Analysis and Intervention in Developmental Disabilities, 6,* 1-19.

Sidman, M., & Tailby, W. (1982). Conditional discrimination vs. matching to sample: An expansion of the testing paradigm. *Journal of the Experimental Analysis of Behavior, 37,* 5-22.

Sigurdardottir, Z.G., Green, G., & Saunders, R.R. (1990). Equivalence classes generated by sequence training. *Journal of the Experimental Analysis of Behavior, 53,* 47-63.

Skinner, B.F. (1972). The generic nature of the concepts of stimulus and response. In B.F. Skinner, *Cumulative record: A selection of papers* (3rd ed., pp. 458-478). Des Moines, IA: Meredith. (Original work published 1935)

Spencer, T., & Chase, P. (in press). Speed analysis of stimulus equivalence. *Journal of the Experimental Analysis of Behavior.*

Spradlin, J.E., Cotter, V.W., & Baxley, N. (1973). Establishing a conditional discrimination without direct training: A study of transfer with retarded adolescents. *American Journal of Mental Deficiency, 77,* 556-566.

Spradlin, J.E., Saunders, K.J., & Saunders, R.R. (1992). The stability of equivalence classes. In S.C. Hayes & L.J. Hayes (Eds.), *Understanding verbal relations* (pp. 29-42). Reno, NV: Context Press.

Steirn, J.N., Jackson-Smith, P., & Zentall, T.R. (1991). Mediational use of internal representations of food and no-food events by pigeons. *Learning and Motivation, 22,* 353-365.

Tomonaga, M., Matsuzawa, T., Fujita, K., & Yamamoto, J. (1991). Emergence of symmetry in a visual conditional discrimination by chimpanzees (*Pan troglodytes*). *Psychological Reports, 68,* 51-60.

Wulfert, E., Greenway, D.E., & Dougher, M.J. (1994). Third-order equivalence classes. *Psychological Record, 44,* 411-439.

Wulfert, E., & Hayes, S.C. (1988). Transfer of a conditioned ordering response through conditional equivalence classes. *Journal of the Experimental Analysis of Behavior, 50,* 125-144.

Zentall, T.R., & Hogan, D.E. (1974). Abstract concept learning in the pigeon. *Journal of Experimental Psychology, 102,* 393-398.

Zentall, T.R., Sherburne, L.M., & Steirn, J.N. (1992). Development of excitatory backward associations during the establishment of forward associations in a delayed conditional discrimination by pigeons. *Animal Learning and Behavior, 20,* 199-206.

Stimulus Class Formation in Humans and Animals
T.R. Zentall and P.M. Smeets (Editors)
© 1996 Elsevier Science B.V. All rights reserved.

11

Some Implications of a Stimulus Control Topography Analysis
for Emergent Behavior and Stimulus Classes

William V. Dube and William J. McIlvane
(dedicated to Barbara Ray and Murray Sidman)

E. K. Shriver Center for Mental Retardation

When behavior analysts speak of different "response topographies," these words are widely recognized as referring to variations in the behavior emitted as the subject responds to programmed or naturally occurring environmental contingencies. Typically, response topography refers to variations in motoric aspects of behavior. When depressing a response key, for example, touches with the left versus the right index finger are different response topographies. Although the recording circuitry in standard testing procedures rarely differentiates response topography variations, they are often readily detectable by watching the subject behave.

A comprehensive behavioral analysis must describe not only the responses that are emitted but also the environmental events that occasion their emission -- the stimulus control of behavior. Surprisingly, behavior analysis has no generally accepted and well-defined technical term that refers to variations in the environmental events that occasion behavior. Perhaps this is due to the fact that the behavior analytic researcher explicitly arranges the environment in which the subject behaves. From the researcher's perspective, variations in environment, when they occur, are under her/his direct control (e.g., when discriminative stimuli are presented or removed).

There are limits, however, to the degree to which the experimenter can know about and control critical environmental events. As Ray and Sidman wrote in 1970, "All stimuli are [complex] in the sense that they have more than one dimension or aspect to which a subject might attend. To ask the experimenter to be aware of all possibilities is already, perhaps, an impossible demand" (p. 199). To this we add that there is no reason to suppose that subjects always attend to the same stimulus dimension or aspect as they are behaving. Indeed, there is good reason to suppose that variation in the stimulus control of behavior -- even in a constant environment -- is the rule rather than the exception (see below). For this reason, "stimulus control topography" (SCT) has been introduced into the language of behavior analysis (Ray, 1969; McIlvane & Dube, 1992; McIlvane, Dube, & Callahan, 1996). The term is intended to provide the field with reasonable language for talking about global and local variations in stimulus control that avoids some of the history and pitfalls of other possible terms (e.g., the "distal" versus the "proximal" stimuli). The term is also intended to suggest that variations in the stimulus control of behavior might be amenable to direct or indirect analysis.

We have found the concept of stimulus control topography to be useful when talking, writing, and thinking about our studies of discrimination learning with individuals with developmental limitations (e.g., severe mental retardation). For example, we have sometimes been able to better understand what were at first puzzling failures to learn by viewing the subject's performance as reflecting multiple and competing forms of stimulus control (e.g., de Rose, Riberio, Reis, & Kledaras, 1992; McIlvane, Kledaras, Dube, & Stoddard, 1989; McIlvane,

Kledaras, Stoddard, & Dube, 1990; McIlvane, Kledaras, Iennaco, & Dube, in press). In this chapter, we will briefly review the SCT formulation and discuss its application to some current issues in the experimental analysis of emergent behavior in stimulus equivalence research. Although the foundation for such an analysis has been in place for some time, there has yet to be a detailed consideration of equivalence research from an explicit SCT perspective. In doing so, our discussion will be in large part what Skinner (1957) termed "an exercise in interpretation." Although there is a substantial and growing empirical foundation for the multiple-SCT analysis of discrimination performances, its current application to equivalence research involves certain assumptions. Only experimental analysis will determine whether these assumptions ultimately prove to be useful.

SCT analysis: Further background and rationale

The term "stimulus control topography" first appeared in a study by Barbara Ray (1969). Ray trained monkeys to perform a go-left/go-right simultaneous discrimination with color and form stimuli displayed on side-by-side keys. Subjects were trained, for example, to press the left key when both keys displayed either red fields (R) or vertical lines (V), and to press the right key when both keys displayed either green (G) or horizontal lines (H). After the original discriminations were established, subjects were presented with "conflict compounds" of superimposed lines and colors, with reversed contingencies for one set of stimuli. To continue the example above, one type of conflict-compound training presented R+H and G+V, with reinforcers following left-key presses for R+H and right-key presses for G+V. Here, the reinforcement contingencies for the colors were the same as in the original training, but the contingencies were reversed for the lines. Presenting conflict compounds disrupted discrimination at first, but the conflict-compound discrimination was quickly acquired.

When performance was accurate with the conflict-compound stimuli, Ray tested stimulus control by the color and line elements presented separately. In the example above, one might predict that control by the colors would remain consistent with the original training, because the contingencies for the colors did not change during the conflict-compound training. But what about the lines? Relative to the original training, the conflict-compound contingencies were reversed; how did this affect the stimulus control exerted by the lines? If the conflict-compound contingencies had changed the form -- the topography -- of the stimulus-response controlling relations in the example above, then H would have came to control a response to the left and V a response to the right. But instead, tests with the lines alone showed that they still controlled the original responses (H right, V left). In fact, over many replications of the procedures, Ray found that stimulus control immediately following conflict-compound training was typically consistent with the original discriminations for *all* elements. She concluded that the conflict-compound contingencies changed the *frequency* with which some of the original controlling relations occurred, but did not alter their *topography*. Thus, when performance was accurate with conflict compounds (e.g., R+H left, G+V right), the frequency of stimulus control by H and V fell to zero or near-zero, but the form, or topography, of the controlling stimulus-response relations remained unchanged (H right, V left). Ray's study indicated that controlling stimulus-response relations are analogous to response-reinforcer relations in that they "may change in probability of occurrence without any accompanying change in topography" (p. 540).

Our definition of stimulus control topography (SCT) entails a modest extension of Ray's original suggestion and is consistent with Stoddard and Sidman's (1971) use of the term. We stress especially the analogy to response topography. The concept draws a direct parallel between controlling stimulus-response and response-reinforcer relations: In the analysis of an operant class, response topography distinguishes among various forms of a response that produce the same outcome. SCT distinguishes among various forms of stimulus control that result in the same measured response. Just as many different response topographies can fulfill the requirements of a given reinforcement contingency (e.g., pressing a key with the left or right hand), so may different SCTs produce accurate discrimination performance. Moreover, just as contingencies can be arranged to select certain response topographies over others, the SCT formulation implies that one should be able to arrange the environment to select or at least restrict the range of stimuli that control behavior.

The concept of the SCT was advanced initially in the context of a research program that examined a broad range of issues related to stimulus control, including the first matching-to-sample based studies of equivalence classes (Sidman & Cresson, 1973). Related findings from this program that supported the SCT formulation have been described elsewhere (McIlvane, 1992; McIlvane & Dube, 1992; Stoddard & McIlvane, 1989). One of the major themes that emerged from this research program was the possibility in any experiment that the controlling stimuli that actually controlled the subject's responses sometimes differed from those intended by the experimenter (Sidman, 1969; Stoddard & Sidman, 1971; Touchette, 1969). That is, every experimental situation has the potential for generating a number of different, and possibly competing, SCTs. The potential for multiple bases of stimulus control had previously been acknowledged in discrimination learning theories, as in, for example, Harlow's (1950) proposal that learning requires the elimination of error factors, or Zeaman and House's (1963) theory that the initial stage of discrimination acquisition is learning to attend to the relevant stimulus dimension among multiple possibilities. The SCT analysis differs from earlier formulations like Harlow's and Zeaman's by proposing explicitly that multiple topographies may (a) coexist in the same performance baseline and (b) occur and perhaps stabilize at different frequencies (cf. Bickel & Etzel, 1985; Ray & Sidman, 1970). This idea is central to the analyses presented below.

The analogy between response topography and SCT may raise a question about the role of topographical classification in the functional analysis of behavior inspired by Skinner. In behavior analysis, the operant class is defined by functional relations and not by response topography. The role of topography, however, depends upon the goals of the research under consideration. For many analyses that examine response-reinforcer relations, variations in topography are made irrelevant by defining the response as a switch closure. For research with other goals, however, attention to response topography becomes necessary. A clear example is in response shaping, where contingencies of reinforcement are dependent upon topographic variation. With respect to stimulus control, the role of topography also depends on the experimental goal. Some research questions may be answerable without the need for the experimenter to discriminate between certain SCTs. For equivalence research, however, we will argue for the importance of attention to SCT. For example, different SCTs that produce the same result during baseline development may produce much different results when outcome tests are given.

Multiple SCTs and matching-to-sample baselines

In this section, we will apply the concept of multiple SCTs to the matching-to-sample procedures used extensively in stimulus control experimentation. In a two-choice matching problem, chance-level accuracy scores indicate that the reinforcement contingencies have captured one or more forms of stimulus control that are different from those that the experimenter (or teacher) is trying to establish. In the typical matching-to-sample procedure, sources of "irrelevant" (from the experimenter's perspective) stimulus control include variables such as the locations of comparison stimuli, absolute (i.e., nonrelational) physical properties of stimuli, similar features in nonidentical stimuli, and so forth. Chance-level scores may be produced by either a single SCT that occurs on every trial, as illustrated in Figure 1A, or by multiple SCTs that occur with different frequencies, as shown in Figure 1B.

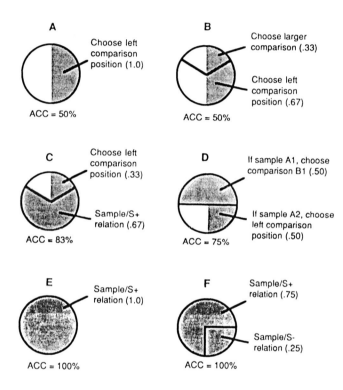

Figure 1. Analyses of single and multiple stimulus control topographies (SCTs) and resulting matching-to-sample accuracy scores. The circles represent the entire population of SCTs for one experimental session. Labels outside the circles give descriptive names for SCTs; the numbers in parentheses and the heavy black lines that divide the circles indicate the proportion of trials on which various SCTs occur. The shaded areas indicate the proportion of trials that would be scored as correct in two-choice matching to sample; the number at the bottom of each circle shows the overall accuracy score for the entire session (ACC). See text for details.

Intermediate accuracy scores, above chance levels but short of perfection, *necessarily* reflect multiple SCTs. Because a score of 83%, to take the example in Figure 1C, is higher than chance level, it indicates that stimulus control by the relevant relations between sample and comparison stimuli occurred on at least some trials. Because the score is lower than 100%, however, it also shows that other irrelevant forms of stimulus control occurred on other trials. As Sidman (1980; "Type D control") has pointed out, multiple SCTs and the resulting intermediate accuracy scores may also reflect perfect conditional control by sample stimuli. An example is shown in Figure 1D, where one sample controls selecting a specific comparison stimulus, and the other sample controls selecting a comparison display location.

Perfect or near-perfect accuracy scores indicate that stimulus control is consistent with the experimenter-specified contingencies. The controlling stimuli are either those deemed relevant by the experimenter, or they are irrelevant stimuli that are perfectly correlated with the relevant stimuli (e.g., Stikeleather & Sidman, 1990). As with chance-level scores, perfect scores may be produced by a single SCT, as suggested in Figure 1E. Perfect scores are also like chance-level scores, however, in that they may reflect more than one SCT. For example, correct responses in matching to sample may reflect either sample/S+ or sample/S- controlling relations (e.g., Carrigan & Sidman, 1992; Cumming & Berryman, 1965; Stromer & Osborne, 1982). These two different SCTs (a) both meet the requirements of the programmed contingency and (b) are indistinguishable to the recording circuitry, because each leads to a touch of the positive comparison stimulus. Moreover, these two SCTs typically cannot be differentiated through gross visual observation; they must be inferred from the results of other tests (see below). Such tests may indicate that matching-to-sample training has established *both* sample/S+ and sample/S-relations, as suggested in Figure 1F (e.g., Dixon, Dixon, & Spradlin, 1983; Stromer & Osborne, 1982).

SCT frequency of zero

Given that multiple SCTs may occur with different frequencies during experimental sessions, it seems important to take into account that a particular SCT may have been established but it may fail to occur because of competition from other SCTs. For example, consider a child performing a matching-to-sample task (to simplify the example, a two-choice task) where correct responses always produce a penny. Early in training, some responses may be controlled by the locations of stimuli, perhaps a "position bias" for selecting any stimulus that appears on the left side of the display. On average, half of these responses will be reinforced adventitiously on an intermittent variable ratio (VR) 2 schedule. Thus, the child's behavioral repertoire may come to include a position-controlled operant (i.e., a stimulus-response-reinforcer behavioral unit) that we will call "left-touch-penny." After continued training with differential reinforcement contingencies, the sample and comparison stimuli may come to control selections, and the operant "sample/comparison-touch-penny" may become established. The generic "sample/comparison' designation is used to include the possibility of both sample/S+ and sample/S- SCTs. A perfect accuracy score of 100% for one session indicates that the position operant did not occur during that session. That is, the frequency of "left-touch-penny" was zero, even though its discriminative stimulus, the left position, was still present on every trial. In baseline development, it often happens that a subject's first accuracy score of 100% is followed by one that is somewhat lower, but perhaps still within the limits of most learning criteria. If the accuracy score in the following session is 90%, one possibility is that both the "sample/comparison-touch-penny" and the "left-touch-penny" operants occurred during that session, on 80% and 20% of the trials, respectively. Our point is that a SCT frequency of zero does not mean that that SCT has been eliminated from the subject's behavioral repertoire, but rather may be the result of competition from other SCTs.

Multiple SCTs and concurrent operants
    In the above example, every matching-to-sample trial presented the discriminative stimuli for two different operants, the left position that controlled one, and the sample and comparison that controlled the other. Seen from the multiple-SCT perspective, the matching-to-sample procedure makes the discriminative stimuli for two or more different operants simultaneously and repeatedly available to the subject. When viewed this way, quantitative analyses of behavioral choice (Herrnstein, 1970; Williams, 1988) have relevance for understanding the development and maintenance of discrimination baselines.
    Experimental analyses of behavioral choice often make use of concurrent operants procedures in which the subject is presented with two or more stimuli that are discriminative for different schedules of reinforcement. The subject in such an experiment is continually "choosing" between response options with different probabilities of reinforcement. Thus, the matching-to-sample and concurrent-operants procedures have in common repeated choices between or among simultaneously available discriminative stimuli for different operants. In a well-designed matching-to-sample procedure, reinforcement is maximized only by the exclusive occurrence of operants controlled by the sample/comparison relations. That is, matching to sample may be characterized as arranging concurrent ratio schedules for competing SCTs. In the example above, continuous reinforcement (CRF) for "sample/comparison-touch-penny" and VR 2 for "left-touch-penny." Maximization by exclusive choice of the richer schedule is the common result in studies of behavioral choice with concurrent ratio schedules (e.g., Herrnstein & Loveland, 1975; although Schroeder [1975] has reported that children with mental retardation may not always maximize on concurrent ratio schedules). In the matching-to-sample procedure, perfect maximization will result in a perfect accuracy score; that is, the per-session frequency of "sample/comparison-touch-penny" will be the same as the number of trials in the session, and the frequency of irrelevant SCTs like "left-touch-penny" will be zero.
    A maximization account makes a testable prediction: If reinforcement schedule disparity is the underlying mechanism for improving accuracy scores in matching-to-sample baseline development, then increasing the number of comparisons should hasten acquisition. The ratio of relevant-to-irrelevant reinforcement probabilities is 2:1 for a two-choice task, 4:1 for a four-choice task, and so forth. One complicating factor, however, is that increasing the number of comparison stimuli comes with several costs: The number of sample-comparison relations to be learned simultaneously increases; larger stimulus arrays require more sustained and orderly observing behavior; and, if training is by trial and error, the initial probability of reinforcement for correct responses is reduced. The costs of increasing the number of comparisons will outweigh the benefits at some point. This issue may be especially important with developmentally limited subjects like small children and individuals with mental retardation.

Increases in the frequency of irrelevant SCTs
    A change in the experimental conditions may produce an increase in the frequency of SCTs that have fallen to zero or near-zero from a previously higher rate (e.g., McIlvane et al., 1989; Ray, 1969). One possibility is the elimination of differential reinforcement on some or all trials, as is commonly done in equivalence experiments to prepare the subject for probe trials. If the current reinforcement rate for the relevant SCT ("sample/comparison-touch-penny") becomes lower than the historical reinforcement rate for irrelevant SCTs (e.g., "left-touch-penny"), one possible result is an increase in the frequency of the latter. For example, Saunders, Saunders, Kirby, and Spradlin (1988, Experiment 2) reported that extensive training, and in one

case procedural modification, was necessary before their subjects with mental retardation could maintain accurate performance in "no-feedback" conditions (cf. Galvão, Calcagno, & Sidman, 1992).

Another type of change that may produce an increase in irrelevant SCTs is the reintroduction of stimulus conditions that have been absent for some time, in a way that parallels spontaneous recovery, or Epstein's (1985) analysis of resurgence in response topographies. The training results in Devany, Hayes, and Nelson (1986) offer an example of a resurgence-like effect with SCTs. To be consistent with current equivalence conventions, we have changed the task designations in Devany et al. (1986) to training AB and AC, and testing BC and CB; where, for example, AB matching means selecting comparison stimuli B1 and B2 conditionally upon sample stimuli A1 and A2, respectively. Training was conducted by a "three-step" method: First, subjects received a series of trials that each displayed sample A1 with comparisons B1 and B2, and touching B1 was correct on every trial. Note that because sample A1 was present on every trial, it was therefore irrelevant to the discrimination. Then, when accuracy with sample A1 was high, a series of trials displayed sample A2 with the same comparisons, and touching B2 was correct on every trial. Again, the sample, A2, was irrelevant. Finally, when accuracy with sample A2 was high, the A1-sample and A2-sample trials were mixed together. The introduction of this "mix" condition usually produced a decrease in accuracy, particularly with the lower-functioning children. As we have pointed out elsewhere (McIlvane, Dube, Kledaras, Iennaco, & Stoddard, 1990), such a decrease is not surprising because the first two conditions were likely to produce simple comparison-stimulus discriminations in which the sample stimuli were irrelevant, that is, a SCT one could call "touch the same comparison stimulus that was correct on the previous trial."

After the AB discrimination was trained, the AC discrimination was also trained in the same way, and with similar results. The final step of baseline development was a "mix" condition that alternated irregularly between AB and AC trials. Even though subjects had previously demonstrated high accuracy on both the AB and AC tasks in isolation, accuracy fell when this final mix condition was introduced. For the lower-functioning subjects, these accuracy decreases were often to chance levels and for a substantial number of trials. This outcome was not merely due to "forgetting" errors on the AB trials because they had not been presented for some time. If the errors occurred only on AB trials, overall accuracy scores would have been at least 75% (with equal numbers of AB and AC trials), but the reported scores were much lower than that. A reasonable interpretation is that the reintroduction of AB trials, with their B1/B2 comparison displays, set the occasion for a resurgence of an "old" SCT, that is, one that had been frequent at the start of training but subsequently became infrequent. An example of such a SCT is what we have called "touch the same stimulus that was correct on the previous trial." If this behavior occurred on both AB and AC trials, the chance-level accuracy scores reported by Devany and colleagues would result. With continued training, the irrelevant SCT would again be reduced in frequency and accuracy would increase. The potential for changes in stimulus displays to temporarily "resurrect" old SCTs has implications for equivalence testing that will be discussed in the next section.

The problem of delayed emergence: Multiple SCTs and behavioral momentum

Delayed emergence refers to a pattern of results on equivalence tests, typically without differential consequences, where performance is initially inconsistent with the experimental classes but, with repeated testing, eventually becomes consistent. Delayed emergence has been observed in a variety of subject populations and with varied testing procedures (e.g., Devany et al., 1986; Fields, Adams, Verhave, & Newman, 1990; Sidman, Kirk, & Willson-Morris, 1985; Sidman, Willson-Morris, & Kirk, 1986; Spradlin, Cotter, & Baxley, 1973). Although delayed emergence is typically observed in a minority of cases, it has been reported often enough to require an explanation.

Sidman's (1992a, 1994) recent analysis of delayed emergence may be summarized as follows: The experimental stimuli in any experiment belong to many different equivalence classes (all may be the same color, all appear in the same positions, all bear some relation to reinforcement, etc.); these classes may come from extraexperimental histories or they may be an unintended result of the experimental contingencies. Baseline training "breaks down" those equivalence relations that are inconsistent with the baseline reinforcement contingencies. On test trials, when subjects are given stimulus displays with combinations of stimuli different from those in the baseline, they may again select comparison stimuli because of equivalence relations that are different from those that the experimenter is trying to establish. Given a reinforcement history for across-trial consistency in conditional discriminations (i.e., that there is only one "correct" comparison for any given display), subjects eventually come to respond in the only way that can be consistent on every trial -- the equivalence classes that are defined by the baseline contingencies (see Sidman, 1994, pp. 274-279).

The multiple-SCT analysis of baseline development can be applied to the testing phase in equivalence paradigms. In describing baseline development, we proposed that experimentally irrelevant SCTs may occur early in training, but that they eventually fall to frequencies near zero as training progresses and reinforcement is maximized. When equivalence test trials are introduced, novel stimulus displays are presented without differential reinforcement contingencies. The introduction of novel displays may set the occasion for new SCTs or for an increase in the frequency of irrelevant SCTs with a remote reinforcement history.

For example, suppose AB and AC training is followed by BC and CB testing. AB and AC baseline training trials require discrimination of B and C stimuli only when they are displayed simultaneously as comparison stimuli. Implicit in this paradigm, therefore, is the assumption that stimuli discriminated simultaneously will also be discriminated successively. If the simultaneous-discrimination context is an important feature of the baseline comparison stimuli, however, then new SCTs may arise on initial BC and CB test trials because subjects are suddenly required to make successive discriminations between or among the B and C stimuli when they are presented as samples for the first time (e.g., Sidman, 1994, pp. 525-527; Sidman et al., 1982). This outcome may be more likely if irrelevant SCTs were reinforced adventitiously very early in training when the A stimuli were first presented as samples.

Other features of equivalence tests that may set the occasion for new or irrelevant SCTs include novel stimulus juxtapositions; stimuli displayed in new locations (cf. Iversen, Sidman, & Carrigan, 1986; Sidman, 1992b); stimuli displayed in new temporal sequences (when sample stimuli are displayed before comparisons); and, as Sidman (1992a, 1994) and others have noted, preexperimentally established equivalence classes (e.g., Watt, Keenan, Barnes, & Cairns, 1991) or irrelevant equivalence classes that were established during the experiment because the stimulus features that controlled responding were different from those intended by the experimenter (e.g., Stikeleather & Sidman, 1990; Barnes, 1990).

We propose that in delayed emergence: (a) Initially inconsistent equivalence test results reflect multiple SCTs. (b) Equivalence experiments are designed so that equivalence classes are demonstrated when the SCT that occurs on baseline trials also occurs on test trials; that is, the

SCT of the equivalence relations the experimenter is trying to demonstrate is the same as the SCT that the experimenter has tried to establish in baseline training (typically, sample/S+ selection). (c) Increasing consistency with continued testing results from decreasing frequency of SCTs that compete with the baseline/tested SCT, in a way that parallels increasing accuracy during baseline acquisition.

At this point, we come to the central question for any account of delayed emergence: Why does behavior change in the absence of differential consequences on test trials? Given that initial test results reflect multiple SCTs, why does the frequency of irrelevant SCTs decrease relative to that of the baseline/tested SCTs? Maximization of reinforcement may be one factor, especially in experiments where baseline trials at least occasionally result in differential consequences during repeated testing. But maximization alone does not seem sufficient to account for the change (as in baseline training) because the reinforcement contingencies are the same for all SCTs that occur on test trials that do not provide differential consequences. Further, delayed emergence has been reported in experiments where baselines were not maintained during testing.

One possible answer to the question of delayed emergence may come from an analysis of *behavioral resistance to change*. From the multiple-SCT perspective, Nevin's (Nevin, Mandell, & Atak, 1983; Nevin, 1992) rigorous and original program of research on behavioral momentum seems relevant to the problem of delayed emergence. The momentum analysis makes analogies between the relationships described in the physics of motion and the psychology of behavioral persistence. The momentum of a moving body is defined in classical mechanics as the product of mass and velocity. The degree to which an outside force can perturb the motion of a moving body depends upon its momentum; increasing mass while holding velocity constant increases the resistance to change. Nevin (1992) suggests a direct parallel in the domain of behavior. He argues that rate of responding is analogous to velocity, and the resistance of that rate to change by a perturbing operation (prefeeding, reduced reinforcement, alternative reinforcement, punishment, etc.) can be used to index the analogue of mass.

To illustrate the momentum analysis, consider a procedure in which different rates of reinforcement are obtained in two alternating components that are signaled by distinctive cues (a multiple schedule). Research by Nevin, his colleagues, and others has shown that resistance to change (a) is less in the component that has the leaner schedule and (b) appears to be determined by the stimulus-reinforcer relation of the reinforcement contingencies. The behavioral momentum analysis has been confirmed in studies with laboratory animals and also with typically and atypically developing humans (see Nevin, 1992 for an integrative summary).

To return to the issue of delayed emergence, inconsistent results on initial equivalence tests may indicate multiple SCTs. Behavioral momentum theory proposes that behavior controlled by stimuli correlated with a higher rate of reinforcement will be more persistent than behavior controlled by stimuli correlated with a lower rate of reinforcement. Because subjects typically do not qualify for equivalence tests until baseline performances are accurate and reliable, the relevant SCT will have a higher rate of reinforcement than irrelevant SCTs. Thus, momentum theory predicts that the baseline/tested SCT should have greater resistance to change than irrelevant SCTs.

Equivalence testing conditions usually involve (a) reduced overall levels reinforcement relative to baseline training and (b) nondifferential reinforcement contingencies on test trials. These features seem analogous to perturbing operations that have been used in studies of behavioral momentum, for example, decreasing the effectiveness of reinforcement by prefeeding, or degrading a reinforcement contingency by presenting noncontingent reinforcers during sessions. The manipulations in both types of experiments may be predicted to decrease behavioral frequencies: response frequencies in momentum experiments, and SCT frequencies in equivalence experiments (although response frequencies may also decrease during equivalence tests). For many subjects in the typical equivalence experiment, the greater momentum of the baseline/tested SCT leads to immediate emergence of the equivalence classes. For some subjects, however, the initiation of equivalence testing leads to the appearance or reappearance of one or more irrelevant SCTs and a temporary decrease in baseline SCT frequency; the decrease occurs because of the forced-choice nature of the matching-to-sample procedure. As testing continues, if irrelevant SCTs are less resistant to change than the baseline/tested SCT, then the frequency of irrelevant SCTs should be more likely to decrease than that of the baseline/tested SCT. Given that the equivalence testing contingencies are sufficient to maintain continued responding, decreasing competition from irrelevant SCTs would result in an increase in the frequency of the more persistent baseline/tested SCT.

This analysis predicts that the rate of emergence will be related to the frequency of reinforcement for baseline trials immediately prior to (or during) equivalence testing. Greater disparities between reinforcement frequencies for relevant and irrelevant SCTs should produce greater differences in behavioral momentum and thus more rapid emergence. This prediction could be tested by varying the amount of baseline overtraining (i.e., additional practice following acquisition) prior to equivalence tests, or by alternating blocks of baseline maintenance trials with blocks of test trials and manipulating the baseline reinforcement frequencies.

A momentum analysis also suggests that the rate of emergence during equivalence testing may be related to the rate of baseline acquisition. Above, we speculated that delayed emergence should be less likely when the baseline training phase of an equivalence experiment is extended by overtraining after acquisition. In contrast, delayed emergence may become more likely when persistent errors necessitate extensive baseline training prior to acquisition, because persistent errors may indicate a prolonged reinforcement history for competing and irrelevant SCTs during training. This possibility suggests that the duration of equivalence testing should be related to the duration of baseline acquisition. This relation seems especially important for the interpretation of negative findings. To return briefly to the example of Devany et al. (1986), we note that almost all of the mentally retarded subjects' accuracy scores during the first four blocks of equivalence testing were indistinguishable from their scores during the first four blocks of the final "mix" baseline condition. Seen from this perspective, the test data are uninterpretable because the test duration was insufficient. In fact, had the equivalence test criterion, 9 correct of 10 consecutive responses within the first 40 trials, been applied to the final mix condition, seven of the eight retarded children would have failed baseline acquisition. When baseline training or equivalence testing are extended, test criteria may need to be adjusted to decrease the probability of meeting a criterion by chance.

To conclude this section, we note that our SCT analysis of delayed emergence differs from Sidman's (1994) in that it does not require the assumption that selections scored as errors, whether during baseline development or equivalence testing, are due to relations of equivalence that are different from those designated by the experimenter. Any irrelevant form of stimulus control could produce the hypothesized effect.

Equivalence classes in conflict

The multiple-SCT analysis also seems pertinent to studies where equivalence tests follow experience that establishes the prerequisites for conflicting stimulus class membership. In such studies (a) "original" experimental equivalence classes are established, (b) one or more of the baseline conditional discriminations are reversed, and (c) the equivalence tests are then repeated: Are results for the second set of tests consistent with original equivalence classes or do results change to be consistent with the reversed baseline? Results with individuals with mental retardation and typically developing children have ranged from completely consistent reversals on equivalence tests to disruption of previously established classes and inconsistent conditional control (Dube, McIlvane, Mackay, & Stoddard, 1987; Dube, McIlvane, Maguire, Mackay, & Stoddard, 1989; Dube & McIlvane, 1995; Pilgrim, Chambers, & Galizio, 1995; Spradlin et al., 1973). By contrast, Saunders, Saunders, Kirby, and Spradlin (1988) found that probe performance on one- or multi-node test trials did not reverse following reversal of one nodal baseline relation for two of three adults with mild mental retardation (results with the third subject were inconsistent). Finally, Pilgrim and Galizio (1990, 1995) found that typically intelligent adults reversed their selections on symmetry tests for the reversed baseline relations, but, as in Saunders and colleagues' study, results on one- or two-node tests were consistent with the prereversal equivalence classes.

From the perspective of a SCT analysis, what happens during reversal training? As a first step to formulating an answer, we will once again consider the parallel between stimulus control topography and response topography. When a reinforced operant response occurs, it becomes a part of the organism's reinforcement history, and a history cannot be altered. In response shaping, for example, gradual changes in reinforcement contingencies may establish new response topographies, but the old topographies remain a part of the subject's behavioral repertoire and they may reoccur under certain conditions. In terms of stimulus control, reversal training need not eliminate SCT(s) that have been established, but rather may establish one (or more) new SCTs and create conditions where the frequency of the previously established SCTs falls to zero (cf. Stoddard & Sidman, 1971). As in response shaping, as long as the new behavior is maintained, the old behavior may never reoccur. If, however, conditions change so as to reintroduce stimuli that have previously controlled the old behavior, then there is some probability that the old behavior may be exhibited. This probability may be modulated by state (e.g., motivation), subject (e.g., developmental level, preexperimental history), and procedural variables (e.g., duration of reversal training, reinforcement contingencies during testing).

By this analysis, we interpret positive reversal results as an indication that the recent training history and the contingencies of reinforcement during testing were sufficient to demonstrate new equivalence classes on test trials. Inconsistent test results may reflect multiple SCTs, perhaps including those established by both the original training and the reversal training. For example, matching-to-sample reversals, where former S+ stimuli become S-, seem likely to encourage sample/S- control, at least on some occasions. Intermediate or chance-level scores on test trials may indicate that a particular trial type produces different SCTs at different times. As a speculative example, a specific equivalence-probe trial display may control a sample/S+ SCT when it follows nonreversed baseline trials and a sample/S- SCT when it follows reversed baseline trials. Baseline disruptions as testing begins also indicate that multiple SCTs are occurring in test sessions (e.g., Pilgrim, Chambers, & Galizio, 1995).

What, then, can account for the findings where baselines are reversed but equivalence test results remain consistent with prereversal contingencies? One possibility (a) parallels that described immediately above in that reversal training establishes baselines with multiple SCTs, but (b) differs from that above in that the multiple SCTs occur consistently on different trial types during testing. That is, the reversed contingencies establish a new SCT on the affected trial type(s), and the nonreversed contingencies maintain the old SCT(s). Spradlin, Saunders, and Saunders (1992) proposed that "Procedures involving the reversal of key prerequisites provide the basis for more than one set of relations to be demonstrated on test trials" (p. 40); to this we might add, "and the basis to maintain more than one set of relations (SCTs) on baseline trials." With respect to results like Pilgrim and Galizio's, symmetry probes displaying the sample/comparison combinations that were reversed may set the occasion for the new SCT that was established during reversal training with those stimuli. The transitivity/equivalence probes may set the occasion for old SCTs that were established prior to reversal training. A study by Stikeleather & Sidman (1990) provides indirect support for this interpretation by showing that equivalence classes may be defined by the order in which the stimuli were introduced into the training regimen. That is, stimuli may be members of "older" and "newer" classes.

In our view, findings such those reported by Saunders and colleagues (1988) and Pilgrim and Galizio (1990, 1995) are theoretically challenging for behavior analysis because the field has not yet accorded the problem of conflicting reinforcement histories the attention it deserves. One can see the current work as revisiting the same conceptual problem addressed by Ray (1969), this time in a relational learning framework. The earlier studies of conflicting histories in simple discrimination also reported variations in outcome across populations (Ray, 1969; Huguenin & Touchette, 1980), and challenged the field to account for such variations in stimulus control topographies. Unfortunately, those studies were not followed up. Perhaps relational learning will provide a more attractive context for studying the variables that determine the extent to which conflicting histories influence SCT development.

Experimental analysis of multiple SCTs

In this section we will briefly discuss some experimental techniques that may be helpful for identifying, separating, or manipulating multiple SCTs in matching-to-sample baselines. These procedures are among the currently available tools for empirical tests of the analyses we have proposed.

Delayed sample presentation

In a commonly used simultaneous matching-to-sample procedure, the display area is blank during the intertrial interval (ITI), and the sample stimulus is presented alone at the start of the trial. A touch to the sample is required, and then the comparison stimuli are presented along with the sample (e.g., Sidman & Tailby, 1982). When the sample stimulus is presented, the response of touching it may be controlled merely by its presence, and not by its other features that are important for accurate matching. In simple terms, the subject may respond to the sample stimulus merely because somethin g is there; if so, the resulting SCT may be called "control by presence alone." Such responses may be reinforced by the presentation of comparison stimuli that function as discriminative stimuli and thus also as conditioned reinforcers.

If control by presence alone occurs only during sample presentation, the subject may be perfectly accurate in simultaneous matching procedures where the sample remains displayed throughout the trial. Once established, however, control by presence alone may also occur when the comparison stimuli are presented. When responding controlled by presence alone occurs soon after the onset of stimuli, it is sometimes called impulsive responding, especially when subjects are developmentally limited (e.g., Lowry & Ross, 1975). If an irrelevant SCT such as presence alone occurred on every comparison selection, accuracy scores would be at chance levels. Multiple SCTs that included both relevant control by sample/comparison relations and irrelevant

SCTs like presence alone would produce intermediate accuracy scores.

We have examined irrelevant SCTs associated with the comparison display in subjects with mental retardation who had persistent, intermediate matching accuracy scores (McIlvane et al., 1989; McIlvane, Kledaras, et al., 1990). These studies used a "delayed sample presentation" procedure. The comparison stimuli were presented first, and a short delay of a few seconds followed. Any responding at this point prolonged the delay, and the sample stimulus was presented only after a few seconds passed without a response.

Note that the delayed-sample procedure was not designed to increase observation of the sample stimuli (in cases where the experimenter or teacher wants to encourage better observation of sample stimuli, one potentially useful procedure is to require a differential observing response, e.g., Eikeseth, & Smith, 1992; Saunders & Spradlin, 1989, 1990, 1993). Rather, it was designed to reduce irrelevant and competing stimulus control over comparison selection. When the delayed-sample procedure was implemented, intermediate accuracy scores often improved immediately to high levels. This outcome implies that control by the sample stimuli had been established but was occurring with a relatively low frequency because of competing irrelevant SCTs. Typical in such cases was responding during the delay initially, and the frequency of these responses usually diminished with continued exposure to the procedure. Responding during the delay could not have been controlled by sample/comparison relations because no sample stimulus was present; such responding had to have been controlled by some irrelevant feature of the comparison display, as with a presence-alone SCT. Because responses to the comparison array alone had no programmed consequences, the delayed-sample procedure allowed the selective extinction of the presence-alone SCT. Relevant control by the sample stimulus when it was finally presented may have been encouraged because of the immediate history of extinction for any responses controlled by presence alone. Nevertheless, control by presence alone may still occur when the sample stimulus appears, and such control may be reflected in failures to improve accuracy with the delayed-sample procedure.

Delayed sample presentation may be useful in stimulus equivalence research, particularly with developmentally limited subjects in whom control by presence alone may be more likely. In some cases the procedure may help to produce the very high baseline accuracy scores that are necessary for meaningful equivalence tests. In addition, an experimental context that allowed for equivalence testing with the delayed-sample procedure could be useful (see below). For example, it seems possible that accurate baselines with the standard matching-to-sample procedure may involve presence-alone control by sample stimuli with some frequency. Although such control may not interfere with accuracy on baseline trials, it may affect the results if it occurs on test trials that display former sample stimuli as comparisons for the first time.

Successive conditional discrimination procedures

One feature of typical matching-to-sample procedures that may foster multiple SCTs is the simultaneous display of several different stimuli. Multiple SCTs may result in part because experimental contingencies rarely exert tight control over the response topography of observing behavior. One way to improve control over observing behavior is to present the stimuli individually, as in successive discrimination procedures. A second potential advantage for successive procedures is that they eliminate one type of contextual disparity between training and test trials in the standard procedure: Stimuli presented only in simultaneous discriminations (as comparisons) during baseline training are not suddenly presented successively (as samples) on test trials, and vice versa.

Adapting successive conditional discrimination procedures for stimulus equivalence research poses several problems. One type of procedure, a "go/no-go" procedure, presents two stimuli on each trial, one sample and one comparison (e.g., D'Amato & Colombo, 1985). Each sample is followed by the correct comparison on some trials and by the incorrect comparison on other trials. For example, a subject trained to perform baseline AB matching might be required to press a response key within 3 s ("go") on trials presenting A1 and B1, or A2 and B2, and not to press for 3 s ("no go") on trials presenting A1 and B2, or A2 and B1. A potential measurement problem may arise on equivalence tests where untrained performances with novel combinations of stimuli must be evaluated without differential consequences. Long response latencies have been observed on equivalence probe trials, particularly in the early stages of testing (e.g., Saunders, Wachter, & Spradlin, 1988). With go/no-go procedures, no-go responses are recorded on trials where response latencies exceed a certain value.

"Go-left/go-right" procedures (e.g., D'Amato & Worsham, 1974) might seem to solve the problem of defining responses by their latencies because they require a response on every trial, as in the standard matching-to-sample procedure. For example, on trials presenting the sample and one comparison (e.g., A1 and B1), pressing a key on the right is reinforced; on trials with the sample and the other comparison (A1 and B2), pressing a key on the left is reinforced. AB training would establish the following (sample-comparison-correct key): A1-B1-right, A1-B2-left, A2-B2-right, A2-B1-left. Similarly, BC training would establish B1-C1-right, B1-C2-left, B2-C2-right, B2-C1-left. Go-left/go-right procedures, however, seem unsuitable for many of the tests required in equivalence paradigms because the baseline training reinforces responses following all sample-comparison combinations. To continue the example, responses to the left, the right, or both keys could be predicted on AC transitivity tests: On a trial that presented A1-C1, the training history of A1-B1-right and B1-C1-right would predict a response to the right (if A1-B1 and B1-C1, then A1-C1), while the A1-B2-left and B2-C1-left history would predict a response to the left (if A1-B2 and B2-C1, then A1-C1).

In a study of auditory equivalence classes (Dube, Green, & Serna, 1993), we avoided the problems outlined above by requiring a response on every trial, and by presenting the sample and both comparisons on every trial (cf. Wasserman, 1976). The comparisons, however, were presented not simultaneously but successively. As each comparison was presented, a different portion of a computer touchscreen was emphasized visually, and the subject responded by touching the area that had corresponded to one of the previously shown comparisons on that trial (over trials, every comparison was paired equally often with every area). This procedure could be implemented with any combination of auditory or visual stimuli. An all-visual AB trial, for example, could begin with the presentation of sample A1 for 3 s in the center of the display area, followed by B1 for 3 s in the upper left corner, then B2 in the upper right, and finally B3 in the lower left (on other AB trials, the comparison stimuli would appear in different corners). After the stimulus presentations, the subject could select comparison B1 by touching the upper left corner of the display area. Auditory stimuli could be accompanied by the appearance of some neutral stimulus like a plain gray square in the response locations, as in our study. This procedure has the advantage of allowing implementation and interpretation of the full range of tests specified by the equivalence paradigm. It does, however, have the disadvantage of requiring the subject to remember the comparison locations for the duration of the trial, and thus may require modifications for use with developmentally limited humans or nonhuman subjects.

Blank-comparison procedures

Blank-comparison procedures were developed to allow the independent measurement of sample/S+ and sample/S- relations in matching-to-sample procedures with visual comparison stimuli (McIlvane, Withstandley, & Stoddard, 1984; McIlvane, Kledaras, Lowry, & Stoddard, 1992). In the blank-comparison procedure, one of the comparison display areas is "blank;" it is obscured by a plain (black) field large enough to cover any of the stimuli that could appear there. On some trials, the comparisons are the S+ and a blank; on other trials, the comparisons are the S- and a blank. Because the blank serves as both S+ and S-, the requirements for conditional discrimination are maintained. On trials that present the sample, correct stimulus, and the blank, a response to the displayed stimulus documents sample/S+ control. On other trials with the sample, incorrect stimulus, and the blank, a response to the blank documents sample/S- control. In both tabletop and computer-implemented settings, we have found that fading procedures are a reliable means to convert standard two-choice matching to blank-comparison matching, even with subjects who have severe developmental disabilities (McIlvane et al., 1984, 1992).

Blank-comparison matching is established by presenting an equal number of sample/S+ and sample/S- trials, so that the blank comparison stimulus is neutral with respect to the reinforcement contingencies. Our studies with this procedure thus far have examined variables relevant to exclusion (e.g., McIlvane et al., 1987) and feature-based stimulus classification (e.g., Serna & Wilkinson, 1995), and these studies have maintained equal proportions of sample/S+ and sample/S- trials. The procedure, however, offers an interesting possibility for equivalence research because it allows the experimenter to control the relative proportions of sample/S+ and sample/S- SCTs and the reinforcement frequencies of each. Experimental manipulations could examine the effects of different proportions or reinforcement frequencies of baseline SCTs on emergent performances (cf. Carrigan & Sidman, 1992; Johnson & Sidman, 1993). The blank-comparison procedure may also be useful in equivalence studies where baseline discriminations are reversed, again because the procedure allows the experimenter to control the relative presentation and reinforcement frequencies of different types of sample/comparison SCTs. For example, we raised the question of whether Pilgrim and colleagues' (1995) results with children reflected a shift from sample/S+ to sample/S- control on the baseline relations that were reversed. The blank-comparison procedure could be used to ask whether the results are affected if the reversed baseline relations are presented only on sample/S+ trials.

CONCLUSION

Is the SCT analysis testable?

We have proposed that equivalence outcomes result when (a) baseline training establishes the experimentally relevant SCT, and (b) this SCT occurs with a high frequency. The pattern of data that would support this analysis is a relation between the degree of experimental control over the definition and frequency of the baseline SCT and the rate and proportion of positive equivalence outcomes. This relation leads to two predictions: First, one should be able to reduce the occurrence of delayed emergence and equivalence failures by instituting procedures that increase the coherence between the subject's and experimenter's SCT definition. Some of the procedures described above could be useful in such an effort. Another way to encourage control by experimenter-specified stimulus differences or stimulus relations is to give subjects experience with a variety of stimuli. This was the approach taken in the study by Schusterman and Kastak (1993) that has provided the most convincing data thus far for equivalence in nonhumans. Their subject, a California sea lion, was trained with many sets of stimuli to encourage concordance with the experimenter's definition of the relevant stimulus aspects and possibly to adapt the animal to the introduction of novel sample-comparison combinations that occurs on equivalence tests. Their positive results, following training likely to reduce competition from irrelevant SCTs, stand in contrast to the negative outcomes obtained in previous studies with nonhuman subjects who did not receive comparable training.

The second prediction is that (a) when baseline contingencies permit multiple SCTs, and delayed emergence and equivalence failures do occur, then (b) procedures that eliminate the irrelevant SCTs in the baseline or from the test trials should produce immediate increases in equivalence outcomes. Although they were not conducted in the context of the equivalence paradigm, our studies with the delayed sample presentation procedure (described above) and a related "delayed S+" procedure (implemented in the context of simple, simultaneous visual discriminations) illustrate the type of effect that would support our second prediction. Figure 2 schematically illustrates the general form of the data we have obtained with these "delayed-presentation" procedures in studies with subjects who have mental retardation (McIlvane et al., 1989, McIlvane, Kledaras, et al., 1990; McIlvane et al., in press).

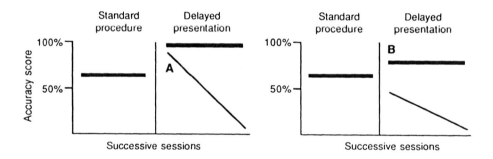

Figure 2. Schematic diagram of findings with delayed-presentation procedures. Heavy black lines represent accuracy scores on successive sessions with standard procedures (left portion of each plot) and after implementation of delayed-presentation procedures (right portions). Thin black lines on the right represent the proportion of trials on which subjects respond during the delay. A: Cases where the only irrelevant SCT is "presence alone." B: Cases with multiple irrelevant SCTs that include presence alone. See text for further details.

The heavy lines in Figure 2 marked "Standard procedure" represent asymptotic and intermediate accuracy scores. In the cases where delayed-presentation procedures have been effective, such scores have ranged from slightly above chance levels (e.g., McIlvane et al., in press) to approximately 90% (McIlvane et al., 1989). To review briefly, our analysis is that such accuracy scores reflect competition between relevant and irrelevant SCTs, including the irrelevant SCT we described above as "control by presence alone." The initiation of delayed-presentation procedures produced sudden jumps in accuracy scores for many subjects, as suggested by the heavy lines in the portions of Figure 2 marked "A" and "B" (the thin lines illustrate the decreasing frequency of responses controlled by presence alone). When accuracy scores improve immediately to perfect or near-perfect levels (Figure 2, A), our conclusion is that presence alone was the only irrelevant SCT. When scores improved suddenly but remained less than perfect (B), we conclude that presence alone was one of multiple irrelevant SCTs. The important point for the present discussion is that the sudden increase in accuracy scores illustrates independence of the relevant and irrelevant SCTs. Although the presence-alone SCT depressed overall accuracy scores, the low scores did not mean that stimulus control by relevant SCTs was not established. Rather, relevant and irrelevant SCTs had independently manipulable frequencies.

In application of the SCT analysis to equivalence research, an important experimental question will be whether procedures that isolate and separate irrelevant SCTs will produce a pattern of data similar to the immediate change in accuracy scores shown above: Can such procedures be used to demonstrate experimental control over delayed emergence and equivalence outcome failures? Such a program of research will be challenging because there may be multiple irrelevant SCTs. Analyses may require the implementation of more than one of the procedures discussed above (delayed presentation, successive discrimination, and blank comparison), either in succession or in combination. This research will benefit from continued efforts to expand the arsenal of procedures for first assessing and then eliminating the various irrelevant SCTs that may interfere with experimental demonstrations of equivalence.

Some possible advantages of the SCT perspective

Two possible advantages of the SCT approach to equivalence research can be described. In our view, one advantage is conceptual: The analogy between stimulus control topographies and response topographies focuses on behavior and discourages the reification of equivalence classes. From the SCT perspective, a failure to show equivalence outcomes in a particular individual or population may be approached as a problem in subject-vs-experimenter stimulus definition rather than as a limitation in the subject's ability to form classes. In cases where equivalence test scores are intermediate, the results can be described as conflicting SCTs rather than as incompletely formed classes. When changing some of the baseline performances does not change all of the related emergent performances, the outcome can be interpreted as reflecting multiple SCTs rather than as a failure to produce a structural reorganization of previously established equivalence classes. In short, the SCT analysis encourages us to treat equivalence classes as patterns of behavior, and not as things that "form" and subsequently exist somewhere. The former conceptualization seems to be a more advantageous starting point from which to pursue a behavioral analysis aimed at discovering the variables of which emergent behavior is a function.

Perhaps a greater potential advantage of the multiple-SCT interpretation is the conception of the matching-to-sample procedure as one that continually presents the subject with discriminative stimuli for concurrently available response options. This characterization provides the basis for a link between two well-developed and vigorous research areas that have been notably separate: "stimulus-control" research (stimulus equivalence, transfer of discriminative functions, exclusion, errorless learning, etc.) and quantitative analyses of behavioral choice and momentum. Because the SCT perspective makes this relation apparent, it may lead to research that integrates these previously disparate research areas, and ultimately a better understanding of the acquisition and maintenance of stimulus control.

AUTHORS NOTES

Manuscript preparation was supported in part by NICHD grants 25995, 25488, 28141. We thank Murray Sidman and Richard Serna for comments on the manuscript, and Aimee Smith for assistance with manuscript preparation. Address correspondence to either author, Behavioral Science Division, E. K. Shriver Center, 200 Trapelo Road, Waltham, MA 02254, or Internet: wdube@shriver. org.

REFERENCES

Barnes, T. (1990). *Equivalence without symmetry? A stimulus artifact.* Unpublished M. A. thesis, Northeastern University, Boston, MA.

Bickel, W. K., & Etzel, B. C. (1985). The quantal nature of controlling stimulus-response relations as measured in tests of stimulus generalization. *Journal of the Experimental Analysis of Behavior, 44,* 245-270.

Carrigan, P. F., & Sidman, M. (1992). Conditional discrimination and equivalence relations: A theoretical analysis of control by negative stimuli. *Journal of the Experimental Analysis of Behavior, 58,* 183-204.

Cumming, W. W., & Berryman, R. (1965). The complex discriminated operant: Studies of matching-to-sample and related problems. In D. I. Mostofsky (Ed.), *Stimulus generalization* (pp. 284-330). Stanford, CA: Stanford University Press.

D'Amato, M. R., & Colombo, M. (1985). Auditory matching-to-sample in monkeys (*Cebus apella*). *Animal Learning and Behavior, 13,* 375-382.

D'Amato, M. R., & Worsham, R. W. (1974). Retrieval cues and short-term memory in capuchin monkeys. *Journal of Comparative and Physiological Psychology, 86,* 274-282.

de Rose, J. C., Ribeiro, I. G., Reis, M. J. D., Kledaras, J. B. (1992). Possible effects of the procedure to teach conditional discriminations on the outcome of tests for stimulus equivalence and transfer of functions. *Experimental Analysis of Human Behavior Bulletin, 10,* 10-11.

Devany, J. M., Hayes, S. C., & Nelson, R. O. (1986). Equivalence class formation in language-able and language-disabled children. *Journal of the Experimental Analysis of Behavior, 46,* 243-257.

Dixon, M. H., Dixon, L. S., & Spradlin, J. E. (1983). Analysis of individual differences of stimulus control among developmentally disabled children. In K. D. Gadow & I. Bialer (Eds.), *Advances in Learning and Behavioral Disabilities* (Vol. 2, pp. 85-110). New York: JAI Press.

Dube, W. V., Green, G., & Serna, R. W. (1993). Auditory successive conditional discrimination and auditory stimulus equivalence classes. *Journal of the Experimental Analysis of Behavior, 59,* 103-114.

Dube, W. V. & McIlvane, W. J. (1995). Stimulus-reinforcer relations and emergent matching to sample. *Psychological Record, 45,* 591-612.

Dube, W. V, McIlvane, W. J., Mackay H. A., & Stoddard, L. T. (1987). Stimulus class membership established via stimulus-reinforcer relations. *Journal of the Experimental Analysis of Behavior, 47,* 159-175.

Dube, W. V., McIlvane, W. J., Maguire, R. W., Mackay, H. A., & Stoddard, L. T. (1989). Stimulus class formation and stimulus-reinforcer relations. *Journal of the Experimental*

Analysis of Behavior, 51, 65-76.

Eikeseth, S., & Smith, T. (1992). The development of functional and equivalence classes in high-functioning autistic children: The role of naming. *Journal of the Experimental Analysis of Behavior, 58*, 123-133.

Epstein, R. (1985). The spontaneous interconnection of three repertoires. *Psychological Record, 35*, 131-141.

Fields, L., Adams, B. J., Verhave, T., & Newman, S. (1990). The effects of nodality on the formation of equivalence classes. *Journal of the Experimental Analysis of Behavior, 53*, 345-358.

Galvão, O., Calcagno, S., & Sidman, M. (1992). Testing for emergent performances in extinction. *Experimental Analysis of Human Behavior Bulletin, 10*, 18-20.

Harlow, H.F. (1950). Analysis of discrimination learning by monkeys. *Journal of Experimental Psychology, 40*, 26-39.

Herrnstein, R. J. (1970). On the law of effect. *Journal of the Experimental Analysis of Behavior, 13*, 243-266.

Herrnstein, R. J., & Loveland, D. H. (1975). Maximizing and matching on concurrent ration schedules. *Journal of Experimental Analysis of Behavior, 24*, 107-116.

Huguenin, N. H. & Touchette, P. E. (1980). Visual attention in retarded adults: Combining stimuli which control incompatible behavior. *Journal of Experimental Analysis of Behavior, 33*, 77-86.

Iversen, I. H., Sidman, M., & Carrigan, P. (1986). Stimulus definition in conditional discrimination. *Journal of the Experimental Analysis of Behavior, 45*, 297-304.

Johnson, C., & Sidman, M. (1993). Conditional discriminations and equivalence relations: Control by negative stimuli. *Journal of the Experimental Analysis of Behavior, 33*, 333-347.

Lowry, P. W., & Ross, L. E. (1975). Severely retarded children as impulsive responders: Improved performance with response delay. *American Journal of Mental Deficiency, 80*, 133-138.

McIlvane, W. J. (1992). Stimulus control analysis and nonverbal instructional technology for people with mental handicaps. In N. R. Bray (Ed.), *International review of research in mental retardation* (Vol. 18, pp. 55-109). New York: Academic Press.

McIlvane, W. J., & Dube, W. V. (1992). Stimulus control shaping and stimulus control topographies. *Behavior Analyst, 15*, 89-94.

McIlvane, W. J., Dube, W. V., & Callahan, T. D. (1996). A behavior analytic perspective on attention. In R. Lyon and N. Krasnegor (Eds.), *Attention, Memory, and Executive Function* (pp. 97-117). Baltimore, MD: Brookes.

McIlvane, W. J., Dube, W. V., Kledaras, J. B., Iennaco, F. M., & Stoddard, L. T. (1990). Teaching relational discrimination to individuals with mental retardation: Some problems and possible solutions. *American Journal on Mental Retardation, 95*, 283-296.

McIlvane, W. J., Kledaras, J. B., Dube, W. V., & Stoddard, L. T. (1989). Automated instruction of severely and profoundly retarded individuals. In J. Mulick and R. Antonak (Eds.), *Transitions in Mental Retardation* (Vol. 4, pp. 15-76). Norwood, NJ: Ablex.

McIlvane, W. J., Kledaras, J. B., Iennaco, F. M., & Dube, W. V. (in press). High probability stimulus control topographies with delayed S+ onset in a simultaneous discrimination procedure. *Journal of the Experimental Analysis of Behavior.*

McIlvane, W. J., Kledaras, J. B., Lowry, M. W., & Stoddard, L. T. (1992). Studies of exclusion in individuals with severe mental retardation. *Research in Developmental Disabilities, 13*,

509-532.

McIlvane, W. J., Kledaras, J. B., Munson, L. C., King, K. A., de Rose, J. C., & Stoddard, L. T. (1987). Controlling relations in conditional discrimination and matching by exclusion. *Journal of the Experimental Analysis of Behavior, 48*, 187-208.

McIlvane, W. J., Kledaras, J. B., Stoddard, L.T., & Dube, W. V. (1990). Delayed sample presentation in MTS: Some possible advantages for teaching individuals with developmental limitations. *Experimental Analysis of Human Behavior Bulletin, 8*, 31-33.

McIlvane, W. J., Withstandley, J. K., & Stoddard, L. T. (1984). Positive and negative stimulus relations in severely retarded individuals' conditional discriminations. *Analysis and Intervention in Developmental Disabilities, 4*, 235-251.

Nevin, J. A. (1992). An integrative model for the study of behavioral momentum. *Journal of the Experimental Analysis of Behavior, 57*, 301-316.

Nevin, J. A., Mandell, C., & Atak, J. R. (1983). The analysis of behavioral momentum. *Journal of the Experimental Analysis of Behavior, 39*, 49-59.

Pilgrim, C., Chambers, L., & Galizio, M. (1995). Reversal of baseline relations and stimulus equivalence: II. children. *Journal of the Experimental Analysis of Behavior, 63*, 239-254.

Pilgrim, C. & Galizio, M. (1990). Relations between baseline contingencies and equivalence probe performances. *Journal of the Experimental Analysis of Behavior, 54*, 213-224.

Pilgrim, C. & Galizio, M. (1995). Reversal of baseline relations and stimulus equivalence: I. adults. *Journal of the Experimental Analysis of Behavior, 63*, 225-238.

Ray, B. A. (1969). Selective attention: The effects of combining stimuli which control incompatible behavior. *Journal of the Experimental Analysis of Behavior, 12*, 539-550.

Ray, B. A., & Sidman, M. (1970). Reinforcement schedules and stimulus control. In W. N. Schoenfeld (Ed.), *The theory of reinforcement schedules* (pp. 187-214). New York: Appleton-Century-Crofts.

Saunders, R. R., Saunders, K. J., Kirby, K. C., & Spradlin, J. E. (1988). The merger and development of equivalence classes by unreinforced conditional selection of comparison stimuli. *Journal of the Experimental Analysis of Behavior, 50*, 145-162.

Saunders, K. J., & Spradlin, J. E. (1989). Conditional discrimination in mentally retarded adults: The effects of training the component simple discriminations. *Journal of the Experimental Analysis of Behavior, 52*, 1-12.

Saunders, K. J., & Spradlin, J. E. (1990). Conditional discrimination in mentally retarded adults: The development of generalized skills. *Journal of the Experimental Analysis of Behavior, 54*, 239-250.

Saunders, K. J., & Spradlin, J. E. (1993). Conditional discrimination in mentally retarded subjects: Programming acquisition and learning set. *Journal of the Experimental Analysis of Behavior, 60*, 571-585.

Saunders, R. R., Wachter, J., & Spradlin, J. E. (1988). Establishing auditory stimulus control over an eight-member equivalence class via conditional discrimination procedures. *Journal of the Experimental Analysis of Behavior, 49*, 95-115.

Schroeder, S. (1975). Perseveration in concurrent performances by the developmentally retarded. *Psychological Record, 25*, 51-64.

Schusterman, R. J., & Kastak, D. (1993). A California sea lion (Zalophus californianus) is capable of forming equivalence relations. *Psychological Record, 43*, 823-839.

Serna, R. W., & Wilkinson, K. M. (1995). Methods for assessing feature-class membership in series of graded stimuli [Abstract]. *Proceedings of the 28th Annual Gatlinburg Conference* on Research and Theory in Mental Retardation and Developmental Disabilities, 78.

Sidman, M. (1969). Generalization gradients and stimulus control in delayed matching-to-sample. *Journal of the Experimental Analysis of Behavior, 33,* 285-289.

Sidman, M. (1971). Reading and auditory-visual equivalences. *Journal of Speech and Hearing Research, 14,* 5-13.

Sidman, M. (1980). A note on the measurement of conditional discrimination. *Journal of the Experimental Analysis of Behavior, 33,* 285-289.

Sidman, M. (1992a). Equivalence Relations: Some Basic Considerations. In S. C. Hayes & L. J. Hayes (Eds.), *Understanding verbal relations* (pp. 15-28). Reno, Nevada: Context Press.

Sidman, M. (1992b). Adventitious control by the location of comparison stimuli in conditional discriminations. *Journal of the Experimental Analysis of Behavior, 58,* 173-182.

Sidman, M. (1994). *Equivalence relations and behavior: A research story.* Boston: Authors Cooperative.

Sidman, M., & Cresson, O. (1973). Reading and crossmodal transfer of stimulus equivalences in severe mental retardation. *American Journal of Mental Deficiency, 77,* 515-523.

Sidman, M., Kirk, B., & Willson-Morris, M. (1985). Six-member stimulus classes generated by conditional discrimination procedures. *Journal of the Experimental Analysis of Behavior, 43,* 21-42.

Sidman, M., Rauzin, R., Lazar, R., Cunningham, S., Tailby, W., & Carrigan, P. (1982). A search for symmetry in the conditional discrimination of rhesus monkeys, baboons, and children. *Journal of the Experimental Analysis of Behavior, 37,* 23-44.

Sidman, M., & Tailby, W. (1982). Conditional discrimination vs. matching-to-sample: An expansion of the testing paradigm. *Journal of the Experimental Analysis of Behavior, 37,* 5-22.

Sidman, M., Willson-Morris, M., & Kirk, B. (1986). Matching-to-sample procedures and the development of equivalence relations: The role of naming. *Analysis and Intervention in Developmental Disabilities, 6,* 1-19.

Skinner, B. F. (1957). *Verbal behavior.* New York: Appleton-Century-Crofts.

Spradlin, J. E., Cotter, V. W, & Baxley, N. (1973). Establishing a conditional discrimination without direct training: A study of transfer with retarded adolescents. *American Journal of Mental Deficiency, 77,* 556-566.

Spradlin, J. E., Saunders, K. J., & Saunders, R. R. (1992). The stability of equivalence classes. In S. C. Hayes & L. J. Hayes (Eds.), *Understanding verbal relations* (pp. 29-42). Reno, NV: Context Press.

Stoddard, L. T., & McIlvane, W. J. (1989). Generalization after intradimensional discrimination training in 2-year old children. *Journal of Experimental Child Psychology, 47,* 324-334.

Stoddard, L. T., & Sidman, M. (1971). Stimulus control after intradimensional discrimination training. *Psychological Reports, 28,* 147-157.

Stikeleather, G., & Sidman, M. (1990). An instance of spurious equivalence relations. *Analysis of Verbal Behavior, 8,* 1-11.

Stromer, R., & Osborne, J. G. (1982). Control of adolescents' arbitrary matching-to-sample relations. *Journal of the Experimental Analysis of Behavior, 37,* 329-348.

Touchette, P. E. (1969). Tilted lines as complex stimuli. *Journal of the Experimental Analysis of Behavior, 12,* 211-214.

Wasserman, E. A. (1976). Successive matching-to-sample in the pigeon: Variations on a theme by Konorski. *Behavior Research Methods and Instrumentation, 8,* 278-282.

Watt, A., Keenan, M., Barnes, D., & Cairns, E. (1991). Social categorization and stimulus equivalence. *Psychological Record, 41,* 33-50.

Williams, B. A. (1988). Reinforcement, choice, and response strength. In R. C. Atkinson, R. J. Herrnstein, G. Lindzey, & R. D. Luce (Eds.), *Stevens' handbook of experimental psychology, Volume 2: Perception and motivation* (pp. 167-244). New York: J. Wiley & Sons.

Zeaman, D., & House, B. J. (1963). The role of attention in retardate discrimination learning. In N.R. Ellis (Ed.), *Handbook of mental deficiency, psychological theory and research* (pp. 159-223). New York: McGraw-Hill.

V

EQUIVALENCE CLASSES:
VERBAL BEHAVIOR

Stimulus Class Formation in Humans and Animals
T.R. Zentall and P.M. Smeets (Editors)
© 1996 Elsevier Science B.V. All rights reserved.

12

Naming and the Formation of Stimulus Classes

Robert Stromer and Harry A. Mackay

Eunice Kennedy Shriver Center and Northeastern University

Experiments by Sidman and colleagues were pivotal in the study of the equivalence of psychological events (Sidman, 1971; Sidman & Cresson, 1973; Sidman, Cresson, & Willson-Morris, 1974). Current research on stimulus classes generally, and equivalence classes in particular, is broadly based, reflecting its potential both for clarifying basic learning processes and solving problems of social concern. Much of the applied work, for example, has centered on the usefulness of the concepts and methods involved for improving the technology of teaching rudimentary communication skills to individuals with intellectual limitations (see reviews by Mackay, 1991; Mackay, Stromer, & Serna, in press; McIlvane, 1992; Remington, 1994; Shafer, 1993; Stromer, 1991; Stromer, Mackay, & Stoddard, 1992). The development of that teaching technology will benefit from close examination of the relationships between equivalence phenomena and verbal behaviors involving stimuli that are heard, spoken, signed, written and pictured. This chapter examines methods and data relevant to that endeavor and provides a framework for the analysis of some of those relationships.

The framework proposed is in the tradition of the experimental analysis of behavior (Goldiamond, 1962, 1966; Keller & Schoenfeld, 1950; Sidman, 1986, 1994; Skinner, 1935, 1950, 1957, 1968). We present its procedural and conceptual basis in the next section. We then critically examine the methods and their results in an effort to clarify the conditions under which functional relationships develop among verbal events and their referents. Finally, we focus on developmental issues and the role of collateral naming in stimulus class formation.

THE EXPERIMENTAL ANALYSIS OF NAMING AND STIMULUS CLASS FORMATION

Stimulus classes are defined by both procedural and functional criteria (Goldiamond, 1962, 1966; Keller & Schoenfeld, 1950; Sidman, 1986, 1994; Skinner, 1935). Stimulus classes are often inferred when the procedure relates two or more stimuli to a common event, traditionally, an action or a spoken word. The functional evidence of a stimulus class comes when the manipulation of one such stimulus event affects the other(s) in the same way. A distinction may be drawn between arbitrary classes, in which the stimuli have no physical features in common, and feature classes, in which the stimuli share physical attributes (cf. McIlvane, Dube, Green, & Serna, 1993; and see chapters in this volume by Astley & Wasserman; Roberts; Zentall). Our focus is on the arbitrary classes known as equivalence classes. In these classes, the relations among the stimuli can be shown to possess the properties of *reflexivity*, *symmetry*, and *transitivity*. The critical tests for these properties (Sidman, 1986, 1994; Sidman & Tailby, 1982; and see chapters in this volume by Saunders, Williams, & Spradlin; Pilgrim & Galizio) examine whether training that establishes arbitrary conditional relations among stimuli also produces other performances suggesting that: (a) each stimulus is conditionally related to itself (reflexivity), (b) the conditional and discriminative stimuli (sample and comparison stimuli, respectively) are interchangeable (symmetry), and (c) the conditional stimulus in one relation and the discriminative stimulus in a second are related to each other because each was related to a common stimulus (transitivity).

Stimulus classes have been distinguished from response classes that derive from procedures in which two or more responses (e.g., actions or spoken words) are related to a common stimulus. However, the importance of this distinction may be reduced by Sidman's (1994) reformulation of equivalence relations that incorporated responses, like names, and also other events like reinforcing stimuli within such classes. It now seems useful to begin a cohesive analysis of functional stimulus classes, equivalence classes, and other phenomena sometimes viewed in terms of response classes, including naming and other forms of differential responding (cf. Kirby & Bickel, 1988). As context for such analysis, the following sections consider methodological and conceptual matters in detail.

Procedures

Figures 1 and 2 illustrate three typical methods for examining the role of naming in the formation of equivalence classes. The procedure on the left in Figure 1 involves matching-to-sample tasks in which a common dictated sample stimulus provides the basis for class formation. For simplicity, three-key displays are shown; sample stimuli appear on the center key and comparison stimuli on the two side keys. The "A"B matching trials involve the dictated samples "dog" ("A1") and "cat" ("A2"); the comparisons are pictures of dog (B1) and cat (B2). When the sample is "A1," touching B1 (+) results in the delivery of a reinforcer, touching B2 does not. On other trials, the sample is "A2" and touching B2 (not B1) is reinforced. The training of "A"C matching is similar, except the comparisons are the printed words DOG (C1) and CAT (C2): On those trials, if "A1" is the sample, touching C1 is reinforced; if "A2," touching C2 is reinforced. The BC and CB tests provide the critical evidence for stimulus classes, the emergence of new matching performances without explicit reinforcement. During the BC test, for example, a subject should select the word DOG when the sample is the picture of a dog because each was related to the sample "dog" in training. The emergence of these performances permits the inference that the trained relations are symmetrical and transitive. The matching of the stimuli that are identical adds a demonstration of reflexivity. In addition, a subject who already responds discriminatively to words heard (e.g., by touching corresponding pictures, imitating), and orally names visual stimuli, also may demonstrate picture and word naming on the test trials shown at bottom left (cf. Baer, 1982).

In the procedure shown on the right in Figure 1, the bases for class membership are again common sample stimuli, but these samples are pictures instead of dictated words. The other stimuli for each potential class are also visual, two printed words. The AB matching task involves pictures of a dog (A1) and cat (A2) and the comparisons DOG and CAT. In AC matching, the samples are the same pictures but the comparisons are different words: If picture A1 is the sample, selecting SEB is reinforced; if picture A2, selecting TIP is reinforced. The formation of stimulus classes would be inferred if, during BC and CB tests, a subject correctly matched DOG and SEB to one another and CAT and TIP to one another. In addition, if the subject has a history of oral naming, we can assess whether the pictures and words used in training are named appropriately and consistently, even though the contingencies of reinforcement never required listening to or saying anything.

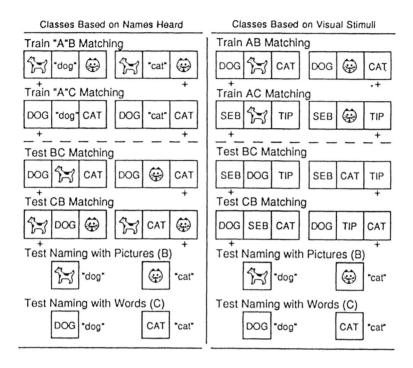

Figure 1. Left: During "A"B and "A"C training, matching-to-sample trials involve the dictated sample stimuli "dog" and "cat." The comparison stimuli are pictures of dog and cat or the printed words DOG and CAT. respectively. During BC and CB matching tests, samples and comparisons are pictures and printed words. Right: During AB and AC training, trials involve picture samples, and the comparisons are either DOG and CAT or SEB and TIP, respectively. During BC and CB tests, samples and comparisons are printed words. In oral naming tests for both procedures, individual pictures and printed words are presented.

Figure 2 shows a procedure in which potential classes are based on names said by a subject. Stimuli such as the pictures and words may share class membership because each is related to a single oral name, a common response. In this example, a subject learns to say "dog" when shown the picture of a dog or the word DOG, and to say "cat" when shown the picture of a cat or the word CAT. As before, the BC and CB tests provide the crucial evidence for class formation. If the pictures and words are matched to one another, then these tests provide a basis for inferring that the stimuli in each class are related by equivalence. The receptive "A"B and "A"C matching tasks assess whether the referent-"name" relations established by direct training are bidirectional.

Conceptual approaches

Horne and Lowe (1996; see also Dugdale & Lowe, 1990) suggest that the formation of equivalence classes may require explicit or implicit verbal mediation. At the core of their account

Classes Based on Names Said

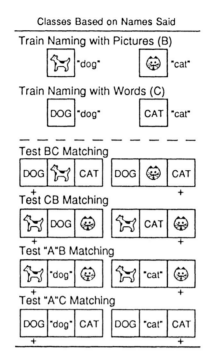

Figure 2. During training, the subject learns to say "dog" when shown the picture of a dog and the printed word DOG, and to say "cat" when shown the picture of a cat and the word CAT. During BC and CB matching-to-sample tests, sample and comparison stimuli are pictures and printed words. During "A"B and "A"C testing, the samples are the dictated names "dog" and "cat," and the comparison stimuli are pictures of dog and cat or the words DOG and CAT, respectively.

is the "naming relation," a synthesis of the behaviors of an individual as speaker and as listener. The naming relation is considered the basic unit of verbal behavior. The implication is that teaching receptive "name"-referent performances should yield the corresponding expressive referent-"name" performances without further teaching. Teaching and testing in the reverse order should have a similar effect; establishing new expressive performances should yield the receptive ones. Such performances may be elaborated by an individual's interactions with the natural environment establishing, for example, stimulus classes involving the names heard and said (e.g., "shoe" spoken by different individuals) and a range of corresponding referents (e.g., several different shoes and pictures of shoes). These classes may be based on common features (e.g., the shape of shoes) or on arbitrary trained relations. Among the arbitrary classes are those that satisfy the criteria for stimulus equivalence.

Horne and Lowe (1996) suggest that the "higher order bidirectional" naming relation is both necessary and sufficient for positive outcomes on tests of equivalence, even in learning situations that do not require hearing or saying a word. From this standpoint, each of the experimental approaches outlined in Figures 1 and 2 should give rise to emergent matching *and* also naming in individuals who enter an experiment capable of the naming relation. However, this approach has a fundamental problem: It assumes that the origins of the complex behavioral repertoire from which equivalence relations may be inferred are presumed to lie in another repertoire, called the naming relation, which need not involve overt behavior. In contrast, others (e.g., Hayes, 1991; Hayes & Hayes, 1992; Mackay, 1991; Sidman, 1986, 1990, 1994) suggest that naming may be sufficient but is not necessary for the formation of equivalence classes. Verbal mediation by names is not required but can facilitate the acquisition of equivalence relations. The conditions under which such facilitation may occur are not clear. However, the approach that is most likely to foster the understanding of any functional relations that develop among the behavioral repertoires concerned is readily apparent:

As Shimoff noted, "An experimental analysis of behavior generally seeks causes of behavior in the environment, not in other behavior" (1984, p. 1; cf. 1986). This means that the origins of stimulus classes in general and equivalence relations in particular do not lie in naming relations. Likewise, the origins of naming relations do not lie in equivalence relations. The origins of both, and any functional relations between them, will be found in environment-behavior relations, such as contingencies of reinforcement, that give rise to the stimulus control involved. The danger of straying too far from this credo is that data may be misinterpreted, overlooked, or both (cf. Perone, 1988). With the focus removed from environment-based relations, one may fail to appreciate fully the complex repertoires called concepts, categories, equivalence, and naming relations. The implications may be profound, particularly if the aims of a basic research program include application (Stromer, 1996b, p. 250).

Sidman's laboratory behavioral analyses of equivalence and oral naming were relevant for both learning theory and application (Sidman, 1971; Sidman & Cresson, 1973; Sidman et al., 1974). He taught rudimentary reading skills to the individuals with mental retardation who participated. An account of the equivalences demonstrated by these subjects that depends on verbal mediation largely ignores research illustrating the application of learning principles in homes, schools, and clinics. Fortunately, any controversy over whether naming is necessary for class formation has not prevented the growth of a diverse list of areas for applied analyses of equivalence research (e.g., Cowley, Green, & Braunling-McMorrow, 1992; de Rose, de Souza, Rossito, & de Rose, 1992; Kennedy, Itkonen, & Lindquist, 1994; Lynch & Cuvo, 1995; Maydak, Stromer, Mackay, & Stoddard, 1995; Osborne & Gatch, 1989; Stromer, Mackay, Howell, McVay, & Flusser, 1996).

A verbal mediation account also ignores how the variables at the core of fundamental learning principles operate in the natural and laboratory environments of nonhumans. There are obvious differences in the performances of humans and nonhumans. Nevertheless, it seems clear that the behavior of nonhumans reflects many of the stimulus control phenomena routinely demonstrable in humans, even some that may underlie stimulus equivalence (e.g., Dube, McIlvane, Callahan, & Stoddard, 1993; Sidman, 1994; Wasserman & DeVolder, 1993; Zentall & Urcuioli, 1993; and see chapters in this volume). Pigeons, for example, show feature stimulus classes (Herrnstein & Loveland, 1964) and arbitrary stimulus classes (Vaughan, 1988; cf.

Sidman, 1994). Especially noteworthy is Schusterman and Kastak's (1993) study of equivalence in a sea lion which suggests that spoken verbal skills are not necessary components of the performances involved. Other research also illustrates promising approaches to the analysis of the role of vocal behavior (e.g., sufficiency, necessity) in emergent performances that involve classes of stimuli and responses (e.g., Manabe, Kawashima, & Staddon, 1995; McIntire, Cleary, & Thompson, 1987; Pepperberg, 1990, this volume). Given all these considerations, a focus on issues that concern generality of principle and procedure may give the theoretical debate about the role of naming a positive and productive direction that does not divert attention from needed experimental analyses.

Of course, questions concerning the function of a subject's verbal behavior in an operant learning situation that does not require such behavior are not limited to studies of stimulus classes. For example, Bentall, Lowe, and Beasty (1985) examined the relationship between the schedule performances and verbal behavior of children and concluded that: "the development of verbal behavior greatly alters human operant performance and may account for many of the differences found between human and animal learning" (p. 165). As Perone (1988) put it, however:

The key question is not whether this conclusion is correct or even reasonable, but rather whether it is justified on the basis of the data. ... When the laboratory behavior of human subjects differs from that of nonhumans, it is tempting to attribute the differences to the humans' complex verbal and cognitive abilities. More constructive, perhaps, would be to regard such [differences] in the same way as one would regard discrepancies among nonhuman studies -- simply as instances in which the controlling environmental contingencies remain to be identified (p. 74).

This same constructive behavioral approach is also relevant to analyses of differences among humans who participate in research on class formation. The approach minimizes neither the need for analyses of relationships between verbal and nonverbal repertoires nor the "uniqueness" of the verbal repertoire of humans and their proclivity to use it. Just because "behavior can occur in nonverbal subjects does not mean that it does remain nonverbal in verbally capable subjects; that rats press bars nonverbally does not imply that college students also press bars nonverbally" (Shimoff, 1986, p. 20). Verbal behavior is not an ultimate cause of nonverbal behavior, just as nonverbal behavior is not an ultimate cause of verbal behavior. "The ultimate causes of behavior -- at least for a behavioral analysis -- are in the environment" (Shimoff, 1986, p. 22). Behavior analysis helps one appreciate, for example, "that the mere possession of an extensive verbal repertoire is not sufficient to ensure that behavior is rule-governed" (Pouthas, Droit, Jacquet, & Wearden, 1990, p. 30), rather than contingency-shaped (cf. Kendler & Kendler, 1962; Luria, 1961; Reese, 1992). As to the present context, notions of "verbal or relational control" (Hayes & Hayes, 1992), "naming relations" (Horne & Lowe, 1996), and "equivalence" may serve as useful descriptors of the complex behaviors produced by the protocols used in research with humans (e.g., Barnes, 1994; cf. Sidman, 1986). However, little is gained by adopting such complex behavioral outcomes as explanatory processes. Parsimony remains on the side of an account that is based directly on environment-behavior relations. The following provides relevant illustrations.

STIMULUS CLASSES WITH AND WITHOUT NAMES

In this section, we examine basic findings of research using variants of the procedures described earlier. Relevant general concerns include clarification of the conditions under which auditory-visual, visual-visual, and referent-"name" procedures generate stimulus classes. Further, are the methods equally effective in doing so? Do procedures that establish receptive "name"-referent relations also give rise to expressive referent-"name" relations, and vice versa, even when the relevant performances are not required by the reinforcement contingencies?

Effects of training auditory-visual relations

The human's unique capacity for orally naming environmental events, and the ubiquity of contingencies of reinforcement for doing so, raise questions about the role of naming in the formation of stimulus classes. Sidman's original studies involving individuals with mental retardation illustrate the basic issues. In Sidman (1971; see Figure 1, left), the subject matched pictures to dictation ("A"B) and named the pictures (B) upon entering the study. The only direct teaching, which involved matching words to dictation ("A"C), then led to the emergent matching of pictures and printed words (BC and CB), and oral naming of the words (C). These results were replicated in Sidman and Cresson (1973; Figure 1, left) but with less capable subjects. Because oral naming of printed words emerged in these studies, a natural question concerned whether the naming produced or facilitated the class formation. However, these studies leave the role of naming unclear because the names were dictated to and spoken by the subject. Either or both in combination could be important.

The protocol used by Sidman et al. (1974) was more instructive. It involved teaching "A"B and BC matching, then testing "A"C and CB matching, and naming of the B and C stimuli. The possibility that "A"C matching would emerge in the absence of the oral naming of the C stimuli was of major interest and this indeed happened. The receptive "A"C matching emerged first and then naming improved markedly across the rest of the experiment. The results, therefore, suggest that oral naming was not required for the emergence of the receptive matching performances ("A"C) involving dictated names as samples and textual stimuli as comparisons.

Dixon (1978) replicated aspects of Sidman's early studies and pointed the way toward further laboratory investigations. Individuals with mental retardation were taught to match four nonsense forms to the auditory sample "la," and another four to the sample "dee." In testing, the subjects matched the visual stimuli in each set to one another, performances consistent with the formation of experimentally defined classes. Dixon did not assess oral naming. However, Sidman and Tailby (1982) did so in a similar study with eight normally capable children. The children learned to match sets of three different visual comparisons to each of two dictated words (Greek letter names) as samples ("A"B, "A"C, and "A"D matching). All children then matched the visual stimuli to one another (e.g., BC, CB, and CD), thereby suggesting that the relations among stimuli were symmetric and transitive. In addition, seven of the eight named the stimuli, just like subjects in Sidman's earlier studies. Sidman, Kirk, and Willson-Morris (1985) extended these findings by showing the formation of six-member classes, each class involving one dictated name and five visual stimuli. Of the eight subjects who formed classes, six also named the five visual stimuli in each class by its corresponding dictated name. Although most children in the latter two studies showed emergent oral naming, some children did not (cf. Green, 1990), suggesting that naming may not be necessary for class formation.

Effects of training only visual-visual relations

Spradlin, Cotter, and Baxley (1973) explored the possibility that training with only visual stimuli in matching tasks that neither involve nor require names may establish arbitrary stimulus classes. Figure 3 illustrates trials of the kind used in their research (Experiment 2 at left, 3 at right). In Experiment 2, AB and CB matching were established initially; thus, common comparisons provided a basis for relations between the A and C samples. The experiment did not use the typical tests for the properties of equivalence relations (e.g., tests of AC and CA matching), but rather resembled a study of functional equivalence classes (Goldiamond, 1962, 1966; cf. Sidman, 1994). The rationale follows: If, through training, one pair of conditional stimuli (A1 and A2) come to control new discriminative responses (D1 and D2), then the other pair of conditional stimuli (C1 and C2) should also control these discriminative responses. Accordingly, the A samples were related to new comparisons in AD matching, followed by the critical test for CD matching. All three participants with mental retardation matched the C and D stimuli with high accuracy (see also Urcuioli, Zentall, Jackson-Smith, & Steirn, 1989).

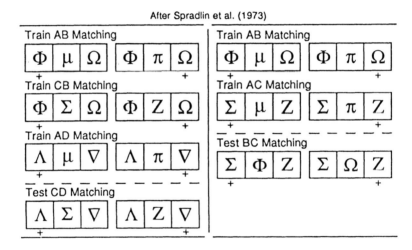

Figure 3. Left: During AB and CB matching-to-sample training trials, the sample stimuli are from two different sets of forms; the comparison stimuli are the same in both tasks. The AD training trials involve one pair of familiar samples and a new set of comparisons. During CD testing, trials involve the second pair of samples and the new comparisons. Right: During AB and AC training trials, the samples are the same forms in both matching tasks; the comparisons differ. During BC testing, forms (B) that appeared as comparisons during training are now presented as samples, with familiar comparisons.

The procedure in Spradlin et al.'s (1973) Experiment 3 resembled those of Sidman (1971) and Sidman and Cresson (1973) more closely. After training with AB and AC matching, BC matching was tested. Two of the three subjects showed BC matching, one immediately and one after repeated testing. The third subject never showed BC matching. The authors suggested that procedural factors probably were responsible for these mixed results. The subjects were not given both AB and AC trials as a baseline at the time of BC testing, a procedure that may not be conducive to the formation of stimulus classes for some subjects. In a later section, we examine in detail three other studies that used variants of Spradlin et al.'s procedure and also failed to establish visual stimulus classes (Barnes, McCullagh, & Keenan, 1990; Devany, Hayes, & Nelson, 1986; Eikeseth & Smith, 1992).

Subsequent research has shown that purely visual classes are readily demonstrated when test trials are interspersed among baseline trials. This procedure was used by Stromer and Osborne (1982), for example, in a study similar to Spradlin et al.'s, and three subjects immediately passed tests for stimulus classes. A fourth did so after repeated tests. Other studies with normally capable children and individuals with mental retardation also demonstrate reliable formation of visual stimulus classes (Haring, Breen, & Laitinen, 1989; Lazar, Davis-Lang, & Sanchez, 1984; Saunders, Saunders, Kirby, & Spradlin, 1988; Saunders, Wachter, & Spradlin, 1988; Sidman et al., 1985; Sidman, Willson-Morris, & Kirk, 1986; Wetherby, Karlan, & Spradlin, 1983).

Comparing auditory-visual and visual-visual training

The data from most previous studies suggest that matching tasks that involve auditory samples and visual comparisons may be easier to learn than tasks in which both the samples and comparisons are visual. Sidman and Cresson's (1973) assessment data suggest that normally capable children and older individuals with mental retardation may enter an experimental or teaching situation showing better auditory-visual than visual-visual matching. Other relevant data come from the few studies that report the results of subject-screening. Dixon (1978) gave an auditory-visual matching task as preliminary training to 16 individuals with mental retardation and 12 (75%) met the acquisition criterion required for further participation. In contrast, Dixon and Spradlin (1976) and Stromer and Osborne (1982) used arbitrary visual-visual matching tasks as preliminary training and only 6 of 22 (27%) and 13 of 22 (59%) individuals continued in the respective studies.

If subjects learn an experimental baseline of auditory-visual matching faster than one involving visual-visual matching, are related differences in class formation also observed? The answer appears to be yes, under some conditions: Subjects with mental retardation may form classes more readily when the stimuli are related in training to a common auditory stimulus rather than to another visual stimulus (Green, 1990; Sidman et al., 1986). However, normally capable children aged 5 years may show no such differential effects (Sidman et al., 1986). Green's data are also significant with respect to the controversy about the role of naming. Unlike Sidman's (1971) and Sidman and Cresson's (1973) results, the receptive "A"B and "A"C training in Green's study produced stimulus classes but only two of five subjects named the stimuli consistently.

Green's (1990) study also is relevant to the earlier discussion suggesting that the omission of trials involving critical baselines may put some subjects at a disadvantage during testing. The protocol ensured high accuracy on the arbitrary matching baselines immediately before testing, but the test trials were not mixed among baseline trials. Whereas classes involving auditory stimuli emerged rapidly, the visual stimulus classes for most subjects emerged only with repeated training and testing. Perhaps the testing procedure interacted with another general feature of the training that is known to cause difficulties for visual stimulus class formation: Training tasks like Green's, which involve common visual sample stimuli (e.g., AB and AC), may be less likely to yield class formation than training tasks that involve common visual comparison stimuli (e.g., AB and CB). This difference has been shown in studies of five-member classes (Saunders, Wachter, & Spradlin, 1988; Spradlin & Saunders, 1986) but not three-member classes in subjects with mental retardation (Stromer & Osborne, 1982; de Rose, this volume; and for related studies with nonhumans, Urcuioli, this volume).

Effects of training oral naming

The production of a common name may provide the basis for relations among the visual stimuli that are named. Suppose, for example, that a subject is taught to name the arbitrary forms A1 and B1 "zeta," and to name A2 and B2 "eta" (Figure 4, top). Would such training yield AB (form) matching? The answer is a qualified yes. Eikeseth and Smith (1992, Phase 3) demonstrated this kind of outcome in two of three children with autism. Details of that study are described later. For the present, note that these children had been trained to name stimuli earlier in the study. That experience may have helped them succeed on the AB test just described.

Eikeseth and Smith's (1992) results resemble those of earlier mediation studies which suggest that verbal and nonverbal repertoires may function independently. For example, Figure 4 (lower left) depicts the design of a study by Birge (1941; as cited in Reese & Lipsitt, 1970, pp. 226-227). In Phase 1, children aged about 8 to 10 years were taught to name A1 and B1 "towk" and to name A2 and B2 "meef." In Phase 2, A1 and A2 were the stimuli in a simultaneous discrimination in which selections of A1 were reinforced and selections of A2 were not. Phase 3 tested discriminative performance with B1 and B2. If the children selected B1, it would suggest that Phase 1 may have established A1 and B1 as one stimulus class and A2 and B2 as another. Training in Phase 1, however, did not suffice to produce these outcomes reliably in Phase 3; about 54% of the children showed the expected test outcomes. More children succeeded when they were required to name the stimuli aloud during simultaneous discrimination training in Phase 2 (77%), testing in Phase 3 (62%), or in both of these phases (85%).

Similar results were reported by Kendler (1972) with kindergarten children using letter-like forms and familiar spoken words (Figure 4, lower right). After training in Phase 1, A1 and B1 were called "one," and A2 and B2 were called "two." Phase 2 established a conditional position discrimination: If A1, respond left; if A2, respond right. Phase 3 then tested if B1 and B2 would also control responding left and right, respectively. Only about 64% of the children who were not required to name B1 and B2 aloud showed this new discrimination. In contrast, about 80% of the children who were required to name performed the untrained discrimination reliably.

Taken together, these findings suggest a possibly important role for dictated auditory stimuli and their spoken (by the subject) counterparts in class formation. The possibility may even gain special interest in light of the deficiencies shown by some individuals with mental retardation in forming visual classes (Green, 1990; MacDonald, Dixon, & LeBlanc, 1986; Sidman et al., 1986; Spradlin & Saunders, 1986). It may not be coincidental that such individuals also display production deficiencies (cf. Flavell, Beach, & Chinsky, 1966; Kendler, 1972). For example, persons with developmental delays may name stimuli readily but fail to use these names as helpful mediators in tasks like delayed matching to sample, unless explicit instructions are given to do so (Bonta & Watters, 1981; Constantine & Sidman, 1975; Gutowski, Geren, Stromer, & Mackay, 1995; Mackay & Ratti, 1990).

The problem of crossmodal transfer of stimulus control
    Studies of class expansion provide further data concerning names and their role in stimulus classes. The success of different procedures appears to depend on the nature of the existing classes and whether the stimuli to be added to the classes are auditory or visual. In one of three related studies, Spradlin and Dixon (1976) examined the addition of an auditory stimulus to classes of visual stimuli in two subjects. The aim was to (a) establish two classes of four visual stimuli in which all conditional relations were trained directly, (b) establish matching to dictation with one stimulus from each class serving as the correct comparisons (e.g., "voo"-A1 and "zi"-A2), and then (c) test whether the dictated samples controlled selections of the remaining members of each class (e.g., "voo"-B1 and "zi"-B2). Both subjects failed to show transfer after only one auditory-visual conditional relation had been trained; two were needed. In a similar study, Dixon and Spradlin (1976) found that after initial training, only three of the six subjects showed the transfer of auditory stimulus control which suggested class expansion; additional training was required by the others. In contrast, Saunders, Wachter, and Spradlin (1988) found that auditory stimulus control developed rapidly in four subjects who had previously acquired two eight-member classes of visual stimuli. After learning to match just one stimulus from each class to a dictated stimulus, three of the four subjects also matched all remaining stimuli to the respective names with no further teaching.
    The preceding studies show the integration of auditory-visual and visual-visual relations. Nonetheless, an apparent incompatibility of the two kinds of stimulus control may prevent immediate transfer. This conclusion must be tentative because the formal analyses remain to be done. However, comparison of the findings of Spradlin and Dixon (1976) and Dixon and Spradlin (1976) with those of Saunders, Wachter, and Spradlin (1988), suggests that the method used to establish a class of visual stimuli may affect how rapidly an auditory stimulus can be added. Perhaps the direct training of visual-visual relations may be particularly likely to produce independent conditional discriminations (cf. Sidman, 1994, pp. 317-318; Stromer et al., 1992). The question about the role of oral naming also remains: At the end of their study, Spradlin and Dixon found that the subjects named all members of one class "voo" and the other class "zi." Neither Dixon and Spradlin nor Saunders, Wachter, and Spradlin assessed oral naming.
    A study by Anderson and Spradlin (1980) contrasts with the studies described above, providing evidence of the independence of verbal and nonverbal behavior in a subject with mental retardation. The stimuli were six groups of common objects (Cars, Bowls, Hats, Dolls, Shoes, and Books) that formed classes of stimuli with common features. There were six to nine different exemplars of each class. An initial test verified that the six groups of items functioned as classes: Objects assigned to the Car class were matched to one another, as were those assigned to the Bowl class, and so on. After this test, the focus of the study shifted to teaching names for the stimuli. Would the subject trained to name some members of a class also give the same name to the rest? This outcome occurred after the subject learned to name only one item from each of the Car and Bowl classes. However, this transfer of stimulus control occurred after names had been learned for three items of the Shoe and Book classes, four items of the Hat class, and five items of the Doll class. Probes for receptive matching were conducted throughout the study; accuracy on these probes was almost always less than 50%. Such independence may have been due partly to the absence of relevant baseline trials during the referent-"name" and "name"-referent tests.
    To summarize, it appears that auditory-visual matching will be acquired more rapidly than visual-visual matching, and also be more likely to yield stimulus classes. Not enough is

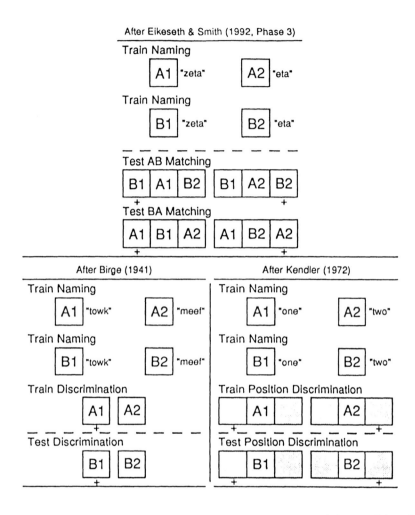

Figure 4. Procedures for assessing class formation based on referent-"name" relations: Training of oral names is similar in each example: Subjects supply one name for each of two forms (A1 and B1), and a second name for each of two other forms (A2 and B2). The procedures for testing class formation then differ. Matching to sample (top): After familiarization with matching tasks, AB and BA test trials are presented in which the A and B stimuli appear as samples and comparisons for the first time. Simultaneous discrimination (left): After training on a simple simultaneous discrimination between A1 and A2, discrimination between B1 and B2 is assessed. Position discrimination (right): After training on a left-right discrimination with A1 and A2 as conditional stimuli, discriminative performance with B1 and B2 is assessed.

known about the effects of referent-"name" procedures to permit firm conclusions, but one should expect difficulties in class formation unless subjects "use" the names they are taught.

Furthermore, the acquisition of auditory-visual "name"-referent relations does not reliably produce the referent-"name" relations of expressive performances, nor vice versa. Of course, the independences that occur among auditory-visual and visual-visual relations and oral naming come as no surprise. Such results are consistent with prior research involving a variety of language tasks and both normal children and individuals with intellectual handicaps (e.g., Guess & Baer, 1973; Lamarre & Holland, 1985; Lee, 1981; Lee & Pegler; 1982; Partington & Bailey, 1993; Smeets & Striefel, 1976; Stromer, 1996a; Stromer & Mackay, 1992a; Watkins, Pack-Teixteira, & Howard, 1989). Finally, the evidence concerning whether subjects come to name visual stimuli that serve as comparisons in auditory-visual matching tasks is mixed.

DEVELOPMENTAL STATUS AND STIMULUS CLASS FORMATION

Understanding the roles of names heard and names said in the formation of stimulus classes will require extensive further study. The literature does not yet answer questions about the developmental variables that may be important in the formation of arbitrary stimulus classes. Work with preverbal infants has just begun (Lipkens, Hayes, & Hayes, 1993) and many questions remain with older children. Research so far suggests that linguistic competence may be correlated with performance on the tasks used in equivalence research. In particular, poor performances on those tasks by young subjects who also did poorly on some language assessment have been used to support the hypothesis that language plays a crucial role in the formation of equivalence classes.

Horne and Lowe (1996) and Hayes (Hayes, 1991; Hayes & Hayes, 1992) have been most explicit about the relationship of developmental status to class formation. Horne and Lowe give special status to the repertoire of the normally developing child, presumably aged 4 to 5 years. They suggest that such children have learning histories that give rise to the naming relation described earlier, a repertoire that is both necessary and sufficient for positive outcomes on tests of equivalence. Some aspects of Hayes' theory (Hayes, 1991; Hayes & Hayes, 1992) are consistent with Horne and Lowe's notions about naming relations. For example, Hayes describes a learning history that may give rise to a kind of symmetry (or bidirectionality) of the stimulus control involved in receptive "name"-referent and expressive referent-"name" tasks. Hayes' account, moreover, suggests that sufficient exposure to such learning tasks may result in the new process, "verbal or relational control," a kind of learning set that accounts for the rapid transfer between the tasks. The two views also differ. For example, the normal child aged 2 years (rather than 4 to 5) displays the performances from which verbal control may be inferred. Also, for Hayes, the formation of equivalence classes may be facilitated but is not necessarily mediated by the events in verbal relations.

The data

Three studies often are used to support verbal mediation accounts of stimulus equivalence. Close examination of these studies may be instructive because all three used similar procedures. Devany et al. (1986) studied three groups of four children: Children in the normal group were aged 2-1 (years-months) to 2-11 (MAs 19 to 37 months), those in the retarded/language group were aged 2-8 to 4-4 (MAs 19 to 36 months), and those in the retarded/no-language group were aged 2-7 to 4-4 (MAs 14 to 30 months). Using non-automated methods, each child learned arbitrary matching with six visual stimuli (A1, B1, C1, A2, B2, C2), that differed in shape and color. All trials began with the experimenter saying, "Touch the one that goes with this one." A three-step procedure was used to teach AB matching. In Step 1, trials were presented in blocks that always involved the nominal sample A1, the correct comparison B1+, and the negative comparison B2-. Trials continued until B1+ was selected reliably regardless of its location on the left or right. Step 2 was similar except the trials involved A2 as the nominal sample and the correct and incorrect comparisons were B2+ and B1-, respectively. In Step 3, the two types of trials were mixed, requiring a conditional discrimination for the first time. This three-step procedure was then repeated to establish AC matching. Subjects were given tests for equivalence after meeting criteria on a mixed baseline of AB and AC trials.

The tests assessed BC and CB matching in four 10-trial blocks. No baseline trials were presented and the child was given a reinforcer after every third or fourth trial for cooperation, attending, etc. During testing, the four normal children performed the BC and CB matching with high accuracy. The two columns on the left in Figure 5 show the results for the four children (Al, Be, Ca, and Da) with retardation and language and the four children (An, Ba, Cr, and De) with retardation but without language. All the children with language whether normal (not shown) or with retardation passed the tests for equivalence. However, all four of the children without language failed these tests.

Subjects in Barnes et al. (1990; cf. Barnes, Browne, Smeets, & Roche, 1995) were two normal children (aged 4-7 and 3-4), and four with hearing deficits (aged 4-10 to 8-1). Only two of the latter four children had verbal ages greater than 2 years. The stimuli were the same as in Devany et al. (1986) and the children were "asked to indicate which of the two comparison stimuli 'goes' with this one (the sample)" (p. 23). The two normal children passed the BC and CB tests. Figure 5 (middle) shows that three of the children with hearing loss also passed the tests; only Claudia (Cu) failed. Notably, however, Claudia received the tests twice and scored zero during the first tests. Such performance reflects perfect conditional discrimination but reliable selection of the incorrect one of the two comparison stimuli presented (e.g., selecting B2 when the sample was A1).

Eikeseth and Smith's (1992) subjects were four children with autism, aged 3-6 to 5-6 and with MAs of <2-4 to 3-8. The stimuli were Greek letters and printed words and all trials began with the experimenter saying, "Point to same." In Phase 1, testing began after AB and AC matching were established. Figure 5 (right) shows data for tests given to each child. First the baseline performances were accurate (open bars). Then, in blocks of BC and CB trials, all the children did poorly (shaded bars). After additional testing verified that baseline performance remained accurate, symmetry of the AB and AC relations was tested (BA and CA trials). Symmetry test scores (striped bars) were high for Trey (Tr) and Joe (Jo), but Rory's (Ro) scores varied from 70% to 90% correct, and Danny's (Da) were all 40% correct. In the final tests, scores were again low on the BC and CB trials but perfect on baseline trials.

Chronological age and performance

How do the preceding studies compare with others that may suggest a relationship between chronological age and success in equivalence experiments? Barnes et al.'s (1990) data are consistent with studies using children aged 4 to 6 years in stimulus class research (e.g., Lazar et al., 1984; Pilgrim, Chambers, & Galizio, 1995; Sidman et al., 1985; Sidman et al., 1986; Stikeleather & Sidman, 1990; Wetherby et al., 1983). Almost all normal children in this age range readily form classes even when all samples and comparisons are visual stimuli (for failures with children aged 4 to 5, see Dugdale & Lowe, 1990). Barnes et al. (1995) also

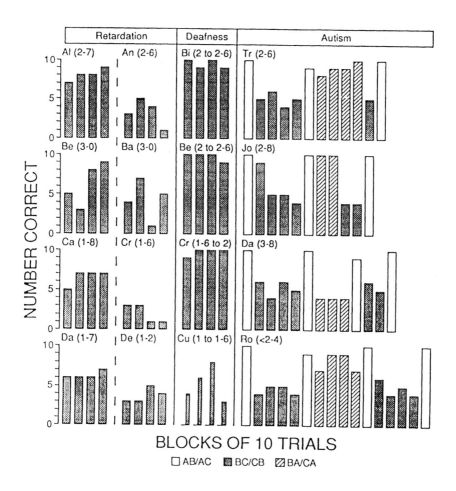

Figure 5. Data adapted from portions of studies by Devany et al., (1986; Retardation), Barnes et al., (1990; Deafness), and Eikeseth and Smith (1992; Autism). Each bar represents the number of correct trials out of 10 given in consecutive blocks of a particular test. Subjects' names are abbreviated above each set of bars; numbers within parentheses reflect mental ages (in years-months) or verbal ages (middle column). Pairs of bars are shown for Subject Cu (middle column, bottom): The bar on the left of each pair shows a score (all zero) for each of the first four blocks of test trials; the bar on the right of each pair shows a score for the second four blocks of test trials.

reported success using a three-step method like that used by Devany et al. (1986) to teach AB and AC matching to children aged 2-11 to 6-2. In contrast, young normal children, aged 2 to 3 years may experience difficulty even in acquiring the baseline performances for studies of equivalence. For example, Augustson and Dougher (1991) attempted to establish arbitrary matching in five children using computer presentation of black-white stimuli, and a three-step teaching method like Devany et al.'s. Whereas two children aged 4-7 and 6-4 learned the task, all younger children failed at Step 3 when the contingencies actually required a conditional discrimination (cf. McIlvane, Dube, Kledaras, Iennaco, & Stoddard, 1990).

Even when children aged 2 to 3 years do learn a baseline of arbitrary matching, they may not pass tests for equivalence (e.g., BC and CB). Horne and Lowe (1996) summarize a study of 29 children taught a baseline of AB and AC matching. The stimuli were vertical and horizontal lines (A), the colors green and red (B), and a cross and a triangle (C). All 10 children aged 4 to 5 passed tests for equivalence. However, only 6 of 12 children aged 3 to 4 passed the tests; and only 1 of 7 aged 2 to 3 did so. In contrast, recall that all four normal children aged 2 to 3 years succeeded in Devany et al. (1986). If language development, which may be expected to increase with age in normal children, is an important variable, the results of the two studies seem to differ in the level of development that may be needed. Devany et al.'s data suggest that the repertoire of the normal 2 year old is sufficient; Lowe and colleagues' data seem to put this age at about 4 years. Clearly, the relationship between age and performance on tasks that provide the prerequisites for equivalence relations requires more analysis.

Language and disability

Do the results of the studies by Devany et al. (1986), Barnes et al. (1990), and Eikeseth and Smith (1992) implicate language or disability? Devany et al.'s subjects (aged 2-8 to 4-4) with mental retardation, who were judged to be verbal, passed tests of equivalence. Presumably the verbal repertoires of these children corresponded roughly to their mental ages of 19 to 36 months. In contrast, children (aged 2-7 to 4-4) with mental retardation who were judged to be nonverbal did not pass the tests. These data suggest that verbal skills at a 2-year level may be important to success on the equivalence procedures used. We hasten to add, however, that further research is needed to (a) specify empirically the behavioral basis for clinical judgments that children may be "language-disabled," and (b) to examine several procedural variables that could have contributed to Devany et al.'s findings. For example, the role of verbal instructions merits attention. Recall also that even older, "language-able" persons with mental retardation have difficulties when the procedures do not maintain relevant baseline performances during testing (Green, 1990; Spradlin et al., 1973; see also Dube & McIlvane, this volume).

The data from Barnes et al. (1990) suggest that neither deafness nor verbal age is related to success on tests of equivalence. The four hearing impaired children had IQ scores in the normal range, suggesting that their mental ages were comparable to their chronological ages of 4-10 to 8-1. Their verbal ages, however, were estimated to be in the 1-0 to 2-6 range. The differing results for the two children with verbal ages less than 2 years are noteworthy: Clare (Cr) succeeded on the equivalence tests but Claudia did not. Claudia's data, however, may tell us more about the procedures used than about language because her conditional discrimination performance was perfect but inappropriate on the initial tests. Indeed, Claudia's test results for the first four sessions may reflect class formation which was based on Reject rather than Select conditional relations (Carrigan & Sidman, 1992; cf. Sidman, 1987; de Rose, this volume). The data for Eikeseth and Smith's (1992) subjects further complicate matters. Except for Rory, these children with autism possessed verbal skills beyond the 2 year level seen as critical by Devany et al. (1986) but none passed the equivalence tests.

Overall, the studies examined in this section suggest that language and success on the tasks used in equivalence research are related in some way. Much remains to be clarified, however. What aspect of language may be important? What role do subjects' sensory capabilities, developmental status, or levels of adaptive functioning play? It is important also to do more than mere correlational analyses. A behavior analysis of such developmental phenomena (Baer, 1970; Sidman, 1994) will emphasize functional analysis of the performances from which stimulus classes are inferred and acknowledge the contingencies of reinforcement on which they are based.

Behavioral analysis

If, after training, the results of appropriate tests support inferences about equivalence relations, we are obligated to search for the origins of these relations in the contingencies of reinforcement. Negative results require the same analytic approach if appropriate interpretations of the data are to be made (cf. Sidman, 1994, pp. 419-421). Such an analysis suggests several variables that may have contributed to the differences among subjects in the three studies using the three-step training method (Barnes et al., 1990; Devany et al., 1986; Eikeseth & Smith, 1992), including: (a) the verbal instructions used; (b) the use of a testing procedure that did not include trials of the critical baselines; (c) the discriminability of the baseline trials from the probe trials; and (d) because no baseline trials were used, the procedures, arguably, extinguished responses to the comparisons used in tests.

Appreciation for subject variables and analysis of the stimulus control involved in matching tasks could converge in productive ways. For example, Eikeseth and Smith's (1992) results are surprising because the data for Trey and Joe suggest symmetry of the relations among stimuli but not equivalence (cf. Devany et al., 1986, p. 252). These findings (cf. Maguire, Stromer, & Mackay, 1995; Stromer & Osborne, 1982) remind us that the performances that provide the basis for inferences about equivalence may be independent under some conditions (cf. Pilgrim et al., 1995; Pilgrim & Galizio, this volume). One may recall in this respect the earlier discussion of the notion that naming and the production of classes of stimuli may be separate outcomes of the same contingencies. Are such findings related to language level, developmental disability, or some combination of these? How might these variables interact with experimental contingencies to produce unexpected forms of stimulus control? In this regard, a "microanalysis" of the errors that occurred during testing might be informative (e.g., Bickel & Etzel, 1985; Dube & McIlvane, this volume; Stromer, McIlvane, Dube, & Mackay, 1993). For example, stimulus and position biases are just two possible sources of stimulus control that might account for the strikingly similar accuracy scores on BC and CB trials before and after the other tests (see Figure 5).

Furthermore, it is difficult to examine Eikeseth and Smith's (1992) data from children with autism without considering the possibility that restricted stimulus control rather than language or naming difficulty may underlie some performances (Litrownik, McInnis, Wetzel-Pritchard, & Filipelli, 1978). Usually, the notion of restricted stimulus control concerns situations where only some of the elements of a complex stimulus control responding. However, in an extension to the present context, it may be suggested that control is restricted or "narrowed" to the particular stimulus arrays used in training. Subjects may have succeeded on BA and CA symmetry tests because they involved the same stimuli used in training AB and AC matching, whereas novel combinations of the stimuli were involved in the BC and CB tests (cf. Stromer & Osborne, 1982). Other analyses might consider the multiple sources of stimulus control in matching tasks (e.g., the separate stimulus control functions of samples and comparisons), and effects of compound stimulus control. The point here is that anomalies like restricted stimulus control frequently are reflected in the performance not only of children with autism, but also those with mental retardation, learning disabilities, and even normal individuals (cf. Burke, 1991). A restricted stimulus control account of difficulty in producing equivalence relations would be more firmly founded on research than one based on language deficiency and be more likely to produce direct solutions for practical problems.

COLLATERAL NAMING AND STIMULUS CLASS FORMATION

We devote special attention to the topic of collateral naming because the analysis of such behavior may clarify the role of verbal mediation in class formation. We highlight this form of naming because so little is known about its origins and because it has great potential for application (Gutowski et al., 1995). We focus first on differential naming that may arise spontaneously during performance of a task like visual-visual matching, even though subjects are given no relevant experimental history of naming. We then turn to the role of such naming when subjects do have a relevant experimental history. Finally, we discuss the possible sources of stimulus control that may be involved.

Naming without a relevant experimental history

In research summarized by Horne and Lowe (1996, pp. 218-219), 17 of the 29 children taught AB and AC matching tasks with visual stimuli (vertical and horizontal lines, green and red, cross and triangle) passed the tests of equivalence. Tape recordings also showed that all 29 children named the individual stimuli ("up," "down," "green," "red," "triangle," and "cross"), although the procedure did not require it. Moreover, all 17 who passed the equivalence tests "had previously, during training, intraverbally named [cf. Skinner, 1957] the correct sample-comparison pairs" (e.g., "up green," "up triangle," "down red," and "down cross"). Some children even repeated these intraverbals (e.g., saying "up green up green up green") whereas for others a contraction produced a common name for the stimuli in a particular class (e.g., saying "up" when the vertical line, green, or triangle was presented). Such collateral naming by these 17 children was considered the critical determinant of their success on tests of equivalence. Horne and Lowe contend that subjects' tendency "to name the stimuli, either overtly or covertly," can account for most demonstrations of equivalence.

These data differ markedly from studies with matching-to-sample procedures in which children either supply no oral names on direct posttests or use different names for stimuli in the same class (cf. Green, 1990; Lazar et al., 1984; Sidman & Tailby, 1982; Sidman et al., 1986). One can argue, of course, that posttest results may not reflect what a subject might say during a training session (Stoddard & McIlvane, 1986) or would say, if asked. Spontaneous verbal behavior may be recorded directly (cf. Horne & Lowe, 1996); however, within-session recordings were seldom made in studies conducted at the Shriver Center because subjects rarely said anything (cf. Sidman, 1994). This was also true in at least one study conducted in the Parsons labs with individuals who had mental retardation (Stromer & Osborne, 1982). Some of those subjects talked freely before and after the sessions; but they rarely spoke during the sessions and when they did it was never task related. The tactic of prompting verbal behavior during sessions holds promise for analyses of rule-governed behavior but interpretation of the results must acknowledge the demand characteristics of such procedures (cf. Wulfert, Dougher, & Greenway, 1991).

The conditions that give rise to spontaneous naming require study. Sidman (1994) suggests that spontaneous naming may be related to the length of the intertrial intervals used;

intervals longer than the 1.5 s to 3 s we typically use may encourage talking. However, the particular length needed is not clear. Pilgrim et al. (1995), for example, used 20-s intertrial intervals and none of the normal children (aged 4 to 7) studied either supplied common names or exhibited intraverbal naming (C. Pilgrim, personal communication, August 27, 1995). Being given the time to talk, of course, is not enough: An individual learning history will determine first whether a subject will have something to say and say it, and then whether the saying will be functionally related to what is done next. Naming may occur, for example, if the stimuli are familiar to subjects, if tabletop procedures are used (perhaps especially if the experimenter gathers the data), or if verbal instructions encourage talking about the stimuli and the task at hand. Nevertheless, the mere presence or absence of collateral verbal behavior like naming should not be used to explain the presence or absence of nonverbal matching that may also be observed.

Naming with a relevant experimental history

Figure 6 summarizes the results of Eikeseth and Smith's (1992) study. They are described here to illustrate a promising approach to the analysis of the relationship of naming to stimulus class formation (Sidman, 1994). The analysis may also apply to aspects of language development (Baer, 1970; cf. Lipkens et al., 1993). Data from Phase 1 were described earlier and are summarized at the left in Figure 6. After training with the AB and AC visual matching tasks, none of the children passed the BC and CB tests. In addition, none named the stimuli spontaneously. The remainder of Figure 6 shows the varying results of the other four Phases of the study.

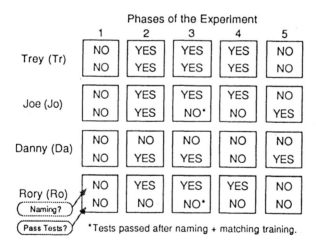

Figure 6. Matrix that summarizes findings from the Eikeseth and Smith (1992) study. The YES or NO entry on the top in each cell reflects whether a subject (listed at left) orally named the stimuli to be matched during the test conditions of each phase of the experiment (list across top). The YES or NO on the bottom in each cell reflects whether a subject passed the series of tests for class formation.

The procedure for Phase 2 added a naming requirement to the AB and AC tasks used in Phase 1, replicating Saunders and Spradlin's (1990, 1993) naming studies. The children were first taught to name A1, B1, and C1, "lambda," and A2, B2, and C2, "xi." After this training, the AB and AC matching tasks were repeated but with the requirement to name each sample and each comparison. This method thus provided an additional basis for the emergence of BC and CB matching. The B and C stimuli were now related not only to a common visual sample (A1 or A2) as in Phase 1 but also to a common spoken name ("lambda" or "xi"). As Figure 6 shows, Trey, Joe, and Danny now passed these tests; Rory did not. In contrast, Trey, Joe, and Rory named the stimuli during testing, even though there were no contingencies for doing so; Danny did not.

In Phase 3, Eikeseth and Smith (1992) used new stimuli to examine if classes now would result if a common name for stimuli in the same class was used during training. The children were taught to name D1, E1, and F1 "zeta" and D2, E2, and F2 "eta." For Rory oral naming was replaced by the construction of two patterns of blocks. Only Trey and Danny passed the critical tests of DE, DF, EF, and FE matching which now assessed the formation of stimulus classes. Notably, Trey used names; Danny did not. In contrast, Joe and Rory failed the tests for class formation although both named the stimuli. After additional training on the DE and DF matching tasks with naming required, both Joe and Rory did the EF and FE matching tasks more accurately than before.

Phase 4 was designed to expand the DEF classes by teaching two new visual matching tasks (EG and FH) without any naming requirement. Would this training produce five-member stimulus classes (DEFGH)? Only Trey succeeded on the tests for class expansion although he, Joe, and Rory all produced names and Danny did not.

Finally, Phase 5 repeated Phase 1 with new stimuli, attempting to establish new visual classes in the absence of a naming requirement. In this instance, Joe and Danny formed the new classes, Trey and Rory did not. As in Phase 1, however, none of the children named the stimuli.

In view of these data, Eikeseth and Smith's (1992) main conclusion was appropriately cautious (cf. Horne & Lowe, 1996, p. 225): "naming may remediate failures to develop untrained conditional relations, some of which are indicative of stimulus equivalence" (p. 123). The relationship between spontaneous naming and success on tests for equivalence was weak at best; the strongest positive relationship occurred during Phase 2 when there were two bases for passing the tests. Even there, however, it should not be assumed that sample naming caused comparison selection: The results "do not allow a conclusion beyond that dictated by parsimony: that both performances were the result of the training procedures" (Saunders & Spradlin, 1990, p. 249).

Behavioral analysis

How naming may be related to the formation of stimulus classes will be elucidated by analyses of the stimulus control involved (cf. Gutowski et al., 1995): First, naming may enhance the discriminative control exercised by the sample stimuli presented. In other words, differential naming may have positive effects because it ensures discrimination (or observation) of the particular sample stimuli involved, perhaps especially when the procedure involves auditory-visual matching and the subject names (imitates) the samples heard (e.g., Constantine & Sidman, 1975; Glat, Gould, Stoddard, & Sidman, 1994). From this perspective, naming may not play a role that is unique to the demands of situations that give rise to stimulus classes. Instead, these names would function just like the nonverbal differential responses that are used to enhance delayed matching performance (e.g., Lowenkron, 1984; Parsons, Taylor, & Joyce, 1981; Torgrud & Holborn, 1989; Stromer & Dube, 1994).

A second possibility is that any positive effects of naming in a visual matching task may reflect a shift in the basis for performing the task. For example, in a visual matching task, names produced by the subject, rather than the visual samples presented, may exert conditional control of comparison selection; thus, performance may involve auditory-visual rather than visual-visual conditional relations. This possibility merits consideration because it appears, as noted earlier, that classes that include auditory stimuli may form more rapidly than exclusively visual classes (Green, 1990; Sidman et al., 1986).

A third possibility is based on observations that the naming of a sample stimulus may be followed by the production of the same name when the comparisons appear; the name thus may provide a common supplemental stimulus that links the sample and the comparison whose selection satisfies the reinforcement contingencies (for additional discussion of issues raised by this possibility see McIntire et al., 1987; and the commentaries by Hayes, 1989; Saunders, 1989). If names serve such a mediating function, one might predict high accuracy on a delayed-matching form of the task, surpassing that to be expected on the basis of the two preceding accounts. This account therefore may suggest ways in which delayed matching to sample could be used in the analysis of whether a name may perform a mediating function rather than, or in addition to, the observing function discussed earlier (e.g., Bonta & Watters, 1981; Constantine & Sidman, 1975; Gutowski et al., 1995; Mackay & Ratti, 1990). Similar analyses might also explain how the intraverbal naming described by Horne and Lowe (1996) may develop and function.

Skinner (1968) outlined the complexity of the reinforcement contingencies operating in situations involving potential mediating events like names, viewing them as precurrent behavior (Parsons et al., 1981; Torgrud & Holborn, 1989). Precurrent behavior is indirectly related to the prevailing contingencies because its occurrence increases the likelihood that some other current behavior will be reinforced. In this respect, the contingencies of reinforcement in delayed matching apply to discriminative behavior involving two situations, one occurring at the time of sample presentation and a second at the time of comparison presentation. If the contingencies are to be satisfied, the successive discrimination required among samples (perhaps involving names) must affect the simultaneous discrimination required among comparisons. Further, each stimulus must serve different functions within and perhaps across trials, being the sample and positive comparison on some and the negative comparison on others.

Notably, this flexibility in the function of stimuli as samples and comparisons suggests that they may be substitutable for each other, a notion implicating class formation in certain delayed matching tasks. For example, it may be suggested that if names are to serve as mediators, they may have to belong in classes with their respective visual referents, the corresponding sample and comparison stimuli. Indeed, such classes may prove to be equivalence classes (cf. Sidman, 1994). The role of these stimulus classes seems clear in some tasks, for example, one in which a written list of names mediates later retrieval of the corresponding objects (e.g., Stromer et al., 1996). Less obvious is how stimulus classes that include oral names may be involved in the delayed matching of identical pictures (e.g., Constantine & Sidman, 1975). Appropriate analysis would have to focus on specification of the sample and comparison events that occur within a particular trial and recognize the bidirectional relations among the receptive and expressive aspects of events that occurred (cf. Dugdale & Lowe, 1990; Hayes, 1991; Mackay & Sidman, 1984). For example, a visual sample may occasion a spoken name and that name may function later as the conditional stimulus controlling the selection of a comparison. More broadly, the analysis of whether differential behavior like naming serves mediating or only observing functions will be relevant to topics like say-do correspondence, self-control, and rule-governed behavior (e.g., Catania, Matthews, & Shimoff, 1990; Kirby & Bickel, 1988; Stokes & Baer, 1977).

In general, then, one might conclude that training with receptive "name"-referent or expressive referent-"name" tasks may produce stimulus classes. However, neither is prerequisite for, nor a necessary outcome of, the formation of classes (e.g., Lazar et al., 1984; Sidman et al., 1986). Further, collateral oral naming may facilitate performance on matching tasks (Eikeseth & Smith, 1992; Saunders & Spradlin, 1990, 1993; cf. Dugdale & Lowe, 1990), but the nature of the stimulus control involved is unclear: Nonverbal differential responses may achieve the same effects as naming in such matching tasks (Eikeseth & Smith, 1992; Saunders & Spradlin, 1989; cf. Parsons et al., 1981; Torgrud & Holborn, 1989).

FUTURE DIRECTIONS

Subjects who can match and even name a variety of stimuli would be candidates for exploring other methods of producing stimulus classes. One line of research has focused on names produced textually rather than orally, that is, via construction of words from arrays of letters or via writing. Such studies illustrate the general effect of learning to produce the stimuli that are involved in matching-to-sample tasks. The original studies (Mackay, 1985; Mackay & Sidman, 1984) and more recent ones suggest that establishing such naming performances may give rise to equivalence classes and also other forms of naming. In overview, our studies illustrate emergent oral and written naming of individual stimuli (Maydak et al., 1995; Stromer & Mackay, 1992a, 1992b, 1993; Stromer et al., 1996) and the oral and written production of sequences of stimuli (Mackay, Kotlarchyk, & Stromer, 1996; Stromer, 1996a). We add, however, that as teaching methods become more complex, the possibilities increase for the development of stimulus control that disrupts or prevents class formation. In an unpublished study, for example, one subject persistently failed to name sets of printed words, even though the corresponding pictures were named and these pictures and the words were matched to the same dictated names and to one another. The subject named those words correctly only after learning to spell them, thus adding to our previous data suggesting the value of incorporating spelling instruction into educational programming (e.g., Stromer et al., 1992).

Another area of inquiry, virtually unexamined so far, would explore the role of observational-learning procedures in the formation of stimulus classes. MacDonald et al. (1986), for example, demonstrated that subjects with mental retardation may acquire the bases of arbitrary stimulus classes via observation. To illustrate, consider an experimenter working with a pair of subjects. Subject 1 is taught to match the printed words DOG and CAT and their respective pictures to the dictated names "dog" and "cat" (Set 1 stimuli) while Subject 2 observes. Subject 2 is taught to match the words PIG and COW and their respective pictures to the dictated names "pig" and "cow" (Set 2) while Subject 1 observes. Both subjects then are tested on all tasks. In addition to the performances explicitly taught, would each subject learn from observing the training given to the other? Would each prove capable of the matching and naming performances with both sets of stimuli?

Additional research is needed using stimulus situations in which two or more discriminable and potentially functional stimuli (redundant cues) may control behavior. The use of such complex training situations is of interest because relations between the redundant stimuli may be established even though these relations are not explicitly required (e.g., Barnes, Smeets, & Leader, this volume; Clarke, Remington, & Light, 1986; Maguire et al., 1995; Maguire, Stromer, Mackay, & Demis, 1994; Schenk, 1993; Smeets & Striefel, 1994; Stromer & Stromer, 1990). To illustrate, suppose that a subject is presented a matching task in which two multi-element sample stimuli are used; one sample consists of the dictated word "dog" and a picture of a dog, the other "cat" and a picture of a cat. The comparison stimuli are the printed words DOG and CAT and the subject is reinforced for matching each to its appropriate sample. Such procedures, often encountered in everyday teaching situations, may produce broad learning outcomes because each element of each sample may come to exert the same discriminative control. These outcomes, for example, might include matching printed-word comparisons to either dictated words or to pictures (cf. Mackay, 1991; Stromer et al., 1992).

Another avenue of research, that also resembles commonly used instructional methods, involves the notion that differential reinforcers may become class members that are interchangeable with the samples and comparisons to which they have been related (Dube, McIlvane, Mackay, & Stoddard, 1987; Dube, McIlvane, Maguire, Mackay, & Stoddard, 1989; for related studies with nonhumans, see Urcuioli, this volume). Applied researchers also have demonstrated the potential for enhancing learning through the addition of verbal stimuli, like spoken category names, among the events used as reinforcers (e.g., Wolery, Doyle, Ault, Gast, Meyer, & Stinson, 1991). For example, subjects might be taught to match the pictures of an apple, a banana, a carrot, and a beet to their corresponding dictated names. In addition to the praise given following correct picture selections, however, the experimenter may differentially add the food's category name: "Good, the banana is a fruit" or "Good, the carrot is a vegetable." If such consequences were common across training with several stimuli, they could provide the basis for the development of superordinate arbitrary classes.

This example suggests how equivalence classes involving pictures of foods and their printed and spoken names may be brought under the contextual control of category names (Sidman, 1986). Studies using such higher-order procedures are important because they highlight the relevance of equivalence for research and theory on category learning (e.g., Anglin, 1977; Rosch, Mervis, Gray, Johnson, & Boyes-Braem, 1976). Higher-order procedures are also relevant to studies of contextually-controlled verbal repertoires (Silverman, Anderson, Marshall, & Baer, 1986; cf. Hall & Chase, 1991; Stoddard & McIlvane, 1986). These methods may serve to examine, for example, how different verbal responses to a picture of a dog, like "Seb" and "golden retriever," come under contextual control of stimuli like "pet name" and "breed." The analysis thus suggests additional ways to examine intraverbal naming (Skinner, 1957; cf. Partington & Bailey, 1993; Watkins et al., 1989) and its relation to class formation. To take full advantage of these possibilities, a thorough understanding of the contingencies of reinforcement and the stimulus control in simple and complex preparations will be required.

Avoiding pitfalls of the past

Finally, future research on the classic problem of the relationship of equivalence and verbal behavior should consider carefully the methods and conceptual approaches used earlier. Sometimes framed as a problem of "mediated generalization," prior research flourished using adults (Jenkins, 1963; Jenkins & Palermo, 1964) and children (Gibson, 1969; Reese & Lipsitt, 1970; Stevenson, 1972). That research was inspired in part by the writings of Miller and Dollard (1941) on the relationship between verbal and nonverbal behavior:

Response-mediated generalizations play an important role in social behavior, where many of the most important categories are culturally rather than innately determined. To begin with a humble example, the Roman numeral III, the Arabic numeral 3, and the written word three are innately quite distinctive as cues. But training in our society has attached the same cue-producing responses to each of these patterns of stimulation. The most obvious of these cue-producing responses is the verbal one; but there are a host of other responses, such as holding up three fingers, which tend to occur in minimal form, supply additional cues common to these three stimuli, and mediate generalization from any one to the others (p. 76).

This 50-year-old passage is remarkable in the way it captures current research issues. It is also noteworthy because Miller and Dollard (1941) acknowledged that differential verbal behavior provided only one of several ways of producing mediated generalization. They also recognized that the stimuli produced by responding may play a crucial role. Even so, early research placed little emphasis on analysis of the stimulus control involved. As Sidman (1994, p. 85) noted, moreover, research with adults "fell victim to limitations that are inherent in the experimental practices and theoretical orientation of methodological behaviorism ... that still characterize much of experimental psychology today." Research on children's verbal and nonverbal behavior conducted prior to Sidman (1971) may be characterized in a similar way (Gibson, 1969; Reese & Lipsitt, 1970; Stevenson, 1972).

We now have a better appreciation of the role that stimuli play in mediated generalization, equivalence, and other phenomena involving stimulus classes: Sidman's analysis liberated the area of inquiry from the constraints and shortcomings of earlier commitments to theoretical accounts that emphasized the role of verbal mediating responses. Such theories simply accounted for too little of the data and also raised questions about where the verbal mediators came from. We look forward to continued behavior analytic research that follows the lead provided by Sidman's studies of equivalence relations because they promise also to illuminate the nature of those relations that involve verbal events.

AUTHOR NOTE

This chapter was prepared with support from the National Institute of Child Health and Human Development (Grant HD25995) and the Massachusetts Department of Mental Retardation (Contract No. 100220023SC). We thank Dermot Barnes, William Holcomb, and Murray Sidman for their helpful comments on a draft of the paper.
Address correspondence to: Robert Stromer, Behavioral Sciences Division, Eunice Kennedy Shriver Center, 200 Trapelo Road, Waltham, MA 02254 (phone: 617-642-0165; email: RStromer@Shriver.org).

REFERENCES

Anderson, S. R., & Spradlin, J. E. (1980). The generalized effects of productive labeling training involving common object classes. *Journal of the Association for the Severely Handicapped, 5,* 143-157.

Anglin, J. M. (1977). *Word, object, and conceptual development.* New York: Norton.

Augustson, K. G., & Dougher, M. J. (1991). Teaching conditional discrimination to young children: Some methodological successes and failures. *Experimental Analysis of Human Behavior Bulletin, 9,* 21-24.

Baer, D. M. (1970). An age-irrelevant concept of development. *Merrill Palmer Quarterly, 16,* 238-245.

Baer, D. M. (1982). Applied behavior analysis. In G. T. Wilson & C. M. Franks (Eds.), *Contemporary behavior therapy: Conceptual and empirical foundations* (pp. 277-309). New York: Guilford.

Barnes, D. (1994). Stimulus equivalence and relational frame theory. *Psychological Record, 44,* 91-124.

Barnes, D., Browne, M., Smeets, P., & Roche, B. (1995). A transfer of functions and a conditional transfer of functions through equivalence classes in three- to six-year-old children. *Psychological Record, 45,* 405-430.

Barnes, D., McCullagh, P. D., & Keenan, M. (1990). Equivalence class formation in non-hearing impaired children and hearing impaired children. *The Analysis of Verbal Behavior, 8,* 19-30.

Bentall, R. P., Lowe, C. F., & Beasty, A. (1985). The role of verbal behavior in human learning: II. Developmental differences. *Journal of the Experimental Analysis of Behavior, 43,* 165-181.

Bickel, W. K., & Etzel, B. C. (1985). The quantal nature of controlling stimulus-response relations as measured in tests of stimulus generalization. *Journal of the Experimental Analysis of Behavior, 44,* 245-270.

Bonta, J. L., & Watters, R. G. (1981). Use of manual signs in delayed matching-to-sample with developmentally disordered, speech deficient children. *Behavior Research of Severe Developmental Disabilities, 2,* 51-66.

Burke, J. C. (1991). Some developmental implications of a disturbance in responding to complex environmental stimuli. *American Journal on Mental Retardation, 96,* 37-52.

Carrigan, P. F., & Sidman, M. (1992). Conditional discrimination and equivalence relations: A theoretical analysis of control by negative stimuli. *Journal of the Experimental Analysis of Behavior, 58,* 183-204.

Catania, A. C., Matthews, B. A., & Shimoff, E. H. (1990). Properties of rule-governed behaviour and their implications. In D. E. Blackman & H. Lejeune (Eds.), *Behaviour analysis in theory and practice: Contributions and controversies* (pp. 215-230). Hove, UK: Lawrence Erlbaum.

Clarke, S., Remington, B., & Light, P. (1986). An evaluation of the relationship between speech skills and expressive signing. *Journal of Applied Behavior Analysis, 19,* 231-239.

Constantine, B., & Sidman, M. (1975). Role of naming in delayed matching-to-sample. *American Journal of Mental Deficiency, 79,* 680-689.

Cowley, B. J., Green, G., & Braunling-McMorrow, D. (1992). Using stimulus equivalence procedures to teach name-face matching to adults with brain injuries. *Journal of Applied Behavior Analysis, 25,* 461-475.

de Rose, J. C., de Souza, D. G., Rossito, A. L., & de Rose, T. M. S. (1992). Stimulus equivalence and generalization in reading after matching to sample by exclusion. In S. C. Hayes & L. J. Hayes (Eds.), *Understanding verbal relations* (pp. 69-82). Reno, NV: Context Press.

Devany, J. M., Hayes, S. C., & Nelson, R. O. (1986). Equivalence class formation in language-able and language-disabled children. *Journal of the Experimental Analysis of*

Behavior, 46, 243-257.

Dixon, M. H. (1978). Teaching conceptual classes with receptive label training. *Acta Symbolica, 9*, 17-35.

Dixon, M. H., & Spradlin, J. E. (1976). Establishing stimulus equivalences among retarded adolescents. *Journal of Experimental Child Psychology, 21*, 144-164.

Dube, W. V., McIlvane, W. J., Callahan, T. D., & Stoddard, L. T. (1993). The search for stimulus equivalence in nonverbal organisms. *Psychological Record, 43*, 761-778.

Dube, W. V., McIlvane, W. J., Mackay, H. A., & Stoddard, L. T. (1987). Stimulus class membership established via stimulus-reinforcer relations. *Journal of the Experimental Analysis of Behavior, 47*, 159-175.

Dube, W. V., McIlvane, W. J., Maguire, R. W., Mackay, H. A., & Stoddard, L. T. (1989). Stimulus class formation and stimulus-reinforcer relations. *Journal of the Experimental Analysis of Behavior, 51*, 65-76.

Dugdale, N., & Lowe, C. F. (1990). Naming and stimulus equivalence. In D. E. Blackman & H. Lejeune (Eds.), *Behaviour analysis in theory and practice: Contributions and controversies* (pp. 115-138). Hove, UK: Erlbaum.

Eikeseth, S., & Smith, T. (1992). The development of functional and equivalence classes in high-functioning autistic children: The role of naming. *Journal of the Experimental Analysis of Behavior, 58*, 123-133.

Flavell, J. H., Beach, D. R., & Chinsky, J. M. (1966). Spontaneous verbal rehearsal in a memory task as a function of age. *Child Development, 37*, 283-299.

Gibson, E. J. (1969). *Principles of perceptual learning and development.* New York: Appleton-Century-Crofts.

Glat, R., Gould, K., Stoddard, L. T., & Sidman, M. (1994). A note on transfer of stimulus control in the delayed-cue procedure: Facilitation by an overt differential response. *Journal of Applied Behavior Analysis, 27*, 699-704.

Goldiamond, I. (1962). Perception. In A. J. Bachrach (Ed.), *Experimental foundations of clinical psychology* (pp. 280-340). New York: Basic Books.

Goldiamond, I. (1966). Perception, language, and conceptualization rules. In B. Kleinmuntz (Ed.), *Problem solving: Research, method, and theory* (pp. 183-224). New York: Wiley.

Green, G. (1990). Differences in development of visual and auditory-visual equivalence relations. *American Journal on Mental Retardation, 95*, 260-270.

Guess, D., & Baer, D. M. (1973). An analysis of individual differences in generalization between receptive and productive language in retarded children. *Journal of Applied Behavior Analysis, 6*, 311-329.

Gutowski, S. J., Geren, M., Stromer, R., & Mackay, H. A. (1995). Restricted stimulus control in delayed matching to complex samples: A preliminary analysis of the role of naming. *Experimental Analysis of Human Behavior Bulletin, 13*, 18-24.

Hall, G. A., & Chase, P. N. (1991). The relationship between stimulus equivalence and verbal behavior. *The Analysis of Verbal Behavior, 9*, 107-119.

Haring, T. G., Breen, C. G., & Laitinen, R. E. (1989). Stimulus class formation and concept learning: Establishment of within- and between-set generalization and transitive relationships via conditional discrimination procedures. *Journal of the Experimental Analysis of Behavior, 52*, 13-25.

Hayes, S. C. (1989). Nonhumans have not yet shown stimulus equivalence. *Journal of the Experimental Analysis of Behavior, 51*, 385-392.

Hayes, S. C. (1991). A relational control theory of stimulus equivalence. In L. J. Hayes & P. N. Chase (Eds.), *Dialogues on verbal behavior* (pp. 19-40). Reno, NV: Context Press.

Hayes, S. C., & Hayes, L. J. (1992). Verbal relations and the evolution of behavior analysis. *American Psychologist, 47*, 1383-1395.

Herrnstein, R. J., & Loveland, D. H. (1964). Complex visual concept in the pigeon. *Science, 146*, 549-551.

Horne, P. J., & Lowe, C. F. (1996). On the origins of naming and other symbolic behavior. *Journal of the Experimental Analysis of Behavior, 65*, 185-241.

Jenkins, J. J. (1963). Mediated associations: Paradigms and situations. In C. N. Cofer & B. S. Musgrave (Eds.), *Verbal behavior and learning: Problems and processes* (pp. 210-245). New York: McGraw-Hill.

Jenkins, J. J. & Palermo, D. S. (1964). Mediation processes and the acquisition of linguistic structure. In U. Bellugi and R. Brown (Eds.), The acquisition of language. *Monographs of Social Research and Child Development, 29*, No. 1, 141-169.

Keller, F. S., & Schoenfeld, W. N. (1950). *Principles of psychology.* New York: Appleton-Century-Crofts.

Kendler, T. S. (1972). An ontogeny of mediational deficiency. *Child Development, 43*, 1-17.

Kendler, H. H., & Kendler, T. S. (1962). Vertical and horizontal processes in problem solving. *Psychological Review, 69*, 1-16.

Kennedy, C. H., Itkonen, T., & Lindquist, K. (1994). Nodality effects during equivalence class formation: An extension to sight-word reading and concept development. *Journal of Applied Behavior Analysis, 27*, 673-683.

Kirby, K. C., & Bickel, W. K. (1988). Toward an explicit analysis of generalization: A stimulus control interpretation. *The Behavior Analyst, 11*, 115-129.

Lamarre, J., & Holland, J. G. (1985). The functional independence of mands and tacts. *Journal of the Experimental Analysis of Behavior, 43*, 5-20.

Lazar, R. M., Davis-Lang, D., & Sanchez, L. (1984). The formation of visual stimulus equivalences in children. *Journal of the Experimental Analysis of Behavior, 41*, 251-266.

Lee, V. L. (1981). Prepositional phrases spoken and heard. Journal of the Experimental *Analysis of Behavior, 35*, 227-242.

Lee, V. L., & Pegler, A. M. (1982). Effects on spelling of training children to read. *Journal of the Experimental Analysis of Behavior, 37*, 311-322.

Lipkens, R., Hayes, S. C., & Hayes, L. J. (1993). Longitudinal study of the development of derived relations in an infant. *Journal of Experimental Child Psychology, 56*, 201-239.

Litrownik, A. J., McInnis, E. T., Wetzel-Pritchard, A. M., & Filipelli, D. L. (1978). Restricted stimulus control and inferred attentional deficits in autistic and retarded children. *Journal of Abnormal Psychology, 87*, 554-562.

Lowenkron, B. (1984). Coding responses and the generalization of matching to sample in children. *Journal of the Experimental Analysis of Behavior, 42*, 1-18.

Luria, A. R. (1961). *Language and cognition.* New York: Wiley.

Lynch, D. C., & Cuvo, A. J. (1995). Stimulus equivalence instruction of fraction-decimal relations. *Journal of Applied Behavior Analysis, 28*, 115-126.

MacDonald, R. P. F., Dixon, L. S., & LeBlanc, J. M. (1986). Stimulus class formation following observational learning. *Analysis and Intervention in Developmental Disabilities, 6*, 73-87.

Mackay, H. A. (1985). Stimulus equivalence in rudimentary reading and spelling. *Analysis and*

Intervention in Developmental Disabilities, 5, 373-387.
Mackay, H, A. (1991). Stimulus equivalence: Implications for the development of adaptive behavior. In R. Remington (Ed.), The challenge of severe mental handicap: An applied behaviour analytic approach (pp. 235-259). London, England: Wiley.
Mackay, H. A., Kotlarchyk, B. J., & Stromer, R. (1996). Stimulus classes, stimulus sequences, and generative behavior. Manuscript submitted for publication.
Mackay, H. A., & Ratti, C.A. (1990). Position/numeral equivalences and delayed position recognition span. American Journal on Mental Retardation, 95, 271-282.
Mackay, H. A., & Sidman, M. (1984). Teaching new behavior via equivalence relations. In P. H. Brooks, R. Sperber, & C. MacCauley (Eds.), Learning and cognition in the mentally retarded (pp. 493-513). Hillsdale, NJ: Erlbaum.
Mackay, H. A., Stromer, R., & Serna, R. W. (in press). Generalization and transfer of stimulus control. In S. Soraci & W. J. McIlvane (Eds.), Perspectives on fundamental processes in intellectual functioning. Norwood, NJ: Ablex.
Maguire, R. W., Stromer, R., & Mackay, H. A. (1995). Delayed matching to complex samples and the formation of stimulus classes in children. Psychological Reports, 77, 1059-1076.
Maguire, R. W., Stromer, R., Mackay, H. A., & Demis, C. A. (1994). Matching to complex samples and stimulus class formation in adults with autism and young children. Journal of Autism and Developmental Disorders, 24, 753-772.
Manabe, K., Kawashima, T., & Staddon, J. E. R. (1995). Differential vocalization in budgerigars: Towards an experimental analysis of naming. Journal of the Experimental Analysis of Behavior, 63, 111-126.
Maydak, M., Stromer, R., Mackay, H. A., & Stoddard, L. T. (1995). Stimulus classes in matching to sample and sequence production: The emergence of numeric relations. Research in Developmental Disabilities, 16, 179-204.
McIlvane, W. J. (1992). Stimulus control analysis and nonverbal instructional methods for people with intellectual disabilities. In N. W. Bray (Ed.), International review of research in mental retardation (Vol. 18, pp. 55-109). New York: Academic Press.
McIlvane, W. J., Dube, W. V., Green, G., & Serna, R. W. (1993). Programming conceptual and communication skill development: A methodological stimulus class analysis. In A. P. Kaiser & D. B. Gray (Eds.), Enhancing childrens' communication (Vol. 2, pp.242-285). Baltimore, MD: Brookes.
McIlvane, W. J., Dube, W. V., Kledaras, J. B., Iennaco, F. M., & Stoddard, L. T. (1990). Teaching relational discriminations to individuals with mental retardation: Some problems and possible solutions. American Journal on Mental Retardation, 95, 283-296.
McIntire, K. D., Cleary, J., & Thompson, T. (1987). Conditional relations in monkeys: Reflexivity, symmetry and transitivity. Journal of the Experimental Analysis of Behavior, 47, 279-285.
Miller, N. E., & Dollard, J. (1941). Social learning and imitation. New Haven, CN: Yale University Press.
Osborne, J. G., & Gatch, M. B. (1989). Stimulus equivalence and receptive reading by hearing-impaired preschool children. Language, Speech, and Hearing Services in Schools, 20, 63-75.
Parsons, J. A., Taylor, D. C., & Joyce, T. M. (1981). Precurrent self-prompting operants in children: "Remembering." Journal of the Experimental Analysis of Behavior, 36, 253-266.

Partington, J. W., & Bailey, J. S. (1993). Teaching intraverbal behavior to preschool children. *The Analysis of Verbal Behavior, 11*, 9-18.

Pepperberg, I. M. (1990). Cognition in an African Gray parrot (Psittacus erithacus): Further evidence for comprehension of categories and labels. *Journal of Comparative Psychology, 104*, 41-52.

Perone, M. (1988). Laboratory lore and research practices in the experimental analysis of human behavior: Use and abuse of subjects' verbal reports. *The Behavior Analyst, 11*, 71-75.

Pilgrim, C., Chambers, L., & Galizio, M. (1995). Reversal of baseline relations and stimulus equivalence: II. Children. *Journal of the Experimental Analysis of Behavior, 63*, 239-254.

Pouthas, V., Droit, S., Jacquet, A.-Y., & Wearden, J. H. (1990). Temporal discrimination of response duration in children of different ages: Developmental changes in relations between verbal and nonverbal behavior. *Journal of the Experimental Analysis of Behavior, 53*, 21-31.

Reese, H. W. (1992). Rules as nonverbal entities. In S. C. Hayes, L. & J. Hayes (Eds.), *Understanding verbal relations* (pp. 121-134). Reno, NV: Context Press.

Reese, H. W., & Lipsitt, L. P. (1970). *Experimental Child Psychology.* New York: Academic Press.

Remington, B. (1994). Augmentative and alternative communication and behavior analysis: A productive partnership? *Augmentative and Alternative Communication, 10*, 3-13.

Rosch, E., Mervis, C. B., Gray, W. D., Johnson, D. M., & Boyes-Braem, P. (1976). Basic objects in natural categories. *Cognitive Psychology, 8*, 382-439.

Saunders, K. J. (1989). Naming in conditional discriminations and stimulus equivalence. *Journal of the Experimental Analysis of Behavior, 51*, 379-384.

Saunders, K. J., & Spradlin, J. E. (1989). Conditional discrimination in mentally retarded adults: The effects of training the component simple discriminations. *Journal of the Experimental Analysis of Behavior, 52*, 1-12.

Saunders, K. J., & Spradlin, J. E. (1990). Conditional discrimination in mentally retarded adults: The development of generalized skills. *Journal of the Experimental Analysis of Behavior, 54*, 239-250.

Saunders, K. J., & Spradlin, J. E. (1993). Conditional discrimination in mentally retarded subjects: Programming acquisition and learning set. *Journal of the Experimental Analysis of Behavior, 60*, 571-585.

Saunders, R. R., Saunders, K. J., Kirby, K. C., & Spradlin, J. E. (1988). The merger and development of equivalence classes by unreinforced conditional selection of comparison stimuli. *Journal of the Experimental Analysis of Behavior, 50*, 145-162.

Saunders, R. R., Wachter, J., & Spradlin, J. E. (1988). Establishing auditory stimulus control over an eight-member equivalence class via conditional discrimination procedures. *Journal of the Experimental Analysis of Behavior, 49*, 95-115.

Schenk, J. J. (1993). Emergent conditional discrimination in children: Matching to compound stimuli. *The Quarterly Journal of Experimental Psychology, 46B*, 345-365.

Schusterman, R. J., & Kastak, D. (1993). A California sea lion (Zalophus californianus) is capable of forming equivalence relations. *Psychological Record, 43*, 823-839.

Shafer, E. (1993). Teaching topography-based and selection-based verbal behavior to developmentally disabled individuals: Some considerations. *The Analysis of Verbal Behavior, 11*, 117-133.

Shimoff, E. (1984). Post-session questionnaires. *Experimental Analysis of Human Behavior Bulletin, 2,* 1.

Shimoff, E. (1986). Post-session verbal reports and the experimental analysis of behavior. *The Analysis of Verbal Behavior, 4,* 19-22.

Silverman, K., Anderson, S. R., Marshall, A. M., & Baer, D. M. (1986). Establishing and generalizing audience control of new language repertoires. *Analysis and Intervention in Developmental Disabilities, 6,* 21-40.

Sidman, M. (1971). Reading and auditory-visual equivalences. *Journal of Speech and Hearing Research, 14,* 5-13.

Sidman, M. (1986). Functional analysis of emergent verbal classes. In T. Thompson & M. D. Zeiler (Eds.), *Analysis and integration of behavioral units* (pp. 213-245). Hillsdale, NJ: Erlbaum.

Sidman, M. (1987). Two choices are not enough. *Behavior Analysis, 22,* 11-18.

Sidman, M. (1990). Equivalence relations: Where do they come from? In D. Blackman & H. Lejeune (Eds.), *Behavior analysis in theory and practice: Contributions and controversies* (pp. 93-114). Hove, UK: Erlbaum.

Sidman, M. (1994). *Equivalence relations and behavior: A research story.* Boston, MA: Authors Cooperative.

Sidman, M., & Cresson, O., Jr. (1973). Reading and crossmodal transfer of stimulus equivalences in severe retardation. *American Journal of Mental Deficiency, 77,* 515-523.

Sidman, M., Cresson, O., Jr., & Willson-Morris, M. (1974). Acquisition of matching to sample via mediated transfer. *Journal of the Experimental Analysis of Behavior, 22,* 261-273.

Sidman, M., Kirk, B., & Willson-Morris, M. (1985). Six-member stimulus classes generated by conditional-discrimination procedures. *Journal of the Experimental Analysis of Behavior, 43,* 21-42.

Sidman, M., & Tailby, W. (1982). Conditional discrimination vs. matching-to-sample: An expansion of the testing paradigm. *Journal of the Experimental Analysis of Behavior, 37,* 5-22.

Sidman, M., Willson-Morris, M., & Kirk, B. (1986). Matching-to-sample procedures and the development of equivalence relations: The role of naming. *Analysis and Intervention in Developmental Disabilities, 6,* 1-19.

Skinner, B. F. (1935). The generic nature of the concepts of stimulus and response. *Journal of General Psychology, 5,* 427-458.

Skinner, B. F. (1950). Are theories of learning necessary? *Psychological Review, 57,* 193-216.

Skinner, B. F. (1957). *Verbal behavior.* New York: Appleton-Century-Crofts.

Skinner, B. F. (1968). *The technology of teaching.* New York: Appleton-Century-Crofts.

Smeets, P. M., & Striefel, S. (1976). Acquisition and cross modal generalization of receptive and expressive signing skills in a retarded deaf girl. *Journal of Mental Deficiency Research, 20,* 251-260.

Smeets, P. M., & Striefel, S. (1994). Matching to complex stimuli under nonreinforced conditions: Errorless transfer from identity to arbitrary matching tasks. The Quarterly *Journal of Experimental Psychology, 47B,* 39-62.

Spradlin, J. E., Cotter, V. W., & Baxley, N. (1973). Establishing a conditional discrimination without direct training: A study of transfer with retarded adolescents. *American Journal of Mental Deficiency, 77,* 556-566.

Spradlin, J. E., & Dixon, M. H. (1976). Establishing conditional discriminations without direct training: Stimulus classes and labels. *American Journal of Mental Deficiency, 80,* 555-561.

Spradlin, J. E., & Saunders, R. R. (1986). The development of stimulus classes using match-to-sample procedures: Sample classification versus comparison classification. *Analysis and Intervention in Developmental Disabilities, 6,* 41-58.

Stevenson, H. W. (1972). *Children's learning.* New York: Appleton-Century-Crofts.

Stikeleather, G., & Sidman, M. (1990). An instance of spurious equivalence relations. *The Analysis of Verbal Behavior, 8,* 1-11.

Stoddard, L. T., & McIlvane, W. J. (1986). Stimulus control research and developmentally disabled individuals. *Analysis and Intervention in Developmental Disabilities, 6,* 155-178.

Stokes, T. F., & Baer, D. M. (1977). An implicit technology of generalization. *Journal of Applied Behavior Analysis, 10,* 349-367.

Stromer, R. (1991). Stimulus equivalence: Implications for teaching. In W. Ishaq (Ed.), *Human behavior in today's world* (pp. 109-122). New York: Praeger.

Stromer, R. (1996a). *On the benefits of direct teaching of spelling in children's language arts instruction.* Manuscript submitted for publication.

Stromer, R. (1996b). On the experimental analysis of naming and the formation of stimulus classes [commentary]. *Journal of the Experimental Analysis of Behavior, 65,* 250-252.

Stromer, R., & Dube, W. V. (1994). Differential observing of complex sample stimuli and delayed matching performance: A brief report. *Experimental Analysis of Human Behavior Bulletin, 12,* 17-20.

Stromer, R., & Mackay, H. A. (1992a). Delayed constructed-response matching improves the spelling performances of students with mental retardation. *Journal of Behavioral Education, 2,* 139-156.

Stromer, R., & Mackay, H. A. (1992b). Spelling and emergent picture-printed word relations established with delayed identity matching to complex samples. *Journal of Applied Behavior Analysis, 25,* 893-904.

Stromer, R., & Mackay, H. A. (1993). Delayed identity matching to complex samples: Teaching students with mental retardation spelling and the prerequisites for equivalence classes. *Research in Developmental Disabilities, 14,* 19-38.

Stromer, R., Mackay, H. A., Howell, S. R., McVay, A. A., & Flusser, D. (1996). Teaching computer-based spelling to individuals with developmental and hearing disabilities: Transfer of stimulus control to writing tasks. *Journal of Applied Behavior Analysis, 29,* 25-42.

Stromer, R., Mackay, H. A., & Stoddard, L. T. (1992). Classroom applications of stimulus equivalence technology. *Journal of Behavioral Education, 2,* 225-256.

Stromer, R., McIlvane, W. J., Dube, W. V., & Mackay, H. A. (1993). Assessing control by elements of complex stimuli in delayed matching to sample. *Journal of the Experimental Analysis of Behavior, 59,* 83-102.

Stromer, R., & Osborne, J. G. (1982). Control of adolescents' arbitrary matching-to-sample by positive and negative stimulus relations. *Journal of the Experimental Analysis of Behavior, 37,* 329-348.

Stromer, R., & Stromer, J. B. (1990). The formation of arbitrary stimulus classes in matching to complex samples. *Psychological Record, 40,* 51-66.

Torgrud, L. J., & Holborn, S. W. (1989). Effectiveness and persistence of precurrent mediating behavior in delayed matching to sample and oddity matching with children. *Journal of the Experimental Analysis of Behavior, 52,* 181-191.

Urcuioli, P. J., Zentall, T. R., Jackson-Smith, P., & Steirn, J. N. (1989). Evidence for common coding in many-to-one matching: Retention, intertrial interference, and transfer. *Journal of Experimental Psychology: Animal Behavior Processes, 15,* 264-273.

Vaughan, W., Jr. (1988). Formation of equivalence sets in pigeons. *Journal of Experimental Psychology: Animal Behavior Processes, 14,* 36-42.

Wasserman, E. A., & DeVolder, C. L. (1993). Similarity- and nonsimilarity-based conceptualization in children and pigeons. *Psychological Record, 43,* 779-793.

Watkins, C. L., Pack-Teixteira, L., & Howard, J. S. (1989). Teaching intraverbal behavior to severely retarded children. *The Analysis of Verbal Behavior, 7,* 69-81.

Wetherby, B., Karlan, G. R., & Spradlin, J. E. (1983). The development of derived stimulus relations through training in arbitrary-matching sequences. *Journal of the Experimental Analysis of Behavior, 40,* 69-78.

Wolery, M., Doyle, P. M., Ault, M. J., Gast, D. L., Meyer, S., & Stinson, D. (1991). Effects of presenting incidental information in consequent events on future learning. *Journal of Behavioral Education, 1,* 79-104.

Wulfert, E., Dougher, M. J., & Greenway, D. E. (1991). Protocol analysis of the correspondence of verbal behavior and equivalence class formation. *Journal of the Experimental Analysis of Behavior, 56,* 489-504.

Zentall, T. R., & Urcuioli, P. J. (1993). Emergent relations in the formation of stimulus classes by pigeons. *Psychological Record, 43,* 795-810.

Stimulus Class Formation in Humans and Animals
T.R. Zentall and P.M. Smeets (Editors)
© 1996 Elsevier Science B.V. All rights reserved.

13

Controlling Factors in Conditional Discriminations and Tests of Equivalence

Júlio C. de Rose

Universidade Federal de São Carlos, Brazil

In a famous short story, Jorge Luis Borges provides a fictional illustration of the importance of stimulus classes for human thinking and language. Funes, "the memorious", remembered every leaf of every tree of every wood, and also every time he had perceived or imagined it. Funes could easily remember an entire day of his life, but, because his memory was so complete, this took another entire day. Although praising the mnemonic talent of his character, Borges acknowledges that it entailed a serious limitation: Funes was not capable of thinking: "*Pensar es olvidar diferencias, es generalizar, abstraer. En el abarrotado mundo de Funes no había sino detalles, casi inmediatos.*" (To think is to forget differences, to generalize, to abstract. In the overly replete world of Funes there was nothing but details, almost contiguous details, Borges, 1956, p.116). Because Funes was unable to "forget differences," it was difficult for him to understand, for instance, that the generic symbol dog applied to so many disparate individuals, of varying sizes and shapes, and he was disturbed by the fact that a dog at 3:14 (seen in profile) had the same name that the dog at a quarter past three (in a frontal view). For Funes, therefore, every experience was unique, every stimulus was singular, having no relation whatsoever to other stimuli. He could not think because he could not form stimulus classes.

Real organisms are able to "forget" differences: Stimuli that are physically different may exhibit similar control over responses and, therefore, comprise a stimulus class. Although current stimuli may be never exactly identical to those previously experienced, organisms react to them based on their relation to stimulus classes. Some classes are based on stimulus similarity or on common features. Other classes comprise stimuli with no physical resemblance: the spoken word "dog", a picture of a dog, and the printed word *dog*, may constitute a stimulus class due to arbitrary relations established by a verbal community. For most English-speaking persons, the relations between these stimuli are equivalence relations, so that the spoken word, printed word, and picture constitute a class of equivalent stimuli.

Sidman and Tailby (1982) adapted the definition of equivalence from mathematical set theory in order to provide behavioral criteria to assess whether a relation between stimuli is an equivalence relation. In set theory, a relation of equivalence is defined by three properties, reflexivity, symmetry, and transitivity. Sidman and Tailby applied this definition to the relation between stimuli established by the conditional discrimination procedure commonly known as arbitrary matching to sample, in which selection of a particular comparison stimulus is reinforced conditionally upon the presence of a given sample. In the simplest case, two comparison stimuli (B1 and B2) are presented on every trial. Each trial displays also a sample stimulus, either A1 or A2. When A1 is the sample, selections of B1 are reinforced, and selections of B2 go unreinforced. When the sample is A2, selections of B2 are reinforced, and selections of B1 go unreinforced. This conditional discrimination is conventionally abbreviated as AB, implying that each sample of set A is conditionally related to one comparison stimulus of set B. Although conditional discrimination arrangements can be very complex, discussion in this chapter will, unless otherwise stated, be confined to procedures in which the number of samples (in successive trials) equals the number of comparisons, all comparisons are presented in every trial, and the relation between each sample and the respective comparison is arbitrary.

Assuming that a conditional discrimination establishes a relation between each sample and the comparison stimulus selected in its presence (abbreviated, in the simplest case, as A1rB1 and A2rB2), this relation would have the property of reflexivity if each stimulus bore the relation to itself (A1rA1, etc.). Thus, if A1 was presented as a sample, and A1 and A2 as comparisons, the subject should be able to select A1 without specific training, and likewise to select an identical stimulus when A2, B1 and B2 were presented as samples. Symmetry would be demonstrated by reversibility of sample and comparison functions, that is, conditional discrimination AB should emerge, in the absence of further training. Demonstration of transitivity would require training of another conditional discrimination, BC. Transitivity would be inferred by the emergence of conditional discrimination AC. Emergence of conditional discrimination CA, on the other hand, would logically imply both symmetry and transitivity of the trained conditional relations, and is sometimes accepted as an abbreviated test of equivalence. Another commonly used training design is to train conditional discriminations AB and AC, and then test the emergence of conditional discriminations BC and CB. These would logically imply symmetry and transitivity of the trained relations. This training design is the simplest case of a "one-to-many" design, in which each sample is related to many comparisons. In a "many-to-one" design, on the other hand, each comparison is related to many samples: The simplest case would be to train conditional discriminations BA and CA, and then test emergent conditional discriminations BC and CB. In both cases, a thorough demonstration of equivalence would require a separate demonstration of reflexivity, but this is sometimes omitted.

Stimulus equivalence attracted considerable attention for at least two reasons. First, equivalence relations present notable generative properties. Training two conditional discriminations, AB and BC, may result in at least four emergent conditional discriminations: BA, CB, AC and CA. As Sidman and Tailby (1982) showed, a stimulus can be added to an existing equivalence class if it is conditionally related to a member of the class. Therefore, training, for instance, conditional relation DC, could add D to the equivalence class, so that all the remaining relations between D and the original class members would emerge. Also, training a conditional relation between members of two equivalence classes produces merger of the classes, giving rise to emergent relations involving all possible pairs comprising a member of each class (Sidman, Kirk & Wilson-Morris, 1985). Thus, training a few conditional discriminations may produce the emergence of many more relations. The equivalence paradigm may thus originate economic and efficient ways to build or remediate complex relational repertoires, in educational or therapeutic settings (e.g., Cowley, Green & Braunling-McMorrow, 1992; de Rose, Souza, Rossito & de Rose, 1992; de Rose, Souza & Hanna, in press; Lynch & Cuvo, 1995; Maydak, Stromer, Mackay & Stoddard, 1995; Stromer, Mackay & Stoddard, 1992).

Second, several investigators have argued that equivalence relations constitute a model for semantic meaning. According to Sidman (1986) if stimuli like the spoken word dog, the picture of a dog, and the printed word dog, are demonstrated to be equivalent, then they will have the same meaning. Moreover, as Fields, Reeve, Adams and Verhave (1991) showed, class membership may extend to stimuli that are physically similar or have common features. Therefore, if the spoken word "dog" and the printed word dog are equivalent to a picture of a dog, they may be also equivalent to pictures of other dogs, to real dogs, and possibly also to the class of real dogs, to the sound of a barking dog, the smell of dogs, etc. Moreover, functions acquired by a member of an equivalence class may transfer to the other members of the class (e.g., de Rose, McIlvane, Dube, Galpin & Stoddard, 1988; Dougher, Augustson, Markham, Greenway & Wulfert, 1994; Hayes, Kohlenberg & Hayes, 1991; Wulfert & Hayes, 1988). Thus, symbols may, to some extent, acquire the controlling functions of their referents. Studies have also shown that membership in equivalence classes can shift depending on contextual stimuli (Bush, Sidman, & de Rose, 1989; Lazar & Kotlarchyk, 1986; Wulfert & Hayes, 1988). All these findings indicate that stimulus equivalence can serve as a model for the experimental study of the acquisition of meaning and its contextual dependence.

As discussed in several chapters of this volume, the nature and determinants of stimulus equivalence are still controversial (see also Barnes, 1994; Boelens, 1994; Hayes & Hayes, 1989; Hayes, 1991; Horne & Lowe, 1996; Sidman, 1994). One of the major controversies concerns the role of language in equivalence class formation. Horne and Lowe (1996) claim that emergent conditional discriminations are a product of verbal behavior. They argue that verbally competent human subjects trained in conditional discriminations will tend to name the stimuli, even when this is not required by the contingencies. They will often produce a common name for a sample and the comparisons related to it. Naming, in their view, is a bi-directional relation, produced by contingencies operating in the early development of humans, that synthesize speaker and listener behavior. Hence, speaker behavior is controlled by a given stimulus object, so that the individual produces the object's name, and listener behavior is controlled by the object's name, so that the individual orients to the object (or objects in the same class) and responds appropriately to it. Therefore, a subject, upon saying the name of the sample, will exhibit self-listening behavior, that would include orienting to the comparison that has the same name and responding to it. More complex forms of naming may also give rise to emergent conditional discriminations, as in a study by Beasty (1987, as cited in Horne and Lowe, 1996) in which children learned conditional discrimination AB (faced with a green and red comparison stimuli, select the green one in the presence of a vertical line sample and the red one in the presence of a horizontal line sample) and conditional discrimination AC (faced with a triangle and a circle as comparison stimuli, select the triangle in the presence of the vertical line sample and the circle in the presence of the horizontal line sample). Many children, specially the older ones, produced some form of "intraverbal naming" in which the name of the sample was followed by names of the other stimuli related to it. For instance, when facing the vertical sample, a child might say, "up, green, triangle". In a test for equivalence, the same child, when faced with the green sample and the triangle and the circle as comparison stimuli, likewise uttered a string of names involving also "green, triangle", which arguably controlled listening behavior to triangle in the presence of green, that is, orienting to triangle and selecting it. This would, then, be a rudimentary form of rule-governed behavior, or, as Horne and Lowe prefer, verbally controlled behavior. Furthermore, Horne and Lowe claim that stimulus equivalence is not found in the absence of some form of overt or covert naming (see Stromer & Mackay, this volume, for a discussion of the evidence supporting this claim).

If emergent conditional discriminations are always controlled by verbal behavior, the excitement raised by equivalence findings would hardly be justified, and, as Horne and Lowe (1996) argue, the construct of stimulus equivalence would not be necessary. However, one of the aspects that attracted attention in the initial findings about equivalence was exactly the occurrence of complex generative performances in individuals with very limited language skills, that were not likely to engage in verbal reasoning or to exhibit verbal mediation at all (see Sidman, 1994;

Stromer, 1996; Stromer & Mackay, this volume). This, together with recent findings with nonhumans (to be discussed below; see also chapters in this volume by Pepperberg, Urcuioli, and Zentall), suggests that the contingencies of conditional discriminations can generate equivalence relations, in the absence of verbal mediation.

On the other hand, I will argue that a necessary step toward solving the controversies over the nature of equivalence and its necessary pre-requisites may be to examine the nature of controlling relations in trained conditional discriminations and in untrained conditional discriminations (as those presented in tests for equivalence). This may show the need to reevaluate data showing seemingly failures or successes in equivalence tests. I will also suggest that similar performances may be brought about by different controlling factors, including, for language-able humans, verbal behavior. Verbal behavior may control subsequent behavior, generating response topographies similar to those that would be shaped by contingencies (Skinner, 1969), and this may happen also in the conditional discrimination paradigm. Hence, it may be necessary to distinguish between (a) conditional discriminations that emerge by reflexivity, symmetry, and transitivity of trained relations, documenting stimulus equivalence, and (b) emergent conditional discriminations that are verbally controlled. These may not be mutually exclusive, and both can be present in language-able humans.

CONDITIONAL DISCRIMINATIONS

Select and reject relations

When a subject performs with perfect accuracy in a two-choice conditional discrimination, whenever sample A1 is presented, comparison B1 is selected, and whenever sample A2 is presented, comparison B2 is selected. As Constantine (1981) has shown, however, these selections may be controlled by at least two distinct relations, select and reject. In a select relation, selection of, for instance, B1 is controlled by the relation between the sample and the S+ itself (a sample-S+ relation). In this case, comparison B2, the S-, may be irrelevant and may not even be noticed by the subject. The reject controlling relation, on the other hand, is between the sample and the S- (a sample-S- relation). In this case, B2 (the S-) controls responding away from itself, so that the subject selects the other available alternative, B1. Although B1 is selected, it is not the controlling stimulus and may be irrelevant and not even noticed by the subject. Actually, when a conditional discrimination is controlled by a reject relation, the subject may still reject the S- when a novel stimulus or a "blank" alternative is substituted for it (Constantine, 1981; McIlvane, Kledaras, Munson, King, de Rose & Stoddard, 1987; Stromer & Osborne, 1982; Zentall, Edwards, Moore, & Hogan, 1981).

The experimenter may use special training procedures to deliberately produce either select or reject relations (Johnson & Sidman, 1993; McIlvane et al., 1987). When no such special procedures are employed, the contingencies do not specify the type of relation that will be learned, and each particular conditional discrimination may be either a select or reject relation, or both. Therefore, although the subject consistently selects comparison B1 in the presence of sample A1, the controlling relation may be between A1 and B1 (select) or between A1 and B2 (reject). Likewise, sample A2 may be related to comparison B2 (select relation) or to comparison B1 (reject relation). Both relations may be present at the same time, so that in the presence of sample A1, comparison B1 controls selection of itself and comparison B2 controls responding away from itself (cf., Stromer & Osborne, 1982), but this is not necessary, because reinforcement contingencies will be met by either relation alone.

Therefore, the stimulus that is selected in the presence of a given sample is not necessarily the one that is conditionally related to it. Yet, predictions about relations derived by reflexivity, symmetry and transitivity should be based not on the observable selection response, but on the pairs of stimuli that are conditionally related (Carrigan & Sidman, 1992; R. Saunders & Green, 1992). However, as Carrigan and Sidman (1992) showed, if a reject relation is reflexive, symmetrical and transitive, the expected performance in emergent conditional discriminations will differ markedly from the performance derived from select relations.

Derived relations based on select and reject baseline relations

In a two-choice conditional discrimination, if the relation is select, there will be a relation between A1 and B1, abbreviated as A1rB1, and a relation between A2 and B2, abbreviated as A2rB2, where r stands for a select relation. If, however, the relation is reject, there will be a relation between A1 and B2, A1rB2, and likewise, A2rB1, where r stands for a reject relation. Both relations would yield the same observable outcome in baseline trials: the subject selects comparison B1 given sample A1, and comparison B2 given sample A2.

If the select relation is reflexive, each stimulus will bear the relation to itself. Therefore, in tests for reflexivity, each stimulus presented as a sample will control selection of an identical comparison. The analogy with mathematical set theory also allows us to assess whether the reject relation is reflexive. In this case, each stimulus would also bear the reject relation to itself, and thus, in a reflexivity test, each stimulus presented as a sample would control the rejection of the identical comparison. Therefore, select and reject relations will yield opposite outcomes in tests for reflexivity (Carrigan & Sidman, 1992). These predictions were confirmed in a study of Johnson & Sidman (1993), that used training procedures to bias subjects toward reject relations.

In tests for symmetry, the two relations will yield identical outcomes. If r is select, then A1rB1 and A2rB2 will, by symmetry, yield B1rA1 and B2rA2: the observed outcome will be selection of comparison A1 given sample B1, and of comparison A2 given sample B2. If r is reject, then the acquired relations A1rB2 and A2rB1 will yield, by symmetry, B2rA1 and B1rA2, with the observed outcome that the subject rejects comparison A1 in the presence of sample B2, thus selecting the other available comparison, A2, and rejects comparison A2 in the presence of sample B1, thus selecting A1.

The outcomes of transitivity tests are more complex. In order to verify transitivity it is necessary to train another conditional discrimination, BC. If the controlling relations are exclusively select, one has relations A1rB1, B1rC1, A2rB2, and B2rC2, yielding, by transitivity, A1rC1 and A2rC2, with the observable outcome that the subject selects C1 in the presence of A1, and C2 in the presence of A2. If the controlling relations are exclusively reject, one has relations A1rB2 and B2rC1, and A2rB1 B1rC2. The relations that emerge by transitivity, A1rC1 and A2rC2 will imply that the subject selects C2 in the presence of A1 (rejecting C1), and selects C1 in the presence of A2 (rejecting C2).

When a stimulus is related to two or more other stimuli it is said to be a node. Thus, when relations AB and BC are trained, the potential classes have only one node. In this case, the B stimuli are nodes, whereas the A and C stimuli are "singles", i.e., they are each related to only one other stimulus (Fields, Verhave & Fath, 1984). If another relation, CD, is trained, the number of nodes is increased to two (the B and C stimuli). This does not alter the pattern of transitivity outcomes for select relations: the subject will be expected to select D1 in the presence of A1 and D2 in the presence of A2. For select relations, demonstrations of transitivity in principle should be independent of the number of nodes. The analysis of Carrigan and Sidman (1992) predicts, however, that for reject relations the pattern of transitivity results will "flip-flop" every time a node is added. After training conditional discrimination CD, the acquired reject relations will be: A1rB2, B2rC1, and C1rD2, yielding by transitivity relation A1rD2, and, likewise, A2rB1, B1rC2, C2rD1, yielding, by transitivity, A2rD1. Consequently, the subject will reject D2 in the presence of A1 (selecting D1) and reject D1 in the presence of A2 (selecting D2). Thus, with two nodes, the transitivity outcomes expected from reject relations are identical as those expected from select relations. In general terms, transitivity of reject relations, will, with an odd number of nodes, result in choices of X2 in the presence of A1 and of X1 in the presence of A2; with an even number of nodes, the subject will select X1 in the presence of A1 and X2 in the presence of A2.

Johnson and Sidman (1993), using special procedures to establish exclusively reject relations, found the outcomes expected from this analysis, for one-node and two-node baseline relations. Carrigan and Sidman (1992) point out that these predictions can be made only when baseline training results in a single type of relation, either select or reject. Because both types of relation will satisfy conditional discriminations contingencies, the experimenter may be often unaware of the relation that produced them. If training results in only one type of relation, either select or reject, the pattern of test results itself may reveal what type of relation is present. If the resulting control is mixed, with select relations holding between some pairs of stimuli and reject relations between other pairs, no consistent pattern of results can be predicted on the basis of equivalence, and if any consistent results are found, they must be attributed to extraneous factors.

A procedural parameter that logically affects the likelihood of select or reject relations is the number of comparison stimuli. In the common two-choice conditional discrimination, the subject may achieve accurate performance either by learning one select relation or one reject relation (select the S+ or reject the S-). However, in a three-choice conditional discrimination, there will be two S-, so that the subject would need to learn two different reject relations (rejecting both S-) in the presence of a given sample, whereas only one select relation would suffice. For this reason, Sidman (1987) argued that baseline conditional discriminations in experiments on equivalence need to involve at least three choices.

Although increasing the number of comparisons should result in a higher proportion of select relations, this may not completely rule out reject relations. Consider, for instance, the hypothetical acquisition of a three choice conditional discrimination, in which the subject learns initially to make a response in the presence of sample A1, then he or she learns to respond in the presence of sample A2 and finally a response is learned in the presence of sample A3. One may assume that the relations involving samples A1 and A2 are likely to be of the select type. However, once these two relations have been learned, the subject may respond in the presence of sample A3 by exclusion (Dixon, 1977; McIlvane and Stoddard, 1981; McIlvane et al., 1987). Ferrari, de Rose and McIlvane (1993) demonstrated that exclusion can take place in a conditional discrimination with four comparisons, if three of them have been already related to other samples.

When a conditional relation is learned through exclusion, selection of the correct comparison is, at least initially controlled by a reject relation, and sometimes subjects do not develop select relations after more extended practice (e.g., Cameron, Stoddard & McIlvane, 1993; Dixon, 1977). Hence, the use of three or more comparisons do not rule out the possibility that performance in a conditional discrimination could involve select relations for some samples and reject relations for others, because the relations that are acquired first are likely to be of the select type, and exclusion may take place after some relations are learned.

This analysis suggests that some apparent failures in equivalence tests may be attributed to the acquisition of reject relations during baseline training, or to the acquisition of a mixed control, involving select relations for some samples and reject relations for others. This is especially likely to happen when baseline conditional discriminations involve only two samples and two comparisons, but it can possibly happen also when more samples and comparisons are used.

Generalized conditional responding (arbitrary assignment)

K. Saunders & Spradlin (1990, 1993) presented data suggesting that conditional responding is a generalized skill. They used several training procedures to establish arbitrary conditional discriminations, each involving two samples and two comparisons, in retarded subjects who appeared to be incapable of learning this task by trial and error. Acquisition of the first conditional discrimination required special training procedures and a large number of trials. Each new additional conditional discrimination, however, tended to require less special training and fewer trials. Eventually, most of their subjects acquired conditional discriminations quickly by trial and error. After the subjects had acquired several conditional discriminations by trial and error, they were given trials with two new samples and two new comparisons, with no programmed reinforcing consequences. They showed generalized conditional responding, consistently selecting one comparison stimulus in the presence of one of the samples, and the other comparison stimulus in the presence of the other sample. K. Saunders and Spradlin (1990) point out that "subjects with a history of responding conditionally tend to respond conditionally" (p. 248). In other words, when presented with an unreinforced conditional discrimination task, subjects with this history may arbitrarily assign each comparison to a sample.

Harrison and Green (1990) showed that normal adults and children can respond conditionally even without an experimental history of reinforced conditional responding. Their subjects were presented with two choice-conditional discrimination trials in which, for each sample, there was only one comparison consistently present. Responses were followed by no programmed consequence other than presentation of the next trial. Most of their subjects quickly developed conditional responding, and for some subjects, the relations acquired in this way proved to be symmetrical and transitive.

Saunders, Saunders, Kirby & Spradlin (1988) showed that conditional responding acquired by arbitrary assignment can also give rise to equivalence relations. In one of their studies, for instance, subjects had previously formed four equivalence classes. They were then presented with unreinforced conditional discrimination trials, with two samples and two comparisons. The samples were drawn from the first two classes and the comparisons were drawn from the third and fourth classes. Subjects arbitrarily assigned one comparison to each sample. Subsequent tests showed that the original classes merged on the basis of this arbitrary assignment.

If subjects can develop conditional responding in the absence of differential consequences, they may do so as well in tests of the defining properties of equivalence. Conditional responding consistent with equivalence may arise either by arbitrary assignment or because subjects can detect consistencies in the arrangements of samples and comparisons presented across blocks of trials (cf. Harrison & Green, 1990). Tests for equivalence may, therefore, produce false-positive effects, and thus, results should be viewed with caution, specially when obtained in a two-choice format, or when frequency of presentation of different comparisons in the presence of a given sample is unbalanced.

Non-arbitrary relations

Emergent conditional discriminations are regarded as deriving from trained conditional discriminations that are reflexive, symmetrical and transitive. However, there may be other relations between stimuli that may give rise to consistent performance in tests. For instance, stimuli may be physically similar or may share common features. These idiosyncratic common features may serve as a basis for selection on test trials. Horne and Lowe (1996) present a hypothetical example in which all stimuli of one class resemble the letter R. In tests for emergent relations, subjects could perform consistently based on this non-arbitrary relation. In this case, performance controlled by non-arbitrary relations would be congruent with that expected if subjects formed equivalence classes. The conclusion that trained conditional relations possessed the properties of an equivalence relation would be misleading, however, because test results did not depend on the baseline conditional discriminations, but on non-arbitrary relations between stimuli. Many other relations between stimuli may, conceivably, control consistent selections in test trials. A compelling example is reported by Stikeleather and Sidman (1990). Their subjects responded consistently in tests even to stimuli that could not be equivalent on the basis of the trained conditional discriminations. Inspection of the training procedures, however, revealed that subjects could have been responding to the stimuli based on the order in which they were introduced in the training sequence, and this possibility was supported by verbal reports of one subject.

No matter how careful an experimenter might be in selecting stimuli and controlling for possible non-arbitrary relations among them, it may be virtually impossible to avoid competing control by such relations in tests for equivalence involving conditional discriminations. If such extraneous relations come to exert partial or total control over test performance, "spurious" equivalence relations may be found (cf. Sidman, 1987; Stikeleather & Sidman, 1990), if they are congruent with expected performance; otherwise, if they are not congruent with the expected performance, then test results may show competing control over selections (cf., Dube & McIlvane, this volume; Sidman et al., 1985).

Verbal control

Common naming

After training a conditional discrimination in which auditory samples are related to visual comparisons, human subjects often come to produce the auditory stimulus as a name for the related visual stimulus (e.g. Ferrari et al., 1993; Lipkens, Hayes & Hayes, 1993). For instance, when subjects are trained in auditory-visual conditional discriminations with the auditory stimulus as a node (training, say AB and AC and testing BC and CB) they may take each A stimulus (often a non-sense word) as a name for the related B and C stimuli. According to Horne and Lowe (1996), in an equivalence test, given, for instance stimulus B1, the subject would name it, and this would control subsequent listener behavior. Listener behavior includes, given a name, orienting toward the corresponding object and responding appropriately to it. Therefore, subjects would be likely to orient toward C1 (which has also been given the same name) and select it. Common naming can, therefore, control responding in tests of equivalence, yielding outcomes consistent with symmetry, transitivity and reflexivity of the baseline relations.

Even when baseline conditional discriminations involve only visual stimuli, subjects may produce a common name for stimuli that are conditionally related, and production of these names in equivalence tests would, according to Horne and Lowe (1996), account for selections consistent with equivalence. Moreover, it has been reported that, when subjects do not show equivalence class formation after baseline training, the addition of naming training can bring about the classes (Dugdale & Lowe, 1990; Eikeseth & Smith, 1992). This is especially likely when baseline conditional discriminations are all visual-visual, so that the experimenter does not provide an auditory stimulus that the subject can readily use as a name for the visual stimuli. When this name is provided in subsequent training, it often brings about consistent performance in equivalence tests. Actually, naming training may produce accurate performance on equivalence tests even when no baseline conditional discriminations are trained (Eikeseth & Smith, 1992).

Control by rules

Human subjects may detect regularities, or contingencies, and formulate them verbally, so that these verbal formulations, or rules, will control their subsequent behavior. The processes involved in rule formulation and how the repertoire of rule following is established are controversial, but there is no doubt that contingencies in baseline conditional discriminations may give rise to rules that may subsequently control performance in equivalence tests. A rudimentary form of rule use is what Horne and Lowe (1996) call intraverbal naming. Subjects may produce idiosyncratic names for the stimuli and string them together according to the experimentally designed classes. Later, in equivalence tests, a subject that has consistently stringed together the names of A1, B1 and C1, for instance, is likely to do the same when B1 is presented as a sample, and this will control selection of comparison stimulus C1. Horne and Lowe cite studies from their laboratory in which children produced these forms of intraverbal naming, and also more elaborate forms of rules, in which they state the conditional relations between stimuli, saying something like "___ goes with ____." "Goes with" is a verbal formulation of an equivalence relation, and it is not surprising that subjects able to state conditional relations in this way demonstrate formation of equivalence classes. Subjects with a more sophisticated verbal repertoire, like college students, are often able to verbally state complex networks of relations among stimuli and to perform accordingly.

Wulfert, Dougher and Greenway (1991) used a "protocol analysis" (cf. Erikson & Simon, 1984) in which subjects were instructed to "think aloud" as they learned baseline relations AB, AC and AD, and they subsequently were tested for equivalence. Wulfert et al. showed that subjects who demonstrated equivalence stated verbally the relations between stimuli, and during equivalence tests usually stated the relation of the sample and comparison to the nodal stimulus. On the other hand, subjects that failed to demonstrate equivalence produced other kinds of verbalizations, the most common being reference to sample and correct comparison as a compound.

In a later study by Dickins, Bentall & Smith (1993), subjects were trained to name stimuli, using names that conflicted with the classes presumably generated by the conditional discriminations. In tests for emergent conditional discriminations, they found that subjects tended to match stimuli according to the names they had learned for them, rather than the baseline conditional discriminations. In this case, test results may have reflected the conflict between classes established by common naming and other classes possibly established by baseline conditional discriminations. Subjects who learned "neutral" names, that did not conflict with equivalence classes based on baseline conditional discriminations, on the other hand, when tested for equivalence, tended to perform according to the classes presumably generated by the baseline conditional discriminations. These results suggest that classes established by common naming may either prevent the formation of conflicting equivalence classes based on conditional discrimination training, or may exercise stronger control than the later classes during tests.

All these studies show that verbal formulations by the subjects are often correlated with the outcomes of equivalence tests. Verbal formulations compatible with experimentally designed classes are usually accompanied by consistent performance in tests for class formation. Verbal formulations incompatible with experimentally designed classes are often accompanied by failure in equivalence tests. When verbal formulations arise "spontaneously" in the conditional discrimination, rather than being directly trained, it is not clear whether the verbal formulations control selections in equivalence tests, or whether both verbal formulations and selections in tests are jointly controlled by other variables. Also, as will be discussed later, the frequent occurrence of verbal formulations does not constitute proof that equivalence does not occur in the absence of verbal control (see also Stromer & Mackay, this volume).

Limitations of equivalence tests based on emergent conditional discriminations

From the above discussion one can conclude that several conflicting factors may interact in untrained conditional discriminations designed to test for class formation. After a history of responding conditionally, subjects may tend to respond conditionally in untrained conditional discriminations, and they may consistently assign a comparison to each sample for a number of reasons, of which the experimenter may be unaware. Because the task involves a forced-choice between a restricted number of alternatives, there is much potential for false positive effects and for interference with class formation by undesired controlling factors.

The range of confounding factors increases when one takes into account negative test results. For instance, Dube and colleagues (Dube, McIlvane, Mackay & Stoddard, 1987; Dube, McIlvane, Maguire, Mackay & Stoddard, 1989) using specific reinforcers correlated with choices of the members of each potential class, have found that the reinforcer itself becomes a member of the class. Because in most studies the same reinforcer is contingent on selection of members of all classes, it follows that all classes will possess a common member, and they may therefore collapse into a single class. Thus, failure in some tests might be attributed to the formation of a single equivalence class, encompassing all stimuli used in training, with the common reinforcer functioning as a nodal stimulus. Sidman (1994) suggests two additional elements that are typically related to all training stimuli, and thus may strengthen the tendency for the formation of a single all-encompassing class, the defined response (usually common to members of all classes) and the experimental context.

If this reasoning is correct, tests of equivalence may produce negative evidence either because conditional discrimination training did not produce equivalence classes, or because the training resulted in larger classes involving all experimental stimuli. Also, as noted earlier, negative test results may be obtained because baseline training results in a mixture of select and reject relations, or because there is interference from non-arbitrary common features, or because of incompatible verbal control. False positive effects may be found when arbitrary assignment or unintended relations between stimuli are convergent with expected performance. Even for genuine positive results there may be two different controlling factors, at least for language-able humans, because equivalence may be generated by contingencies of conditional discrimination training or may be verbally controlled.

The next section will discuss some experimental findings that illustrate the complexity of the controlling factors in untrained conditional discriminations.

INTERPRETATION OF SOME PUZZLING EFFECTS

Nodality and training design

A common finding in the equivalence literature is that more training and testing is required to form equivalence classes as the number of nodes increase (Fields, Adams, Verhave & Newman, 1990; Sidman et al., 1985). Fields, Adams, Verhave & Newman (1993; see also Fields, Landon-Jimenez, Buffington & Adams, 1995) suggest that even after classes have been formed, stimuli within a class vary in their degree of relatedness, so that relatedness is inversely proportional to the number of nodes intervening between stimuli. Fields et al. (1993) trained two-choice conditional discriminations AB, BC, CD, and DE, and verified the formation of two equivalence classes. They then trained subjects to type a combination of keystrokes on a computer keyboard in the presence of A1 and another combination in the presence of A2. In subsequent probes some subjects showed a complete transfer of discriminative control to all class members, whereas other subjects showed what appeared to be decreasing rates of transfer as the number of nodes separating stimuli from A1 and A2 increased. Fields et al. (1993) interpreted the decreasing rate of transfer as indicating a decrease in the relatedness of stimuli within the same equivalence class.

Sidman (1994) suggested that the effects of number of nodes on equivalence tests may arise, at least partially, from a mixture of select and reject relations: "As conditional discriminations are added to a baseline, the probability increases that a subject's bases for choice will vary -- it becomes more likely that some comparisons will be chosen by selection and others by rejection. Such inconsistency can be expected to increase the variability among test outcomes as the number of nodes increases." (Sidman, 1994, p. 540). Sidman suggests that effects of nodal number may be smaller after training in conditional discriminations with three or more stimuli, because this would increase the likelihood of select relations. A study of Kennedy (1991) has indeed showed decreasing effects of nodal number when the number of comparisons in baseline conditional discriminations increase from two to three.

A series of studies conducted in our lab is relevant to this issue. Table 1 summarizes the relevant procedural features and outcomes of each experiment. In Experiment 1, college students were trained in a series of two-choice conditional discriminations. For one group, the training design involved a single node (uninodal design). For two subjects in the group, the design was one-to-many, with each nodal sample related to several different comparisons (conditional discriminations AB, AC, AD, AE, and AF). For two other subjects, the design was many-to-one, with each nodal comparison related to several samples (conditional discriminations BA, CA, DA, EA, and FA). Another group had a training design with four nodes (multinodal design, with conditional discriminations AB, BC, CD, DE, and EF, for five subjects, and BA, CB, DC, ED, and FE, for six other subjects). A simple simultaneous discrimination was also trained between A1 and A2, so that subjects learned to select A1 (the S+) and not A2 (the S-). Probes were then conducted to verify transfer of discriminative functions, that should result in emergent simple discriminations (cf. Boelens & Smeets, 1989; de Rose et al., 1988; Smeets, 1994) involving stimulus pairs B1/B2, C1/C2, D1/D2, E1/E2, and F1/F2, and for equivalence formation (probing for untrained conditional relations FA, EA, DA, and CA). Based on the previous results of Fields and colleagues (Fields et al., 1990; Fields et al., 1993; Fields et al., 1995), one would expect the uninodal design to be more effective for class formation than the multinodal design, and the data confirmed this prediction: All four subjects in the uninodal group showed equivalence and transfer of functions whereas no subject in the multinodal group showed either equivalence or transfer of function. Experiment 2 was an attempt to replicate this first study. Because differences were not found between the one-to-many and many-to-one training designs, only the one-to-many design was used with the uninodal group, in this and the following studies. Only one training design was used with the multinodal group (training conditional discriminations AB, BC, CD, DE, and EF). A few other procedural changes, not considered relevant at the time, were made. To reduce the time required for conditional discrimination training, each new conditional discrimination was taught using an on-screen verbal prompt, with the phrase "if this is here" written below the sample, and the phrase "pick this", written below the correct comparison, whereas trial and error training was used in the Experiment 1. Because of software differences, subjects in Experiment 1 pressed keys in the computer's keyboard to make selections, whereas in Experiment 2 they used a mouse to move an arrow-shaped cursor, placing it on the comparison to be selected and then clicking the mouse button. The unexpected outcome of Experiment 2 was that all subjects of both groups showed equivalence and transfer of functions. Apparently, then, a multinodal design could be as effective as the uninodal design. We then speculated that some of the procedural changes that were initially considered to be irrelevant, could have biased subjects toward select relations. In Experiment 2, it was possible that the written prompt resulted in control by the relation between the sample and the S+ (select relation), because the prompt stated this relation verbally. Also, the topography of the selection response in Experiment 2

Table 1
Response topography, number of choices, training procedure, and number of subjects that formed classes in the uninodal and multinodal groups, in experiments comparing the effectiveness of uninodal and multinodal training designs.

| | | | | Subjects Forming Classes | |
Exp.	Response Topography	Choices	Training Procedure	Uninodal	Multinodal
1	Keyboard	2	Trial/Error	4/4	0/11
2	Mouse	2	Prompt	4/4	6/6
3	Touch Stim.	3	Trial/Error	4/4	0/4
4	Keyboard	2	Prompt	7/7	2/8
5 Gr K	Keyboard	2	Prompt	--	1/5
5 Gr M	Mouse	2	Prompt	--	4/5

Note. These experiments will be numbered sequentially, for convenience, although most of them have been reported separately; Experiments 1 and 2 were presented in a brief report by de Rose, Ribeiro, Reis and Kledaras (1992). Experiment 3 was reported in a thesis by Ribeiro (1994), and Experiment 4 has been reported by de Rose, Thé and Kato (1995).

involved moving an arrow and placing it over the S+, and this could increase the likelihood that the S+ would be the controlling stimulus, giving rise to select relations (de Rose, Ribeiro, Reis & Kledaras, 1992).

If failure of the multinodal group to show class formation was due to a mixture of select and reject relations in the baseline task, it is possible that, as Sidman suggested, an increase in the number of comparisons could produce select relations, thus resulting in class formation for subjects with multinodal training. To verify this, in Experiment 3 (Ribeiro, 1994) four children were trained with conditional discriminations AB, BC, CD, and DE (multinodal group) and four other children in conditional discriminations AB, AC, AD, and AE (uninodal group) using procedures similar to those used in Experiment 1. Each conditional discrimination involved three samples and three comparisons, and the children made selections by touching the stimulus on the computer monitor. All subjects in the uninodal group showed equivalence and transfer of function, but no subject in the multinodal group showed either effect. Thus, a training design with several nodes seemed to be less effective than a uninodal design even with three-choice conditional discrimination training. A possible explanation for these results is that the increase in the number of comparisons did not completely rule out reject relations in the baseline task. Thus, even if most learned relations were select, if a few reject relations were present in the multinodal group, this would be sufficient to prevent the demonstration of equivalence classes.

Two subsequent studies were conducted to verify effects of the written prompt and the topography of selections. In Experiment 4 (de Rose, Thé & Kato, 1995), an on-screen prompt in the initial trials was used to train college students in conditional discriminations involving two samples and two comparisons. Subjects selected stimuli through keyboard presses. All seven subjects in the uninodal group showed equivalence and transfer of functions. Of the eight subjects in the multinodal group, two showed equivalence and transfer of functions, four showed neither equivalence nor transfer of functions, and two showed somewhat mixed results. Thus, most subjects of the multinodal group did not show class formation even when they were trained with an on-screen prompt.

Experiment 5 studied the other procedural variable suggested by de Rose et al. (1992), response topography. A multinodal design was used for two groups of college students. Group K made selections using the keyboard, and Group M made selections using the mouse. Of the five subjects of group K, only one showed equivalence and transfer of functions, whereas four of the five subjects in Group M showed both equivalence and transfer of functions.

Although the results of this series of studies are not conclusive, an inspection of Table 1 reveals some consistent findings. With the uninodal training, equivalence and transfer were found for all subjects, and were not affected by the variations in the procedure. With the multinodal design, on the other hand, very few subjects showed equivalence and transfer when the response topography did not involve the mouse. However, in our two experiments in which subjects made selections using the mouse, eight of nine subjects showed equivalence and transfer of functions (Experiment 2, and Experiment 5, Group M). In these two conditions, training was conducted with an on-screen prompt. Experiment 3 and 5 (Group K) showed, however, that the on-screen prompt is not sufficient to increase the effectiveness of the multinodal design. It is possible, however, that both the onscreen prompt and use of the mouse are necessary. Other features of our procedures should also be examined, to verify if they interact with training design.

A possible explanation for these results is that procedural variations can affect the likelihood of select and reject relations in baseline conditional discriminations. This seems a very plausible conjecture, because conditional discrimination contingencies can be met by either select or reject relations, or by a mixture of both; assuming that behavioral control is determined, and not capricious, the likelihood of particular controlling relations must be a function of procedural features, interacting with the subject's history. For instance, a response topography requiring the subject to move the mouse so as to place an arrow-shaped cursor on the S+, may increase the likelihood of observing the S+, resulting, therefore, in select relations. This would explain why, when subjects use the mouse, multinodal and uninodal designs are equally effective in producing class formation. If this response topography has such a biasing effect, however, it is not clear why the uninodal design seems to be effective regardless of response topography. To address these issues, we are currently attempting to assess the pattern of select and reject relations, in order to verify how it is affected by response topography and how it interacts with training design. It is interesting to note, though, that a few published studies appear to support our hypothesis. Fields et al. (1995) used a multinodal design with college students as subjects, and showed that only two of twelve subjects showed equivalence. The subjects in their study made selections by typing particular keys on the keyboard. However, Kennedy, Itknonnen, and Lindquist (1994), in a study with moderately retarded adults as subjects and a multinodal training design, found that all three subjects showed equivalence. They also used prompts to train the conditional discriminations. The stimuli were printed words, and the subjects were required to circle the sample word and read it, and then selected a comparison stimulus by circling it and reading it. The requirement of circling and reading successively the sample and the selected comparison explicitly requires control by the S+ in the presence of each sample.

Regardless of why seemingly "minor" variations, like the topography of the selection response, affect the outcomes of equivalence tests, the fact that they have such an effect shows how sensitive to procedural variables conditional discrimination performance may be.

Complex interactions between training design and procedural features also have been found in studies comparing effects of many-to-one and one-to-many training designs. R. Saunders and colleagues showed consistent effects of training design on class formation, with mildly retarded subjects trained in two choice conditional discriminations (R. Saunders, K. Saunders, et al., 1988; R. Saunders, Wachter, & Spradlin, 1988; Spradlin & R. Saunders, 1986). In these studies, all subjects trained with a many-to-one design showed equivalence class formation, whereas most subjects trained with the one-to-many design did not. In a subsequent study, K. Saunders, R. Saunders, Williams and Spradlin (1993) found that the outcomes of the many-to-one design were affected by instructions given to the subjects and the particular stimulus set used. In the earlier studies, at the start of each new conditional discrimination, subjects were told names for the stimuli and received the instruction: "When the (sample name) comes up, you press the button under the (comparison name)". K. Saunders et al. (1993) found that, in the absence of such instructions, the many-to-one design was as ineffective as the one-to-many design for equivalence class formation. They reasoned that instructions could have affected performance via anticipatory naming of the correct comparison stimulus. With the many-to-one design, in the presence of each sample belonging to the same prospective class, the subject would produce a common name, the name of the comparison stimulus related as a node to all the samples. This common name could then foster equivalence class formation (see also Urcuioli, Zentall & DeMarse, 1995; Urcuioli, Zentall, Jackson-Smith & Steirn, 1989; Zentall & Urcuioli, 1993, for similar findings with pigeons). However, when they attempted to replicate these results using other sets of arbitrary stimuli, K. Saunders et al. (1993) found that with some sets of stimuli, subjects formed equivalence classes in the absence of instructions. It is not clear whether these successes in the absence of instructions (a) were due to the fact that subjects had already formed classes with earlier sets (with instructions), (b) were specific to certain stimulus sets, or (c) were due to repeated exposure to equivalence "problems" with different stimulus sets.

Other studies suggest that training design may interact also with the number of stimuli in the prospective classes. Stromer and Osborne (1982) compared the effectiveness of one-to-many and many-to-one training designs, with retarded adolescents, and found that most subjects trained with both designs showed equivalence. In their study, however, the number of stimuli in each prospective class was limited to three, as opposed to four per class in the studies of R. Saunders and colleagues. In general, studies with retarded subjects that used the one-to-many design have showed equivalence formation when the number of stimuli per class was limited to three (e.g., Green, 1991; Sidman, Wilson-Morris & Kirk, 1986).

The results of K. Saunders et al. (1993) show that verbal control needs to be added to the list of variables that can influence performance in emergent conditional discriminations, interacting with training variables and other procedural features. In the next section I will argue that verbal control is but one of the variables that may influence emergent performance. Verbal control may supplement, or even circumvent control by conditional discriminations contingencies. For this reason, it may be useful to distinguish between contingency-generated equivalence and verbally controlled derived relations.

Stimulus equivalence vs. verbally controlled derived relations

When relations between stimuli are verbally formulated, either through common naming or more complex rule-like formulations, subjects are likely to perform tests for equivalence as if baseline conditional relations possessed the properties of an equivalence relation (Dugdale & Lowe, 1990; Eikeseth & Smith, 1992; Horne & Lowe, 1996; Wulfert et al., 1991). However, this performance may not tell much about the status of baseline conditional discriminations, because "emergent" conditional relations may occur even in the absence of a baseline of conditional discrimination (cf. Eikeseth & Smith, 1992). Emergent conditional discriminations will occur, in such case, either because verbal relations formulated by the subject, such as common naming, intraverbal naming or "___ goes with ___," may themselves be equivalence relations, or because the subjects are able to formulate rules that control further selections. These verbally controlled relations need to be distinguished from stimulus equivalence, in which conditional relations possess the properties of reflexivity, symmetry and transitivity.

It cannot be doubted that verbal control can give rise to emergent performance consistent with the properties of equivalence relations. Evidence for contingency-generated equivalence has, on the other hand, been disputed. Some of the major controversies surrounding this question (see also Stromer & Mackay, this volume) will now be surveyed.

Subjects unable to name do not form equivalence classes.

Humans

Devany, Hayes and Nelson (1986) compared formation of equivalence classes in three groups of children, matched for mental age: normal children, language-able retarded children, and language-unable retarded children. They trained AB and AC two-choice conditional discriminations and found that both normal children and language-able retarded children showed emergent BC and CB conditional discriminations, whereas retarded children with no language showed chance performance in BC and CB conditional discriminations. The study by Devany et al. is often cited as a demonstration that children without language are incapable of forming equivalence classes (cf. Dugdale & Lowe, 1990; Horne & Lowe, 1996) although the authors themselves admitted that the study did not provide definite evidence on this issue. In fact, as has been pointed out elsewhere (e.g., McIlvane & Dube, 1996; R. Saunders & Green, 1996; see also Stromer & Mackay, this volume), methodological shortcomings of this study limit its validity as a demonstration that language is required for equivalence formation. All subjects received verbal instructions and prompts in training and presumably also in testing, and these could not be useful for the non-verbal subjects. Tests were conducted in a single session, mixing BC and CB trials, with no baseline trials interspersed, making it impossible to verify maintenance of accurate baseline performance. Only one test session was conducted, and the verbal subjects showed delayed emergence of equivalence in the course of this session. Because non-verbal subjects required considerably more training in conditional discriminations, emergence of conditional discriminations might also require more extensive testing.

Barnes, McCullagh and Keenan (1990) compared equivalence formation in children with and without hearing impairment, using a procedure similar to that of Devany et al. (1986). Two hearing impaired subjects had verbal development scores below age two, and two others were rated above age two. The two subjects with verbal scores above age two showed equivalence formation, as well as one subject rated below age two. The fact that the subject who did not form equivalence had the lowest verbal score led Barnes et al. to conclude that their study showed a correlation between verbal development and equivalence formation. As they admit, however, this is based on data from only one subject who did not show equivalence. Moreover, even highly capable subjects may fail to form equivalence initially but they may show it after more extensive testing or other interventions, such as cycling between training and testing conditions or testing pre-requisite emergent relations (cf. Lazar, Davis-Lang & Sanchez, 1984; Sidman et al., 1985; Wulfert & Hayes, 1988). None of these interventions were attempted by Barnes et al. (1990). It is important to note, also, that one of the subjects that Barnes et al. included in the set of least verbally-developed subjects showed equivalence (see Stromer & Mackay, this volume, for further discussion of these data). Therefore, the studies of Devany et al. (1986) and Barnes et al. (1990) provide little empirical support for the claim that non-verbal humans are not able to form equivalence.

Non-humans

Many investigators have tested properties of equivalence in non-human animals, with negative results often reported (D'Amato, Salmon, Loukas & Tomie, 1985; Lipkens, Kop & Matthijs, 1988; Sidman, Rauzin, Lazar, Cunningham, Tailby & Carrigan, 1982). Some apparently positive results have been criticized because, in fact, purportedly emergent performances may have been directly trained (McIntire, Cleary & Thompson, 1987; Vaughan, 1988). Even studies conducted with chimpanzees that had received extensive language-training showed that conditional discriminations were not symmetrical (but see Tomonaga, 1993; and Tomonaga, Matsuzawa, Fujita & Yamamoto, 1991). Dugdale and Lowe (1990) report studies conducted with Sherman and Lana, two chimpanzees that had previously received extensive language training. They showed that conditional discriminations acquired by these subjects were not symmetrical. Yamamoto and Asano (1995) attempted to train symmetrical responding in Ai, another language-trained chimpanzee, and showed some indication of transitivity, but in an equivalence test (combined symmetry and transitivity), again results were negative.

In spite of these negative or not totally convincing results, recent studies seem much more promising. Schusterman and Kastak (1993) trained a California sea lion in symmetrical and transitive responding with 12 three-member stimulus classes, and subsequently tested for equivalence class formation with 18 other classes. After training with conditional discriminations, AB and BC, the subject was able to perform the untrained conditional discrimination CA, significantly above chance, showing correct performance in the first trial in 16 out of 18 potential classes. Manabe, Kawashima and Staddon (1995) trained budgerigars to emit differential vocalizations in the presence of two stimuli. These stimuli were then used as comparisons, related in a conditional discrimination to two different sample stimuli. In the presence of each sample, the birds eventually emitted the vocalization trained in the presence of the corresponding comparison. This may be considered a transfer of discriminative functions acquired by the comparison stimuli to the related samples, which is consistent with the notion that samples and comparisons had become equivalent (see Sidman, 1994). Studies with pigeons have showed that different samples related to the same comparison stimulus in a many-to-one paradigm, may be equivalent, whereas equivalence has not been found after training with a one-to-many paradigm (Urcuioli et al., 1995; Urcuioli et al., 1989; Zentall & Urcuioli, 1993). If such evidence continues to grow, it will eventually force the conclusion that equivalence can be found in other species. It will also put to rest the controversy on the necessity of language for equivalence class formation.

Naming tests

When baseline conditional discriminations include an auditory-visual relation, in naming tests the auditory sample is often given by the subjects as the name of all visual stimuli related to it. Two outcomes from these tests have been taken as indication that naming is not necessary for equivalence: one is that common naming of the visual class members (usually with the auditory sample given as the common name), although frequent, is not always obtained. The other outcome, reported by Sidman, Cresson and Wilson-Morris (1974) and Sidman and Tailby (1982) is that a few subjects, even though eventually able to name the stimuli, provide collateral evidence that the names were evoked by the naming test itself and were not being produced while the subjects were performing in conditional discriminations.

When baseline conditional discriminations are visual-visual, and the stimuli are arbitrary, baseline relations do not provide a "name" for the stimuli. Nevertheless, stimulus equivalence is often found, and subsequent naming tests often do not yield common names for class members (Green, 1990; Lazar et al., 1984; Sidman et al., 1986). Lowe and colleagues (Dugdale & Lowe, 1990; Horne & Lowe, 1996; see also Stoddard & McIlvane, 1986) maintain that post-experimental naming tests cannot be taken as valid indicators of naming during baseline and testing sessions, because post-experimental interviews may fail to evoke the very names uttered by the subjects during the experimental sessions. For instance, Dugdale & Lowe (1990) report studies in which verbal utterances were recorded during experimental sessions and compared with names given in post-experimental interviews. Session recordings showed that subjects assigned common names to class-members or stated verbally the relations between stimuli, whereas in post-experimental interviews they often gave names different from the ones produced during the sessions or failed altogether to name the stimuli. Moreover, Dugdale and Lowe (1990) and Horne and Lowe (1996) report several studies in which children who did not name during sessions also did not show equivalence, but most of these subjects came to form equivalence classes after they were trained to name. Thus, the arguments of Lowe and colleagues against naming tests are based on the lack of agreement between naming in post-experimental tests and spontaneous overt naming occurring during the sessions.

Sidman (1994) has noted that in his laboratory "spontaneous" overt naming during experimental sessions is rarely observed. He wondered whether the use of a very short intertrial interval may diminish subjects' opportunities for naming, giving them "little time to think." Also, the subjects in the studies by Lowe and colleagues have been predominantly normally developing pre-school children, who may display a readiness to engage in overt verbalizations while solving problems (cf. Vygotsky, 1978). The subjects in the studies by Sidman and colleagues, on the other hand, have often included moderately or severely retarded subjects, with considerably impaired language repertoires. As Sidman (1994) noted, these subjects are not likely to engage in lengthy verbal chains while solving problems, yet they often show good evidence of equivalence class formation. Stromer and Mackay (this volume) review the literature showing that developmentally disabled subjects are not likely to use verbal mediation even after being trained to do so. It does not seem reasonable, therefore, to postulate that such subjects will spontaneously engage in verbal mediation in equivalence tests, specially when all stimuli are visual and no name has been provided by the experimenter.

Even bright subjects may not depend on verbal formulations to perform in equivalence tests, as an example provided by Sidman (1994) indicates: An adolescent learned seven two-choice conditional discriminations arranged to establish two six-node equivalence classes. He then performed accurately in tests for equivalence, in the absence of feedback. Furthermore, he said, after a testing session, that he knew he was selecting the correct stimuli, but he did not know why. This subject's report suggest that it is possible to form equivalence classes in the absence of a conscious overt or covert verbal formulation.

Relations between equivalence and verbal control

The example provided by Sidman (1994) suggests that the relation between equivalence and verbal control may be parallel to the relation between contingency-shaped and rule-governed behavior. Verbally controlled performance in equivalence tests indeed may be considered as rule-governed, which does not require an explanation different from other kinds of rule-governed behavior. The fact that a significant portion of the behavior of verbally competent humans may be under control of rules does not signify, however, that these behaviors are acquired exclusively by means of rules. As Skinner (1969) pointed out, it is not likely that human behavior lost the sensitivity to contingencies. Rule-governed behavior can, nevertheless, be similar in topography to contingency-shaped behavior, although the controlling variables are different and may be revealed by the sensitivity of the behavior to other manipulations.

Similarly, the contingencies of conditional discriminations may give rise to equivalence relations, producing emergent conditional discriminations. Similar topographies may be generated by verbal control. The verbal behavior controlling performance in conditional discriminations may be directly trained by the experimenter, or may be generated by the conditional discrimination contingencies together with the past history of the subject (particularly the history of verbally describing problem-solving situations). Subjects who lack an appropriate history of such behavior, may tend to form equivalence classes controlled exclusively by conditional discrimination contingencies. For subjects with a more elaborate verbal history, these contingencies may interact with verbal behavior.

The interaction between contingencies and verbal behavior will be similar to the one observed between contingency-shaped and rule-governed behavior. Some behaviors may be originally shaped by the contingencies. Once they have been acquired, the subject may be able to verbally describe the contingencies, and these verbal descriptions may act as rules that may acquire partial or even total control over the behavior. On the other hand, individuals may acquire behaviors controlled by rules, but once they are emitted, their consequences come to acquire partial or total control over them.

Cognitive psychologists have traditionally emphasized conscious rule-control of human learning (see, however, Smolensky, 1988). They admit that performance acquired in this way, may become automatized with continued practice (cf. Schiffrin, 1988). Because continued practice involves continued exposure to the direct consequences of the behavior, automatization may refer to the same phenomena that behavior analysts interpret as rule-governed behavior falling under partial or total control of the contingencies involving the direct consequences of the behavior.

Although behavior analysts acknowledge that new behavior may be acquired under the control of rules, they maintain that behavior may also be shaped by the consequences that it produces. As Skinner (1969) pointed out, contingency shaped behavior may be "intuitive", and not readily amenable to a verbal formulation. As in the verbal report of Sidman's subject, the individual may just do it, without necessarily knowing why. However, after continued exposure to the contingencies, humans may formulate them verbally and their behavior may fall at least partially under control of these rules.

Thus, for behavior analysts, learning may proceed both from verbally controlled to contingency-shaped, and from contingency-shaped to verbally controlled. Perhaps, a similar distinction applied to the equivalence paradigm, may suggest novel approaches to understanding some of the discrepant findings that have been reported. Perhaps, also, theoretical controversies will be resolved only after methodological progress enables researchers to disentangle the several competing sources of control in trained and emergent conditional discriminations, and to use other research paradigms to provide convergent evidence that may circumvent the limitations of the conditional discrimination paradigm.

AUTHOR NOTE

The experiments summarized in this chapter were supported by Fundação de Amparo à Pesquisa do Estado de São Paulo (Grant # 92/2320-4) and Conselho Nacional de Desenvolvimento Científico e Tecnológico (Grant # 520917/93-6). Preparation of the manuscript was supported by the Graduate Program in Special Education of Universidade Federal de São Carlos, and by Grant HD25995 from the National Institute of Child Health and Human Development. The author is indebted to Joanne Kledaras, Bill Dube, Bill McIlvane, Deisy de Souza, Olivia Kato, and Bob Stromer, for many valuable contributions to this chapter. Thanks also to Luiz Ricardo Barros, Goretti Fonseca, Josineide Alves, Ricardo Botta, Mariana L. Garcia, Alessandra Ladvig, Heloisa Menezes, and Aline Torres for assistance with data collection. Address correspondence to Julio de Rose; Departamento de Psicologia; Universidade Federal de São Carlos; 13565-905 São Carlos, SP; Brazil (internet: djcc@power.ufscar.br).

REFERENCES

Barnes, D. (1994). Stimulus equivalence and relational frame theory. *Psychological Record, 44*, 91-124.
Barnes, D., McCullagh, P. D., & Keenan, M. (1990). Equivalence class formation in non-

hearing impaired children and hearing impaired children. *Analysis of Verbal Behavior,*
     8, 19-30.
Beasty, A. (1987). The role of language in the emergence of equivalence relations: A
     developmental study. *Index to Theses with Abstracts, 39*, p. bC.
Boelens, H. (1994). A traditional account of stimulus equivalence. *Psychological Record, 44*, 587-
     605.
Boelens, H., & Smeets, P. (1990). An analysis of emergent simple discrimination in children.
     Quarterly Journal of Experimental Psychology, bC, 135-152.
Borges, J. L. (1956). *Ficciones.* Buenos Aires: Emecé.
Bush, K. M., Sidman, M., & de Rose, T. (1989). Contextual control of emergent equivalence
     relations. *Journal of the Experimental Analysis of Behavior, 51*, 29-45.
Cameron, M. J., Stoddard, L. T., & McIlvane, W. J. (1993). Exclusion vs. selection training
     of conditional relations in individuals with severe intellectual disabilities. *Experimental*
     Analysis of Human Behavior Bulletin, 11, 50-51.
Carrigan, P. F., Jr., & Sidman, M. (1992). Conditional discrimination and equivalence
     relations: A theoretical analysis of control by negative stimuli. *Journal of the*
     Experimental Analysis of Behavior, 58, 183-204.
Constantine, B. J. (1981). *An experimental analysis of stimulus control in simple conditional*
     discriminations: A methodological study. Unpublished doctoral dissertation: Northeastern
     University.
Cowley, B. J., Green, G., & Brawnling-McMorrow, D. (1992). Using stimulus equivalence
     procedures to teach name-face matching to adults with brain injuries. *Journal of Applied*
     Behavior Analysis, 25, 461-475.
D'Amato, M. R., Salmon, D. P., Loukas, E., & Tomie, A.. (1985). Symmetry and transitivity
     of conditional relations in monkeys (*Cebus apella*) and pigeons (*Columba livia*). *Journal*
     of the Experimental Analysis of Behavior, 44, 35-47.
de Rose, J. C., McIlvane, W. J., Dube, W. V., Galpin, V. C., & Stoddard, L. T. (1988).
     Emergent simple discrimination established by indirect relation to differential
     consequences. *Journal of the Experimental Analysis of Behavior, 50*, 1-20.
de Rose, J. C., Ribeiro, I. G., Reis, M. J. D., & Kledaras, J. B. (1992). Possible effects of the
     procedure to teach conditional discriminations on the outcome of tests for stimulus
     equivalence and transfer of functions. *Experimental Analysis of Human Behavior Bulletin,*
     10, 10-11.
de Rose, J. C., Souza, D. G., & Hanna, E. S. (in press). Teaching reading and spelling:
     Exclusion and stimulus equivalence. *Journal of Applied Behavior Analysis.*
de Rose, J. C., Souza, D. G., Rossito, A. L., & de Rose, T. M. S. (1992). Stimulus
     equivalence and generalization in reading after matching to sample by exclusion. In S. C.
     Hayes & L. J. Hayes (Eds.), *Understanding verbal relations* (pp. 69-82). Reno, NV:
     Context Press.
de Rose, J. C., Thé, A. P., & Kato, O. M. (1995). *Effects of nodal structure on equivalence*
     class formation and transfer of discriminative functions. Paper presented at the 21st
     Annual Convention of the Association for Behavior Analysis, Washington, DC.
Devany, J. M., Hayes, S. C., & Nelson, R. O. (1986). Equivalence class formation in
     language-able and language-disabled children. *Journal of the Experimental Analysis of*
     Behavior, 46, 243-257.

Dickins, D., Bentall, R. P., & Smith, A. B. (1993). The role of individual stimulus names in the emergence of equivalence relations: The effects of interpolated paired-associates training of discordant associations between names. *Psychological Record, 43,* 713-724.

Dixon, L. S. (1977). The nature of control by spoken words over visual stimulus selection. *Journal of the Experimental Analysis of Behavior, 27,* 433-442.

Dougher, M. J., Augustson, E., Markham, M. R., Greenway, D. E., & Wulfert, E. (1994). The transfer of respondent eliciting and extinction functions through stimulus equivalence classes. *Journal of the Experimental Analysis of Behavior, 62,* 331-351.

Dube, W. V., McIlvane, W. J., Mackay, H. A., & Stoddard, L. T. (1987). Stimulus class membership established via stimulus-reinforcer relations. *Journal of the Experimental Analysis of Behavior, 47,* 159-175.

Dube, W. V., McIlvane, W. J., Maguire, R. W., Mackay, H. A., & Stoddard, L. T. (1989). Stimulus class formation and stimulus-reinforcer relations. *Journal of the Experimental Analysis of Behavior, 51,* 65-76.

Dugdale, N. A., & Lowe, C. F. (1990). Naming and stimulus equivalence. In D. E. Blackman & H. Lejeune (Eds.), *Behavior analysis in theory and practice* (pp. 115-138). Hove: Lawrence Erlbaum.

Eikeseth, S., & Smith, T. (1992). The development of functional and equivalence classes in high-functioning autistic children: the role of naming. *Journal of the Experimental Analysis of Behavior, 58,* 123-133.

Eriksson, K. A., & Simon, H. A. (1984). *Protocol analysis: Verbal reports as data.* Cambridge, MA: MIT Press.

Ferrari, C., de Rose, J. C., & McIlvane, W. J. (1993). Exclusion vs. selection training of auditory-visual conditional relations. *Journal of Experimental Child Psychology, 56,* 49-63.

Fields, L., Adams, B. J., Verhave, T., & Newman, S. (1990). The effects of nodality on the formation of equivalence classes. *Journal of the Experimental analysis of Behavior, 53,* 345-358.

Fields, L., Adams, B. J., Verhave, T., & Newman, S. (1993). Are stimuli in equivalence classes equally related to each other? *Psychological Record, 43,* 85-105.

Fields, L., Landon-Jimenez, D. V., Buffington, D. M., & Adams, B. J. (1995). Maintained nodal distance effects in equivalence classes. *Journal of the Experimental Analysis of Behavior, 64,* 129-145.

Fields, L., Reeve, K. F., Adams, B. J., & Verhave, T. (1991). Stimulus generalization and equivalence classes: A model of natural categories. *Journal of the Experimental Analysis of Behavior, 55,* 305-312.

Fields, L., Verhave, T., & Fath, S. (1984). Stimulus equivalence and transitive associations: A methodological analysis. *Journal of the Experimental Analysis of Behavior, 42,* 143-157.

Green, G. (1990). Differences in the development of visual and auditory-visual equivalence relations. *American Journal of Mental Retardation, 95,* 260-270.

Harrison, R. J., & Green, G. (1990). Development of conditional and equivalence relations without differential consequences. *Journal of the Experimental Analysis of Behavior, 54,* 225-237.

Hayes, S. C. (1991). A relational control theory of stimulus equivalence. In L. J. Hayes & P. N. Chase (Eds.), *Dialogues on verbal behavior.* Reno, NV: Context Press.

Hayes, S. C., & Hayes, L. J. (1989). The verbal action of the listener as a basis for rule-governance. In S. C. Hayes (Ed.), *Rule-governed behavior: Cognition, contingencies, and instructional control.* New York: Plenum.

Hayes, S. C., Kohlenberg, B. S., & Hayes, L. J. (1991). The transfer of specific and general consequential functions through simple and conditional equivalence relations. *Journal of the Experimental Analysis of Behavior, 56*, 119-137.

Horne, P. J., & Lowe, C. F. (1996). On the origins of naming and other symbolic behavior. *Journal of the Experimental Analysis of Behavior, 65*, 185-241.

Johnson, C., & Sidman, M. (1993). Conditional discrimination and equivalence relations: Control by negative stimuli. *Journal of the Experimental Analysis of Behavior, 59*, 333-347.

Kennedy, C. H. (1991). Equivalence class formation influenced by the number of nodes separating stimuli. *Behavioral Processes, 24*, 219-245.

Kennedy, C. H., Itkonnen, T., & Lindquist, K. (1994). Nodality effects during equivalence class formation: An extension to sight reading and concept development. *Journal of Applied Behavior Analysis, 27*, 673-683.

Lazar, R., Davis-Lang, D., & Sanchez, L. (1984). The formation of visual stimulus equivalences in children. *Journal of the Experimental Analysis of Behavior, 41*, 251-266.

Lazar, R., & Kotlarchyk, B. J. (1986). Second-order control of sequence-class equivalences in children. *Behavioural Processes, 13*, 205-215.

Lipkens, R., Hayes, S. C., & Hayes, L. J. (1993). Longitudinal study of the development of derived relations in an infant. *Journal of Experimental Child Psychology, 56*, 201-239.

Lipkens, R., Kop, P. F. M., & Matthijs, W. (1988). A test of symmetry and transitivity in the conditional discrimination performances of pigeons. *Journal of the Experimental Analysis of Behavior, 49*, 395-409.

Lynch, D. C., & Curvo, A. J. (1995). Stimulus equivalence instruction of fraction-decimal relations. *Journal of Applied Behavior Analysis, 28*, 115-126.

Manabe, K., Kawashima, T., & Staddon, J. E. R. (1995). Differential vocalization in budgerigars: Toward an experimental analysis of naming. *Journal of the Experimental Analysis of Behavior, 63*, 111-126.

Maydak, M., Stromer, R., Mackay, H. A., & Stoddard, L. T. (1995). Stimulus classes in matching to sample and sequence production: The emergence of numeric relations. *Research in Developmental Disabilities, 16*, 179-204.

McIlvane, W. J., & Dube, W. V. (1996). Naming as a facilitator of discrimination. *Journal of the Experimental Analysis of Behavior, 65*, 267-272.

McIlvane, W. J., Kledaras, J. B., Munson, L. C., King, K. A., de Rose, J. C., & Stoddard, L. T. (1987). Controlling relations in conditional discrimination and matching by exclusion. *Journal of the Experimental Analysis of Behavior, 48*, 187-208.

McIlvane, W. J., & Stoddard, L. T. (1981). Acquisition of matching-to-sample performances in severe retardation: Learning by exclusion. *Journal of Mental Deficiency Research, 25*, 33-48.

McIntire, K. D., Cleary, J., & Thompson, T. (1987). Conditional relations by monkeys: Reflexivity, symmetry and transitivity. *Journal of the Experimental Analysis of Behavior, 47*, 279-285.

Ribeiro, I. G. (1994). *Aprendizagem conceitual em crianças com dificuldades de aprendizagem: Efeitos da distancia nodal sobre a formação de classes de estimulos.* [Conceptual learning in children with learning difficulties: Effects of nodal distance on equivalence class formation.] Unpublished Master's thesis: Universidade Federal de São Carlos.

Saunders, K. J., Saunders, R. R., Williams, D. C., & Spradlin, J. E. (1993). An interaction of instructions and training design on stimulus class formation: Extending the analysis of equivalence. *Psychological Record, 43,* 725-744.

Saunders, K. J., & Spradlin, J. E. (1990). Conditional discrimination in mentally retarded adults: the development of generalized skills. *Journal of the Experimental Analysis of Behavior, 54,* 239-250.

Saunders, K. J., & Spradlin, J. E. (1993). Conditional discrimination in mentally retarded subjects: Programming acquisition and learning set. *Journal of the Experimental Analysis of Behavior, 60,* 571-585.

Saunders, R. R., & Green, G. (1992). The nonequivalence of behavioral and mathematical equivalence. *Journal of the Experimental Analysis of Behavior, 57,* 227-241.

Saunders, R. R., & Green, G. (1996). Naming is not (necessary for) stimulus equivalence. *Journal of the Experimental Analysis of Behavior, 65,* 312-314.

Saunders, R. R., Saunders, K. J., Kirby, K. C., & Spradlin, J. E. (1988). The merger and development of equivalence classes by unreinforced conditional selection of comparison stimuli. *Journal of the Experimental Analysis of Behavior, 50,* 145-162.

Saunders, R. R., Wachter, J. , & Spradlin, J. E. (1988). Establishing auditory stimulus control over an eight-member equivalence class via conditional discrimination procedures. *Journal of the Experimental Analysis of Behavior, 49,* 95-115.

Schiffrin, R. M. (1988). Attention. In R.C.Atkinson, R. M. Herrnstein, G. Lindzey & R. D. Luce (Eds.). *Stevens' handbook of experimental psychology, 2nd edition. Vol. 2: Learning and cognition.* New York: John Wiley & Sons.

Schusterman, R. J., & Kastak, D. (1993). A california sea lion (Zalophus Californianus) is capable of forming equivalence relations. *Psychological Record, 43,* 823-839.

Sidman, M. (1986). Functional analysis of emergent verbal classes. In T. Thompson & M. D. Zeiler (Eds.), *Analysis and integration of behavioral units.* Hillsdale, NJ: Lawrence Erlbaum Associates.

Sidman, M. (1987). Two choices are not enough. *Behavior Analysis, 22,* 11-18.

Sidman, M. (1992). Equivalence relations: Some basic considerations. In S. C. Hayes & L. J. Hayes (Eds.), *Understanding verbal relations,* (pp. 15-27). Reno, NV: Context Press.

Sidman, M. (1994). *Equivalence relations and behavior: A research story.* Boston, MA: Authors Cooperative.

Sidman, M., Cresson, O., Jr., & Wilson-Morris, M. (1974). Acquisition of matching-to-sample via mediated transfer. *Journal of the Experimental Analysis of Behavior, 22,* 261-273.

Sidman, M., Kirk, B., & Wilson-Morris, M. (1985). Six-member stimulus classes generated by conditional-discrimination procedure. *Journal of the Experimental Analysis of Behavior, 43,* 21-42.

Sidman, M., Rauzin, V., Lazar, R., Cunningham, S., Tailby, W., & Carrigan, P. (1982). A search for symmetry in the conditional discriminations of rhesus monkeys, baboons, and children. *Journal of the Experimental Analysis of Behavior, 37,* 23-44.

Sidman, M., & Tailby, W. (1982). Conditional discrimination vs. matching to sample: An extension of the testing paradigm. *Journal of the Experimental Analysis of Behavior, 37,* 5-22.

Sidman, M., Wilson-Morris, M., & Kirk, B. (1986). Matching-to-sample procedures and development of equivalence relations: The role of naming. *Analysis and Intervention on Developmental Disabilities, 6,* 1-19.

Skinner, B. F. (1969). *Contingencies of reinforcement: A theoretical analysis.* New York: Appleton-Century-Crofts.

Smeets, P. M. (1994). The stability of emergent simple discrimination in children. *Journal of Experimental Child Psychology, 57,* 397-417.

Smolensky, P. (1988). On the proper treatment of connexionism. *Behavioral and Brain Sciences, 11,* 1-74.

Spradlin, J. E., & Saunders, R. R. (1986). The development of stimulus classes using match-to-sample procedures: Sample classification versus comparison classification. *Analysis and Intervention in Developmental Disabilities, 6,* 41-58.

Stikeleather, G., & Sidman, M. (1990). An instance of spurious equivalence relations. *Analysis of Verbal Behavior, 8,* 1-11.

Stoddard, L. T., & McIlvane, W. J. (1986). Stimulus control research and developmentally disabled individuals. *Analysis and Intervention in Developmental Disabilities, 6,* 155-178.

Stromer, R. (1996). On the experimental analysis of naming and the formation of stimulus classes. *Journal of the Experimental Analysis of Behavior, 65,* 250-252.

Stromer, R., Mackay, H. S., & Stoddard, L. T. (1992). Classroom applications of stimulus equivalence technology. *Journal of Behavioral Education, 2,* 225-256.

Stromer, R., & Osborne, J. G. (1982). Control of adolescents' arbitrary matching-to-sample by positive and negative stimulus relations. *Journal of the Experimental Analysis of Behavior, 37,* 329-348.

Tomonaga, M. (1993). Tests for control by exclusion and negative stimulus relations of arbitrary matching-to-sample in a "symmetry-emergent" chimpanzee. *Journal of the Experimental Analysis of Behavior, 59,* 215-229.

Tomonaga, M., Matsuzawa, T., Fujita, K., & Yamamoto, J. (1991). Emergence of symmetry in a visual conditional discrimination by chimpanzees. *Psychological Reports, 68,* 51-60.

Urcuioli, P. J., Zentall, T. R., & DeMarse, T. (1995). Transfer of derived sample-comparison relations by pigeons following many-to-one versus one-to-many matching with identical training relations. *Quarterly Journal of Experimental Psychology, 48B,* 158-178.

Urcuioli, P. J., Zentall, T. R., Jackson-Smith, P., & Steirn, J. N. (1989). Evidence for common coding in many-to-one matching: Retention, intertrial interference, and transfer. *Journal of Experimental Psychology: Animal Behavior Processes, 15,* 264-273.

Vaughan, W., Jr. (1988). Formation of equivalence sets in pigeons. *Journal of Experimental Psychology: Animal Behavior Processes, 14,* 36-42.

Vygotsky, L. S. (1978). *Mind in Society: The Development of Higher Psychological Processes.* Cambridge, MA: Harvard University Press.

Wulfert, E., Dougher, M. J., & Greenway, D. E. (1991). Protocol analysis of the correspondence of verbal behavior and equivalence class formation. *Journal of the Experimental Analysis of Behavior, 56,* 489-504.

Wulfert, E., & Hayes, S. C. (1988). Transfer of a conditional ordering response through conditional equivalence classes. *Journal of the Experimental Analysis of Behavior, 50,* 125-144.

Yamamoto, J., & Asano, T. (1995). Stimulus equivalence in a chimpanzee (*Pan troglodytes*). *Psychological Record, 45,* 3-21.

Zentall, T. R., Edwards, C. A., Moore, B. S., & Hogan, D. E. (1981). Identity: The basis for both matching and oddity learning in pigeons. *Journal of Experimental Psychology: Animal Behavior Processes, 7,* 70-86.

Zentall, T. R., & Urcuioli, P. J. (1993). Emergent relations in the formation of stimulus classes by pigeons. *Psychological Record, 43*, 795-810.

Stimulus Class Formation in Humans and Animals
T.R. Zentall and P.M. Smeets (Editors)
© 1996 Elsevier Science B.V. All rights reserved.

14

Stimulus Classes and Stimulus Relations:
Arbitrarily Applicable Relational Responding as an Operant

Steven C. Hayes, Elizabeth V. Gifford, and Kelly G. Wilson

University of Nevada

Humans show remarkable forms of stimulus control based upon seemingly arbitrary relations among stimuli. Normal adults who are told that a beautiful bottle contains poison will probably avoid that bottle, perhaps for life. Humans told a novel name for a novel object will now orient toward the object given the name. Normal adults shown the word "style" and then offered the comparisons "fashion" and "stile" will probably select the former over the latter although the former is topographically dissimilar (Razran, 1939; Reiss, 1946).

The research interest in equivalence and other derived stimulus relations documents the fascination such performances have for behavioral psychologists. As with any behavior, a satisfactory behavior analytic account of these performances requires a specification of the nature of the activity and the antecedent, consequential, motivative, and other variables involved in its manipulation and prediction. This chapter offers one such analysis and explores some of its implications for our understanding of human stimulus control.

DERIVED STIMULUS RELATIONS AND LANGUAGE

There is a strong empirical relationship between language and derived stimulus relations (e.g., Devany, Hayes, & Nelson, 1986; see Horne & Lowe, 1996, for a recent review). From the beginning, behavioral work in derived stimulus relations has been closely connected to language training and usage (e.g., Sidman, 1971). Understanding language is a sought after prize for all of psychology. The relationship between equivalence and language has energized the behavioral investigation of derived stimulus relations -- but it has also complicated it. An empirical relationship does not mean that derived stimulus relations are produced by language or are mediated by language, although some have taken that position for specific theoretical reasons (e.g., Horne & Lowe, 1996).

When two dependent variables are correlated, one conservative place to begin is to examine whether both are measures of the same basic phenomenon. It seems at least plausible that the correlation between verbal abilities and the capacity of humans to relate events seemingly arbitrarily may occur because both are forms of the same general activity. Such a point of departure is a conservative place to begin because it does not assume that topographical differences are functional differences until this has been demonstrated.

If the two areas do overlap functionally, then when we ask questions about verbal behavior perhaps we are dealing with issues of derived stimulus relations and vice versa. Our own work on "Relational Frame Theory" (RFT) has attempted to integrate such diverse phenomena as stimulus equivalence, naming, mutual exclusion, rule-governance, verbal behavior, understanding, and the like. RFT takes the view that the defining component of all these activities is relational stimulus control and, furthermore, that such stimulus control is susceptible to an operant account. In this chapter, we will lay out the basic premises of RFT and discuss the ways in which it informs an understanding of complex stimulus control among verbally competent humans.

DEVELOPING A GENERIC DESCRIPTIVE LANGUAGE FOR DERIVED STIMULUS RELATIONS

Most of the work on derived stimulus relations has been done on stimulus equivalence. There are several preparations used to establish stimulus equivalence in an experimental setting, but by far the most popular is matching-to-sample. In arbitrary matching-to-sample a sample stimulus appears with an array of comparison stimuli, one of which is then selected. The stimulus arrangements and responses required vary. In most of our own studies, subjects are instructed to select among the stimuli by pressing one of three keys on a computer keyboard. For example, they could be instructed to press the number one if they wish to select the stimulus to the left, two for the stimulus in the middle, and three for the stimulus on the right. In the example screen portrayed in Figure 1, below, the sample stimulus is "zibble." If the subject wanted to select "porget," they would press the number two on the keypad. Say that the subject was reinforced

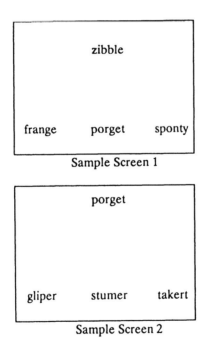

Sample Screen 1

Sample Screen 2

Figure 1. An example of an experimental task in a simple equivalence study.

for selecting "porget," (e.g., points, money, "correct" feedback) and in a later trial (Sample Screen 2, Figure 1) for selecting "gliper" when "porget" was the sample. Even with such a small set of trained discriminations, we could expect to see several interesting outcomes. The subject would now be likely to select "zibble" from an array if "porget" were the sample (i.e., symmetry), "gliper" from an array given "zibble" as the sample (i.e., transitivity), and "zibble" from an array when "zibble" is also the sample (i.e., reflexivity). Such relations are typically described as possessing properties of symmetry, reflexivity and transitivity, and the entire outcome is called "stimulus equivalence" (Sidman & Tailby, 1982).

If there were no derived relation other than equivalence, transitivity, symmetry and reflexivity would suffice as a way of describing the major properties of derived stimulus relations. However, an increasing number of studies have generated patterns of derived responding that are difficult to describe in these terms (Dymond & Barnes, 1995; Green, Stromer, & Mackay, 1993; Steele & Hayes, 1991). The relation of "larger than" is an example. If A is larger than B, however, we could not say that B is larger than A: the relation is not symmetrical. Green, et al. (1993) point similarly to the example of order. If B follows A and C follows B, some but not all of the properties of equivalence hold. For example, transitivity holds true - C also follows A - but symmetry does not - A does not follow B. Ordering relations are nonreflexive, asymmetrical, transitive, and connected (Green, et al., 1993). Because we wish to speak of all possible derived relations that might be established among events, we have adopted a language that is more generic than that which is applied to equivalence or other specific relations.

Generic Alternatives to the Descriptive Terms for Stimulus Equivalence

Mutual entailment

Mutual entailment refers to the derived bidirectionality of some stimulus relations: it is a generic term for what is called "symmetry" in stimulus equivalence. "Mutual entailment" applies when in a given context A is related to B, and as a result B is related to A. The particular derived relation depends upon the relation specified. For example, if you are told that A is better than B, you will probably derive that B is worse than A. If you do, you are showing what we mean by "mutual entailment."

Combinatorial entailment

Combinatorial entailment refers to instances in which two or more relations showing mutual entailment mutually combine. Combinatorial entailment is the generic term for what is called "transitivity" and "equivalence" in stimulus equivalence. Combinatorial entailment applies when, in a given context, if A is related to B, and B is related to C, then A and C are mutually related in that context. For example, if I tell you that the consequence behind door number one is less than the one behind door number two, and that the consequence behind door number two is less than the consequence behind door number three, then a derived mutual relation of less than/more than is entailed between door number one and door number three.

Transformation of stimulus function

Several studies have shown that stimulus functions transfer through the members of equivalence classes. Transfer has been shown with conditioned reinforcing functions (Hayes, Brownstein, Devany, Kohlenberg, & Shelby, 1987, Hayes, Kohlenberg, & Hayes, 1991), discriminative functions (Hayes, et al., 1987), elicited conditioned emotional responses (Dougher, Augustson, Markham, Greenway, & Wulfert, 1994), extinction functions (Dougher, et al., 1994), and self-discrimination functions (Dymond & Barnes, 1994), among others. However, changes in stimulus functions occurring when relations other than equivalence are involved make the term "transfer of stimulus functions" too limited for generic use.

Consider the following: Imagine that a blue border around a computer screen has been trained to serve as a cue for opposite relations. Details on the procedures used to establish this kind of control can be found in Steele and Hayes (1991) or Dymond and Barnes (1995; in press). Typically, sets of stimuli that are non-arbitrarily related are presented and different relational responses are reinforced. For example, given a short line as a sample, and short, medium, or long lines as comparisons, selecting the long line is reinforced when the border color is blue, but selecting the short line is reinforced when the border color is red. Once different relational responses are under contextual control, stimuli that have no such obvious formal dimensions between them may be used.

Suppose, given such training, a subject learned in the presence of the blue border (the contextual cue for selecting an opposite) to select stimulus A2 given stimulus A1 as the sample. Now further suppose stimulus A1 is given a conditioned punishing function, for example by pairing it with a loss of points. RFT would predict, under these conditions, that A2 may have *reinforcing* functions without any history of having a reinforcing function directly trained. A *transfer* of function from A1 to A2 would mean that A2 would also have a punishing function; however, A2's acquisition of a reinforcing function would more properly be called a *transformation* rather than a transfer. We now know that this prediction is correct at least under some circumstances, since Dymond and Barnes (1995) have recently empirically demonstrated a transformation of response functions through derived relations of greater than/less than.

Reflexivity

A more generic term for reflexivity is unnecessary. We have discussed elsewhere some difficulties with using the term in relations other than equivalence, since its defining properties do not distinguish between those due to derived stimulus relations and formal similarity (Steele & Hayes, 1991).

IS DERIVING STIMULUS RELATIONS OPERANT BEHAVIOR?

The terms in the preceding section are simply descriptive, not theoretical (Malott, 1991). They constitute a generic vocabulary for the description of derived relations among related events, and thus are relevant to any theory that attempts to explain the full range of derived stimulus relations. These terms make the description of RFT quite simple, however.

RFT takes the view that mutual entailment, combinatorial entailment, and the transformation of stimulus functions are themselves learned operant behavior, under both antecedent and consequential stimulus control. Stimulus equivalence, from this perspective, is a learned response class, and it is but one of many similar relational responses.

Stating the essence of RFT is easy. Several things complicate the picture, however, and because of these complications some behavior analysts seem to find the position both difficult to understand and difficult to embrace. First, several technical details are needed to define deriving stimulus relations as learned behavior. If these behaviors are operants, they are somewhat unusual operants. None of these details, in our view, are so extraordinary as to exclude this kind of behavior from our usual behavioral analysis, but others may disagree, especially if they usually think of operants in structuralistic and physicalistic terms. Second, our operant perspective on derived stimulus relations has major implications for the behavioral analysis of other topics. Our analysis, while conservative at the level of process, is liberal at the level of implications. Third, because derived stimulus relations are acquired quite early and naturally, a fully adequate empirical analysis has been difficult to achieve, from whatever theoretical viewpoint. For example, it is quite difficult to work with infants, and yet if these relational behaviors are operants, some of them can be acquired in infancy. Finally, all theories of derived stimulus relations in humans have a hard time dealing adequately with the overlap between these phenomena and verbal behavior. Verbal behavior is often given almost mystical powers by behavior analysts and verbally-based explanations have a great deal of intuitive appeal even when they are technically inadequate.

These complications call for varied responses. In this chapter we will first examine the evidence that derived stimulus relations show the properties normally expected of operant behavior. Second, we will deal with the technical details needed to view deriving stimulus relations as learned behavior. We will try to show that none of these details disqualify any behavior, including this kind, from being categorized as operant behavior. Finally, we will show that the implications of RFT - liberal though they may be - flow nonarbitrarily from its conservative behavioral roots.

If It Acts Like a Duck, Maybe It Is a Duck

It is easiest to show that behavior is operant when it can be originated, maintained, modified, or eliminated in the laboratory. Many naturally occurring behaviors, however, are difficult to bring into the laboratory in such a highly controlled fashion. Still, we can look at the characteristics of these naturalistic behaviors to see if they have some of the properties expected of operants. Four such properties seem relevant: first, they should develop over time rather than emerging in whole cloth; second, they should have a flexible form; third, they should be under antecedent stimulus control; and fourth, they should be under consequential control.

If derived stimulus relations are based upon operant behavior, they should show these four characteristics. Although much work remains to be done, there is some supporting evidence for each of them (see Hayes, 1994, for a discussion of the evidence along these dimensions).

Development over time

Derived stimulus relations do indeed develop over time in very young children. In one of the few existing longitudinal studies, Lipkens, Hayes, and Hayes (1993) found that relatively simple derived relations such as mutual entailment were present by 16 months of age, but that more elaborated derived relations such as combinatorial entailment emerged later (see Lipkens, et al., 1993, for a detailed account of the development of derived relations in an infant).

This sort of development can also be reproduced within an individual subject in the training of a particular equivalence class. Fields, Adams, Verhave, and Newman (1990), for example, have shown that simpler derived relations (i.e., those separated by a single node in training) emerge more rapidly than relations among stimuli that involve more extended combining of relations (i.e., those separated by more than one node in training). Thus, equivalence relations do not seem to emerge in whole cloth either over the development of these relational responses in an infant, or in the learning of a particular set of relations in an adult with these repertoires in place.

Flexibility

The flexibility of operants is one of their hallmarks. Several studies show that relations among members of an equivalence class are quite changeable, and even once formed, relations among stimuli in a class may change individually or en masse depending on the conditions. For example, having provided training sufficient to generate equivalence classes, we can change all of the baseline conditional discriminations, and new relations will emerge among the stimuli consistent with these altered baseline relations (e.g., Spradlin, Cotter, & Baxley, 1973). However, if we change only a small number of the baseline discriminations, some of the derived relations will change while others will remain intact (e.g., Pilgrim & Galizio, 1995). The dissociation between symmetrical and equivalence relations seen in studies such as Pilgrim and Galizio's "raise questions about the functional substitutability of stimuli that is a defining feature of stimulus equivalence, and thus, perhaps, about the integrated nature of 'equivalence' as a behavioral unit" (Pilgrim & Galizio, 1995, p. 226). These findings suggest that relating one event to another and combining relations among events are flexible behaviors under specific environmental control.

Antecedent stimulus control

It has long been known that the composition of specific equivalence classes can come under contextual control (e.g., Wulfert & Hayes, 1988). It is also possible to develop many specific forms of derived stimulus relations such as sameness, opposition, difference, more than, less than, and sequencing relations, and in turn to bring all these under contextual control (e.g., Dymond & Barnes, 1995; Green, et al., 1993; Lipkens, 1992; Steele & Hayes, 1991). These latter findings speak both to the antecedent control possible with equivalence and also to its flexibility discussed in the previous section (see also Spradlin, Saunders, & Saunders, 1992, on the flexibility and contextual control of equivalence relations).

Consequential control

The weakest evidence right now is that deriving stimulus relations is under consequential control. Two studies have provided supportive data. Wilson and Hayes (in press) provided conditional discrimination training sufficient to establish three four-member equivalence classes. Later training reorganized the same stimuli into three new classes. When the derived relations emerging from this later conditional discrimination training were punished, there was a resurgence of the older derived relations, exactly what one sees with directly trained operant responses. That is, when an operant response ceases to produce reinforcement or begins to produce punishment, responding becomes more variable and earlier topographies reemerge (e.g., see Epstein & Skinner, 1980; Mowrer, 1940; Rawson, Leitenberg, Mulick, & Lefebvre, 1977 for examples of resurgence of directly trained responses). Derived stimulus relations seem to operate in the same manner.

In another experiment, Leonhard and Hayes (1991) gave subjects matching-to-sample training that would normally give rise to equivalence. During testing some of these subjects were then given testing trials 50% of the time which could not be answered consistently with the derived relations that had emerged (i.e., all answers were "incorrect"), while other subjects had normal testing. These inconsistent testing items greatly reduced symmetry and equivalence on the normal tests trials. More importantly, when all subjects were then trained and tested normally with a new set of stimuli, those with a history of odd test items in earlier training showed much less equivalence class formation in the new class. Leonhard and Hayes argued that one of the proximate consequences for deriving equivalence is making sense of the test items, and that inserting items that cannot be answered via equivalence punishes not just the specific class, but also subsequent classes.

What Kind of Operant? Overarching, Relational, Arbitrarily Applicable

If derived stimulus relations are operants, they have several important features: They are overarching, relational, and arbitrarily applicable. These dimensions do not, however, disqualify these behaviors as operants, nor do they constitute new "kinds" of operants based on these dimensions.

They are overarching, purely functional operants

Operant behavior is classified functionally, based on its history. The form or topography of a response is insufficient to determine its status in a functional analysis.

These truisms of behavior analysis are more theoretical than practical in most instances. Many operants can be well defined topographically, and a great deal can be done with behavior as a topographical entity. It is not by accident, for example, that applied behavior analysts have become experts in "behavioral definitions" and "direct observation systems" although the huge majority of these definitions and systems are based on topographical descriptions of behavior. Behavioral assessors seem more likely to assess "hitting" than "attention getting." Similarly, a bar press is defined entirely by the effect of activity upon the bar, but in fact the overwhelming majority of bar presses involve "pressing" motions. A sensitive bar might be moved by sneezing, coughing, or even heavy breathing, but for all practical purposes these can be ignored. Even if they are included, there is still some limit to the number of things that could possibly deflect a bar.

If derived relational responses are operants, they are operants that have few topographical features that define them, either in terms of the stimuli or the responses involved. Researchers often call such operants "generalized" or "overarching," or "higher order" (Branch, 1994; Catania, 1996). These qualifiers are not really necessary, because the idea of response classes with an infinite variety of forms is built right into the concept of the operant. However, the qualifiers are used because the overlap between topographical and functional classes of behavior-environment interactions may cause confusion, and such qualifiers reemphasize the purely functional nature of the behavior at issue. For present purposes, we simply claim that relational operants are hardly unique in their purely functional quality, and thus there should be nothing surprising to behavior analysts.

There are several examples of purely functional operants. For example, it is possible to successfully shape the production of random numerical sequences (Neuringer, 1986; Page & Neuringer, 1985) by giving feedback to an individual about the randomness shown in instance after instance of numerical strings. By definition, a random numerical string cannot be defined in anyway by the topographical features of the string: this is precisely what is meant by "randomness." Yet randomness can be learned, and it can be learned as an operant. Purely functional classes are not limited to humans. Non-humans can learn to produce novel response topographies when reinforcement is provided only when such topographies occur (Pryor, Haag, & O'Reilly, 1969). Similarly, behavior analysts have claimed that it is possible to shape "generalized attending" (McIlvane, Dube, Kledaras, Iennaco, & Stoddard, 1990; McIlvane, Dube, & Callahan, 1995), though what is being attended to will vary.

There are many more examples, but perhaps the best known overarching operant class is generalized imitation. Generalized imitation does not refer to a class of topographically similar behaviors on the part of the imitating person; rather, it refers to a functional relation between a model, an imitator, and a history of differential consequences for imitating. A virtually unlimited variety of response topographies can be substituted for the topographies used in the initial training leading to a robust imitative repertoire (e.g., Baer, Peterson, & Sherman, 1967; Gewirtz & Stengle, 1968). It is the relation between the varying form of the model's behavior and the covarying form of the individual's behavior that defines a generalized imitative repertoire.

How does such a generalized or overarching response class come about? Studies by Bear, et al. (1967) identify the process. Subjects were shaped to emit responses formally similar to the model's behavior. The behaviors used were simple and easily discriminable, and a variety of imitative responses of varying topography were reinforced. Once the relevant "do like the experimenter does" response was brought under control with one behavior (say arm raising), other behaviors were introduced (jumping up and down, vocalizing, etc.). With enough variety and exposure to reinforcement, imitative responding generalized to nonreinforced responses (tapping a window, etc.). Bear et al. concluded "for children with truly imitative repertoires, induction has occurred, such that (1) relatively novel behaviors can be developed before direct shaping, merely by providing an appropriate demonstration by a model, and (2) some imitative responses can be maintained, although unreinforced, as long as other imitative responses are reinforced" (1967, p. 407).

The operant approach to imitation is by now relatively uncontroversial within behavior analysis.For example, Dinsmoor recently stated the operative process this way: "When a number of correspondences have been reinforced between the actions of an experimental subject and the actions of a model, the correspondence itself may become a governing factor in the relation between the two actions, extending to new topographies of behavior" (1995, pp. 264-265).

In other words, a non-arbitrary relation called "correspondence" has been directly trained. "Doing-what-others-do-behavior" can include any topography. This requires a training history that allows the child to come under control of the relevant contingencies. For example, if only one specific imitative response was ever trained, it is unlikely that generalized imitation would occur, whatever the length of training. By varying the contextual dimensions (e.g., having the model do various things), while maintaining consistent reinforcement and gradually introducing more novel or difficult response forms, the functional class can be acquired. Eventually, through enough exposure to opportunities to imitate a variety of behaviors under various conditions, the relevant response and contextual dimensions are discriminated. At this point, the response task itself is reinforced, not just the form of a particular instance of imitating, and as a result reinforcement for the class will maintain the performance of nonreinforced responses of the same kind (Peterson & Whitehurst, 1971).

The example of generalized imitation is often used by modern behavior analysts as a kind of archetype for the acquisition and functioning of overarching operant classes (Pelaez-Nogueras, 1996; Catania, 1996). We argue that relating as an overarching class is formed in just this way: with enough exemplars across multiple situational contexts, relating--responding to one event in terms of another--is abstracted, and derived relational responding emerges as an overarching operant class. While the notion of generalized relating may appear unusual, we see it as a straightforward application of a behavior analytic approach.

They are relational operants
Although obvious, it bears pointing out that deriving relations among events is a relational

operant, i.e., the response task is responding to one event in terms of another. Relational Frame Theory relies on the fact that organisms can respond relationally to various stimulus events--they can be trained to abstract both the task of relating and the formal dimension along which this relationship is relevant. For example, mammals, birds, and even insects can readily be trained to select a stimulus as "the dimmest" of several options (see Reese, 1968, for a review of studies of this kind). The behavior of complex organisms, in other words, may be brought under the stimulus control of the abstracted property of stimulus relationship along a formal stimulus dimension. Training in such relational responding involves multiple opportunities to discriminate the relevant stimulus relation. For example, suppose an animal is presented with two objects. Selecting the larger one or the longer one is not reinforced--only selecting the dimmer one. Multiple trials may be required to acquire control by the appropriate dimension (relative luminosity, not relative size or shape).

Consider what may now occur with the development of arbitrary stimulus relations. Suppose a person is taught A-B and later B-A relations. With one exemplar the specific formal characteristics of each relation will dominate (e.g., "given green box pick red circle and given red circle pick green box"). With additional and diverse exemplars, discriminative control becomes increasingly refined, and there is a gradual exclusion of an increasing number of irrelevant formal characteristics. As more and more formal properties are excluded, through exposure to an increasingly rich history of differential reinforcement across varying complex stimuli, eventually the behavior of relating itself is discriminated (something more like "given that this thing is related to that one, that one is related to this one").

We can see no reason that the critical features of the response task of relating (which we describe as mutual entailment, combinatorial entailment, and transformation of stimulus function) cannot be discriminated and come under antecedent stimulus and consequential control. In the same way that exemplars with imitation can lead to a situation in which "correspondence itself may become a governing factor . . . extending to new topographies of behavior" (Dinsmoor, 1995, pp. 264-265), exemplars with relating can lead to a situation in which relating itself becomes the important factor, extending to new specific instances. When this has occured, relational responding is abstracted to the point that it can be arbitrarily applied to any stimulus set.

Several studies have suggested that stimulus control may include features of response tasks (e.g., McIlvane et al., 1990; Saunders & Spradlin, 1990, 1993). The benefits of varying stimuli to sharpen stimulus control along relevant dimensions are widely discussed, e.g., "training sufficient examplars" and "training loosely" (Goldstein, 1995, p. 385; see also Duncan, 1958) . Features of response tasks themselves may, with a proper history, come to exert control over behavior. The process by which this occurs closely resembles the abstractive process we believe is responsible for the development of overarching and arbitrarily applicable relational responding.

These relational operants are arbitrarily applicable

As relational responding is freed via abstraction from particular formal properties of the relata, it must be under the control of some sort of contextual cue serving as a discriminative stimulus for the relevant response.

Modeling again provides a demonstration. Peterson and Whitehurst (1971) showed that the imitative response was brought under the control of particular conditioned stimuli such as the command "Do this," and in some cases in the presence of particular models or reinforcement delivery. In normal children, imitation is gradually brought under the control of model similarity, observed reinforcement, and so on, because these cues predict reinforcement for imitative behavior.

What predicts reinforcement for particular kinds of relational responding? Some cues are obvious. A great deal of relational training occurs in the context of language training. Words often serve as cues indicating that particular relational responses are functional in a given context. For example, suppose a child is told "this is called a ball." If this is called a ball, then a ball is this. That is, the words "is called" quite reliably predicts reinforcement for symmetry in this context.

The matching-to-sample procedure used in stimulus equivalence studies is not a procedure that children are unfamiliar with. It is common for children's workbooks or playtime magazines to have samples and comparisons on a page, and the child is to draw a line connecting those that are related. Even the test situation can be an important source of stimulus control in the experimental procedures commonly used (Devany et al., 1986; Leonhard & Hayes, 1991).

When different types of relating have been abstracted and brought under the control of cues that go beyond the formal properties of the related events, relational responding is arbitrarily applicable: it can occur whenever these contextual cues are discriminated as relevant for the purpose of responding, regardless of the formal nonarbitrary properties of the related events. In the real world, however, relational responding is usually not arbitrarily applied. When any two events are related--are responded to in terms of one another--there are many stimulus dimensions along which to relate them. An apple and an orange may be related along the dimension of shape, of food category, of vitamin quotient, of juggling utility, or any other number of properties. Nonverbal objects carry many inherent stimulus features available for relational responding. However, in the natural use of human language, the relevant relational response is not limited to these formal dimensions. Rather, formal dimensions may serve as a cue for relational responding that may occur in other contexts without the support of formal stimulus relations at all. According to this approach, then, stimulus equivalence is only an arbitrarily applied example of actions that involve formal properties under other circumstances.

HOW MIGHT DERIVED RELATIONAL RESPONDING AS AN OPERANT CLASS BE TAUGHT?

At its core, RFT is a rather simple behavioral theory. It claims merely that derived relating is learned operant behavior that has some unusual but not unique characteristics (it is a purely functional operant abstracted from a particular history that can be brought to bear arbitrarily). The specific history needed to acquire such an operant is a matter for empirical research, not armchair theorizing, but we have several times pointed to some aspects of the history that seem plausible and researchable.

It is interesting that functional psycholinguists who study the acquisition of language include pre-language development of nonverbal relational training (which some describe as a "case grammar"). This prerequisite learning is thought to organize the world into "the concepts of action" (Bruner, 1983, p. 34). Nonverbal abstracting and relating is a necessary part of this training. Bruner says it this way: "The child must master the conceptual structure of the world that language will map" (1983, p. 39). While we disagree with the idea of a nonverbal "conceptual structure" it does seem likely that nonverbal relating is a prerequisite to verbal relating (see Peleaz-Nogueras, 1996, for a brief review of some of these issues).

This is a plausible notion from the point of view of RFT. Learning nonarbitrary stimulus relations, and gradually arranging conditions under which relational abstraction can take place, could occur in the context of early childhood learning such as learning to play games. Playing provides experience with tasks that are relatively free from fixed structural or formal relations, and yet have clear functional and relational categories. For example, children learn to emit variable topographic responses (i.e., several different ways to play peek-a-boo) within the parameters of specific functional similarities (making something appear and disappear). While these games initially provide contexts for the development of nonverbal abstraction (we play peek-a-boo with nonverbal children), "In time and with increasing abstractness, formats [play contexts] become like moveable feasts. They are no longer tied to specific settings but can be "imposed" by illocutionary devices on a variety of situations. When they reach this more evolved form, they can properly be called speech acts" (Bruner, 1983, p. 121).

The other rich source of relational response acquisition is language training. Imagine a child being taught to respond to such questions as "Which bag has the greater number of toys?" or "Which glass has the greater amount of juice?" The thing that remains consistent across such questions is the relational task and some contextual cues tied to this task (in this case, the words "greater than"). Reinforcement is also provided for displaying the mutually entailed relation in the opposite direction. If the red bag has more toys than the green bag, then the green bag has fewer toys than the red bag.

When the relational response is abstracted and comes under the contextual control of cues other than the related events, it can be applied to stimuli that do not have formal properties that support greater than/less than relations. Suppose that we arbitrarily designate X as greater than Y, and ask "Which is greater: X or Y?" With no formal properties to support making the relational response, the subject must guess. If they guess X and are reinforced, we would expect a perfect performance when we ask "Which is smaller: X or Y?" Having had a rich history of direct reinforcement for making these mutually entailed relational responses, individuals given the relation in one direction will readily derive the relation in the other direction.

Similarly, we seem to teach frames of coordination by direct reinforcement for responses in both directions. Suppose we ask a child "Where is the truck?" and provide reinforcement when they point to a truck. When we point to the truck and ask "What is this?," we provide reinforcement when the child answers "a truck." In a naturally occurring language training history, reinforcement for such bidirectional responding is rich. Combinatorial entailment is simply a more complex case of mutual entailment, with a likewise slightly more complex training history. RFT suggests that a history of direct reinforcement for bidirectional responding leads to a generalization of those bidirectional responses to new stimuli.

There are a variety of response forms that participate in these interactions as they pertain to the acquisition of verbal behavior. Imitative repertoires, echoic repertoires, tacts and mands all describe distinguishable component classes of such training. These behaviors are the functional means by which the culture transmits the structure of language, and through which relational repertoires become fully operational. For example, children must learn not just to relate, but also to echo spoken words so that hearing can lead to speaking. These behaviors, however, would have little utility in themselves without an adequate relational repertoire, any more than the echoing of a parrot leads to effective verbal communication or reasoning.

RELATIONAL FRAMES AND THE NATURE OF VERBAL BEHAVIOR

We can now define our core concept. The many specific varieties of arbitrarily applicable relational responding we term "relational frames." A relational frame:

(1) is a specific type of learned instrumental responding that shows the contextually controlled qualities of mutual entailment, combinatorial mutual entailment, and transformation of stimulus functions;

(2) is due to a history of relational responding relevant to the contextual cues involved; and

(3) is not based solely on direct non-relational training with regard to the particular stimuli of interest, nor solely to non-arbitrary characteristics of either the stimuli or the relation between them.

We use the term relational frame in its noun form for the sake of convenience; however, a relational frame is always "framing events relationally"--it is an action. Arbitrarily applicable relational responding is the generic name for behavior of this kind.

The term frame is used for the same reasons that Skinner used terms like autoclitic frames (1957). The behavioral response is explicitly functional rather than topographical, and can include an infinite variety of stimuli. For example, Skinner (1957), in discussing autoclitic frames, suggests that having learned the response "the boy's gun, the boy's shoe, and the boy's hat, we may suppose that the partial frame the boy's _____ is available for recombination with other responses. The first time the boy acquires a bicycle, the speaker can compose a new unit the boy's bicycle. . . . The relational aspects of the situation strengthen a frame, and specific features of the situation strengthen the response fitted into it" (1957, p. 336). Speaking of a frame in which a particular relational response will occur, such as a frame of opposition or coordination, is no more mysterious or structuralistic (if somewhat more abstract) than the frames referred to by Skinner (see Hayes & Wilson, in press; cf., Boelens, 1994; Sidman, 1994).

Based on our fairly conservative explanation for the correlation between derived relations and language, we argue (Hayes & Hayes, 1989, 1992) that derived stimulus relations and verbal behavior itself are both based upon relational frames. Indeed, it seems to us that the link is so complete that we can define verbal events in these terms.

We will begin with the behavior of the listener. We can think of verbal stimuli as stimuli that have their effects because they participate in relational frames. That is, a stimulus is verbal to the extent that it has its stimulus functions as result of the listener's deriving stimulus relations, and transforming stimulus functions consistent with those relations, as opposed to having its stimulus functions as result of a history of direct training.

Typically, this is a matter of degree. For example, suppose a boy entered a restroom with the word "Caballeros." The word "Caballeros" might have its discriminative stimulus functions based entirely on relational frames. This could happen, for example, if "Caballeros" were placed in a frame of coordination as result of someone saying to the boy "Caballeros means men." The word "means," in this context, is a cue for a relational response of coordination, or equivalence. Participation in such a frame means that some of the stimulus functions of "men" will probably transfer to "Caballeros." If the boy enters a restroom with "Caballeros" on it because of such a relational response, but has never been directly reinforced for doing so, then the functions of the word "Caballeros" would not be discriminative (because the word "discriminative" requires such a direct history). The stimulus functions of "Caballeros" would instead be discriminative-like, based on a transformation of stimulus functions through derived relations. In this case, because all of the relevant functions of the word are derived, it is entirely verbal. If by contrast the boy had only a direct history of reinforcement for entering restrooms with the word "Caballeros" on it, the word would actually be a discriminative stimulus, and therefore (according to our definition) entirely nonverbal.

To see how this is a matter of degree for organisms for whom derived relational responding is at strength, consider the following scenario. Imagine that the boy sees what look like restrooms, but does not know whether to enter the one marked "Caballeros" or "Damas." Say he enters the one marked "Caballeros" and upon entering sees several men. The boy would breath a sigh of relief at having made the appropriate choice, and one might say that he was reinforced for his selection. However, if the boy has had considerable experience with public restrooms and knows that the words "men" and "women" are written on their doors, he would be likely then to relate "Caballeros" to men. Thus "Caballeros" could have some of its functions as result of the boy's direct reinforcement history, and some due to the additional functions that resulted from the boy's subsequent relational response. For example, he might see the word "Caballeros" in a different context and tell his parents "That word means 'men.'" or may be able to find the menswear section by the signs in a department store. We suspect that the reinforcement available for deriving stimulus relations and transferring functions are so great that once the repertoire is at strength, virtually every event has some verbal functions (i.e., derived functions).

Similarly, if the production of stimuli by a speaker is based entirely upon relational frames, then that act is entirely verbal. If the form of a characteristic response is based entirely on a direct history of reinforcement for that form, then the act, while perhaps communicative, is not verbal. In many cases--perhaps most cases in mature speakers--it will be both.

This approach defines verbal behavior entirely functionally, and entirely in terms of the history of the particular individual involved. It fits with Skinner's definition of verbal behavior in some interesting ways: establishing arbitrarily applicable relational responding requires socially mediated reinforcement, for example. This is precisely the sense in which events are arbitrary, with arbitrary meaning conventional in this context. In *Verbal Behavior*, Skinner suggests that upon hearing the sentence, *an amphora is a Greek vase with two handles*, a listener might (1) say, *amphora*, when asked, *what is a Greek vase with two handles called?*, and (2) say, a Greek vase having two handles when asked, *what is an amphora?*, and (3) may point appropriately when asked, *which of these is an amphora?* He goes on to say though, that "these are not the results which occur spontaneously in the naive speaker but rather as the product of a long history of verbal conditioning" (1957, p.360). RFT is our operant account of precisely the sort of "long history of verbal conditioning" that is necessary to establish such a diverse set of responses to a very limited stimulus event such as, *an amphora is a Greek vase with two handles*.

IMPLICATIONS OF RELATIONAL FRAME THEORY

RFT is thus concerned with a particular subset of relational activity--arbitrarily applicable relational responding--an activity that is a learned, abstracted relational response class. What impact do relational frames have on human functioning and upon our understanding of behavior? We believe that the implications are very large. Relational frames enable learned forms of stimulus control that do not otherwise exist, and that can be applied in virtually any situation. This changes the world in which the verbal organism lives. We will address a few brief examples (see Hayes, 1992; Hayes & Wilson, 1993, for others).

Classes versus Relations in Human Stimulus Control

We began our analysis of derived stimulus relations in a most conservative fashion: we have sought to analyze them with the usual principles available in an operant account of behavior. It seems ironic that such a conservative approach could have very dramatic implications. We think it does, however. One of the most striking is the implications of derived relational responding to the concept of the stimulus class.

The concept of class is built right into the operant. As Catania puts it, an operant relation is a "correlation between classes of responses and classes of stimuli" (1973, p. 106). An operant is definable as the correlation of three classes of events (1) a class of stimuli in the presence of which (2) a class of reinforcing stimuli are produced by (3) a class of responding. Members of either of the three classes are defined not by their topographical features, but by their participation in the defining correlation. Importantly, the relations among them are established by a particular contingent and contiguous historical arrangement (or by generalization or induction).

Consider the class of stimuli we call discriminative stimuli (SD). A stimulus is an SD if the occurrence of a class of behaviors is more probable in the presence of that stimulus because reinforcement for such behavior has been more likely in its presence than in its absence. Thus the fact that some stimulus is a member of a class of stimuli that have a discriminative function tells us not only about the effect that the stimulus will on the response, but also the history that produced that functional relation.

Now imagine that we have provided matching-to-sample training sufficient to produce a three-member equivalence class. Imagine further that we give one member of the class a discriminative function, and that we do this in the normal way that stimuli come to have that function. Through the transformation of stimulus functions, other members of the same class will now probably function as if they were SD's, even though reinforcement has not been more likely in the presence of these stimuli than in their absence. As noted earlier, these effects are not discriminative but are "discriminative-like" (Hayes & Wilson, 1993). Schlinger and Blakely (1987) make a similar case regarding the function altering effects of "contingency-specifying stimuli." Thus, the derived functions of events in relational frames do not seem entirely reducible to existing classes of directly established behavioral functions.

Now imagine that a given event is not just a participant in one derived relation, but in hundreds. Let us take an example: the word "MAN." Consider the following questions and note at least one answer for each:

What is "MAN" the same as?
What is "MAN" opposite of?
What is "MAN" composed of?
What is "MAN" faster than?
What came before "MAN"?
What is bad about "MAN"?
What is good about "MAN"?
What is "MAN" a member of?
What is stronger than "MAN"?

In this exercise, contextual cues are provided for frames of coordination, opposition, hierarchical class membership, comparison, time, and so on. As each relation is derived, the stimulus functions of "MAN" change slightly. In addition to directly trained effects, the functions of this stimulus depend upon the specific combinations of derived relations between this stimulus and others that are present in a given moment. This combination is fluid, and the functions that result are both derived and transformed. For example, when the question was asked "What is MAN' opposite of?" some may have answered "animals," "woman," "angels," "NAM" or any of dozens of other answers. In each instance, the stimulus qualities of "MAN" changed. Consider the person who answered "woman." "Woman" itself has many derived relations with other stimuli. If, for this person, the psychologically dominant relation was, say, between "Woman" and "warm" the resulting quality for "MAN" might be a certain harshness, since the underlying relational frame was one of opposition.

We asked nine questions about "MAN." Each brought to bear a different kind of relational frame to another event, and we suppose that some functions of the other event were transformed and attached to "MAN." Although this is a matter of degree, the totality of functions that resulted were dominantly derived or verbal, not direct. Furthermore, although relational frames are classes of responses, it strains behavioral terminology to explain the totality of functions that resulted using simple stimulus class concepts. The stimulus functions of harshness is not in a functional class with warm. If both warm and harsh are in the same class because they are related, then all possible functions are all in one big class. This can be readily assessed by selecting two functions that are not seemingly in a class and asking "what is the relation between these two items?" Verbally competent adults will always have an answer (we argue this is because relational frames are arbitrarily applicable)--they will always be related. If all functions are in a "class" we have saved a behavioral concept by destroying it.

We argue that the concept of stimulus class, as the single dominant process used to explain stimulus functions, is much less relevant in verbal organisms due to the transformational and derived qualities of many stimulus functions. It is anxiety provoking to begin to let go of "stimulus class" as the almost exclusive way of accounting for "stimulus function." Yet our behavior analytic account seems to lead inexorably to this conclusion. It seems likely that many stimuli have their effects due to the psychological relevance of multiple stimulus relations and the functions that are transformed in terms of them. In essence, the functions of stimuli begin to depend more upon networks of derived stimulus relations brought to bear by contextual cues than upon directly established stimulus classes.

In our approach to verbal stimulus functions, the concept of stimulus relation begins to dominate over the concept of stimulus class. In a superficial way, this begins to look rather more like the network theories of meaning found in cognitive psychology than traditional behavior analysis, but our networks of derived stimulus relations are not hypothetical or inferred, they are not structures, and they are not mental events. They are collections of contextually situated actions.

Concept Formation

While classes do not explain all stimulus functions, the processes we have described have implications for the verbal development of categories and classes. Wittgenstein (1953) described the imprecise nature of categorical sets, and such topics have also occupied many behavior analysts (e.g., Williams, 1983; Wasserman & Devolder, 1993). Some argue that categories may be produced by nothing more than simple discriminative control exerted by a certain number of relevant features; others that category formation involves a more complex interaction of different discriminative features, "such that various conjunctions and disjunctions control response probabilities different from the sum of response strengths controlled by their constituent elements . . . understanding the emergence of such unified stimulus compounds may thus constitute a critical part of understanding the nature of concept learning" (Williams, 1983, p. 480).

Some argue, and we concur, that the definition of concepts in complex organisms must consist of stimuli that are not related solely based on perceptual similarity (Lea, 1984). Where generalization occurs based on formal dimensions, primary stimulus generalization is sufficient to explain category membership in many verbal categories. The interesting question involves the behavioral process that permits the development of categories composed of perceptually dissimilar stimuli (Adams, Fields, & Verhave, 1993).

The classic behavior-analytic definition of a concept is offered by Keller and Schoenfeld: "Generalization within classes and discrimination between classes" (1950. p. 155). The basic requirements of this definition can be fulfilled in direct discrimination and generalization training contexts with pigeons and children (Bhatt & Wasserman, 1989; Wasserman & Devolder, 1993). We may also easily directly train humans to discriminate and generalize arbitrary concepts with perceptually dissimilar stimuli (cf., Engelmann & Carnine, 1982). However, relational frames provide a much richer and rapid means for the development and elaboration of concepts.

A verbal concept is a coherent network of derived stimulus relations that allows both the mutual transformation of stimulus functions within that network, and discrimination between that network and others. For example, given the word "hare," normal adults will select the word "rabbit" rather than "hair" because "hare" and "rabbit" participate in a coherent set of derived stimulus relations that are encompassed by the verbal concept, and that can be distinguished from other such sets of stimulus relations, even if the stimuli are formally similar ("hair"). Normal processes of stimulus generalization are part of these verbal concepts, since the related elements have formal properties, but the concept is not limited to such processes.

The Nature of Verbal Reasoning

The interaction of "verbal" stimulus functions with "nonverbal" stimulus functions may become extremely complex. Non-arbitrary events in the previously nonverbal world may have their functions modified via participation in relational networks (see Hayes, 1994), and to that degree they become "verbal." Once these functions are modified verbally, they may themselves serve as cues for additional verbal relational activity.

For example, imagine a situation in which a group of boxes are waiting on the lawn to be placed into a moving van. On what basis are properties of the boxes selected, in order to determine the order in which to move them? According to weight, to size, to fragility of contents? The dimension(s) controlling behavior may be verbally described--may acquire functions by participating in relational frames--and may then in turn constitute the basis for additional responding.

Verbally analyzing the world enables more effective interaction with it. Problems can be defined according to goals, and the properties of the situation relevant to these goals may then control behavior. If the contents of the boxes are particularly valuable, or if the space inside the vehicle is particularly limited, there may be various properties that assume greater relevance or attractiveness. Verbal relations thus allow more efficient commerce with the nonverbal world as it becomes verbally analyzed. This means that verbal reasoning literally begins to transform the nonverbal world into a verbal one with highly abstracted and derived properties. What is typically described as "abstract reasoning" is the selection of verbally accessible and abstracted properties of events, where new relations are derived among sets of established relational responses.

Verbal behavior thus begins to dominate over direct stimulus functions, and to blur the distinction between highly abstract verbal reasoning on the one hand and the simple description of the "nonverbal" (but increasingly verbal) world on the other. Dewey said it this way:

When Aristotle drew a distinction between sensible things that are more noted--known--to us and rational things that are more noted--known--in themselves, he was actually drawing a distinction between things that operate in a local, restricted universe of discourse, and things whose marks are such that they readily enter indefinitely extensive and varied discourse. (1929, p. 145)

Skinner also identified this general process. He says, in speaking on reference and the origins of language:

We cannot echo or imitate blue things or heavy things or truculent things with blue, heavy, or truculent responses. The alternative is to allow one or at most a few properties of each stimulus to acquire control of a separate form of response. No effort is made to respond to all properties of a given stimulus. The most precise result is achieved by the process of abstraction . . . In the present analysis we have spoken of defining properties and of classes of stimuli, and in casual discourse we can name these controlling concepts with suffixes such as "redness," "pyramidality," and so on. In a more sophisticated sense, we may speak of properties common to many instances as concepts, abstractions, universals, notions, and so on, so long as we keep the actual process of demonstration in mind. This is also the point at which the term "idea" might be revived for use through an operational definition. (1957, pp. 127-128)

We think he was on to something.

A BEHAVIORAL PSYCHOLOGY OF LANGUAGE AND COGNITION

There is a huge difference between cognitive psychology and a behavioral psychology of language and cognition: while the former tends to be mechanistic, structuralistic and dualistic, the latter can be characterized as contextualistic, functionalistic, and monistic. Modern behavioral work on derived stimulus relations may be leading increasingly to such topics as rule understanding, reasoning, problem solving, purpose, and the like. As this process unfolds, the broad outlines of a behavioral psychology of cognition is visible. It will stay true to the contextualistic, functionalistic, monistic roots of behavior analysis. Nevertheless, it will challenge some of our old ideas about how stimulus functions are acquired, how concepts are formed, or how problems are solved.

Language researchers in the functionalist tradition have long been dissatisfied with both a behavioral approach to language based simplistically on direct training and imitation, and a cognitive position that appeals to the spontaneous emergence of preformed linguistic structures. Bruner has argued that the job of those developing functional analyses of language is to fill "the gap between an impossible empiricist position and a miraculous nativist one" (1983, p. 39). We agree. The former failed to deal fully with the derived nature of verbal behavior, and the latter with the environmental influences that develop and maintain that quality. We believe that our approach provides an avenue for behavioral psychology to make fuller use of its functionalist tradition in the analysis of the most intriguing and important form of human activity.

REFERENCES

Adams, B. J., Fields, L., & Verhave, T. (1993). Formation of generalized equivalence classes. *Psychological Record, 43*, 553-566.

Baer, D. M., Peterson, R. F., and Sherman, J. A. (1967). The development of imitation by reinforcing behavioral similarity to a model. *Journal of the Experimental Analysis of Behavior, 10*, 405-416.

Bhatt, R. S., & Wasserman, E. A. (1989). Secondary generalization and categorization in pigeons. *Journal of the Experimental Analysis of Behavior, 52*, 213-224.

Boelens, H. (1994). A traditional account of stimulus equivalence. *Psychological Record, 44*, 587-605.

Branch, M.N. (1994). Stimulus generalization, stimulus equivalence, and response hierarchies. In S.C. Hayes, L.J. Hayes, M. Sato, & K. Ono (Eds.), *Behavior analysis of language and cognition* (pp. 51-90). Reno, NV: Context Press.

Bruner, J. S. (1983). *Child's talk: Learning to use language.* New York: Norton.

Catania, A. C. (1973). The concept of the operant in the analysis of behavior. *Behaviorism, 1*, 103-116.

Catania, A.C. (1996). Natural contingencies in the creation of naming as a higher order behavior class. *Journal of the Experiemental Analysis of Behavior, 65*, 267-279.

Dewey, J. (1929). *Experience and nature.* LaSalle, Ill: Open Court.

Devany, J. M., Hayes, S. C., & Nelson, R. O. (1986). Equivalence class formation in language-able and language-disabled children. *Journal of the Experimental Analysis of Behavior, 46*, 243-257.

Dinsmoor, J.A. (1995). Stimulus control: Part II. *Behavior Analyst, 18*, 253-269.

Dougher, M. J., Augustson, E., Markham, M. R., Greenway, D. E., & Wulfert, E. (1994). The transfer of respondent eliciting and extinction functions through stimulus equivalence classes. *Journal of the Experimental Analysis of Behavior, 62*, 331-351.

Duncan, C.P. (1958). Transfer after training with single versus multiple tasks. *Journal of Experimental Psychology, 55*, 63-72.

Dymond, S. & Barnes, D. (1994). A transfer of self-discrimination response functions through equivalence relations. *Journal of the Experimental Analysis of Behavior, 62*, 251-267.

Dymond, S. & Barnes, D. (1995). A transformation of self-discrimination response functions through the arbitrarily applicable relations of sameness, more than, and less than. *Journal of the Experimental Analysis of Behavior, 64*, 163-184.

Dymond, S. & Barnes, D. (in press). A transformation of self-discrimination response functions in accordance with the arbitrarily applicable relations of sameness and opposition. *Psychological Record.*

Engelmann, S. & Carnine, D. (1982). *Theory of instruction: Principles and applications.* New York: Irvington.

Epstein, R. & Skinner, B. F. (1980). Resurgence of responding after the cessation of response-independent reinforcement. *Proceedings of the National Academy of Science, 77*, 6251-6253.

Fields, L., Adams, B. J., Verhave, T. & Newman, S. (1990). The effects of nodality on the formation of equivalence classes. *Journal of the Experimental Analysis of Behavior, 53*, 345-358.

Gewirtz, J. L. & Stengle, K. G. (1968). Learning of generalized imitation as the basis for identification. *Psychological Review, 5*, 374-397.

Goldstein, A.P. (1995). Coordinated multitargeted skills training: The promotion of generalization enhancement. In W. O'Donohue & L. Krasner (Eds.), *Handbook of psychological skills training: Clinical techniques and applications* (Pp. 383-399).

Green, G., Stromer, R., & Mackay, H. A. (1993). Relational learning in stimulus sequences. *Psychological Record, 43*, 599-615.

Hayes, S. C. (1992). Verbal relations, time, and suicide. In S. C. Hayes & L. J. Hayes (Eds.), *Understanding verbal relations* (pp. 109-118). Reno, NV: Context Press.

Hayes, S. C. (1994). Relational frame theory: A functional approach to verbal events. In S. C. Hayes & L. J. Hayes *Behavior analysis of language and cognition* (pp. 9-29). Reno, NV: Context Press.

Hayes, S. C., Brownstein, A. J., Devany, J. M., Kohlenberg, B. S., & Shelby, J. (1987). Stimulus equivalence and the symbolic control of behavior. *Mexican Journal of Behavior Analysis, 13*, 361-374.

Hayes, S. C. & Hayes, L. J. (1989). The verbal action of the listener as a basis for rule-governance. In S. C. Hayes (Ed.) *Rule-governed behavior: Cognitions, contingencies, and instructional control* (pp. 153-190). New York: Plenum.

Hayes, S. C. & Hayes, L. J. (1992). Verbal relations, cognition, and the evolution of behavior analysis. *American Psychologist, 47*, 1383-1395.

Hayes, S. C. & Leonhard, C. (1994). An alternative behavior analytic approach to verbal behavior. *Revista Mexicana de Psicologia, 11*, 60-86.

Hayes, S. C. & Wilson, K. G. (1993). Some applied implications of a contemporary behavior-analytic account of verbal events. *Behavior Analyst, 17*, 289-303.

Hayes, S. C. & Wilson, K. G. (in press). Criticisms of Relational Frame Theory: Implications for a behavior analytic account of derived stimulus relations. *Psychological Record.*

Hayes, S. C., Kohlenberg, B. K., & Hayes, L. J. (1991). The transfer of specific and general consequential functions through simple and conditional equivalence classes. *Journal of the Experimental Analysis of Behavior, 56*, 119-137.

Horne, P.J. & Lowe, C.F. (1996). On the origins of naming and other symbolic behavior. *Journal of the Experimental Analysis of Behavior, 65*, 185-241.

Keller, F. S. & Schoenfeld, W. N. (1950). *Principles of psychology: A systematic text in the science of behavior.* New York: Appleton-Century-Crofts.

Kohlenberg, B. S., Hayes, S. C., & Hayes, L. J. (1991). The transfer of contextual control over equivalence classes through equivalence classes: A possible model of social stereotyping. *Journal of the Experimental Analysis of Behavior, 56*, 505-518.

Lea, S. E. G. (1984). In what sense do pigeons learn concepts? In H.L. Roitblatt, T.G. Bever, & H. S. Terrace (Eds.), *Animal cognition* (pp. 263-276). Hillsdale, NJ: Erlbaum.

Leonhard, C. & Hayes, S. C. (1991). *Prior inconsistent testing affects equivalence responding.* Paper presented at the 17th Annual Convention of the Association for Behavior Analysis, Atlanta, GA.

Lipkens, R., Hayes, S. C., & Hayes, L. J. (1993). Longitudinal study of derived stimulus relations in an infant. *Journal of Experimental Child Psychology, 56*, 201-239.

Lipkens, R. (1992). A behavioral analysis of complex human functioning: Analogical reasoning. Unpublished doctoral dissertation, University of Nevada, Reno.

Malott, R. W. (1991). Equivalence and relational frames. In L. J. Hayes & P. N. Chase (Eds.), *Dialogues on verbal behavior* (pp. 41-44). Reno, NV: Context Press.

McIlvane, W. J., Dube, W. V., Kledaras, J. B., Iennaco, F. M., & Stoddard, L. T. (1990). Teaching relational discrimination to individuals with mental retardation: Some problems and possible solutions. *American Journal on Mental Retardation, 95,* 283-296.

McIlvane, W. J., Dube, W. V., & Callahan, T. D. (1995). Attention: A Behavior Analytic Perspective. In G. R. Lyon, & N. A. Krasnegor (Eds.), *Attention, memory, and executive function* (pp.97-117). Paul H. Brookes: Baltimore, MA.

Mowrer, O. H. (1940). An experimental analogue of "regression" with incidental observations on "reaction formation." *Journal of Abnormal and Social Psychology, 35,* 56-87.

Neuringer, A. (1986). Can people behave "randomly?": The role of feedback. *Journal of Experimental Psychology General, 115,* 62-75.

Page, S. & Neuringer, A. (1985). Variability as an operant. *Journal of Experimental Psychology: Animal Behavior Processes, 11,* 429-452.

Pelaez-Nogueras, M. (1996). Thought without naming. *Journal of the Experimental Analysis of Behavior, 65,* 299-301.

Peterson, R. F., & Whitehurst, G. J. (1971). A variable influencing the performance of generalized imitative behaviors. *Journal of the Experimental Analysis of Behavior, 4,* 1-9.

Pilgrim, C. & Galizio, M. (1995). Reversal of baseline relations and stimulus equivalence: I. Adults. *Journal of the Experimental Analysis of Behavior, 63,* 225-238.

Pryor, K. W., Haag, R., & O'Reilly, J. (1969). The creative porpoise: Training for novel behavior. *Journal of the Experimental Analysis of Behavior, 12,* 653-661.

Rawson, R. A., Leitenberg, H., Mulick, J. A., & Lefebvre M. F. (1977). Recovery of extinction responding in rats following discontinuation of reinforcement of alternative behavior: A test of two explanations. *Animal Learning and Behavior, 5,* 415-420.

Razran, G. H. S. (1939). A quantitative study of meaning by a conditioned salivary technique (semantic conditioning). *Science, 90,* 89-90.

Reese, H. W. (1968). *The perception of stimulus relations: Discrimination learning and transposition.* New York: Academic Press

Reiss, W. H. R. (1946). Genetic changes in semantic conditions. *Journal of Experimental Psychology, 36,* 71-87.

Spradlin, J., Saunders, K. J., & Saunders, R. R. (1992). The stability of equivalence classes. In S. C. Hayes & L. J. Hayes (Eds.), *Understanding verbal relations* (pp. 29-42). Reno, NV: Context Press.

Saunders, K. J., & Spradlin, J. E. (1990). Conditional discrimination in mentally retarded adults: The development of generalized skills. *Journal of the Experimental Analysis of Behavior, 54,* 239-250.

Saunders, K. J., & Spradlin, J. E. (1993). Conditional discrimination in mentally retarded subjects: Programming acquisition and learning set. *Journal of the Experimental Analysis of Behavior, 60,* 571-585.

Schlinger, H. & Blakely, E. (1987). Function-altering effects of contingency-specifying stimuli. *Behavior Analyst, 10,* 41-45.

Sidman, M. (1971). Reading and auditory-visual equivalences. *Journal of Speech and Hearing Research, 14*, 5-13.

Sidman, M. (1994). *Equivalence relations and behavior: A research story.* Boston: Authors Cooperative.

Sidman, M. & Tailby, W. (1982). Conditional discrimination versus matching to sample: An expansion of the testing paradigm. *Journal of the Experimental Analysis of Behavior, 37*, 5-22

Spradlin, J. E., Cotter, V. W. & Baxley, N. (1973). Establishing a conditional discrimination without direct training: A study of transfer with retarded adolescents. *American Journal of Mental Deficiency, 77*, 556-566.

Skinner, B. F. (1957). *Verbal behavior.* N.Y.: Appleton-Century-Crofts.

Steele, D. L. & Hayes, S. C. (1991). Stimulus equivalence and arbitrarily applicable relational responding. *Journal of the Experimental Analysis of Behavior, 56*, 519-555.

Wasserman, E. A., & Devolder, C. L. (1993). Similarity and nonsimilarity-based conceptualization in children and pigeons. *Psychological Record, 43*, 779-793.

Williams, B. A. (1983). Stimulus control and associative learning. *Journal of the Experimental Analysis of Behavior, 42*, 469-483.

Wilson, K. G. & Hayes, S. C. (in press). Resurgence of derived stimulus relations. *Journal of the Experimental Analysis of Behavior.*

Wittgenstein, L. (1953). *Philosophical investigations* (G.E.M. Anscombe, Trans.). Oxford, England: Blackwell.

Wulfert, E. & Hayes, S. C. (1988). The transfer of conditional sequencing through conditional equivalence classes. *Journal of the Experimental Analysis of Behavior, 50*, 125-144.

Author Index

Subject Index

Printed in the United States
113882LV00002B/263/A